From.
Chris + Sherry
Birthday,
Nov. 2016

*"I would wish to be remembered as
a decent human being, and a caring one."*

*- Princess Grace of Monaco, in her last interview on June 22, 1982
two and a half months before her tragic death on September 14
(Interviewed by Pierre Salinger for ABC's 20/20)*

My Days with Princess Grace of Monaco

Our 25-Year Friendship, Beyond Grace Kelly

JOAN DALE

with GRACE DALE

In-Lightning
3319-3151 Lakeshore Rd.
Kelowna, BC V1W 3S9
Canada

info@in-lightning.com

Although every precaution has been taken to verify the accuracy of the information contained herein, the authors and publisher assume no responsibility for any errors or omissions.

Ordering Information:
Ingram
www.ingramcontent.com

Printed in the United States of America

Publisher's Cataloging-in-Publication data

1. Biography   2. Royalty

Dale, Joan, 1931-2005, author
      My days with Princess Grace of Monaco : our 25-year friendship, beyond Grace Kelly / Joan Dale, Grace Dale.

Issued in print and electronic formats.
ISBN 978-1-895885-08-8 (bound)
ISBN 978-1-895885-10-1 (epub)

      1. Dale, Joan, 1931-2005. 2. Dale, Joan, 1931-2005--Friends and associates. 3. Grace, Princess of Monaco, 1929-1982. 4. Grace, Princess of Monaco, 1929-1982--Friends and associates. 5. Americans--Monaco--Biography. 6. Princesses--Monaco--Biography. I. Dale, Grace, 1967-, author II. Title.

DC943.D34A3 2013   944.9'49092   C2013-906460-5
                                                C2013-906461-3

First Edition

10 9 8 7 6 5 4 3 2 1

www.PrincessGrace*of*Monaco.com

FOR THE CHILDREN:

Charles, Gregory, Eric

and

Pamela Grace, Princess Grace's goddaughter,
without whose help and loving support
this book would not have been written

AND FOR THE GRANDCHILDREN

So they may know what it was like to have days with Grace...

DEDICATED TO GRACE, WITH LOVE

My Dear Grace,

I have kept silent all these years since your passing, treasuring in my memory all the wonderful times we spent together, with our children, traveling, walking, having long talks, or just being quiet enjoying each other's company. Few have been aware that I even knew you, or that we shared so much together as friends.

I have written these memoirs for the children, who were too young to remember the good times we all had. My children have suggested that I publish this account so that others might know you as the kind, warm, loving and genuine human being that you truly were. Many books have been written by those who never met you, some of whom were consumed with sensationalism. This is written from my heart to you, whom I admired and loved so much.

You will always be with me. You have inspired me to take time for others, to love and to care about the people of the world. You did your part in living an exemplary life of selfless dedication to serving humanity, and with this book I hope to do my part to ensure that your true legend lives on. I would feel fulfilled if others could be aware of how compassionate and caring you were, and that they could draw strength and inspiration from your fine character in these days of turmoil, suffering, and lost innocence.

With Love Always,

Joan

CONTENTS

PHILANTHROPY:
THE LEGACY OF PRINCESS GRACE

Throughout her twenty-six years as Princess of Monaco, Her Serene Highness Princess Grace was committed to helping people around the world by raising funds and awareness for many charities and countless causes.

In honor of Princess Grace's legacy, a portion of the proceeds from this book will go to the following organizations, whose work was dear to her heart:

Princess Grace Foundation - USA
www.pgfusa.com

Following the death of Princess Grace in 1982, Prince Rainier III established this Foundation to honor her legacy of supporting emerging artists. The Foundation awards grants and scholarships to those gifted in the performing arts, and now also recognizes and supports the philanthropic and humanitarian efforts of those who have attained celebrity and work to shine their spotlight on charitable causes, as Princess Grace did.

The Princess Grace of Monaco Foundation
www.fondation-psse-grace.mc

Founded by Princess Grace in 1964, this Foundation supports local artisans, provides scholarships for those gifted in the arts, and under the presidency of H.R.H. Princess Caroline of Hanover, is now also focused on humanitarian action, especially in aid of sick and handicapped children and their families.

Red Cross Monaco
www.croix-rouge.mc

Now presided over by H.S.H. Prince Albert II, the Monégasque Red Cross was founded in 1948 to provide financial aid, emergency supplies, medical support and relief efforts to people and places in need throughout the world. Princess Grace worked tirelessly to support this organization as its president from 1958-1982.

AMADE
www.amade-mondiale.org

Princess Grace founded AMADE in 1963 to promote the inalienable rights of the child, and protect the most vulnerable children from violence, exploitation or abuse. It supports the welfare of children and communities everywhere by providing access to education and healthcare. AMADE operates in association with consultative status with UNICEF and UNESCO under the present leadership of H.R.H. Princess Caroline of Hanover, who carries on her mother's work and legacy.

INTRODUCTION

Grace was a very appropriate name for one who personified that quality in every sense. She had a charismatic presence, and a beauty that shone brightly from deep within her soul, with a radiance that was dazzling. Even in her exalted position, she always managed to remain humble and down-to-earth.

Princess Grace tried to live life and raise her children in as ordinary a way as possible. She appreciated simple things and quiet intimate moments with family and friends, but she always greeted every person who said hello to her, and went out of her way for others. She was warm, gracious and friendly, contrary to her reputation of being an "ice princess."

Whenever someone asked me what Grace was like, I would say that she was as lovely inside as she was outside. She carried the depth of her beauty on her face. I think she would always have been beautiful in all the different stages of her life, because she never allowed herself to be melancholy. She was the most extraordinary person I have ever encountered, and I hope that some of the qualities that she possessed have become part of me, so that I can help to carry on her legacy of love.

I never intended to make public any part of my very private and personal relationship with Grace and her family. If Grace were alive today, I would probably not be writing this book, because her presence and benevolence spoke for themselves. Since she has been gone, so many untruths have been told about her that it seems the world has forgotten what an extraordinary person she really was. Over the years I have only been able to shake my head at the absolute nonsense that has been printed, which has become more and more outrageous. I have been saddened and enraged by those who would tarnish her memory for gain or notoriety.

I have agonized over making these memoirs public, but I feel I must speak out in Grace's honor. She deserves to be recognized for her generosity, sincerity, integrity, and dedication to a lifetime of service. I share my treasured memories from a deep sense of love and affection for Grace's family, and I trust that they will understand that I have felt compelled to write the truth about my dear friend out of loyalty to her. Mine is a simple story of a warm and beautiful friendship with a warm and beautiful person. I only want to remind the world, and everyone who loved her, of the remarkable woman that was Grace.

Many reading this may say to themselves, "Joan who?" I have often smiled at seeing photographs of myself with Grace that read: "Princess Grace with unidentified woman," or seeing pictures published of Grace that I have been cut out of, when I had been standing right next to her. It took a long time for me to develop the courage to take my own photos at the occasions that we shared together, but everyone knew that I was an avid photographer, and it was natural for me to do so. Of course, these photographs were never intended for publication; they have always been in my family photo albums with my most cherished mementos.

This account is written to the best of my recollection – please forgive me for anything I may have forgotten after all these years. I shall not focus on her childhood or her movie career as Grace Kelly, because I did not know her then. It would suffice to say that she always had something special about her – a radiance that made her a star. Much has been written about Grace subsequent to her death, but although some of these authors have done inexhaustible research and have written with skill, most did not know her personally. I write from a genuine love of a special and wonderful human being, who was like a sister to me.

Grace had a way about her that was endearing, all encompassing, as if she held the key to the universe and its workings. There was always something mysterious about her, something held back, perhaps her own deep sense of self, only to be shared by a few.

All those she came in contact with held her a bit in awe, but always with love and respect. Grace enveloped everyone in her warmth, affection and compassion for all. One felt that she was an angel in disguise – not that she had no faults, but her charm and her ability to laugh at herself made them virtually unnoticeable.

The times I spent with Grace were truly unforgettable. Over the years, I recounted to my parents many of the extraordinary events that we had the good fortune and privilege to be included in. I wrote to them regularly, because in those days we did not make long distance telephone calls, and certainly not overseas calls, unless it was a real emergency. My parents and I always had a tendency to preserve things (a trait that Princess Grace also shared), and I am thankful that they kept all of my letters and newspaper clippings, which now serve to refresh and substantiate my precious memories.

My early letters were somewhat naïve and enthusiastic, as I was in my mid-twenties and wide-eyed at the glamour and glitter of Monaco. Upon reflection, when Grace and I met in the 1950s, it was an era that was more innocent and not as "label conscious," otherwise I don't believe that my husband and I would have dared to invite our royal guests to a barbecue, to dine on folding bridge chairs, and to take them to ordinary restaurants. Perhaps it was this very innocence that cemented my friendship with Grace. We mutually felt a deep sense of trust, respect and a profound bond.

Grace wrote me many long and chatty letters over the years, as well as postcards from wherever she was in the world; she said that I had moved so often over our twenty-five-year friendship that she had started to write my address in her book in pencil! I felt linked to her presence even when we were living across oceans and continents, and I believed that we would always remain close friends until the end of our days, growing old together.

My dear friend, Grace of Monaco, is now gone and unable to speak for herself. Her leaving us in the prime of her life left a deep sense of loss everywhere, as a glowing light was extinguished. She was a genuine human being who loved her friends, her family, and all of the world's children. Princess Grace tirelessly championed countless causes and headed a variety of charities. Throughout her lifetime Grace touched many hearts around the globe, and I believe she was an unrecognized force for peace.

Our planet lacks love, caring and compassion; Grace embodied all of these virtues (a word rarely heard nowadays). As her bereaved husband, Prince Rainier, wrote to me shortly after her death, "Grace was such a beautiful person and such a wonderful human being, full of love and kindness, that maybe she was not meant for this world of violence and misery, and so God took her into His Kingdom." Grace was one of the kindest, most thoughtful and beautiful people who ever walked this Earth. She is very often in my thoughts, and her endearing spirit will never leave me…

THOUGHT FOR THE DAY:

YOU!

We are so happy you are here — Hope your stay will be everything you wish —
Love —
Grace

Mrs. Martin Dale
Hotel de Paris

PART ONE:
THE EARLY DAYS

DAYS OF ACQUAINTANCE

The day that I first met Princess Grace is forever etched in my memory. I was twenty-six years old, one year younger than Grace. My husband, Martin, age twenty-five, had been made Acting Consul at the United States Consulate in Nice, France, and U.S. Representative to the Principality of Monaco. It was April 12, 1957, almost exactly a year after her fairy-tale wedding to the charming Prince Rainier III. Most fairy tales end when the heroine marries her handsome prince, but for Grace, this was just the beginning.

Martin and I went to Monaco quite often and had seen Prince Rainier and Princess Grace on several occasions from a distance. After several "near misses," we wondered when we would actually have the opportunity to meet them. That day finally arrived when we received an invitation to an official reception at the Prince's Palace.

We could hardly contain our excitement as we were chauffeured in the official car of the Consulate with the American flags flying. We drove through the old town of Monaco and arrived at the majestic Palace. The Prince's Chamberlain, the Count d'Aillières, greeted us, as did the Majordomo, wearing his impressive uniform with gold braid and the many ribbons denoting years of service. Uniformed footmen guided us up the grand, horseshoe-shaped marble staircase in the Palace courtyard. We were led through the open air Gallery of Hercules with an elaborately frescoed vaulted ceiling, then down the long marble hallway of the *Galerie des Glaces* (Hall of Mirrors), lined with ancient mirrors and flanked with sculptures, marble busts, and portraits of the Prince's ancestors in gilded frames.

We were ushered into an enormous reception room called the *Salle des Gardes* (Guards' Room). On the walls were huge tapestries of the Prince's coat of arms, depicting two monks with swords outstretched on either side of a red and white shield, with the motto *"Deo Juvante,"* meaning "With God's Help." This commemorates the conquest of Monaco in 1297 by François Grimaldi, a member of an aristocratic family from Genoa, who disguised himself as a monk in order to infiltrate the citadel, thereby ousting a rival family. Originally called *Monoikos*, Monaco is also coincidentally the Italian word for "monk."

The reception room was striking, with dark blue walls, a magnificently carved stone fireplace, stunning chandeliers, with comfortable sofas and chairs interspersed throughout. On the tables were silver-framed portraits of family members, princes and princesses, and kings and queens. The Grimaldis are the longest reigning sovereign family, and Prince Rainier was the most titled monarch in the world, holding one hundred and forty-two titles. He was a distant cousin of Queen Elizabeth, and was also related to many other members of Europe's royal families.

At one time, the Prince's family had ruled over all of the territory east of Monaco toward the Italian border, to an area west of Nice called Les Baux. They had numerous land holdings, which accounted for some of the Prince's many titles. When Grace married Prince Rainier, these titles were also conferred on her: Princess of Château-Porcien, Duchess four times, Countess six times, Marquise four times, Baroness seven times, etc., making her the most titled woman on Earth.

Martin and I felt very nervous as we waited to be presented to the Prince and Princess. We stood anxiously with about fifty other people, whom we did not know because we were quite new to the French Riviera. As diplomats, we were used to being at parties with people we had never met before, who often spoke languages that were not familiar to us. It was fortunate that we both spoke French fluently, and English, which was becoming the common global language.

Prince Rainier and Princess Grace took our breath away when they entered the room; they were a magnificent couple. The Prince looked younger than I had expected, dashingly handsome with a debonair smile. A very nice, charming and dynamic man, he was much better-looking in person than in photographs. Grace's presence filled the room, and she was more beautiful than one could ever imagine. She shone like a brilliant sun on a summer day, and it was this shining quality that touched people when they saw her on the movie screen, in photographs or on television.

Princess Grace looked positively stunning in a dark blue taffeta cocktail dress with a full skirt and cap sleeves, adorned simply with an exquisite Van Cleef & Arpels sapphire and diamond flower brooch. The only other jewelry she wore was her brilliant ten-carat emerald-cut diamond engagement ring by Cartier, which was a testament to the Prince's impeccable taste.

It was easy to see why Grace, who could have chosen almost any man in the world, had married the affable and fascinating Prince, for although somewhat shy, he possessed a magnetic personality. They were a very well-matched couple. Grace could easily have eclipsed most men, with anyone who married her becoming "Mr. Grace Kelly," but not Prince Rainier. He was a very successful man in his own right, who ran Monaco like a mega-corporation. The Prince was extremely intelligent, very quick and witty, and great with repartee. In fact, it was hard to keep up with him at times. As an avid sportsman, he loved car racing, deep-sea diving, skiing, yachting, golf, and shooting. Among his many other talents, he also painted beautifully, was an excellent dancer and musician, and was a true visionary.

On this occasion of our first meeting, Grace and Rainier greeted their guests as we passed through the receiving line. The Prince was addressed as *Monseigneur* (My Lord), or Sir; Grace was addressed as *Altesse* (Highness), or Madame.

Grace seemed to have the most extraordinary ability to remember something about each person being presented to her, especially the citizens of Monaco, known as Monégasques. It amazed me that she was able to recall the names of so many people despite her grueling schedule. She would suddenly say, "Monsieur ____, how was your holiday?" or "Madame ____, is your mother feeling better now?" This was even more remarkable as I found out later that Grace was very nearsighted and could not really recognize people until she got quite close to them, so she obviously had a very quick mind.

When our turn finally came, I curtsied, while Martin bowed to each of them. Meeting Princess Grace in person for the first time, I was truly awestruck. But when she spoke to me, I felt as if a comfortable cloak had enveloped me. Her soft blue eyes, dazzling smile and friendly manner put me immediately at ease. She had an astounding ability to focus all her attention on one person, no matter what was going on around her.

The Prince and Princess wandered separately around the room, speaking with different people, then both ended up talking with us until the reception ended, responding warmly to us right away. I suppose that there were very few young people in the region that they could both get along with and enjoy, especially because Grace's French was not fluent at that time. It was a short evening, as it was just a cocktail reception, but it was delightful and thrilling for both Martin and me. Little did we know that it would be the beginning of a lifelong friendship…

My life had been a whirlwind leading up to our first meeting with Princess Grace and Prince Rainier, but nothing in my background could have prepared me for what was to come. I had graduated in 1953 with Honors from Mills College in California, with a Bachelor of Arts degree in French Literature, and was awarded a Fulbright Scholarship to study International Affairs at the University of Strasbourg in Alsace, France. That's where I fell in love with Martin Dale, a fellow Fulbright Scholar who was doing graduate studies in International Law, after graduating Phi Beta Kappa from Princeton University.

We were married in France in 1954, and moved to Boston, Massachusetts, where Martin got a fellowship to pursue his master's degree from Tufts' Fletcher School of Law and Diplomacy. It was a struggle to make ends meet at times on my meager salary, but Martin and I were a creative team and enjoyed lots of fun and laughter together. We made our own Christmas decorations out of aluminum foil and wrapping paper, and improvised with "beat-the-budget" dinners, usually consisting of canned tuna in one form or another.

Martin was a bright young man with a promising future, whose goal was to enter the United States Diplomatic Service. He endured three straight days of grueling oral and written exams that were required of candidates at that time, and passed with flying colors. In September 1955, after three months in an intensive State Department training course in Washington, D.C., Martin was made Vice Consul of the United States for Marseille, France.

It was around this time that I first became aware of Grace, when we saw her in Alfred Hitchcock's *Rear Window*. We were familiar with James Stewart, but we were totally unprepared for the astonishing effect that Stewart's leading lady, a relative newcomer to films, would have on us. Grace lit up the movie screen like an angel – a luminous star shining brightly. She was radiant and glowing with beauty, class, freshness and charm, with a hint of mystery behind her demure smile. She was mesmerizing on the big screen. As we left the theater, I said to Martin, "Grace Kelly, I must remember that name!"

The following year, she would become Her Serene Highness, Princess Grace of Monaco. It was the wedding of the century, watched on television by thirty million people on April 19, 1956 (quite amazing, as there weren't televisions in every home at that time.) News of the wedding was in all the papers, and everyone around the world had been eagerly anticipating the arrival of the big day.

It was reported that 20,000 people crowded the narrow streets to hail the new Princess of Monaco. Although the wedding was a sacred and solemn ceremony, it became a media circus, with cameras protruding from behind floral arrangements. There were photographers everywhere, pushing and shoving, as they jockeyed for the best vantage point from which to capture the couple. Somehow Grace and Rainier managed to appear regal and serene throughout the entire wedding day, but the Prince finally had to call in the French riot police, as the more than 1,500 reporters crowded into the tiny Principality were getting out of hand.

Grace later confided to me that she and Rainier could not enjoy their wedding with all the people, the media, and the stress. They had wanted a small private wedding in a chapel, but duty prevailed. Grace and Rainier had become public property. Every move was to be reported and scrutinized, making their lives akin to living in a fishbowl. As an American movie star, Grace was accustomed to being in the spotlight, but I don't think she ever could have anticipated how this marriage would forever thrust her and her family into the public eye in the years to come.

Nice – January 24, 1957

Dearest Mum and Dad,

We have great news! Marty has been promoted to Class 6 in the Foreign Service. We hardly expected the promotion, as Marty has only been in the Service for 1½ years, and he is very young, too. I think he was the youngest to receive this promotion. Mr. Wharton, the U.S. Consul General, "urged promotion" in his Efficiency Report. This means a pay increase of $1,000 – therefore we earn about $8,500 per year, including housing.

All love, Joan and Marty

After Martin was transferred to the American Consulate in Nice in November 1956, we began to meet extraordinary people who came to call at the Consulate, such as Aristotle Onassis, the Begum (the Aga Khan's wife), and many others. We soon met Monsieur Pierre Rey, Prince Rainier's financial advisor and

President of the *Société des Bains de Mer* (SBM), the company that owns and operates many of the most important properties in Monaco.

Before our first meeting with Prince Rainier and Princess Grace in April 1957 at the reception at the Palace, Monsieur Rey had been trying to arrange for us to meet them on a number of occasions. I think he was concerned that Princess Grace was perhaps a bit lonely and isolated in her new country, and might appreciate the friendship of Americans who were her own age.

Monsieur Rey had entertained us several times to see if we would be suitable people to be acquainted with Their Serene Highnesses. He invited us to the Monte-Carlo Opera, in the beautiful *Salle Garnier* of the Casino (named for Charles Garnier, who designed the opulent Casino building, as well as the Opera Garnier in Paris). Monsieur Rey had a private box next to the Prince's Box, and we all smiled and nodded to the Prince and Princess from afar. During the intermission, we went to an adjacent private room for champagne and refreshments, where we met Father Francis Tucker, an American priest appointed to Monaco by the Vatican in 1950, who became Prince Rainier's personal chaplain in 1951. Father Tucker had a sparkling personality with great wit, and a decidedly Irish twinkle in his eye. We had a delightful evening, even though we did not actually get to meet the Prince and Princess that night.

On February 8, 1957, Monsieur Rey invited us to be his guests at the *Bal de la Rose* (Rose Ball), a fabulous gala event at the International Sporting Club in Monte Carlo. Thousands of roses were arranged in huge bouquets and garlands everywhere the eye could see. Entering this splendid room was like walking into a dream. There was a spectacular production of ballet and dance, with music led by the renowned bandleader, Aimé Barelli.

We had the honor of being seated at the head table with Monsieur Rey, Grace's mother, Mrs. Margaret Kelly, and Prince Pierre, who was Prince Rainier's father. We were thrilled that we would finally get to meet Their Serene Highnesses that night, but unfortunately, Princess Grace and Prince Rainier had decided not to attend, as it had been only two weeks since she had given birth to Princess Caroline.

Prince Pierre was very pleased that his son had found a princess who personified "grace" in every way, and who had now provided an heir to the throne. Prince Rainier's father was born Count Pierre de Polignac; when he married Princess Charlotte of Monaco, he assumed the title of Prince Pierre along with her surname to carry on the Grimaldi line. Princess Charlotte was Hereditary Princess of Monaco and heiress-presumptive to the throne, until she renounced in favor of their son, Prince Rainier III, the day before his twenty-first birthday (and by Sovereign Ordinance on June 2, 1944, three days later).

Prince Pierre came from a renowned aristocratic French lineage that went back a thousand years. He was a courtly, courteous and distinguished gentleman of old-world nobility, who often wore a striking black cape adorned with all of his medals. His love of beauty led him to preside over many associations that recognized and rewarded those gifted in the arts.

Princess Grace's mother was a lovely and gracious woman. Mrs. Kelly and I walked around the gala together, enjoying looking at all of the beautiful people, and the glorious gowns and jewels they were wearing. She stopped at the Cartier display to admire some magnificent pieces of jewelry. The agent for Cartier opened the case and asked if she would like to see anything. Mrs. Kelly said, "Oh, Joan, do put that brooch on," so the stunning brooch was pinned on the bodice of my white strapless evening gown. It felt extraordinary... I had never worn a piece of jewelry that was so exquisite and obviously very expensive. (The brooch cost $40,000 in 1957, the equivalent of $300,000 today! An average salary was about $5,000 a year at that time.)

Nice – February 12, 1957

Dearest Mum and Dad,

What a wonderful social life we have been having lately! Friday, Mr. Rey invited us to attend, as his guests, the "Rose Ball" at the Sporting Club of Monte Carlo. It is the most brilliant affair of the season, and all the cream of the Côte d'Azur attends. We were seated at the table of honor with Mrs. Kelly (who was placed opposite me), the French Minister to Monaco, Mr. Rey, etc. The photographers buzzed all over all the time, taking photos of Mrs. Kelly. She is a beautiful, charming, polished and interesting woman. Do not believe anything derogatory you may read, as the reporters have been spiteful because the Prince has gotten annoyed at them for intruding on his privacy. We are indeed flattered, because we were invited uniquely because Mr. Rey likes us, and not for our rank (we are too low on the scale for that!). It was a wonderful evening. We had caviar, consommé, lobster, chicken with truffles and foie gras, Genoa asparagus, liqueur ice cream and fruit candies, coffee, and champagne throughout the meal. The floorshow was marvelous. There were beautiful gowns and jewels there, but believe it or not, I was asked to pose for a photo for the Nice newspaper fashion page. I wore the tulle dress and white taffeta coat, plus *moonstone! There was a Cartier display case with three men guarding it, in which Mrs. Kelly, taking my arm, expressed interest. They opened the case and took out a $40,000 emerald and diamond pin. It was placed on my bodice to show it off. Imagine wearing $40,000! It was a wonderful evening, and we were celebrities. All for now.*

Loads of love, Joan and Marty

The next day, I read in the *Nice Matin* newspaper: "Mrs. Dale, wife of the Vice Consul of the USA at Nice, was a symphony in white net lace dress and faille silk coat. Diamond crested combs set off her light blonde hair." I had to laugh because they were actually rhinestones! However, I had been wearing a very large moonstone and diamond pendant that my father had given to me for graduating from college with honors and getting my Fulbright Scholarship – it had originally been part of the Czar of Russia's collection, and I have always treasured it. The newspapers reported that: "The most beautiful jewels in the world were there which sparkled like a fireworks display." I had never experienced such a fantastic evening in my life.

On Sunday, March 3, 1957, Princess Caroline's christening took place at the Cathedral of Monaco, followed by a reception for four hundred and fifty guests at the Palace. We were still quite new to our post in Nice, and Martin had to borrow the white tie and tails and the top hat that were required for the event. We were driven in the chauffeured car of the American Consulate, with the diplomatic flags flying from the front bumpers. It was thrilling, as people turned and stared, wondering who we were.

All of Monaco was bedecked in flags and ribbons, celebrating the heir presumptive to the throne. The christening of Princess Caroline was a sacred and delightful ceremony, with the Cathedral decorated with white and pink flowers. We were seated in the right transept, and the christening itself took place just five feet away from us. We had a wonderful view of the baby, and of the Prince and Princess, but this would prove to be another of our "near misses," with us being so close, yet so far from actually meeting them.

Monsieur Rey subsequently invited us to a dinner that Prince Rainier and Princess Grace were going to attend. We were so excited to go to a private dinner with them, but again, they had to cancel at the last minute. We started to wonder whether we would ever meet Their Serene Highnesses. Then finally, after months of disappointment, we were invited to the Prince's Palace, and I found myself in a receiving line, gazing into the smiling eyes of Princess Grace for the first time... Soon afterward, many more invitations arrived.

Nice – April 27, 1957

Dearest Mum and Dad,

We attended a cocktail party at the Palace given for American journalists. This week we attended the awarding of the Gold American Legion Medal to the Prince, which was televised – and watch for it in Fox Movietone News. Afterwards, there was a cocktail party at the Palace, followed by a ballet at the Opera. We were seated with Their Highnesses in their box, along with Princess Antoinette (the Prince's sister) and assorted Counts and Countesses. They are all very simple and likable people, the Prince and Princess especially. We attended a gala at the Sporting Club, given by the Monégasque Minister of State, as his honored guests. This last Monday we attended luncheon at the Palace. Marty was seated next to the Princess, and afterwards in the Salon I sat and spoke with her at length while Marty spoke to the Prince. We got along famously, and I have been "invited" sometime when they return from their audience with the Pope to see the baby Princess. They really are a charming couple. All the above affairs, incidentally, had to do with entertaining the American Legion, and we were asked only because Marty is Acting Consul. Now that we have our introduction, I hope we shall be invited as friends.

Last Friday we went to the British-American Hospital Ball at the Hôtel de Paris in Monte Carlo. The guests of honor were the Prince and Princess – and you should have seen how people gawked at them. Some American paid a handsome amount to sit at the table adjoining. We were not at Their Highnesses' table, but Marty greeted them at the door, and later when dancing, they stopped to chat.

Good news! The rabbit says, "yes" – so you will be grandparents around the middle of December. We are so excited!!!

All love, Joan and Marty

I felt very fortunate to be in Monaco during the late 1950s. It was an exciting time, and for a twenty-six-year-old, the social scene was a glittering flurry of activity. In early 1957, the Mayor of Monaco had invited us to the *Gala des Colonies Etrangères* (Ball for the foreign community of Monaco). We were seated at the Mayor's table with the legendary undersea explorer Jacques Cousteau, who was the Director of Monaco's famed Oceanographic Museum from 1957 to 1988. We met Jacques Cousteau on many occasions between his travels, and we always enjoyed his brilliance, enthusiasm, humor and lively conversations about conserving the environment, a topic rarely discussed in those days. He felt that animals, marine life and humans are all part of the same ecosystem, and that the very survival of the Earth and humanity depends on the understanding of this connection and interdependency. He was fascinating and very much ahead of his time.

After we met Prince Rainier and Princess Grace, we were invited to numerous cocktail parties, luncheons and dinners at the Palace. We were also included in many exciting special events and activities with them. We felt very honored to receive these personal invitations that were not related to official functions of our diplomatic post.

Nice – May 22, 1957

Dearest Mum and Dad,

We had a very special thrill this last Sunday. We were invited to attend the Grand Prix automobile races in Monaco, by the Prince and Princess. It was not an official invitation, as we were the only foreigners as their guests – so they must like us. We sat in the Prince's Box for the first few rounds of the sports cars, but as the noise was deafening, we adjourned to a new apartment ten stories high, which was arranged for the Prince and his party. The balcony was draped with maroon velvet, and we could watch the whole race above the noise – even so, earplugs were advisable, and the Princess wore them. A television set was provided, along with champagne, sandwiches and cakes – served by the Palace staff in livery and white gloves. We talked at length to the Prince and Princess and told them about our happy event. [We were soon to be parents for the first time.] They were so pleased, and offered loads of advice. Today, Marty received a personally typewritten letter from the Prince, which was exceptionally warm and friendly.

June 7th, the FORRESTAL, our largest aircraft carrier, will put in to Monaco, and a day's special trip is arranged for the Prince and his retinue.

All our love, Joan and Marty

Martin and I were invited along with Grace and Rainier to watch a demonstration of air maneuvers on board the huge aircraft carrier, the USS *FORRESTAL*. It was quite an overwhelming sight to see the enormous ship looming outside the harbor of the tiny Principality. At the time, the American Sixth Fleet was stationed in the Mediterranean, with the great Vice Admiral Charles "Cat" Brown in command. The Prince and Princess were welcomed aboard the *FORRESTAL* with a twenty-one-gun salute in their honor, and then Their Serene Highnesses were taken up in a helicopter for the first time, which was thrilling for them. Grace always had an adventurous spirit and loved to try new and unusual things, so she was game for the helicopter ride, despite her tendency toward motion sickness.

We had a marvelous time on the bridge of the ship with Grace and Rainier, watching the display of mock bombing and rocket attacks by *Demons, Furies, Cougars, Banshees, Sky Raiders* and *Sky Warriors*, including a dive attack on the ship, all of which was sensational. We watched the planes take off and land on an airstrip that looked to me like it was the size of a postage stamp. There were very thick metal cables stretched across the deck at various intervals that were designed to catch the hook at the back of the planes. On one landing attempt, a plane came flying along the deck, missing the first cable, then the second cable, then the third cable… The plane plummeted off the end of the ship and disappeared. We all gasped and held our breath, because pilots have died as a result of going over the edge of aircraft carriers into the water. Somehow, the pilot managed to pull the plane up at the last minute; he came around for another attempt, this time landing perfectly. We were not sure if this had been real or just a daredevil stunt, but we all had our hearts in our throats. These pilots were truly amazing and performed extraordinary aeronautical feats.

Afterwards, we had lunch on board, and then toured the ship with Admiral Arnold, as the sailors looked at Grace in absolute awe. She was stunningly beautiful, and the poor young sailors tried to remain at attention but could not keep their eyes off her. Grace had been a movie star, and was now a real princess. The U.S. Navy was proud to welcome her aboard as an American, and also because Princess Grace and Prince Rainier were perhaps the most famous couple in the world at that time, especially after all the press coverage of their wedding and their constant presence in the global media. Photographs of their visit to the *FORRESTAL* appeared in all the newspapers, and it was a real coup for the U.S. Navy to have them on board. Martin was largely responsible for arranging this spectacular exhibition, and we all enjoyed it immensely.

Martin often attended dinners with Admirals, which we thought was quite ironic because his rank was equivalent to a Lieutenant Senior Grade – whom an Admiral ordinarily would ignore as being too low a station, but being a diplomat offered a certain amount of distinction. When Martin was the Acting Consul in Nice, we were frequently invited on board the U.S. naval ships. Because he was an official dignitary, he would be "piped aboard," meaning that a pipe or whistle was blown to alert the crew that someone important was coming on deck. As Martin came up the gangplank, everyone would see this very young-looking man, who looked even younger than his twenty-five years. They would all look around wondering whom they should salute to. It was very amusing. At the American Consulate in Nice, one of the wealthy old dowagers once walked into Martin's office and said, "I didn't come here to see you, young man, I came to see your father, the Consul!" Being such a young diplomat also had its challenges.

There were a variety of consular duties that Martin was responsible for. Primarily, he assisted American citizens residing abroad, as well as American visitors with such things as lost passports, issuing or renewing passports, as well as granting visas to those living on the Côte d'Azur who wanted to visit or live in the United States. He also had to rescue American tourists who got in trouble with the French authorities, particularly U.S. sailors whom he had to bail out of jail in the middle of the night for drunk and disorderly conduct.

Martin was expected to be a representative of the United States for various events and occasions. He would greet and attend to visiting members of the U.S. Congress, as well as other dignitaries and Foreign Heads of State. At one time, he was called upon to present Princess Grace with the American Millinery Industry's first annual Golden Hat Award as "The Best Hatted Woman in the World." The scroll that Grace received, as quoted in the *New York Herald Tribune*, cited her "good taste in wearing hats suited to the occasion and chosen to enhance her great natural beauty." Protocol required Grace to wear a hat and gloves on many occasions. She loved hats and wore them well, except perhaps for her now-famous choice of the wide-brimmed white hat that she donned on her arrival in Monaco for her wedding. The hat itself was striking. However, all of the photographers and the Monégasques were upset, because it obscured their view of her lovely face.

After receiving several invitations to the Palace for luncheons and dinners, Martin and I decided that we really should return the hospitality. At the time, we lived in a charming old house in Nice called *Villa Les Marguerites*. I was a young and rather inexperienced hostess, so I was extremely nervous about entertaining our royal friends. We invited them to lunch and began by serving martinis. This proved to be a good idea, because the steak that my husband was cooking on the barbecue took longer than it should have. In the end it turned out to be quite crisp, bearing a remarkable resemblance to shoe leather. Grace looked at it and said with a smile, "I always find a meat thermometer to be useful." Of course, she was no longer doing very much cooking at that time.

We sat down for lunch, and everybody was very brave and polite about eating the steak. For dessert, we served a Rum Baba that our neighbor, Ilse, had prepared for us. To make sure that it was really delicious for our special guests, she had added even more rum and syrup than the recipe called for. The waiter we had hired for this special occasion served the dessert to the Prince, but as he withdrew the tilting platter, a thin stream of syrupy rum dripped from the wrist to the shoulder of Prince Rainier's gorgeous suit. I was absolutely mortified. Being a great gentleman, the Prince did nothing until he thought that nobody was watching, then he very quietly mopped his sleeve with his napkin.

It was a warm day, so all of our windows were open. Our neighbor, Ilse, who was also our landlady, had been looking into our house trying to catch a glimpse of the Prince and Princess. She later informed us that she had seen our hired waiter chasing our maid around the kitchen. Fortunately, this occurred behind closed doors!

Despite all the mishaps, we were tremendously gratified that our new royal friends stayed until very late in the afternoon, well past the usual departure time dictated by protocol. We sat cozily around the fireplace, chatting about babies, as I was expecting my first child. Grace was eager to impart her newfound knowledge about Caroline, who was five months old at the time. She had read many books on the subject of motherhood, pregnancy and babies, and was happy to share her valuable experiences with me. We were starting to become friends, and there was a growing bond between us that we both felt.

Grace sent me three books that would prove indispensable to a somewhat apprehensive mother-to-be. One was called *J'Attends un Enfant* (I am expecting a baby), and its advice helped me through all my pregnancies. I was very grateful and touched by such a thoughtful gesture, with a handwritten note: "Hope these might be of some help & that you have fun reading them." It was signed "Grace de Monaco."

In the beginning, protocol required a degree of formality in our relationship. For quite some time, Grace and Rainier would address us as "Mrs. Dale" or "Mr. Dale," and would sign their letters "Grace de Monaco" and "Rainier Prince de Monaco." Eventually, their communication with us became much more relaxed and familiar, beginning with "Dear Joan" or "Dear Martin," and signing off "Love – Grace," and "Love to all, See you soon!! Rainier."

It did not take too long for us to be able to call her "Grace," because she preferred informality for the most part. However, the Prince remained "Monseigneur" or "Sir" for years before we were close enough that I could address him simply as "Rainier," both in person and in writing. (They sweetly had all of our children call them "Aunt Grace" and "Uncle Rainier.")

In many ways, Grace was a very basic and sensible person, very loving and motherly with everyone. She would soon announce that she was expecting her second child, just a few months after Princess Caroline was born, and the due dates for our babies were only three months apart. We enjoyed being pregnant together, which created a special sisterly relationship between us. Grace was very comforting to me during my first pregnancy. She made everything seem natural and gave me support and confidence, as well as a feeling of safety. Without Grace's reassurance, I know that the birth of my first child would have been fraught with fear and anxiety.

Nice – June 1957

Dearest Mum and Dad,

Last week I received a lovely gift of three books, one on baby care by Dr. Spock, another on naming the baby, and a third all about maternity, in French – gifts of Princess Grace of Monaco!! She really is a sweet person and actually takes time to think of others. Last night we were invited to attend a concert at the Palace as special guests of Prince Rainier (pronounced Ren-yay). There were three guests, plus his suite, twelve in all. We heard the concert from the Palace balcony on a gorgeous moonlight night. The lights on Monaco and the blue sea were beyond description, not to mention the ambiance. We had coffee and liqueur, and afterwards champagne. They are lovely people, and the Prince has a wonderful sense of humor. They are leaving for Switzerland soon for the summer, but I am sure we shall see them upon their return. They really do like us. The dress last evening was tuxedo and short evening dress. I wore my gray organdy with the jacket, which you gave me before I left.

All love, Joan and Marty

Grace seemed genuinely pleased to have an American friend that she could talk to. I never heard her complain about her life, although I am certain it was not the fairy-tale existence that most people believed it to be. She said many people had a picture in their minds of her lazily reclining on a chaise lounge, being fed grapes. Nothing could have been further from the truth in her very busy life. It was only years later that I realized how lonely and isolated she must have felt, being in a land where customs were different, where she did not speak the language fluently (that was to change in time), and where her very position as Princess created feelings of awe that set her apart. Grace was a very warm woman who sincerely loved people, but her situation made it difficult for her to get close with anyone other than the Prince.

Those who are born to royal families do not really know what true freedom is. Of course, their wealth and privilege give them the opportunity to have experiences that most people will never have, but there are always restraints placed on their behavior with the demands of decorum, duty and protocol. Even when they are free to be themselves and to have fun, there are usually underlying expectations. This is especially true for those royals who find their every move being photographed and scrutinized in the press, like Grace and Rainier (and eventually all their children). Royals almost never have privacy – there is the constant parade of paparazzi that follows them everywhere, and there are also countless attendants, servants, and members of their retinue who are always around them. Some people might think that it would be wonderful to be waited on hand and foot, but it also means never having one's own personal space.

Although Grace was regal by nature, she nevertheless had known freedom in her childhood and during her acting and modeling career. She was a rather modern and independent woman who enjoyed doing things for herself, even when she became a famous movie star. She could never have imagined the different world that she would encounter upon entering a ruling dynasty. Even the simplest things that most people take for granted were now impossible; for instance, it was considered improper for a princess to "go shopping." Rainier's mother, Princess Charlotte, had clothes and other items brought to the Palace for her to select from. Grace couldn't just go to the kitchen or to a market when she wanted something; instead, she had to ask someone for everything she needed, even while experiencing the constant cravings of pregnancy. This was all rather difficult for her to adapt to, and I am sure that there were times in the early years when she felt somewhat like a prisoner in a gilded cage behind the Palace walls.

Grace was very much in love with her charming Prince, but after the honeymoon was over, Rainier had to attend to the many demands of running a country, and she found herself among strangers, trying to adapt to a rather rigid lifestyle that she was unaccustomed to. Fortunately for Grace, she became pregnant immediately, which was of the utmost importance for the ruling Prince and for the Monégasque people. They had to have an heir to the throne. It also gave her something to focus her energies on: preparing a nursery and planning for motherhood. Grace was a natural mother, which is not necessarily the case for all women.

It was not easy for Grace to adjust to living in a huge Palace. It was indeed magnificent, but rather cold and lonely, walking through the vast and numerous rooms, furnished with opulent antiques dating back hundreds of years. The Palace had priceless paintings by old world masters, gilded ceilings and frescoes everywhere, huge chandeliers, elaborate marble floors with exquisite designs, and marble decorations in every color throughout. The enormous and ornate Palace was akin to living in a museum.

The members of the Palace staff were extremely formal, with their courtly manners and impeccable full-dress uniforms complete with white gloves. Grace grew up in a wealthy family with a few servants in their Philadelphia home, but in America there is a more relaxed attitude. At that time, there were about two hundred and fifty people working at the Palace, which had over two hundred rooms. The staff included the Prince's Cabinet, Secretaries, a general manager called the *Régisseur*, the *Gouverneur* (who oversees the Palace), personal staff, gardeners, electricians, upholsterers, carpenters, painters, a curator of archives, a bookbinder, a housekeeper, and a painting restorer for the centuries of family portraits and priceless works of art. In Grace and Rainier's personal household there was the Majordomo (chief of staff), who supervises the five footmen, three butlers, the Prince's valet, Grace's personal maid, a French chef and his assistant chef, laundresses and seamstresses. Grace and Rainier each had a personal secretary, and Grace had a Lady-in-Waiting, while Rainier had a Chamberlain or Aide de Camp, who were often by their side. Of course, there were also the Palace guards, the *Carabiniers*. Many of those who worked at the Palace of Monaco had been there for years, some for generations – it was a great honor for them, and they took their jobs very seriously.

It took quite some time before Grace won over the hearts and the loyalty of the servants at the Palace with her gentle, courteous and considerate ways. When Grace would suggest a change, the Majordomo, who had been there many years, replied, "We have never before done it that way, Altesse." He did what Grace asked, but, slowly and surely, he would gradually revert back to his way.

Sometimes, the staff would say yes to her request, and then neglect to carry it out.

Grace had a difficult job trying to change the servants' old patterns. Before their marriage, Prince Rainier had lived in a villa outside Monaco, so the Palace had remained empty most of the time, and the staff members were left to their own devices. Grace was determined that she and Rainier would make the Palace their home and live there year-round.

Having a slew of servants should solve all of one's problems; however, the truth is that having servants can create its own unique set of circumstances and challenges. Even though there was a chief of staff, endless difficulties were presented to Grace for solutions. Over the years, many members of the staff went to Grace with their own personal issues, because she was so compassionate. She listened attentively and spoke little, but when she did, it was with a deeply thoughtful and caring comment, or gentle advice, if one wished it. Grace was never brusque or hurried. She always took time for people, no matter how busy she was. She was open, patient and welcoming.

Grace was quietly forceful and determined when she knew something absolutely had to be done, and then almost nothing would stop her. Although she was very tactful, she was one of the most charmingly persuasive people I have ever encountered. She somehow made you feel really good and honored within yourself that you made that decision. Above all else, she was loving, and one could not help but love Grace.

Throughout her life, Grace touched many hearts and souls. She brought light and life to people, as she visited the elderly or those sick in the hospital. Soon after her marriage, she became President of the Monégasque Red Cross, which was just one of her many duties and responsibilities. When I was giving blood to the Red Cross for the first time, Grace insisted on coming with me. She stood beside me, wringing her hands the whole time, looking very concerned. That meant a lot to me, as it was quite early on in our friendship.

Nice – July 25, 1957

Dearest Mum and Dad,

There have been a great many social activities recently – highlight of which was the Red Cross Charity Ball in Monaco. We are not sure, but apparently we were invited at the request of Prince Rainier. Marty had received a few days before a very chatty and friendly letter from His Serene Highness, but protocol *is such that he could never invite the American Vice Consul to sit at his table, except if he were honoring the American something-or-other, and even then the Consul takes precedence. However, we have been squeezed in sometimes, even when we should not have been. We were seated at the Ball at the Monégasque Minister of State's table, with the Governor of our District (Prefet), the French Ambassador to Monaco, the Minister of Public Works, and a Consul General. We probably anger many people, being listed ahead of those with titles and money. We had a wonderful dinner of caviar, consommé, lobster, duck à l'orange, raspberry sundae, candies, champagne, and coffee. If we had paid for it, it would have cost $100 per person! The gowns were exquisite, and Princess Grace was a picture as always. She wore an enormous diamond necklace as her only jewelry.*

The floorshow situated by the sea was terrific, and as the wee hours passed by and the dance floor thinned, the Prince and Princess danced. At about 2:30 a.m. they beckoned us to come to their table, and we talked for quite a while. They are so simple and charming. They have returned to their chalet in Switzerland but will come back here in September – and then we hope to see them. I really feel sorry for the life they lead. The newsmen regale in printing untruths about the Prince and other women, and they are constantly receiving anonymous letters from dangerous or deranged people. A private life is impossible for them.

All our love, Joan and Marty

We were very fortunate to have been invited as guests to the lavish galas and banquets that others paid a fortune to attend – otherwise, we could never have afforded them on Martin's U.S. Government salary. The Red Cross Ball was held at the Monte Carlo Summer Sporting Club, which was built out over the Mediterranean Sea. From the spacious outdoor terrace, the glittering lights of Monaco and Italy could be seen sparkling like diamonds in the night. The atmosphere was festive and brimming with excitement when the Prince and Princess arrived at ten o'clock. Grace was wearing a splendid midnight blue organdy evening gown embroidered in pale blue, with an eye-catching diamond necklace and a white ermine stole. All eyes were upon her as she entered, gliding elegantly across the large dance floor, which was lit softly from underneath the glass tiles.

After dinner was served, the spectacular floorshow began, depicting a mystical ceremony from the time of the ancient Incas. There was a magician, an outstanding juggler, and Edgar Bergen performed his famous ventriloquist act with his dummy, Charlie McCarthy. Actor Van Johnson then introduced singer Eddie Fisher (before he was married to Elizabeth Taylor). A colorful Mexican ballet was presented, culminating in a marvelous fireworks display, after which we danced until the early morning. Over nine hundred guests attended, including the Henry Fondas, Prince George Festetics (godfather to Princess Caroline), and Prince George of Denmark, among others. All proceeds from this annual Ball went to aid the needy of the world, through the Monégasque Red Cross.

In early November, Martin received a handwritten note at the U.S. Consulate in Nice, hand-addressed by the Prince himself, on a notecard bearing an embossed golden crown: "The twelfth of November (12) being Princess Grace's birthday, I am organizing a little birthday dinner in the Palace that evening at 8:30. The Princess and myself would be so pleased if you and Mrs. Dale would join us on this merry occasion. I trust you will be able to free yourself from all and any diplomatic tangles to spend that evening with us!!?" Invitations from the Palace were always formally written in calligraphy by the staff, so it was highly unusual for the Prince to send out a personal invitation.

Prince Rainier wanted to make everything special for his beloved Grace, as she celebrated her second birthday as Princess of Monaco, at the age of twenty-eight. We were extremely honored to be invited to the Palace for Grace's birthday dinner, along with Rainier's father and sister, Prince Pierre and Princess Antoinette, and other members of the De Polignac family. The French Minister of State and his wife were there, along with Monsieur Rey, and Father Tucker. Princess Grace was once again pregnant for the occasion and looked especially radiant, with a motherly glow of love and joy that made her seem positively luminous. Two days later, Grace invited me to tea at the Palace. We had a delightful afternoon, chatting about babies; she gave me lots of encouragement, as I was in the final month of my first pregnancy, filled with a mixture of anxiety and anticipation.

The following week was the Monégasque National Holiday, which comprised two days of glorious annual traditions that were full of pageantry and ceremony. On November 18, there was a cocktail party at the Palace, where Prince Rainier honored the Diplomatic Corps. The next day, we attended a *Te Deum* (Christian hymn of thanksgiving) in the morning, followed by luncheon at the Palace with festivities in the Throne Room. That evening, we attended the Monte-Carlo Opera gala in the Loge of the French Minister of State, followed by champagne with the Prince and Princess.

Our son, Charles, was born on December 10, 1957, in the Clinic Santa Maria in Nice, a small private hospital where babies spent the day in a crib by the mother's bedside. However, at night they were taken to a gas-heated nursery with the other infants. I was a little worried about the safety of the antiquated heating arrangement and was happy to go home after two days.

Grace and Rainier sent a magnificent orchid bouquet and a handsome outfit for the baby, with a handwritten note from the Prince: "With all our most sincere and heartfelt wishes and thoughts for mother and 'junior'. Not forgetting the poor papa, of course!" They also sent a gorgeous, warm and cuddly Dior blanket, which eventually served all my children.

My parents came to Nice for the birth of their first grandchild, and it was wonderful for us to have their help and support with our newborn for six months. It was also a blessing for them to personally share in these experiences, and not have to live vicariously through overseas letters. Martin and I spent the next few weeks reveling in the joys of being new parents, despite the sleepless nights and our lack of social activities. We had been given the greatest gift of all for Christmas – a healthy baby boy!

On February 7, 1958, we again attended the annual *Bal de la Rose* at the International Sporting Club. This time we were guests of the Prince and Princess, and we were very flattered and excited by the invitation to be seated at the head table with them. We waited inside the foyer of the Sporting Club for the arrival of Their Serene Highnesses, preceded by the *Carabiniers*, the Prince's personal guard, who were mounted on motorcycles. Grace, in her eighth month of pregnancy, wore an elegant gown of pale blue satin with silver threads running through it, designed in a way that camouflaged her condition.

We arrived amid an explosion of flashbulbs and such a crush of reporters that I hardly know how we made it to the table! It was my first experience of this sort with the media, which would be repeated each time we went out officially with the Sovereigns. Grace remained calm, smiling and serene, and somehow seemed to take all the jostling in stride. Grace's mother was seated on Prince Rainier's right and I was on his left, with Rainier's father to my left. Princess Grace was in the center of the long table, directly across from Prince Rainier, and in the photographers' haste to get pictures of her, I found battery and camera cases resting on my head and shoulders!

As we dined, we admired the splendid decor of this vast room, whose walls and ceiling had been entirely lined in rose faille material covered in sparkling gray net tulle. Twelve large bronze statues of women carrying enormous bouquets of pink and red roses were scattered around the banquet hall. There were roses everywhere, on all the tables and in every nook and corner – over twenty-four thousand roses were used to create this elegant, fairy-like setting! I had never seen anything to compare with this opulence.

Soft violin music was playing all the while, then came a great surprise: one hundred violinists recruited from all along the Riviera as far as Genoa paraded around the tables of over four hundred guests, stopping to serenade the Princely Table of Honor with Viennese Waltzes. Then followed a delightful ballet, with ballerinas gowned in romantic rose net skirts. At the end of the evening, all the ladies were given bottles of perfume, while a glorious cascade of fireworks called the "Rain of Roses" poured down outside the tall bay windows of the ballroom. We stayed at the Prince's table, chatting and dancing as the evening flew by; it was two o'clock in the morning before we all parted company. It had been an amazing night, the kind that dreams are made of!

Throughout Grace's pregnancies, she always carried on with her duties and responsibilities, seeming to enjoy it all. That was certainly exemplified by her attending the *Bal de la Rose* just a few weeks before giving birth to Prince Albert. The children were all born at home in the Palace, assisted by an attending doctor who came down from Paris. The den of their private apartments was converted into a delivery room for this purpose. Of course, when the heir to the throne is involved, having a child born at home precludes any concern for mistaken identities or other mishaps that can occur in hospitals. (Prince Rainier was also born at the Palace, and was one of the few Princes of Monaco in their 700-year dynasty who lived there full time.)

Grace felt that this was a far nicer way to give birth, as the baby could feel at home and warmly welcomed by the entire family. It was very important for Grace to be as close to her children as possible. She strongly believed that mothers should nurse their babies, a subject which she would champion publicly in years to come.

Prince Albert II was born Albert Alexandre Louis Pierre, Marquis des Baux, on March 14, 1958. A one-hundred-and-one gun salute announced the birth of the heir to the throne of Monaco. Everyone was thrilled to welcome him into the world, and Prince Rainier was overjoyed to have a son. The Grimaldi heirs were named after their ancestors, with names that could be spoken in French as well as in English. Albert II was named after his great-great-grandfather, Albert I of Monaco (1848–1922), known as the "Mariner Prince," who was a pioneer in the science of Oceanography and who founded the world-renowned Oceanographic Museum of Monaco.

When Princess Caroline Louise Marguerite was born on January 23, 1957, she had briefly been the hereditary heir to the throne until her brother came along. The laws of succession favor males, so a female is called an "heir presumptive" until a male – the "heir apparent" – is born. (In the Grimaldi line, there had been another Princess Caroline, married to Prince Florestan of Monaco in 1816.)

Prince Rainier III was born Rainier Louis Henri Maxence Bertrand Grimaldi, Count of Polignac, on May 31, 1923. He was named after Rainier I (1267–1314), who was the first sovereign Grimaldi to rule over the area now known as Monaco. Upon the death of his grandfather, Prince Louis II, on the 9th of May, 1949, Prince Rainier III inherited the throne just three weeks before his twenty-sixth birthday. Rainier's mother, Princess Charlotte, had renounced her claim to the throne in favor of her son five years prior.

When Prince Albert was born, Prince Rainier wrote to Martin: "I want to thank [you] so much for your very kind letter you so very nicely sent me for the birth of little Prince Albert. The 14th of March was a wonderful day that will count in my memory and heart as it will in the history of this little country. The Princess and myself were so touched by the gesture of the U.S. Navy. It was indeed so moving and so delicate that the USS *SALEM* came to honour the little Prince by a gun salute on the day he was a week old. I am writing to Admiral Brown to express to him our most sincere appreciation."

On April 20, 1958, Martin and I attended the baptism of H.S.H. Prince Albert, hereditary Prince, at the Cathedral of Monaco. We were again invited to sit with the Diplomatic Corps in the right transept, as we had for Princess Caroline's christening the year before. We arrived by ten thirty in the morning, and the glorious spring fragrance of white lilacs and tulips filled the Cathedral. It was a quiet, dignified ceremony befitting the joyous occasion. Grace looked radiant, and Prince Rainier was beaming with pride at having a son and heir. Then at half past five in the afternoon, we were invited to a reception honoring the baby prince at the Palace, followed by a gala dinner at the Sporting Club attended by Prince Rainier.

Prince Albert and Princess Caroline were born just fourteen months apart, which ultimately affected Grace's health. She confided to me that she had not truly recovered her stamina from having one child right after the other, in addition to all of the other demands that were constantly being made on her time and energy.

While my mother was visiting me in Nice, she and I were invited to the Palace to see young Caroline and two-month-old Albert in the nursery. It was a delightful afternoon, as we sat with Grace and had tea, which she herself poured. The children were very lively, and Caroline was playing with Albert as if he were a little doll. They were adorable, and obviously very happy children. Albie (as Grace always affectionately called him) kept smiling and laughing, while Caroline would lovingly bring him all kinds of toys. The children received gifts from everywhere, and the multitude of playthings was unbelievable. Knowing Grace, I'm sure she redistributed a lot of those gifts to needy children and orphans.

Grace and I took great pleasure and delight in being new mothers together and enjoying our babies. She and I shared advice and helped each other in many ways. As Martin was a U.S. Government employee, we often went to a nearby American Armed Forces Post Exchange (PX) to buy baby goods for our son, Charles, and also for Princess Caroline and Prince Albert. Grace was very grateful for this, as she had difficulty getting certain items in France at that time. She wrote: "So many thanks for the wonderful parcel of baby goodies – I certainly appreciate it more than I can say... Little Charles must be changing every day now & I know what fun you are having with him..."

Grace loved simplicity, despite the fact that she was surrounded by opulence and by socialites with a penchant for ostentation. Certain members of society were always trying to outdo each other by throwing ever more elaborate parties, competing over illustrious guests, and showing off their homes, jewelry, and clothing with shameless displays of conspicuous consumption.

Most of the lavish parties or soirées were held during the summer months, when the very wealthy would occupy their sumptuous homes on the French Riviera for the few months of "the season." Grace and Rainier were invited to these events but often chose to decline, preferring to spend quiet time together whenever possible. They found it rather taxing to always be the center of attention, to have to smile all the time while carrying on "pleasant" conversations, and to be continually on guard.

Martin and I usually accepted these invitations because he was Acting Consul in Nice. We were also aware that our time on the Côte d'Azur was limited, as we never knew when he would be transferred to a new diplomatic post. We enjoyed having the opportunity to experience these extraordinary parties and the extravagant luxuries that only great wealth can buy.

Many of the palatial villas were located at Saint Jean Cap Ferrat – an affluent peninsula located only twenty minutes by car from Monaco, and not too much farther by yacht. King Leopold II of Belgium had villas there, as did the

Rothschilds at one time; David Niven's stately home at Cap Ferrat had previously belonged to Charlie Chaplin and had gardens descending to the sea.

Somerset Maugham also had a grand home there on nine acres called Villa Mauresque, which he purchased in 1926. The house had an "endless pool" that was unique at that time, where the water cascaded over the edge into a pool below, giving the impression that one could swim straight into the Mediterranean itself. The British author was reputed to be the world's first superstar novelist, having penned many books, including *Of Human Bondage*. He was also a playwright, with four plays running simultaneously in London. He had studied medicine before becoming a writer, and later worked for British Intelligence during WWI.

We were invited to the palatial home of Lady "X" for a luncheon in honor of Somerset Maugham and were very much looking forward to meeting this fascinating man. We drove along a seemingly never-ending driveway, arriving at the imposing pillared facade of her villa that resembled the Parthenon. We rang the bell and waited… and waited… looking at each other, wondering if we had mistaken the date. Finally, the door opened, and a jovial man asked us to enter, explaining that he was a houseguest.

The immense marbled rooms were devoid of people, and we, in our youthful inexperience, began to feel very uncomfortable in this unknown situation. When the houseguest offered us a drink, we requested anything but gin – the Foreign Service had expressly instructed us never to drink gin, because it loosens the tongue, and "loose lips sink ships." We were told that diplomats had to have three things: steel arches (for standing endlessly at receptions), a cast-iron stomach (for unidentifiable "delicacies"), and a "zipped lip" (to avoid inadvertently revealing secrets and classified information). We had arrived promptly at the appointed hour, because our diplomatic training ingrained in us that it was of the utmost importance to be punctual under all circumstances, particularly for engagements at the Palace. We did not realize that at this level of society, an invitation for one o'clock meant that one should arrive "fashionably late" at one thirty at the absolute earliest.

Slowly other guests began to appear, and finally, at around two o'clock, our elegant hostess swept in, carrying a very strange, monkey-like creature from Australia perched on her shoulder. She looked at the houseguest who had let us in and said, "Oh, are you still here? I haven't seen you for weeks!" The villa was obviously so large that one could literally get lost in it!

The luncheon was excellent, but rather strained for us because we didn't know anyone, and the conversation was impossibly superficial, filled with gossip about other people whom we did not know. We left as soon as we could politely slip away. Somerset Maugham also left early, as he was beginning to show signs of decline at age eighty-four, and was not at his best that day.

Most of the villas along the French Riviera were exquisite, especially at night, with lanterns setting a romantic mood in the gardens, illuminating covered colonnaded marble walkways, and lighting fountains and swimming pools. Immaculately uniformed servants served sumptuous feasts, and more than a little flirting took place when a spouse was looking the other way. There was always scandal and intrigue in the air as the rich and famous converged on the glorious Côte d'Azur, France's southern playground.

It did not take us long to realize that true friendship mattered far more than glitter. I am glad that I discovered this early in life so that I would not spend my time searching for what can never truly bring happiness. Grace and I spoke about this; being surrounded by such opulence made us both appreciate simplicity and tranquility as luxuries. Friendship meant a great deal to her, but genuine friends were not easy to come by in her position. We enjoyed getting together for tea at my home, or visiting in their private apartments at the Palace, chatting endlessly about everything and nothing at all.

Grace told me that she was really going to miss me when we moved, as Martin was soon being transferred. We had received word from the Foreign Service that he would be promoted to Second Secretary of Embassy in Paris. At the age of twenty-six, Martin was quickly getting recognized and rising through the ranks of the U.S. Foreign Service.

Just before our move to Paris, Grace and Rainier invited us to see the ranch that they were creating at Mont Agel, in the mountains above Monaco, about thirty-five minutes away. The estate would be called "Rocagel," which the press usually spelled as two words (Roc Agel); however, "Rocagel" always appeared as one word in Grace and Rainier's letters and letterhead.

Prince Rainier drove us in one of his convertibles to the barren land that would soon become their sanctuary. The four of us sat down under the solitary tree to a sumptuous picnic, from the most elaborate and complete picnic basket I have ever seen. The basket overflowed with all sorts of wonderful Monégasque delicacies, accompanied by champagne. There was *pissaladière*, a thin-crusted, onion and anchovy tart with black olives. There were also various sandwiches, including the "pièce de résistance": Grace's favorite, peanut butter and jelly! Peanut butter was not available in France at that time, so she had imported it specially from America. I always giggle at the idea of peanut butter and jelly with champagne, but it was a real treat for us. It was June 1, the day after Prince

Rainier's birthday, so out of the picnic basket came a marvelous birthday cake, complete with candles, for us to celebrate.

We spent the afternoon discussing plans for the house and farm that they were about to build. There had been nothing on the property except a small stone shepherd's hut, which they were going to incorporate into the house to form part of the ground-floor guest suites. Grace and Rainier were eager to have a rather modest and cozy retreat where they could relax and get away from the enormity of the Palace in seclusion; it would become their true family home. Now that they had two babies, Grace wanted a place to nest and nurture her family, and Rainier was willing to move heaven and earth to give it to her as quickly as possible. They must have had a multitude of builders working around the clock, because the next time we saw Rocagel, the transformation was absolutely astounding.

DAYS OF FRIENDSHIP

We left the French Riviera, and traded our beautiful house for an apartment in Paris near the Arc de Triomphe. We settled into the busy Parisian lifestyle, where I spent the next several months walking baby Charles in the nearby *Bois de Boulogne* and enjoying the magnificent "City of Light."

Grace wrote to me at the end of September: "We moved into our house [at Rocagel] three weeks ago and are still trying to push out the painters, plumbers, carpenters, etc. It is quite a job & we have been working very hard indeed but having great fun... I have even planted a garden & much to my surprise - it is growing! ...We expect to be in Paris for a few weeks in October, and I hope we will be able to see you at that time."

Grace and Rainier spent a few weeks each year in Paris, usually in the month of October. Prince Rainier's grandfather had kept an apartment there in the large official legation of Monaco, but this was too much like the grand opulence and formality of the Palace. Rainier wanted more of a home for Grace and the family, in an apartment with a nearby park for the children. Grace enjoyed decorating this apartment, and spent time shopping and going to the Paris fashion houses of Dior, Lanvin, Givenchy and Balenciaga to see their Fall collections. In Paris, Grace and Rainier went to the theater, to museums and shops, and saw friends. They also went to see Rainier's mother at the nearby *Château de Marchais*.

When Grace and Rainier came to Paris, I was invited to their elegant apartment near the *Bois de Boulogne*. I arrived at the door with two shopping bags filled with Gerber's baby food for baby Albert, which I had been able to get at the Armed Forces PX. As I stood waiting at the front door, a very regal lady arrived and glanced at me with these bags in hand, probably thinking that I was a delivery woman. Upon opening the door, the valet said "Your Highness," so I realized it must have been Prince Rainier's imposing mother, Princess Charlotte, whom I had never met. She was escorted to the salon, while I was led to the master bedroom, where Grace was trying on beautiful clothes from a famous Parisian couturier. Grace welcomed me with open arms. We chatted for a while as fitters fussed around her, then I left because I knew they had many official engagements.

Paris – October 30, 1958

Dearest Mum and Dad,

It appears that we might be here for four years, if we wish. Paris is a wonderful city, and it would give Charles a chance to speak French. I received a lovely box of candied Riviera fruit from Grace. I went to their apartment the day before they left and was there while Grace had fittings of some eight Balenciaga gowns, suits, dresses, etc. They were gorgeous. She still is as sweet as ever – and as lovely as ever.

All for now and all our love, Joan, Marty and Charlesie

Martin had been transferred to Paris in order to participate in negotiations on the Friendship, Commerce and Navigation Treaty (FCN) between the United States and France. Ever since 1793, when America repealed the first Friendship Treaty with France due to an incident called the Citizen Genêt Affair, the two countries had been unable to come to terms on a new treaty, despite having been allies in two World Wars! The FCN would fill a huge diplomatic void, and Martin, at the age of twenty-seven, was the only other American at the negotiating table, charged with an enormous task of diplomacy: addressing rights of establishment, insurance, banking, trade, commerce, etc.

Martin was assisting Mr. Herman Walker Jr., the American Counselor of Embassy for Commercial Affairs, who had previously headed the Treaty Division at the U.S. Department of State. Because Mr. Walker had been the head of the division, there was no one in Washington to whom he had to report back, so he had the full authority to negotiate on behalf of the United States. These were very rare circumstances in diplomacy.

Twice a week, Martin and Mr. Walker would negotiate with the large French delegation, and Martin wrote up the reports. Mr. Walker was a brilliant man from the Ozarks, with a master's degree from Harvard and a Ph.D. from Duke University. He spoke some French, having studied at the University of Paris, but he relied heavily on Martin's fluency. Throughout the course of the negotiations, Martin wanted to make sure that he had gotten all of the nuances correct regarding what had been agreed upon, in order to draw up the terms of the Treaty, which would be printed in both languages. For verification, he frequently consulted with his counterpart in the French delegation, Charles de Chambrun, whose family members owned Baccarat Crystal, and were direct descendants of the Marquis de Lafayette. (He would later play an important role in saving Martin from President Charles de Gaulle's vendetta against him.) After a long period of negotiation, the Franco-American Treaty of Establishment was finally signed in Paris on November 25, 1959.

But no sooner had we gotten settled in Paris, than we received word that we were being transferred again! Perhaps Martin was doing his job a little too well, helping to get the French to agree to the terms of a friendship treaty when others had failed to do so for 160 years... I loved living in France and was sad at the thought of leaving. Such was the life of a diplomat and his family, so I would make the most of the time that I had in any one place. I was really looking forward to seeing Grace while we still lived in Europe.

Paris – April 20, 1959

Dearest Mum and Dad,

The Dales are on the move again! You had better come soon as we are going to be transferred to Washington for six months in January, 1960 – then onwards to FORMOSA (Taiwan) for a two-year intensive Chinese language training period. It has taken our breaths away.

The Department wrote that it is a great honor to be chosen to study so difficult a language (ha!), but I am sure that it will be fascinating, and we are both very pleased. I hope we can find a place to live in Washington for 6 months. Life certainly is never dull.

I just had a letter from Grace saying that they would arrive in Paris this week, and she would phone me to arrange to see us and for Charles to play with

Caroline. There is so much to do and to see in Paris and I had better hurry as we only have eight months left here.

All our love, Joan, Marty and Charlesie

Paris was an exciting city, which we loved to explore. Whenever Princess Grace and Prince Rainier were in town, we would always try to think of various new ways of entertaining them – something that would be different from the ordinary. Our royal friends had so many formal events that we thought something fun and informal would be a good idea. We found a delightful Parisian restaurant serving Indonesian Rijsttafel – a type of smorgasbord featuring a selection of exotic and spicy dishes served with rice. It was a long dinner, well accompanied by a variety of drinks, and the four of us were in a merry mood. The restaurant stayed open late for us, then at 2 a.m. we decided to go to a stylish Parisian cellar nightclub. It was great fun, and we all got along famously, laughing and joking the whole night.

Afterwards, we went back to our apartment and asked Grace and Rainier in for a drink, which they accepted, much to our surprise, as it was very late. We enjoyed chatting and drinking cognac for quite a while. The next day Grace called me to say, "It was a delightful evening, and we had such a wonderful time. However, on the way home, Rainier and I got into a terrible argument, but this morning neither of us could remember what it was about!"

Paris – May 5, 1959

Dearest Mum and Dad,

We went to dinner at Grace and Rainier's apartment and had a delightful informal evening with just the two of them. The next day I took Charles over to play with Caroline, and you should have seen how sweet they were together. Charles wanted to play, but Caroline was a little shy. She is very pretty and quite advanced for her age in talking. She is very tall and dwarfed poor Charlesie. Prince Rainier adored Charles and enjoyed amusing him with all sorts of toys and burying his face in Charlesie's tummy to make him giggle. The next day Grace told me that Caroline said, "Caroline put on hat and coat and go find Charles."

Grace is much better now, and her stamina is amazing [she had recently had an appendectomy]. The Prince insisted three times that we all come and stay at "Rocagel," their home on the cliffs behind Monaco. Maybe we shall.

Love always, Joan

On numerous occasions, Martin and I were invited to Grace and Rainier's Paris apartment for casual dinners with just the four of us, which still consisted of several courses. One such dinner began with martinis and foie gras appetizers, followed by turtle soup (which was quite popular in France at that time), partridge with champagne and rice pilaf, cheese, custard, Chianti, coffee, and champagne. We enjoyed these delightful evenings, talking late into the night.

When they moved to an apartment on Avenue Foch, Grace hired interior decorator, George Stacey, who had decorated the New York apartment that she had lived in before her marriage. She wanted him to "do" their new Paris apartment. The Prince was not fond of having a decorator, and was not particularly thrilled with the ceramic stove that Stacey placed in their living room! I was a little amazed by its odd placement, but said nothing.

On May 9, Prince Rainier wrote Martin a note saying how wonderful it was to see us in Paris, and thanking us for the Indonesian meal. He said, "…I hope that before we gather round the Formosan meatballs, we will be able to see you both in Paris and in this part of the world, very soon? All best wishes to both of you and of course this goes for wee Charles!"

FROM THE DESK OF
MARTIN A. DALE

Paris – May 21, 1959

<u>*PERSONAL*</u>

H.S.H. Prince Rainier of Monaco
Your Highness,

Thank you for your letter of May 9th enclosing the documentary notes on the methods of incorporation in the Principality. Please excuse my tardy reply, but I deemed it prudent first to obtain clearance on my project to write a brochure on "Establishing a Business in Monaco." I am pleased to report that my *superiors at the Embassy and the Department of Commerce have given an enthusiastic green light to the project.*

Joan and I were delighted to have seen you and the Princess during your recent visit to Paris, and I only hope that the Indonesian dinner had no ill effects on the Princess. I must admit that we suffered slight malaise as a consequence of our piquant adventure, and we were worried that Princess Grace's appendicitis operation only a few weeks before might have caused her even greater distress. We sincerely hope that we will have the pleasure of your visit in Formosa and promise not to spike the tea.

I am sure you would not believe me if I claimed that Charles is still talking about his afternoon romp with Princess Caroline, if only because you know that he has not yet learned to say much other than "Dada" and "cookie." Caroline is a very beautiful young lady, however, and I hope that Charles will continue to demonstrate such a discerning eye for the opposite sex. We shall all three look forward to playing with Prince Albert in the fall.

Joan joins me in sending you and Princess Grace our best regards,

Sincerely, Martin

The Prince responded to Martin's letter: "I am very pleased with the news concerning the work you wish to do on 'establishing business in Monaco.' Also I am delighted to hear that your superiors are in favour of this work and will encourage you." He said that they were really looking forward to seeing us in Monaco in September, and that Caroline was still talking about "little boy Charles."

Grace and Rainier invited us up to their mountain hideaway of Rocagel to see their newly built retreat. It had been completely transformed, bearing absolutely no resemblance to the place that we had seen the year before. The once-rocky terrain was now a verdant oasis. It had a ranch-like atmosphere on about twenty acres, with a pony enclosure in front of the understated elegance of the *Mas* (a Provençal style farmhouse), which had been built on the site of the original shepherd's hut we had seen previously. It was a charming, unique, and magnificent white house with green shutters and a crow's nest construction on the top overlooking Monaco.

The Prince loved trees, and had actually planted all four hundred of the fruit trees and other shade trees. He loved to do that sort of thing, finding it relaxing and a welcome change of pace from official duties. He would plan where to put the tree, dig the hole himself and then plant it. The trees were now beginning to fill out and grow tall, creating a beautiful and peaceful setting. Rainier had also put in all of the paths around the property, driving the bulldozer himself.

Prince Rainier had a tremendous love of animals. There were farm animals of all sorts on the ranch, and the children reveled in stroking rabbits, cows, sheep, horses, chickens, goats and ponies. The family had a vegetable garden and ate the eggs that came from their own chickens. It was a real farm that they very much enjoyed in their leisure time. (Eventually, Rainier would create his own zoo at Rocagel, complete with exotic cats – Grace used to get very nervous when the Prince let his big female cheetah roam freely in the house! I found it frightening, but the Prince had amazing courage and complete trust of wild animals.)

Rainier wanted to show Martin and me what had been done to the property since we were last there. He drove us around the grounds in his jeep, over a terribly bumpy road that led to a promontory overlooking the spectacular sparkling jewel of Monaco far below. It was breathtakingly gorgeous. However, I was pregnant with my second child and jokingly said, "If this baby is born prematurely due to this incredibly rocky ride, we will call him Rainier!" The Prince laughed. When Prince Rainier found out that I was expecting again, he gave me a very funny plaque showing a rather unhappy pregnant woman that said, "I *should* have danced all night!" (A play on words from the popular song from *My Fair Lady*, "I Could Have Danced All Night.")

A bit shaken from our drive, we returned to the house, which felt comfortable and lived-in even though it had been so recently built. Grace took us on a tour of the fourteen-room home, explaining that it had turned out to be somewhat larger than the cozy retreat they had envisioned. While Grace had been looking over the plans, she had assumed that all the measurements written along the walls were in feet as in America, without realizing that the French measured in meters (which are three times as long). As a result, everything turned out to be much larger than she had imagined it would be! When she saw the foundations laid, she was quite astounded, and told me that she couldn't believe how immense it was. Ultimately, when the house was complete, she and Rainier managed to make it very homey, and one didn't feel the size. It was cozy, like an English country home, and it really was just perfect for them.

Immediately upon entering, we could sense the warm atmosphere, which both Grace and Rainier always managed to create wherever they were. There was a pleasant clutter in the entry hall, which was quite large, with a white marble floor. The immense foyer formed the central hub for the living room, dining room, outdoor terrace, the Prince's study, and the graceful staircase to the second floor.

A black and gold Chinese screen placed crosswise cleverly divided the large living room. The furnishings were a comfortable mix of French and Chinese, the only real unity being the flowered chintz fabric of green and white roses on a black background, covering the sofa and the overstuffed chairs. Fresh flower arrangements abounded, lending a lightness and brightness to the pleasant surroundings. Two paintings by Dufy flanked the simple antique marble mantelpiece. Assorted books lay about, along with Grace's ever-present current needlepoint project, always neatly put away in a cloth bag designed specially for that purpose. (Over the years, the room remained the same – even when I saw it twenty years later, only the chintz coverings had been replaced, but with the identical material.)

The upper bedrooms were large and airy, with bedrooms for the children and their nurse, topped by a cozy "eagle's nest" room. The master bedroom was beautifully decorated, and on the double bed was one of the small baby pillows that Grace took with her on her travels. I never asked Grace why she slept on it, but I have heard that it is excellent for posture and wrinkle-free skin. Judging from Grace's appearance throughout her life, the pillow did a wonderful job.

The guest rooms were on the ground floor of the house, beneath the living room. Their design had incorporated the vaulted ceilings of the original shepherd's hut, which were rough-finished white plaster, making the rooms delightfully cool in the hot summer. An intimate family chapel was also included on the property for the celebration of Sunday Mass.

After our tour of the house, Caroline took us down to her playhouse and served us tea from her miniature tea set. She was a very graceful little princess with sparkling eyes, and we were all quite spellbound by her maturity for a toddler of two-and-a-half. The children went inside the playhouse while we all stood outside looking into the windows. Caroline was serving tea to Charles, who was just under two years old – it was adorable.

Caroline picked some little wildflowers, which she handed to her mommy. Then the children rode around in the pony trap, a small open carriage driven by a nanny. Caroline was very motherly, looking after Charles to make sure he did not fall out. When Charles got down from the pony trap, she took him by the hand and led him all around. It was very sweet. We all enjoyed a delightful afternoon together.

Martin and I spent the next three weeks of September visiting our friends on the French Riviera, and going to the Monte Carlo Beach Club with Grace and the children. Before we returned to Paris, we were invited to Rocagel several more times for casual dinners that lasted until well past midnight. Sometimes after dinner, we went down to the Prince's "cave," a room lined with African masks and souvenirs from his exotic travels, which was next to the guest suites. This is where he kept his drums, which he would play for us – he was an excellent drummer.

Two weeks later, Princess Grace and Prince Rainier came to Paris again, this time for an official visit which included a number of special events that had been planned in their honor. On October 12, 1959, General Charles de Gaulle, President of France, welcomed Their Serene Highnesses to Paris as his illustrious guests for a state visit to the Elysée Palace, the office and residence of the President of the French Republic (the equivalent of the White House). Grace was breathtaking in the finely beaded white Lanvin gown that her father-in-law, Prince Pierre, had given to her as a wedding present. She told me that she had to have the dress slightly altered after her two pregnancies, because she had been extremely thin at the time of her wedding. That night, Grace wore a tiara that featured three detachable clips of large ruby cabochons with diamonds, which she often detached from the tiara to adorn her evening gowns.

Grace could not wear her eyeglasses with a long formal gown, and could not tolerate contact lenses because of her allergies, so she decided to look for the tallest man in the room, which was sure to be President de Gaulle. Standing at about six feet five inches in height, De Gaulle was a commanding and rather imposing figure. He was immediately captivated by Grace and enchanted by her charm, her warmth and her beauty. The President gave this toast, roughly translated as follows:

"Monseigneur, it is my particular pleasure to welcome Your Serene Highness to Paris with Princess Grace and to express the great friendship of France. You are, Monseigneur, the noble representative of a dynasty that has not ceased to maintain with us the most close and trusting relations. This is no doubt a process of the geographic and political nature of things. But they are equally inspired by the best reasons of the spirit and the heart. As for us, we hold precious the evidence such as, for example, the act concluded by your great-grandfather, Prince Albert, to settle our relations, or the fact that during the course of WWI your grandfather, Prince Louis II, believed it his duty to belong to the French

Army as a Brigadier General, or the valiant participation that You even wanted to make in the ranks of our 1st Army in the battle which liberated Europe and carried our flags on the Rhine and the Danube. Yes, Monseigneur, Your visit consecrates communal interests and feelings, which create between our two countries an exemplary association. You mark it today. But let me add, that at the same time, You give us the greatest pleasure. Because we can, in Your presence, address this testimony to You, as heir to the work achieved in the Principality of Monaco by Your illustrious ancestors, You act in Your turn, in favor of letters, of sciences and of arts, and fertilize action that profits human progress. But also we have the opportunity of telling You how much, in France, You are popular and to what point the very widespread image of the charming sovereign family created by You touches us, by the very gracious Princess Grace and Your two young children. I raise my glass in honor of His Serene Highness Prince Rainier, in honor of Her Serene Highness Princess Grace, and in honor of the Principality of Monaco."

On October 13, the Mayor of the City of Paris received Their Serene Highnesses for a reception in their honor at the *Hôtel de Ville*, where the Mayor's palatial offices are. The *Hôtel de Ville* was very impressive and, upon entering, felt as if one were going back in time a few centuries. Two thousand Parisians cheered the Prince and Princess as they ascended a seemingly never-ending grand staircase carpeted in red, flanked by the *Garde Nationale* in full dress uniforms with plumed helmets. The President of the Paris Municipal Council said the marriage of Prince Rainier to Princess Grace "has permitted the most charming of princesses to achieve the peaceful conquest of France."

Following the reception that evening, Grace and Rainier were guests at a formal dinner at the historic *Hôtel de Lauzun* on the Île Saint-Louis, the island in the center of the Seine River. It was an ancient setting, filled with memories of long-forgotten eras. Grace wore a white satin gown with a short, multicolored, long-sleeved top. Her jewelry was very simple: a double strand of pearls gracing her swan-like neck, and matching pearl earrings. The Prince was dashing as ever in white tie and tails, decorated with all of his medals.

Prince Rainier had been awarded more than seventeen medals, including the French *Croix de Guerre* and the Bronze Star for bravery under fire against the Nazis, when he served in the French Army, eventually receiving the rank of Colonel. His grandfather, Prince Louis II, had been a Grand Officer of the Legion of Honor and became Brigadier General in the French Army after serving in WWI. Following a family tradition of loyalty to France, Prince Rainier enlisted as a Second Lieutenant in World War II, serving in Alsace.

Because he spoke English, he was sent to Strasbourg to be a liaison with the U.S. Army Texas Rangers. Among other honors, he also held the Grand Cross of the Legion of Honor of France.

On official occasions, and especially on State visits, Prince Rainier wore his medals as a sign of respect for those who had awarded them to him. Some people in the press accused the Prince of wanting to show off all his decorations, but he was aware that those in high positions got very upset, and were even offended, if he did not wear them. On one occasion, Martin noticed the Prince looking somewhat burdened by all the pomp and circumstance. He said, "Monseigneur, you look a little reluctant today." The Prince replied, "This is my duty. If I had my choice, I would be a gentleman farmer."

Paris – October 24, 1959

Dearest Mum and Dad,

This has been quite an unforgettable week. Grace and Rainier came to our apartment for cocktails, and then we went out to an Hungarian restaurant for a marvelous dinner, complete with zither, violin, cimbalom – and much wine. We tasted all the specialties: goose liver, sausages, goulash, chicken paprika, stuffed cabbage, etc., and by the time we left after midnight we were very gay. Rainier insisted on taking us to an old student haunt of his (where he said he would not dare take his other more stodgy friends). We danced, saw a floorshow, were offered roses by the owner, consumed four bottles of champagne (!) and staggered home at 4:30 a.m. with great hilarity. We all had a grand time together, but the next morning – Oh! We felt terrible. I cannot drink champagne because of the bubbles.

That was the last night that we had our Mercedes – we shall have a lovely dark blue Mercedes 220 (larger car) on November 20th. The Prince was disturbed that we should be carless and promptly offered us the use of his Peugeot car – which of course we declined. He insisted all during the week, even calling Marty at the Embassy to renew the offer, saying, "you are the hardest people to lend a car to!" He seemed hurt, so the result is we are now driving Rainier's car! It is difficult to win his friendship, but once won, it knows no limits. He even wanted us to sail from Cannes and stay with them before we left, and as much as we should like to, it is impossible. It would be too much for me at this point in the pregnancy with 12 days on the ship instead of four, additional traveling, etc. They even offered to have [Grace's dog] Oliver sire [our dog] Fara's puppies – but she comes into heat at the wrong time, unfortunately.

Last Friday was an evening to remember always. We were invited by the Prince and Princess, upon request from Prince Pierre de Polignac, Rainier's father, to join in his birthday celebration at Maxim's! We are so flattered! It was black tie night at Maxim's, and we were two of the ten guests. Grace and Rainier, Prince Pierre, Prince Louis de Polignac (Rainier's cousin and owner of Pommery Champagne and Lanvin-Castillo Couturier and perfumes), the Roger Crovettos (owner of Veuve Clicquot Champagne), Pierre Rey (ex-President of the S.B.M. of Monaco, of whom we have often spoken), ourselves, and the Maharani of Baroda, whose husband is one of the wealthiest men in the world. She is reputed to possess a few billion dollars worth of jewels – and I believe it, judging from what she was wearing that evening. Marty is still dazzled as he remembers holding several million dollars worth when he danced with the Maharani. She is a beautiful woman, very intelligent and mystic, who is divorced from the Maharajah and who managed no mean feat of keeping her son and great wealth. She was wearing an emerald green and gold sari, and around her neck was a three-strand pearl necklace – each pearl being the size of a giant pea and clasped by a 30-carat diamond surrounded by diamonds two to three carats apiece. Her earrings were enormous things of eight-carat diamonds and huge emerald drops, and even though they hung to her shoulders she did not look garish. Her rings were huge diamonds, but the most exceptional item was the clasp on one of her pearl bracelets – it was an emerald the size of a matchbox with about a twenty-carat square-cut diamond inlaid in it! I must say that we have never seen anything like it. I wonder what her other jewels are like.

Grace was dressed very simply in pink satin with small pearl-and-diamond earrings and a small pearl pendant. For their State Reception by General de Gaulle she was dressed like a queen and won all Parisian hearts through her simplicity and sweetness.

To return to Maxim's, our dinner consisted of lobster bisque, filets of sole in cognac, filet of beef with foie gras and truffles, cheese, raspberry sherbet and Prince Pierre's birthday cake – plus champagne. We danced and talked until 2 a.m. (I wore the moonstone and blue lace maternity dress.)

The next day we went over to their apartment to pick up the car and to say "au revoir" for several years. Rainier gave Charles a little steering wheel with horn and gearshift so that he could drive when Daddy drove. It was sweet of him. They have left now, as they are to be received in Rome by the President in a few weeks.

This letter has been full of one topic – but it was thrilling, and we shall have fond memories. We shall really miss our friends.

Incidentally, Albie is extremely handsome and is always smiling through his Irish eyes. Caroline is a sweet little girl and was very taken with Charlesie. All for now. Hope all is well with you.

All our love, Joan, Marty, Charlesie

Martin and I were very flattered to be invited to Prince Pierre's birthday dinner at the exclusive Maxim's of Paris, especially in such illustrious company. Princess Grace had pre-ordered some of Prince Pierre's favorite dishes for our group, including filet of beef. However, Grace did not realize that the Maharani of Baroda was a strict vegetarian for religious reasons, so amid much embarrassment, a replacement dish had to be prepared.

Our dinner continued with lively and interesting conversation, but apparently embarrassment was on the menu for me that evening as well. I was seated next to a gentleman who introduced himself as Roger Crovetto. I cannot drink anything effervescent, so as we spoke, I was very discreetly maneuvering a small gold swizzle stick around in my glass to remove the bubbles from my champagne. Suddenly, Mr. Crovetto said, "Madame, we have spent years putting those bubbles in the champagne, and now you are taking them out." I smiled and said, "Pardon?" He explained, "I am the owner of Veuve Clicquot Champagne!" I must have turned several shades of crimson, but he just laughed. He was one of Prince Rainier's closest friends from boarding school, whom we later got to know quite well. He had a wonderful sense of humor like the Prince, so he was somewhat amused.

A few days earlier, on an October Sunday when the leaves were a glorious myriad of colors, and the slight nip in the air heralded winter, the Prince asked us to join them on a family outing to the gardens of the Palace of Versailles. Prince Rainier drove his black Peugeot 403 – the same one he wanted to lend us. It was not a very large car, so it ended up being quite packed, with Caroline, age two-and-a-half, Charles and Albert, both under two years of age, Grace and Rainier, Martin and myself. The children were well behaved for being so young, though Albert and Charles would occasionally raise quite a little ruckus, but it did not disturb our very competent driver, Prince Rainier.

People passing the car on the road did a double take as some of them recognized the well-known profile of the Prince. I suppose they were surprised that the family was like any other out for a Sunday drive, and not being chauffeured as one might expect. Rainier loved to drive. He was also passionate about car racing, and I think he would have liked being a professional racecar driver if he had not been destined to be a sovereign prince.

We entered the majestic park of the *Château de Versailles* by the lower gate. The gardens were so beautiful in the autumn, and the air was bracing as the kiddies ran and played in the fallen leaves, expending their seemingly inexhaustible energy. We chased after the romping children, watched the gorgeous sunset, and chatted about Their Highnesses' three-day official visit to the French government and President Charles de Gaulle, which had been a fabulous affair. The children nibbled on cookies that we had brought along, and then the Prince drove us back to their apartment, where Charles had dinner with Albert and Caroline while we had cocktails. We left around 7:45 p.m., which was past the children's bedtimes, but it had been a special occasion.

FROM THE DESK OF
MARTIN A. DALE

Paris – November 13, 1959

H.S.H. Prince Rainier of Monaco
Your Highness,

Joan and I are eternally grateful to you for your having let us use your "403" these past few weeks. Although I have used the car as sparingly as possible, I find that we have driven over 200 kilometers and, looking back, I don't know how we could have managed if we had been obliged to use public transportation. There have been no mishaps, but your Minister will probably be surprised when he receives the seven or eight tickets I have collected by parking in bus stops. Please let me know if I should stop now or try for an even dozen.

I am enclosing some duplicates of the color slides, which I took at Rocagel. I seem to have specialized in rear views, and Albert appears to have been very successful in avoiding being photographed, a quality that he will undoubtedly find useful as he grows older. We hope, however, that you will honor us with a front view of all of you that we may gaze at nostalgically as we huddle over the brazier in our bamboo hut while the typhoon rages outside. The motion picture film that I took turned out extremely well, but Kodak refuses to duplicate 8mm color film. Unless we can get it done in the States, we shall have to use it as bait to induce you to visit us in Formosa. The film and the enticing prospect of Formosan meatballs eaten with chopsticks should prove irresistible.

We hope that your official visit to Rome was enjoyable and not too exhausting. You have returned, of course, just in time for the festivities of your National Holiday. Your endurance must be extraordinary; there are very few people with the stamina to take the round of parties to which you are subjected. I say a little prayer every night to thank God that I wasn't born a Prince. But Joan and I want to add our personal congratulations to you on the tenth anniversary of your official accession to the throne and our best wishes for your name day.

Joan and I are very sad at the thought that it may be several years before we have the pleasure of being with you and Princess Grace again. We hope, however, that the time may be shortened by arranging a reunion somewhere in the Far East. Until then, we send you and Grace our fondest personal regards.

Sincerely,
Martin

Prince Rainier enjoyed Martin's humor, and he appreciated that although Martin always remained respectful of the Prince's position, he was never intimidated by it. The Prince loved witty banter, which he carried on in his letters, responding to Martin: "*Cher Monsieur l'Ambassadeur*! ...I am happy that your cinematographic efforts were crowned with success and thus you will have some kind (even if only rear views) of remembrance of Rocagel and us, its inhabitants... How sad that you and Mrs. Dale and Charles are all going off without us being able to wave you off even! Do hope it will not be ages until we meet again – somewhere. Please try and make it so. As I, having been arrived to this post, will not be moving until I go to the ground! We will make sincere and true efforts to get near to you all – Japan would be a rather good meeting spot?! No?... I hope that you will, dear Martin, keep in touch with us and that we will be able to follow you in your diplomatic adventure."

Paris – December 4, 1959

Dearest Mum and Dad,

Yesterday, we received a very warm letter from Prince Rainier saying how sorry he was to see us go and promising to come to Formosa or Japan to see us. He is very sweet and thoughtful to friends. Grace and Rainier also sent us a signed informal photograph of themselves and the children taken at Rocagel. We are so pleased to have it. We are all well and anxious to leave now, although we do have a few regrets about leaving this lovely city.

All love, Joan, Marty, Charlesie

DAYS OF DECISIONS

When we first entered the U.S. Diplomatic Service, Martin had said that he would be interested in a post in China. We had also requested countries around the Mediterranean other than France. We wanted to experience the Mediterranean culture, which was most interesting to us: Greece, Turkey or even North Africa sounded fascinating. Many of the other officers entering the Foreign Service had requested France, but they were posted to all the other countries! It was extraordinary that we were assigned to such special and desirable posts as Marseille, Nice and Paris, and even more amazing that we could speak the language. It had obviously been serendipitous.

SS UNITED STATES
December 20, 1959

Dearest Mum and Dad,

We are having a grand time aboard this ship, despite the heavy seas. We really were sad to leave, as so much of our lives have been spent there, and so many things have happened to us there. We have every reason to return some day for our friends. We received a lovely telegram on board ship: "Bon voyage - Merry Christmas and affectionate thoughts - Rai Grace." It was sweet of them to think of us. See you soon.

Love from us all, Joan

Whenever Rainier and Grace sent a public message to us, either a telegram or a postcard from their many travels, they would often disguise his name by writing either "Rai" or simply "R." This prevented these communications from being intercepted, as Grace is a name that is fairly prevalent, but the name "Rainier" could only be associated with the Prince of Monaco, because it is so unusual. In the early years, Grace used to pronounce his name in a very American fashion: "Ray-neeyay." Over time, she would pronounce it correctly as "Ren-yay." Her delightful voice was unique and endearing, and I missed it very much after we left France.

I felt great comfort and excitement whenever I heard from Grace. It was always touching for me to receive letters from her, as I knew how busy she was. I was honored that she would think of me and take the time to write such long and chatty letters to keep me informed of what was happening in her life and with her family.

Grace wrote me a sweet letter soon after we arrived in the United States: "How exciting about Martin's promotion - that is wonderful news! Please give him our congratulations... Am so sorry to know of little Charles' ankle - It absolutely frightens me to think of what we must go through with boys - Albert hasn't really started to let loose yet, but I'm holding my breath - But boys are lazy, you know, and you mustn't let him make you carry him all of the time as it can't be very good for you... We are both exhausted as we have been very busy - And now I must move the Red Cross into another building & organize the alterations there - I'm beginning to be an authority of French building & decoration - Although it's very likely to be the end of me... I do hope that these last days are not too uncomfortable. We will be thinking of you - Please let us know about the baby, we will be anxious to hear."

We found a house to rent temporarily in Washington, D.C., as we prepared for our transfer to our new post at the U.S. Consulate in Taiwan. The move from Paris was rather stressful because I was eight months pregnant at the time. Soon after we arrived in the USA, we took Charles to see the sights of the capital city, which made quite an impression on a young boy; our rambunctious two-year-old ran up and down the lawn at the Washington Monument until he fell and badly sprained his ankle, causing me to have to carry him everywhere for two weeks during my last month of pregnancy. I was on my own, as Martin was too busy at the State Department to help.

Martin had been promoted to Class 5 and commissioned Consul, the equivalent military rank of a colonel. He was in Washington to attend the State Department's school for foreign languages, undergoing an intensive six-month training program to learn to speak Mandarin Chinese. The Diplomatic Service obviously recognized Martin's penchant for languages, as he had learned to speak and read Russian at Princeton, as well as being fluent in French.

Chinese is extremely difficult for a westerner to learn, so Martin studied diligently day and night, with classes for ten hours a day, six days a week, plus calligraphy studies on Sundays. Chinese is a tonal language, where the same word can mean completely different things depending on the tone one uses. There was a phonetics teacher to make sure that he had the right pronunciation and would not offend someone by inadvertently uttering some kind of insult with the wrong intonation. Martin became so fluent that he even began dreaming in Mandarin!

Martin's teacher was an enormously cultured man who had held very high positions in China before coming to America. He was a Chinese Christian, who had been the publisher of a Chinese Catholic newspaper until the Communists took over China. After long days of classes, he invited Martin to his home for dinners with his wife, followed by private in-depth tutoring in Chinese customs. Eventually, he ceremoniously adopted Martin as his son, which Martin thought was a great honor, until he realized that in Chinese tradition it meant that he would have to look after his teacher for the rest of his life!

During this time, Martin received a very touching letter from Rainier that made us very nostalgic for our life in Europe: "...I do wish that you had been able to drive the car down to Monaco, so that we could have had the pleasure of seeing you before you were off... And what a shame to feel you have left this continent! No more of our picturesque meetings and soirées in Paris! The pleasure of your company, now impossible with distance in ocean, as separation... sad!... *Mais la vie doit continuer pour chacun et tous* [but life must go on for each and for all] and I suppose that you will before long be a very solemn ambassador! And I will be an old crummy Prince full of souvenirs and regrets! We will then have a pack of souvenirs to unfold. How sad and dreary it seems now, and yet we will enjoy it all so much on the moment!... I would so like to find someone that I could have very close to myself to work with, and who would be a good supervisor of the affairs, and who could study and follow through different problems and their solutions. I need this kind of person... but it is so hard to find!"

On February 10, 1960, our second son, Gregory, was born in the midst of a blinding blizzard. My parents came to Washington, D.C., to help take care of the boys. They were eager to spend some time with us while we were in North

America for a few months, as we were expected to spend the next few years in the Far East. I was their only child whom they had very late in life, and they were terribly concerned about us going to the other side of the world.

While we were in Washington, we corresponded often with Grace and Rainier, sharing news and being kept up-to-date on what was happening in Monaco. Grace wrote: "We were so happy to receive the wonderful news of the arrival of your new baby boy and do hope that you are both doing well - It is very exciting & I'm sure Charles must be quite delighted & enthused with all of this excitement - I can imagine your joy and we are both so happy for you... Our congratulations to the proud daddy & grandparents & my warmest wishes to you & to your babe for a long and happy life - with Love - Grace –"

We spent our six months in Washington, D.C., preparing both physically and psychologically for our new post at the Consulate in Taichung, Taiwan, which would be an entirely new and different cultural environment than anything we had experienced before. I had never been to Asia, but I had always been interested in Oriental art and culture, so I was really excited at first. However, our post in Taichung was up in the hills, so we would be quite isolated. I was not sure what I would find there, and as a mother of a newborn baby, I was becoming increasingly anxious about what kind of medical attention there might be, especially in case of an emergency.

I was also missing the life we had in Europe, and particularly the friendship that we had enjoyed with Princess Grace and Prince Rainier. Although they vowed to meet us somewhere in Asia, I was worried that we might not see them again for a long time. It felt like we were moving to the ends of the Earth, far away from everything and everyone that we knew and loved.

When Prince Rainier wrote to Martin saying that he needed someone whom he could trust to work closely with him at solving problems, I encouraged Martin to explore the options of offering his services to the Prince. Martin was a specialist in problem solving, particularly regarding economics.

Martin had received his Masters in Economics and International Finance from the Fletcher School of Law and Diplomacy, jointly administered by Harvard and Tufts Universities. Upon graduating with Honors, his goal had been to enter the United States Diplomatic Service. However this seemed highly unlikely at that time, as Senator Joseph McCarthy had implemented a three-year hiring freeze, fearing that the dreaded Communists had found ways to infiltrate the State Department.

During the McCarthy era of the Cold War, various branches of the United States Government had to revise their hiring practices. The U.S. Foreign Service had therefore established an extremely difficult screening process to weed out potential risks to national security. These intensive security measures consisted of rigorous examinations and stringent background investigations, in order to ensure that only the most outstanding and upright Americans would be recruited.

Martin was put through seventy-two hours of grueling interrogations and written exams designed to see if he would break under pressure, methods that were abolished soon afterward. Once he passed these tests and background checks, he was sworn in as a proud member of the first class of new Foreign Service Officers to be admitted into the U.S. Diplomatic Corps and quickly rose through the ranks, gaining a great deal of recognition.

At the U.S. Embassy in Paris, Martin's superiors had given him approval to write a brochure on "Establishing a Business in Monaco," during which time he discovered that he had an excellent working rapport with Prince Rainier. In creating the brochure, Martin had a chance to explore issues relating to incorporation in the Principality, as well as the relations between France and Monaco. Martin found out that the Prince was quite American in his thinking and in what he wanted for his Principality. They had a strong meeting of the minds, as well as a trusting friendship.

Martin was truly torn and really did not want to leave the U.S. Diplomatic Service, so he had an idea for a temporary solution. With a great deal of reticence, Martin decided to seek permission to take a two-year leave of absence from the Foreign Service in order to work for the Prince.

Prince Rainier responded: "...Now as to your answer concerning my desire to have someone I can trust and depend on right next to me, I was and am still delighted at your reaction! It would be too good to be true, if you could take on a job of this kind. I am really enthusiastic about it. In fact, the moment is so perfectly right. I want to promote the establishment in Monaco of big American firms who want to put up a 'base' company in Europe for their businesses. Over two hundred of these companies have done this in Switzerland during the last year. So getting such a promotion as establishing here big American firms would of course mean economic boom..."

His long letter concluded: "...So I need desperately somebody I can trust, specially to start and develop this economic promotion. If this general working

– and the particular branch that could be yours interests you… please do come and get started. But all this has to be between us, and I want you to be quite frank and clear with me. Materially, I want you to tell me what you would want as salary. I would lodge you and your family here in an apartment *en ville* [in town] that I possess. Your office would be in the Palace, and your title could be worked out… Please think this over rather quickly and tell me your opinion."

FROM THE DESK OF
MARTIN A. DALE

Washington, D.C. – July 3, 1960

H.S.H. Prince Rainier of Monaco
Your Highness,

We learned via the press of the illness and death of Princess Grace's father and share with you both your sorrow at this great loss. Please accept this expression of our deepest sympathy.

The contents of your letter pleased me very much indeed. I am looking forward with keen anticipation to working for and with you. The job, as you describe it, strikes me as both interesting and challenging, and from a more personal point of view, I need not tell you how happy Joan and I are at the prospect of seeing you and Princess Grace again in the very near future.

I am glad that there is no particular urgency about our coming to Monaco. A move of this sort always entails considerable preparation, and our problems are complicated by the fact that Greg is still very much an infant demanding a great deal of attention. I take it from your letter that it would be most convenient to you if we planned to arrive in mid-October. Actually this would also suit us best. I have, therefore, made tentative reservations on the SS INDEPENDENCE scheduled to arrive in Cannes on October 19.

I and Joan send you and Princess Grace our warmest personal regards.

Very Sincerely,
Martin

Grace wrote to me from Rocagel shortly thereafter, saying: "Thank you so much for your lovely message of sympathy, which means a great deal in these difficult days... It's just wonderful that you will be with us and I can't tell you how pleased I am - We are looking forward to it tremendously... Give those babies a big hug for me - With Love - Grace –"

Grace's father, John Brendan "Jack" Kelly, passed away June 20, 1960. Jack Kelly was a self-made millionaire who owned one of the most successful brick businesses on the East Coast of the United States. He was a terrific athlete, having won an unprecedented three Olympic gold medals in rowing for the U.S. Olympic team in 1924 in both single and double sculls, as well as being World Champion in both of these events. At that time, rowing was at the height of its popularity, so he was considered a superstar in the world press.

Jack Kelly was tall, handsome, outspoken, imposing, and a bit of a rough diamond. He was a very wealthy, powerful and prominent businessman who also took an interest in politics, and was certainly a force to be reckoned with. He was extremely competitive and fostered that in his children. His son, John B. Kelly Jr. (called Jack, or "Kell" by the family) was also an Olympic rower, having competed in four Olympic games and winning the bronze medal in single sculls at the Melbourne Olympics in 1956. (Kell went on to ultimately be elected President of the U.S. Olympic Committee.) Both of Grace's sisters were into sports. Her younger sister, Lizanne, was captain of the varsity hockey team at the University of Pennsylvania, and was one of the first female athletes to appear in *Sports Illustrated* in 1955. Even Grace's mother was athletic – a former professional model, Margaret Kelly was the first coach and founder of women's athletics at the University of Pennsylvania.

Jack Kelly expected great things from his children, but Grace was never able to please him, no matter what she did. He never saw Grace as she really was, seeming to hold her in his memory as the quiet middle child who wore glasses and loved to read books, who was never as successful as her siblings, particularly in sports. He had no interest in anyone who wasn't athletic, and he did not really appreciate culture, despite the fact that his brother was a Pulitzer Prize-winning playwright.

Grace loved to swim, but was not truly athletic. She often had allergies that made her sniffle and appear to be sickly. It was well known that Grace's older sister, Peggy, was her father's favorite, which he clearly expressed in *McCall's* in January 1955, "I thought it would be Peggy whose name would be up in lights one day. Anything that Grace could do, Peggy could do better." This was printed shortly before Grace won her Academy Award for Best Actress.

Her father did not respect acting as a career, so Grace was determined to prove herself and make it on her own. After graduating from the American Academy of Dramatic Arts, Grace pursued roles on Broadway. She modeled to support herself, while acting in dozens of live television programs, before becoming a Hollywood movie star. Still, Jack Kelly would take credit for her success, stating that his powerful connections helped make her career. He wasn't even impressed by her marrying a prince; he apparently told Rainier that he didn't think much of royalty, and the Kellys never acknowledged Grace's status as a princess.

Grace had a rather love-starved childhood, and her efforts to impress her father were futile despite her many extraordinary accomplishments. She was in awe of him and had an obsessive quest for her father's approval. This perhaps resulted in her search for a father substitute and her dating older men in her early days, including famous fashion designer Oleg Cassini, who was sixteen years her senior. (Rainier was six years older than Grace.)

Despite her father's feelings toward her, Grace was always loving, devoted and loyal to all members of her family. She dearly loved her sisters, and wrote in July 1960: "...We expect to be here until the beginning of August when we will take our boat out for the first time - My sister [Lizanne] and her husband will come over - They have never been to Monaco and don't know the Mediterranean at all - so I will enjoy showing everything to them –"

As usual, Grace was also concerned for our comfort and well-being regarding our move to Monaco, so she took the time to write with thoughtful suggestions as the time drew nearer: "...I do hope that your trip over will be easy with the children or at least not too difficult or long - It might be a good idea to bring any medicines they are used to - Although our children do well on the French products - except for baby aspirin and vitamin pills which my mother sends me from the States - All Johnson products are available in Monaco & for most other things a French or English product is closely similar - I sometimes have trouble finding the right shoes for Albie & Caroline so I would suggest outfitting Charles for winter shoes before leaving... Looking forward so much to seeing you soon - Love - Grace –"

Grace often imported play clothes for the children through American catalogs, because casual children's clothing was not readily available in Europe at the time. Caroline loved clothes even at an early age, and she had a way of wearing them that was ladylike and graceful. Grace dressed her mostly in skirts, blouses, jumpers or basic dresses unless it was her birthday, when she wore a simple organdy "party dress." Slacks were worn for play or boating.

When Grace went to the U.S., she bought shoes for the children, because children's shoes were very expensive in Europe, and special widths and sizes were not really available. Once, on her return to Monaco from America, she put all the shoes she had bought into one suitcase, which unfortunately got lost.

Grace did not have too much luck with luggage. She laughingly described to me her visit to the newly remodeled Nice airport around 1960. Before her flight, the airport supervisor wanted to proudly show off the modern facilities. As Grace was ready to board her plane, she noticed the baggage handlers loading the luggage, and asked to see how it was done. In those days, there were no conveyor belts into the planes, so the handlers placed one large, sturdy-looking suitcase flat on the ground and used it as a trampoline to bounce the other bags into the plane's cargo hold. To Grace's amazement, and the airport supervisor's horror, Grace suddenly exclaimed, "That's my suitcase!" as they both realized the one being used as a trampoline belonged to Her Serene Highness, Princess Grace of Monaco! Luckily, it was undamaged and was immediately loaded on board, while Grace was hurried into the plane with profuse apologies. I was so much looking forward to seeing Grace again, and enjoying her amusing stories and delightful sense of humor.

As we prepared for our move to Monaco, Prince Rainier wrote several letters in which he outlined the expectations of Martin's position in the Principality: "...Your functions will be in my mind, very close to me, and they will also be very numerous and varied, and as the questions come up. Let me say that, I expect you to have ideas, and if these please me and fulfill a clear necessity for Monaco, then I will want you to put the idea into a living shape (legally, etc., with the collaboration of the technicians). The same will apply to ideas that come from elsewhere and that should be put into an operating form. All this will of course be mainly in the economic and financial domain. So for the moment, I would name you: *'Conseiller Privé de SAS Le Prince pour l'économie'* which enables you to cover a vast field of activities..."

Prince Rainier believed that Martin was the ideal person to help promote and develop Monaco's economy. He would focus on attracting foreign interests, such as American and British companies, and assist international firms to establish foreign corporate headquarters based in Monaco. Prince Rainier greatly admired American ideals, and was deeply committed to modernizing his country: "...As you will well understand, that my constant headache is to notice that in many important domains, this little country is not progressing or even adapting itself to these modern times! And there are many, many domains where Monaco should progress and advance! I count on you, dear Martin, to seek these new sectors and also think of how, when, the Principality should realize this..."

Martin would ultimately be given the title of Economic Advisor and Privy Counselor to the Prince himself. Martin felt very honored that Prince Rainier would offer him such a position, especially as there had never before been a Privy Counselor who was a foreigner, let alone an American.

Prince Rainier personally took it upon himself to make sure that all the arrangements were taken care of for our arrival in Monaco. He was offering to lodge our family in an apartment that he owned in a building just below the Palace, called the Ruscino. This way, Martin would be very close at hand. He wrote to us from Naples two weeks before our departure: "I have checked concerning your apartment in the Ruscino and all is supposed to be en ordre [in order]! But I will have to go and have a look myself on my return. The Frigidaire is ordered and so is the cooker, and the delivery is supposed to be prioritaire après la rentrée des vacances [priority after return from vacation]!! I will of course be in Monaco for your arrival, so as to get things set down exactly as they should be from the start!... At the end of October we are having the General [de Gaulle] for an official day's visit..."

However, when French President Charles de Gaulle found out that Martin was going to work for Prince Rainier, he was absolutely outraged. He deemed it to be against the treaty between France and Monaco for Prince Rainier to engage an American in an official government position. He also felt that having an American diplomat working for the Prince would create too strong an alignment with the United States. There was word that President de Gaulle was launching a "Démarche," a formal diplomatic protest to the U.S. Department of State complaining of Martin's appointment to work in Monaco during a two-year leave of absence, while technically still employed by the American government.

About two weeks before we were to move to Monaco, Martin was called into the office of the Deputy Under Secretary of State for Administration, Loy Henderson, a long-time career diplomat and former U.S. Ambassador, who was looking forward to retiring in four months. We had met him socially in Paris in October 1958. He said to Martin, "You're causing a lot of problems for us, son. You are going to have to decline your offer from Prince Rainier and go to Taiwan as per your orders." Martin responded by saying, "But, sir, I have already given my word to the Prince and feel that I have made a commitment." After a long pause, Loy Henderson said, "Well then, you leave us no choice but to ask for your resignation... and when your work in Monaco is done, of course you'll apply for re-instatement." Martin had received numerous letters of recommendation and commendations as a Foreign Service officer, and he was assured that he would always have a future with the U.S. Diplomatic Service, and that the State Department would welcome him back anytime.

Living close to Grace and Rainier once again was most enticing for us, but serving our country had been a lifelong goal, so it was a difficult decision to make. Martin had always planned to be a career diplomat, and was a rising star in the Diplomatic Corps, having achieved such a high position at such a young age. He was the youngest Consul in the U.S. Foreign Service, and he was still just twenty-eight years old.

Martin resigned with much regret, as he had completely devoted himself to his work. We left with a bit of trepidation, but with mounting excitement as we embarked on the Italian ocean liner, SS *LEONARDO DA VINCI*, en route to Monaco. We sailed from New York on October 4, 1960, with our two young sons, Charles, who was almost three, and Gregory, age eight months, and all of our possessions on board, bound for a new and dazzling life.

Joan said "Yes!" to Martin – newly engaged in Strasbourg, 1954

Grace aboard the aircraft carrier USS *FORRESTAL*, June 7, 1957

Martin and Joan speaking with Prince Rainier at a reception, 1957

Joan Dale meeting Princess Grace for the first time, April 1957

Joan, Martin and Princess Grace with American flag at reception, 1957

Joan and Princess Grace – two young Americans meeting in 1957

Newly built Rocagel overlooking Princess Caroline's playhouse, September 1959
(L to R) Joan, Grace seated, Charles with Prince Rainier at playhouse window,
Caroline picking flowers, Albert on swings

The newly built ranch at Rocagel, September 1959
Charles and Caroline in pony trap with our nanny

Prince Albert, Princess Grace, Prince Rainier, Princess Caroline
A parting gift of remembrance from Prince Rainier:
"To the Dales, with warmest wishes," signed Rainier, Grace 1959

PART TWO:
THE MONACO DAYS

DAYS OF JOY

We arrived in Monte Carlo on October 13, 1960, and were thrilled to find that the Prince had provided a luxurious suite of rooms for us at the sumptuous *Hôtel de Paris*. Large bouquets of flowers and the finest champagne greeted us in our magnificent rooms, along with messages from Grace and Rainier: "We are so happy you are here - Hope your stay will be everything you wish." Grace's sweet note was handwritten on stationery that said, "Thought for the day: YOU!" I think they were truly happy to have us close by, and also to have Charles and Gregory as playmates for their little children. We stayed in the hotel for a glorious two weeks, while the Prince's apartment overlooking the Port of Monaco was being prepared for us.

Martin immediately went to work for the Prince, spending long days going over the logistics of his position, returning home every night at 8:30. While Martin settled into his office at the Palace, Grace invited the boys over to play with Albert and Caroline. She welcomed us with open arms, and I was so happy to be back.

However, the intrigue of living in Monaco was to begin right away, just ten days after our arrival. On October 23, President Charles de Gaulle was coming to the Principality for an official state visit. We were looking forward to the grand social functions surrounding this event, and we were very excited that Martin would at last be able to meet this great man whom he had long admired. Martin's graduate thesis from Princeton University in 1953 was titled, "General

Charles de Gaulle, and the Importance for United States Foreign Policy." At that time, General de Gaulle was considered to be a political has-been, but Martin had predicted that De Gaulle would come back into power, to which his professor had responded, "Not a chance!" Alas, Martin was correct after all. Charles de Gaulle came out of retirement to become President of France in January 1959, which would soon prove to be very unfortunate for Martin, for Prince Rainier, and for Monaco itself.

General de Gaulle was a commanding figure, revered by many as a war hero. His visit was a grand occasion, and all of Monaco was brimming with anticipation. However, to Martin's great disappointment, the General would not allow us to attend the banquet in his honor. President de Gaulle was furious that Rainier had engaged an American as an advisor despite his protests, and said firmly that he would only proceed with his visit to the Principality "on the condition that he would not encounter Mr. Martin Dale!" While the General was there, we were not even supposed to be in the country. Martin tried to make light of the situation, but behind his brave face, he was really quite hurt and very concerned about what this might mean for his future, as Monaco was so closely tied with France.

When Martin was appointed Privy Counselor to the Prince, the newspaper announcements in France, Monaco, and the United States said that this was the first time that an American was to hold such a position at the Palace. From then on, Martin Dale was always referred to as "the American." Rampant anti-Americanism was raging in France, which would get much worse over time. While I could understand the French fearing the influence of the American superpower, and the concern that English words were seeping into their language, it seemed the French had forgotten too soon that without the help of the Americans during and after the war, they would all be speaking German!

De Gaulle told Prince Rainier that the presence on "The Rock" of the American advisor was considered an unfortunate sign of alignment with the United States. He was so opposed to Martin working for the Prince that he argued that it was against the Franco-Monégasque agreement for Rainier to appoint an American as Privy Counselor.

Unbeknownst to us at the time, a powerful campaign was already being launched in France to discredit Prince Rainier's ideas on modernizing his country. Rainier was a true visionary, able to foresee future needs. He wanted to leap forward in economic development and build a firm basis for the Principality's economy, without relying on income from gaming, thus changing Monaco's image from solely being the gambling mecca of the world.

While we had been en route to Monaco, Prince Rainier formed the Monaco Economic Development Corporation (MEDEC), which Martin was made head of. Martin would be in charge of seeking out foreign corporations who would benefit from having management and sales branches in Monaco. The Prince particularly wanted to attract American businesses, which is one reason that he had hired an American for the job. The many advantages of the Principality, not to mention the beauty and reputation of Monte Carlo as a splendid playground for the rich and famous, along with its tax-free status, made it a very attractive location for international businesses. Monaco's exceptional climate, with more than three hundred days of sunshine, and year-round outdoor activities in world-class resort facilities, made it even more alluring.

From the moment he arrived, Martin started to entice large corporations from the United States, France, and all over the world to make their headquarters in Monaco. He was still quite young, and we were very close to the Prince and Princess, publicly and privately – as Privy Counselor for economic affairs, Martin was the highest-ranking official in the Principality. This brought Martin a great deal of attention, both positive and negative.

Many people were pleased to have Martin working towards the economic growth of Monaco, but there were also those who were spiteful, jealous and angry, especially in the French government. None of that was evident at the outset, and we had no idea what was in store for us as we began our new and exciting life in this marvelous country – although, in hindsight, President de Gaulle's initial snub of Martin was just a small taste of what was to come…

Monaco – November 10, 1960

Dearest Mum and Dad,

Please forgive me for the long silence, but I do not even know if I can describe to you all of the things that fill our days in trying to get our apartment outfitted. It could only happen in France! We have really scores of workmen who come in all during each day just to look – they bring no tools with them. They leave and say they will come back tomorrow – they don't, and time drags on. We have just gotten the cupboards in the kitchen (minus shelves, which will be here in two weeks! So not much can be put away). Toilet seats have been installed which are too large and which fall down when Charlesie goes pee-pee!

The upholsterer is madly trying to finish the Opera before the National Feast Day next week, and so we shall not have our wall-to-wall carpeting or sofa until the end of November. Meanwhile we are camping in the apartment, and the floors, being tile, are extremely cold. As a result we all have colds again – for the third time since beginning our trip. Our view is lovely, and when all is finished we shall be comfortable.

Charlesie is already beginning to speak French. He chatters endlessly in English all day long. He remembers you in his prayers and has added Albie and Caroline, with whom he plays weekly. The other night he said, "God bless Caroline and Albie who hit me on the head!"

The Prince and Grace are well, and we have spent several evenings with them. We are invited to sit in their box at the Opera for the National Holiday. Marty finds that he has the highest ranking post here, and many are unhappy, including the French government. However, Marty is doing wonders to patch up ruffled feathers. It is quite a job and not an easy one. One could call it "Tightrope."

Much love from us all, Always, Joan

The Prince had very kindly offered us a waterfront apartment that he owned in the Condamine area just below the Palace. It had a gorgeous view with a lovely balcony overlooking Monaco's harbor with the Mediterranean and the Italian Riviera in the distance.

The Ruscino (pronounced ru-shino) was a new building next to the yacht club, and was not quite complete when we moved in. New apartments in Europe are often turned over to their occupants without light fixtures or other facilities. We encountered a few problems as we tried to get settled, such as needing to have the apartment rewired, and appliances that would not work properly. (It took six visits to install the washing machine!) Everyone wanted us to be pleased with the apartment because of Martin's position, but for quite some time, it was one problem after another.

We finally settled into our two-bedroom apartment, which was charming, although a bit small for the four of us (less than 145 square meters/about 1500 square feet – with no closets!). We were fortunate to quickly find a French nanny for the children named Colette. An Italian couple, Franca and Elio, served us faithfully as cook, maid, and chauffeur for the whole time we were there and were housed in a small apartment on the first floor. We needed help to look after the children because we were expected to attend numerous functions several times a week, often until well past midnight. We were relieved and grateful to have such wonderful people to work with us, since it was difficult to find reliable help.

When Prince Rainier came for his first visit, he said, "Let me see what you have done with the place," so we gave him a quick tour. Upon entering the apartment, there was a den on the right that doubled as a bedroom for the nanny. On the left was a bathroom that also contained a washer and dryer stacked on top of each other. Directly ahead was the kitchen, with a glass-enclosed balcony that served as the children's play area. The dining room, two compact bedrooms and a bathroom were down a corridor to the right.

We showed Rainer the children's bedroom with bunk beds, which he had never seen before. He thought it was a really good idea, but he did not realize that the room was so cramped for the two children that we could not fit two single beds in there. We then went into our master bedroom, which, like all French bedrooms, was very petite. We had a king-size bed that practically filled the entire room. Rainier walked in and said, "Oh my, this could be a *champ de bataille* (a battlefield)!" Perhaps he had never seen a king-size bed before, as this was particular to our American culture. When Grace had shown us their master bedroom at Rocagel, it had one double bed for the two of them, which was typical in Europe.

The living room was long and narrow, resembling a railroad car. Eventually, with some clever arrangement of the furniture, I managed to disguise this aspect. Looking back, I wonder how we squeezed in ten or more children for the annual birthday parties, along with eight or so mothers for tea!

Our apartment was very cozy, and every time the Prince came to visit, he commented on the warm atmosphere and the comfort he felt there. He was used to living in a huge Palace and large villas, so our apartment must have seemed quite homey and pleasant.

Monaco – December 15, 1960

Dearest Mum and Dad,

Our apartment is shaping up. We are still waiting for our sofa to be re-covered – and the two chairs, too. Charlesie's birthday was a great success. Albie and Caroline and Grace came. The children played beautifully, and Charles received lovely gifts – a racing car and track set, plus a big Jeep from Albie and some little cars and things from Caroline. Caroline also brought a little duck and some shoes for Greggie, which she had chosen herself. She adores Greg and sat holding him in her lap for a long time. It was the first time she ever held a baby, and we took photos so I hope they came out. Charles was sweet, and the children were so very good. The cake was delicious and pretty, and the ladies enjoyed tea in the living room on a borrowed sofa! It was a great success.

Every Monday or Thursday evening we are on duty at the Palace, which means that we go there to dinner with the Prince and Princess, Father Tucker, the Aide de Camp, etc., and afterwards we see movies in the private theater in the Palace. These are always black tie affairs, and the movies are excellent first-runs. Then there are receptions we are expected to attend, plus other social engagements. We have been leading a gay life, dining at the Hôtel de Paris with the Maharani of Baroda. All our friends have been very kind to us, and we really are enjoying life here. Marty plays golf with Rainier every week, and is organizing the new job. It is fascinating but hard work. Marty's arrival created quite a stir here and all over France because of his age and his nationality. They haven't gotten over it yet, and even General de Gaulle talked about it to the Prince.

We went on board Onassis's CHRISTINA for cocktails and toured the ship. It is gorgeous and huge. La Callas was there. She is quite a dynamic person and had a great success a few days ago at the opening of La Scala. Tonight we are going to a reception in honor of the marriage of [Belgian] King Baudouin to Fabiola, then on to cocktails with the British Consul.

Have a very happy Christmas, and we shall all be thinking of you. Hugs and kisses from your two sweet boys.

All our love, Joan and Marty

We were often invited to the Palace for luncheons and dinners, including a special American Thanksgiving dinner with turkey, chestnuts, and all the trimmings, prepared specially for Princess Grace, as this was not typical in Europe. Lunches took place at 1 p.m., whether they were formal or informal. For dinners at the Palace, one was expected to arrive promptly at ten minutes before eight, which was sometimes a little challenging with two small children, but Martin and I always managed to make it on time. We would receive an engraved invitation with the Grimaldi crest embossed in gold at the top, with the details of the event, the date and time carefully handwritten in calligraphy, and the required dress: black tie ("smoking"), white tie, cocktail, business attire (*tenue de ville*), morning dress, etc.

When we arrived at the huge ornate formal dining room of the Palace, there would be a small folded place card with our name on it, with a miniature seating map inside showing our place at the table, sometimes with the names of our dinner companions seated directly on our left and right. Husbands and wives were never seated together; guests were seated alternating men and women, with the Prince and Princess sitting opposite one another at the center of the long table (which seated eighteen or more). Of course, the place of honor was to be seated next to the Prince or Princess on either side of them.

At official dinners, people were seated by rank according to protocol. This should have been the case at galas as well, but Martin and I were often seated next to Grace and Rainier, which upset a lot of people who had great wealth and titles. At dinners at the Palace, Grace purposely seated me next to important men who were rather shy or difficult to talk to, because she knew that I was a good conversationalist, especially after my experience in the Foreign Service. The guests were always very interesting people, including a veritable parade of royalty, celebrities, and dignitaries.

Each place setting had a printed menu with the Grimaldi crest embossed in gold, listing what was being served, usually consisting of about five courses. A footman would hold a large silver platter to one's left, from which one would serve oneself, then they removed plates from the right. The Prince was served first, Princess Grace was served second, then everyone else was served down the line in order of precedence. Even with many footmen serving, the last guest would often find himself beginning to eat as the Prince's plate was being taken away. According to protocol, when the Prince was finished with a course, everyone else had to finish as well. This created a hurried frenzy as guests could barely enjoy the delicious food while trying to keep up with the Prince. Sometimes, if a guest was oblivious to what was going on, a hovering footman waited until that person laid their utensils down and then quickly whisked the plate away, whether the guest had finished eating or not! Grace purposely tried to eat very slowly, so no one would feel rushed or uncomfortable.

At a formal dinner at the Palace, one of the Prince's Cabinet Ministers took a tangerine at the end of the meal, but was so engaged in conversation that he left it on his plate. Suddenly noticing a hush all around him, he looked up to see that everyone else had finished, and the footmen were at attention waiting to pull out the guests' chairs. He quickly picked up the tangerine and put it in the pocket of his tuxedo! Grace and Rainier smiled, but other guests pretended not to notice, in pure diplomatic fashion.

Every Monday and Thursday night, a movie was shown in their private cinema. These movie nights were black tie affairs that usually began with dinner in the formal dining room, complete with gleaming silver, crystal, and fine Palace china, and white-gloved footmen in full livery standing behind every chair. These footmen were trained to be so discreet that you couldn't even sense they were there, but they watched for anything that anyone would need throughout the meal and took care of everything immediately.

After dinner, we went to the screening room, where Prince Rainier had a huge, elaborate train set the size of an average living room. It was mounted on a platform and decorated with houses, trees, trestles, hills and miniature figures. All the men loved to play with it while we all stood around watching. (Protocol dictated that no one should be seated if the Prince was standing.)

I believe that the movie theater was in a former stable where Rainier had kept his antique and exotic cars, until his collection outgrew the space and was moved to Rocagel. It was then converted to accommodate one of Grace's great loves: films. The screening room at the Palace was grand and full of very comfortable, overstuffed armchairs, so we did not sit in rows as in a typical movie theater. We were served coffee and after-dinner drinks, while we watched the latest Hollywood releases with the biggest stars of the day. Occasionally, a buffet-style dinner was served in the screening room instead of in the grand formal dining room.

There were many times when Martin and I watched movies alone with Grace and Rainier *en famille*, or the children watched screenings of Disney movies together. Grace and Rainier often invited special guests who were visiting Monaco to attend movie nights, such as Ava Gardner, Greer Garson, Gregory Peck, Cary Grant, Bing Crosby, Alec Guinness, David Niven, and many of Grace's other friends from Hollywood. Occasionally, the guests would include visiting dignitaries, but they usually came for formal luncheons at the Palace, especially if they were royalty.

One of the people that we often socialized with when we first arrived in Monaco was the prominent Greek shipping tycoon, Aristotle Onassis, who was one of the wealthiest men in the world at that time. He had made his fortune operating oil tankers and whaling vessels with his company, Olympic Maritime, and later formed Olympic Airways. He chose Monaco as his home and as his base of operations following his 1952 purchase of a large number of shares in the *Société des Bains de Mer* (SBM), the company that runs the Casino and all of the big hotels in Monaco that are not privately owned.

Aristotle Onassis was a very interesting man; he may not have been very attractive physically, but he was quite magnetic. He was always pleasant if he thought that you could be of service to him in some way, but if not, he would ignore you in favor of someone who could be. Onassis told Martin there are only three things that matter: your clothes, your address, and whom you know!

On several occasions, we were invited on board his yacht, the *CHRISTINA*, which was the largest and most modern of its era. It was absolutely astounding. On the aft deck was a large swimming pool that turned into a mosaic dance floor at the push of a button. It dwarfed the other yachts in the Monaco harbor, with a helicopter landing pad, as well as several motorboats and launches – it even had its own surgical operating room! It had originally been a medium-sized Canadian navy frigate, built in 1943 as a convoy escort for World War II. Onassis purchased the ship for $34,000 and reportedly spent over $4 million in 1954 to convert it into a luxurious yacht with a crew of forty-eight, including three chefs. He lived on board and used it as his floating home in Monaco.

The yacht exuded opulence and extravagance, showcasing his priceless and exquisite collection of art treasures by such artists as El Greco, Gauguin, and Pissarro. We were shown the guest suites named after Greek islands, which were very lavish, with full marble bathrooms resplendent with real gold fixtures, and faucets shaped like fish. Each bathroom had a different type and color of Italian marble: one was a deep green, one was white, another maroon, the next was gray, and each was more spectacular than the last. I always wondered how the ship stayed afloat with all that marble on board!

Ari, as he was known to his friends, had quite a sense of humor, and could be a little crude at times. He liked to embarrass people, and it gave him a feeling of power and satisfaction to make them squirm – essentially, he liked to make people feel uncomfortable while hosting them in the lap of luxurious comfort. Once, when I was sitting on one of the barstools on his yacht, he took my hand and had me rub the white leather upholstery, saying, "Do you know what this is?" It was the softest thing I had ever felt, but I could not imagine it being anything other than perhaps white kidskin. I shook my head, and he said with a smile, "You, my dear, are sitting on a whale's penis!" Apparently, the soft "leather" on the bar stools came from the foreskin of a whale, and the footrests were whales' teeth! I tried not to look as shocked as I felt.

Onassis loved to entertain on his yacht (he had hosted a reception for Grace and Rainier's wedding). His lady friend at the time was the world-renowned Mezzo Soprano, Maria Callas, whom I liked very much. Known as "La Callas," she was not the "prima donna" that the media made her out to be. In fact, she was a very interesting and unpretentious woman. She was lovely, charming, intelligent and easy to talk to, although somewhat shy at times.

In the beginning, we often went out with Grace and Rainier, Onassis and Maria Callas, and did unusual things. The first time Martin and I ever went bowling, it had been a spontaneous suggestion on the part of Onassis, and we were not dressed for it at all. Grace, Maria and I were wearing cocktail dresses, and Rainier, Ari and Martin were in black tie! It was quite an experience, but we all had a good time. The six of us got on very well and had a lot of fun together.

Monaco – January 5, 1961

Dearest Mum and Dad,

Prince Rainier gave Charlesie a beautiful big horse on springs, and he adores it. He and Albie get along famously and scrap and push and roll on each other. Caroline adores Greg and holds and cuddles him.

Xmas eve we went to midnight Mass at the Palace Chapel. It was lovely, and afterwards we had supper at the Palace, which was all candlelit and gorgeous. There were presents for each guest – for Marty, golf balls and a golf score watch, and a lovely blue crystal bead necklace from Mallorca for me from Grace. We gave them a miniature golf set, which they seemed to enjoy. Onassis and Callas were there and a few naval officers. It was fun. Then all during the week there were parties for orphans and the elderly and Monégasque children, where gifts were given, tea served, and we were supposed to attend officially. There was one each day. Then we had the usual dinner at the Palace on Thursday and a movie. New Year's eve, we went with the Prince and Princess to the Hôtel de Paris Gala. It was great fun. Monday, Marty played golf with the Prince. He and Marty play golf once or twice a week and are having great fun together. Tonight we go again to dinner at the Palace.

Monaco is booming with socialites. I have never seen so many well-dressed people united in one place. I believe there are not many places left as chic as this one.

We all send all our love, Joanie, Marty, Charlesie, Greggie

Every year, the Prince and Princess hosted Christmas parties for the children of Monaco. Hundreds of children were invited to the Palace for cake and ice cream, and each child would be given a gift that had been personally selected by Grace herself. It was always extraordinarily touching to see the excitement and gratitude of the children as they received gifts from their very caring Princess, which she lovingly handed to each one of them. As her own children got older, Grace would ask them to present the gifts to the Monégasques.

Albert and Caroline were always given numerous gifts from all over the world, some of which were tremendously extravagant. Aristotle Onassis once gave Albert a motorized toy racing car that he could drive around in – it was red with a white stripe down the center, the colors of the Monégasque flag. Although the children were very blessed with all that they received, Grace wanted them to know that Christmas was a time of giving as well as receiving.

Monaco – February 5, 1961

Dearest Mum and Dad,

Grace and Rainier have left for Switzerland – Gstaad – and have invited us to come up, too, in March for two weeks. Rainier said he would find us a place to stay – a chalet or an apartment – they really do not seem to mind having us around! Marty really is helping him here and is really taking a heavy load. Everyone says how much more relaxed Rainier is since our arrival!

We had them here last Sunday evening for dinner, and we each cooked a special dish – I made Chinese shrimp, Grace made veal scaloppini, Marty made macaroni and cheese, and the Prince made his famous crêpes – they were delicious. He really likes us, because I doubt if he has ever cooked anything away from home. It was a fun evening.

The night before we had attended a gala dinner with them at the Hôtel de Paris – Gene Kelly had danced beforehand in a show with Carol Lawrence (star of "West Side Story"), and it was a marvelous performance. Prince Pierre is inviting us to sit in his box tomorrow for a famous French play, and we are having him here for a drink. We shall now have to begin entertaining – but we still have no dining room chairs, as they are so expensive now. The only inexpensive thing here is food.

All our love, Joan, Marty, Charles, Greggie

It was rare for the Prince and Princess to have a casual and informal dinner with their very busy social schedule. Most dinners at the Palace were very formal occasions, unless we were in Grace and Rainier's private apartments, but even then, there were always white-gloved servants around. We decided to invite

Grace and Rainier to our apartment for a different sort of dinner. We gave the help the night off so that our royal guests would feel more at ease.

Martin and I had spent the first few years of our marriage living in furnished apartments, so we did not have very much furniture of our own. We had ordered everything from an upholsterer who was in the middle of redecorating the entire Monte Carlo Opera House, which meant that our order would take months to complete. We decided to invite Grace and Rainier over for dinner anyway. We had a sofa and some patio furniture, but no dining chairs, so we used folding bridge chairs instead. In retrospect, I think this was rather courageous of us to invite the Prince and Princess into our home under these circumstances, but we were young and naïve. I believe that this simplicity was a welcome change that Grace and Rainier appreciated and which truly endeared us to them.

Grace and Rainier arrived with neat parcels of ingredients, no doubt packaged by the Palace chefs, and we all set to work in my small kitchen. I made an appetizer, Martin contributed a side dish, and Grace prepared the main course. I thought it was delicious, but Grace felt she was a little out of practice, as she had not cooked in quite some time. "I used to make really good veal scaloppini," she said with her charming little pout, "but I think I've lost my knack." The pièce de résistance was dessert, and the Prince did a masterful performance, maneuvering crêpes in a chafing dish to regale us with Crêpes Suzette, with a marvelous sauce that he prepared himself.

These were things that Grace and Rainier normally did not do. It had probably been at least four years since Grace had done any real cooking, because the Palace kitchen was solely the domain of the chef and servants, and they held dominion over their territory! Occasionally she made sandwiches or a birthday cake in the kitchen at Rocagel, but even there, she had a cook.

After dinner, we sat on the balcony and played "*Mille Bornes,*" an exciting French card game depicting an automobile race, which we thought Rainier would enjoy because of his passion for cars and for the Grand Prix. We all had a delightful time, laughing together all evening. I think that what Grace and Rainier enjoyed most is that they could just relax and be themselves when they were with us, and not always have to play the role of Prince and Princess.

They loved to play games of all kinds, which we did most evenings when we were on vacation together. Rainier was very competitive at everything, especially with Martin. He jokingly taunted Martin in a letter from Switzerland: "...I am enchanted concerning your golfing progress... I must admit that I felt that I needed more competition from you!!!! So carry on... Any way my revenge will be on the slopes!" Then in the next letter: "Bravo for your bowling and for the golf score... of course I will be *compréhensif* [understanding] towards your skiing debuts?... but you must catch on so that you can get away from the kids and the noise and come skiing with me and the *moniteur* [instructor]. We are looking forward to your arrival."

Grace and Rainier had taken the children to Schönried, Switzerland, for the month of February, and arranged for us to have a chalet there in March so we could join them on vacation. We were very excited, as we had never skied before. Even when skiing, the Prince was often working, and so was Martin. As Sovereign, the dossiers and affairs of state would follow the Prince wherever he went. Rainier welcomed Martin's ideas and opinions, and they would discuss issues regarding the Principality when they were away from the family.

Martin was very loyal and protective of Prince Rainier. He was also very direct and honest with him, which engendered Rainier's trust, while others tended to be intimidated by the Prince and his position. Rainier wrote in February: "Many thanks for your last long letter, very interesting and instructive. I do appreciate that you speak and write always to me in *complete* and *entire* frankness; that is mainly why I asked you to come and work for and with me!"

Rainier corresponded with Martin frequently by letter and telephone while he was on vacation: "I did not, nor did the Princess, consider your telephone intervention of the other day any interference in our private affairs or lives. On the contrary, I found it very sympathetic and friendly of you to do so. These articles are bad and nasty... I am ready to do what is the best though, as I cannot let this press campaign go on!"

Martin was warning Prince Rainier that the French press had begun an assault against him. The French were very worried that Monaco was starting to lure businesses away from France and taking away valuable taxes from them, particularly as they were still recovering economically after the war. Many articles in French magazines and newspapers were critical of Rainier's economic policies and his politics, and they also directed a constant slew of outrageous slings and arrows at him personally.

While the Prince was away, Martin was working on a wonderful brochure for MEDEC called "Monaco Can Help Your Company." It was written entirely in English, outlining the benefits of establishing headquarters and branches in Monaco, particularly for American and British corporations. This brochure would become extremely popular, especially because it had a metal "coin" on the front, depicting the Grimaldi coat of arms, which many people kept as a souvenir medallion.

According to Monaco's treaty with France, the Prince was required to have a French citizen as Minister of State, who was proposed by the government of France, but who was paid by the Principality. At that time, the position was held by Émile Pelletier, a former member of General de Gaulle's Cabinet. He was rather close to De Gaulle, and frequently kept him apprised of what was happening in Monaco. Out of loyalty to France, Minister Pelletier was trying to hinder the production of the MEDEC brochure, to which Prince Rainier responded: "...As for the objections Pelletier has made concerning the brochure... they seem to me childish and quite *à côté de la situation* and beside the point! For heaven's sake do not let this stop you! Go ahead as scheduled... make this quite clear to him that I have approved this project, and I do not want anything changed!"

Schönried, Switzerland – March 1961

Dearest Mum and Dad,

We are having a delightful time here and are enjoying the wonderful clear air and warm sunny days. The view from our chalet is gorgeous with sharp, snow-covered peaks everywhere. We have seen a great deal of Grace, the Prince and the family – Charlesie and Greggie are there now with the nurse, playing with Albie and Caroline. We have been to their lovely chalet for lunch and dinner, and also we have been out with them to some of the quaint dining places in Gstaad. We have eaten our fill of fondue, grisson (beef dried at 3000 ft. altitude) and other specialties. This is a pretty nice job to be able to take two weeks of winter sports and then a summer vacation, too – however, Marty is working here so one cannot call it a complete rest. Vera Maxwell is here visiting, and so are the Crovettos – owner of Veuve Clicquot champagne and the Metropole Hotel at Beaulieu – and longtime friends of the Prince (Roger went to Le Rosey school in Gstaad with Rainier).

We spent a delightful evening at their chalet in the company of David Niven and his Swedish wife, the Earl of Warwick, a fascinating man, and the Prince de Fürstenburg – the Prince's cousin. I must say we meet interesting people here in this job.

Loads of love from - Joanie, Marty, Charlesie, Greggie

For the next few years, Grace and Rainier invited us to join them on family vacations in Switzerland. Vera Maxwell, a well-known New York fashion designer, was also a frequent visitor, both there and in Monaco. Grace enjoyed her company as a friend and liked to wear her practical designs.

Martin and I would usually take the children to Switzerland in February or March and spend several weeks there. Grace and Rainier had a chalet for themselves just up the hill from the chalet that we rented. It was a beautiful and tranquil place, with lots of snow on the ground but usually not much snow falling, so it was mostly very sunny.

The days began with getting the children ready to go out in the snow by bundling them up in many layers of clothing. Caroline, Albert, Charles and Greg would all sled together, often sitting on each other. (Perhaps this was Albert's early inspiration to form Monaco's Olympic bobsleigh team!) It was fun to watch them on skis for the first time, slipping down the hill and enjoying themselves. They made snowmen, and once even made an igloo with the help of Albert and Caroline's first nanny, Maureen, and Jacqueline, our nurse. Nanny Maureen was an amusing English girl, full of fun and laughter. Our Jacqueline was very artistic and taught the children how to draw and color.

In the evenings, we all got together and often went out to one of the local restaurants for *fondue* or *raclette* (a special cheese that is melted and eaten with boiled potatoes). These evenings were fun, intimate and casual. Sometimes we went down to Gstaad itself, which was not far from our chalet in Schönried. That was where the Prince had attended *Institut Le Rosey*, the prestigious international boarding school, so in some ways it was a homecoming for him. We would go to the Palace Hotel, where Grace and Rainier were recognized, but the Swiss were always nice and kept their distance, allowing them to have a real vacation.

We had cozy family dinners at the Prince's chalet, followed by card games like gin rummy. The Prince loved limericks, the saucier the better, which usually required a bit of wine for me to find my inner poet. We took turns trying to come up with something witty, and the ones we recited about each other would have us all rolling on the floor with laughter. We played charades, which Grace was a master at. She loved games and jigsaw puzzles. In her chalet, there was always a huge table with a puzzle in progress, and as she passed by, she would put in another piece.

Grace was very fond of both Charles and Greg, treating them like her own and including them in most of their family activities. Albert often celebrated his birthday in Switzerland with a party; Grace personally planned all the parties and themes for her children, which was something she loved to do.

Monaco – March 23, 1961

Dearest Mum and Dad,

Here we are again after a delightful holiday and change of air. We returned via the Simplon Tunnel, where one puts the car on a flatcar, stays in the car and travels through a tunnel for 30 minutes – an incredible accomplishment for the builders! We made it in one day, arriving at 10 p.m., after having left at 8:30 a.m. The weather was perfect, and so were the children.

Charlesie is no longer afraid to do things and loves to swing, box, ride real ponies all alone, etc. I attribute this change to Albie and the Prince, who fortunately play rather rough, and Charles has just had to learn to defend himself.

Grace and Rainier returned yesterday, and we were very pleased to be invited to a very small dinner with them and Queen Victoria Eugenia of Spain (Albert's godmother). She is the granddaughter of Queen Victoria, is very regal but is easy to talk to. After dinner (nine people only) Marty played Bridge with the Queen, and I played Canasta with Grace and Rainier. Charles attended Albie's birthday party at Schönried, and we took movies of it. Hope they come out.

By the way there will be an article about Marty and his work in next week's "Newsweek"! Talk about notoriety! The "New York Times" had a long article three weeks ago about Marty and Monaco, and so did "Businessweek." I am so proud of him.

Everyone, incidentally, comments on the moonstone – even the Prince, who loves jewelry. All for now.

All our love, Joan, Marty, Charlesie, Greggie

An article entitled "Monacompanies" in *Newsweek* April 3, 1961, said that Prince Rainier had hired a Yankee to head up a diversification and development program: "He's Martin A. Dale, a slim, 29-year-old Phi Beta Kappa from Princeton who was the youngest consul in the U.S. Foreign Service when he quit to accept Rainier's offer." The article stated that their goal was to attract thirty to fifty leading international corporations within three years. They were planning to create 2.4 million square feet of industrial floor space to accommodate light industry and manufacturing over a five-year period.

In the two weeks prior to *Newsweek's* interview with Martin, three American companies, along with one British and one Swiss company had all agreed to open offices in Monaco. Among them was Timex, a subsidiary of U.S. Time, one of the largest watch manufacturers in the world. The pen manufacturer, Scripto, was already established in Monaco, expecting to produce 25 million ballpoint pens a year in a factory less than 10,000 square feet in size. Twenty-seven companies had already been rejected because they did not meet the criteria or were not reputable firms. Martin was quoted as saying, "Monaco doesn't intend to set itself up as just another tax haven. We can, and will, control this program to a degree no other country has been willing to exert."

One of the major benefits for these companies establishing themselves in the Principality was that they did not have to pay corporate taxes. Monaco was poised to help companies, particularly American companies, to expand in the growing European marketplace. Many international corporations were finding it necessary to manufacture products in the markets that they were destined for, rather than exporting to Europe from the West or the Far East.

Although Monaco did not derive taxes from these companies or from their employees, it stood to gain revenue from a type of "corporate tourism," where board meetings and conventions would be held in Monaco, benefitting the hotels, restaurants, tourist activities, and shops. Executives would also buy real estate in Monaco. One of the requirements for companies to be headquartered there was that they had to hire a Monégasque citizen, so this created jobs for Monégasques in the new international managerial class. Unemployment became virtually non-existent, and the per capita income was and still is one of the highest in the world.

Monaco was turning into a businessman's paradise, and Martin was becoming quite well-known in the business world. Between November 1960 and March 1961, over a dozen important corporations had already set up substantive management headquarters and sales subsidiaries or branches in the Principality, and several new industries had been created. Three new hotel projects were under consideration, including one with three hundred rooms to be built by a major international hotel chain. A monumental convention hall to hold sixteen hundred people, an exposition hall, and a modern air-conditioned office building were all on the drawing board.

In just five months since Martin's arrival, the economic expansion of Monaco was well under way, and Prince Rainier's vision for the growth and modernization of his tiny country was being fulfilled. Rainier wrote to Martin: "Of course I am pleased with your work and what you have already achieved – But I do want more liaison and information to me directly, do not hesitate! I am isolated by my function… So it must be the duty of each and all who work for and with me to diminish this isolation."

Martin's job not only entailed attracting new businesses, but also involved working closely with the Prince regarding city planning and preparing future infrastructure to accommodate the growing economy in the years to come. Since Monaco's development was limited by its small landmass of less than one square mile, Martin suggested creating a large land fill, as had been done in Lower Manhattan. This would allow Monaco to expand its commercial, industrial and housing concerns, so it could literally grow in all directions.

The tiny Principality was about the size of New York's Central Park, surrounded by France on three sides with the Mediterranean Sea as its fourth frontier. There were four main districts in Monaco: Monte Carlo, which includes the famous Casino and the *Hôtel de Paris*; the Condamine by the Port (where we lived); Monaco Ville, the ancient part of Monaco, where the Palace is perched on the naturally fortressed hill, also known as "The Rock"; and Fontvieille, a newer industrial area to the west. Fontvieille was originally a narrow strip of factories by the railroad tracks, built on land that was reclaimed from the sea, which included a stadium – Stade Louis II. Martin proposed to extend the land fill of Fontvieille, which would eventually increase Monaco's size by about twenty percent, providing room for future commercial growth.

Martin was earning a great deal of prestige, and we were both enjoying our close relationship with Grace and Rainier. Sometimes it was a delicate balance for Martin between being a friend and being an employee. There were many official events that we attended with the Prince and Princess as part of his job, and we were also included in many personal and intimate evenings with them as well. On one such occasion, we were privileged to meet Queen Victoria Eugenia of Battenberg, an extraordinary and fascinating lady, who was the grandmother of the present king of Spain, Juan Carlos.

She told us about the day of her wedding to King Alfonso XIII of Spain on May 31, 1906. Right after the marriage ceremony, they rode in their open carriage through the cheering crowds lining the streets of Madrid. Suddenly, someone threw a large bouquet of flowers in front of the coach, which landed on the right-hand side of the vehicle. The bouquet concealed a bomb that exploded, killing thirty-one soldiers and bystanders. At that moment, the king had been pointing to something, causing both the king and queen to lean out on the left-hand side of the carriage, which apparently saved their lives. One of the king's mounted bodyguards was killed right next to them, spattering blood all over the queen's wedding gown. The king immediately got out of the carriage, insisting that the queen be taken back to the Palace. He then mounted the horse of the slain guardsman, and courageously rode alone through the streets of Madrid to show that he was not going to be intimidated. This was the first of several assassination attempts on the king's life.

Monaco – April 1961

Dearest Mum and Dad,

We went out bowling alone with Grace and the Prince last week and had a very gay time. Then we have been to the Palace to several movies and were invited to the Ballet in their box. Cary Grant was visiting them, and we enjoyed him. He is very easy to know. Monday evening – our seventh anniversary! We went to the British-American Hospital Ball at the Hôtel de Paris in their company. We were in a cavalcade of cars from the Palace, and we accompanied Prince Pierre. It was quite thrilling to see the mob cheering and crushing in – incredible!

All for now - All love, Joan, Marty, Charles, Greg

One evening, we were invited to a buffet dinner at the Palace, followed by a movie screening in their large cinema. Cary Grant was one of the guests, and he approached me saying, "May I join you?" He listened intently as we conversed, never taking his eyes off mine. It didn't matter what was going on around us, he just spoke directly to me. That was such a rarity, because in many social situations, people look around to see who else might be there who could benefit them in some way. He was interesting and interested, handsome, graceful in a masculine way, with a divine British accent. He was one of the most charming gentlemen I've ever met.

All of the great stars came to Monaco, and we got to see many of them perform. We enjoyed excellent operas, ballets, and concerts with wonderful singers at the Monte Carlo Opera House. As you entered the opulent Casino building, the Casino was to the left, and the *Salle Garnier* was straight ahead with an elegant bar and a vestibule where you could look out over the sea. There was a staircase up to the Prince's Box, with a private room behind it, where champagne and refreshments were usually served at intermission.

Grace and Rainier often invited us to sit with them in their box, either in the front row next to them, or behind them if they were entertaining an important guest. Many people thought that Grace and I were related, especially when we arrived at the Opera with the Prince and Princess in their Rolls Royce. We were both blonde and wore our hair in a similar way.

In April of 1961, Grace had her hair cut by Alexandre of Paris in his signature "artichoke style," where locks are cut in the shape of leaves nesting one over the other. Grace did not tell Prince Rainier that she was having her elegant hairstyle changed from the shoulder-length French twist that she was known for. That evening, we were at the home of Rainier's father, Prince Pierre, having pre-dinner drinks while waiting for Grace to arrive. Usually, she accompanied her husband, but under some pretext, she sent a message saying that he should go on ahead. It was a shock to everyone when she walked in with very short, wavy hair. She looked beautiful and was very pleased with her surprise. Upon seeing her, the Prince commented that Grace looked like Marilyn Monroe. Howell Conant photographed her with this coiffure for *Look* Magazine, wearing a white satin gown, with a light blue velvet stole by Balenciaga.

Ladies Home Journal of October 1961 said of Grace, "At 31, her complexion is apple blossom, her smile instantaneous and she still appears to have been dipped in pearl right down to her pink fingertips. Her blonde hair is cut short at the neck and bouffant on top in the 'artichoke' style created by Alexandre de Paris. Princess Grace remarked, 'I'd always worn my hair long before. Now that I've had it cut, I don't know whether I like it or not.' Even thus, shorn of her serene chignon, Princess Grace remains swanlike and beautiful. She still has that rose-embowered air of a princess at play, able through her art to make us believe again in Swan lakes, castles and happily-forever-after romance."

No matter what she was wearing or how she wore her hair, Grace was always beautiful. I saw her on many occasions without makeup, with eyeglasses and in casual clothes – she was simply a natural beauty and a real woman. Queen Elizabeth II, after a luncheon with Princess Grace at Buckingham Palace, was reported to have said, "She is the most beautiful person I have ever seen." She turned heads wherever she went, and you simply could not take your eyes off her radiant beauty, regardless of who else was in the room.

On screen and in photos, Grace was absolutely mesmerizing – and even more so in person. Her smile, with vertical laugh lines surrounding her mouth, was genuinely warm, charming and endearing. Her soft blue sparkling eyes, perfect nose (especially in profile), lustrous peaches-and-cream complexion, and her long graceful neck, made her a true vision of exquisite beauty.

Grace had excellent posture, with her back perfectly upright and her head held regally; she usually crossed her legs delicately at the ankles, not at the knee. She was always beautifully composed and elegant, even when she was relaxed and casual. Her only defect was a sway back, which she told me she cleverly disguised with her clothing.

Princess Grace had been very thin when she got married, and she always worried about her weight. In the summer months, when she could get away from all the official functions, she retreated to Rocagel to eat healthily, and abstained from alcohol for several weeks every year.

Grace also visited her family regularly in Philadelphia. Prince Rainier loved going to the United States, where he enjoyed a great deal more freedom and privacy than he did in Europe. In May, he wrote to Martin from America: "Sorry to have been so silent – But as you may well understand being in this fabulous country… one has little or no time to sit down and write… in fact, one has little time to even think…"

Monaco – May 15, 1961

Dearest Mum and Dad,

The Prince and Princess are away. They are having a wonderful time in the U.S. – we just heard from S.A.S. (the Prince) today. He said he went to the Kentucky Derby and "had to bet on a horse called 'Prince Dale' which did not win" to quote him. Can you imagine the coincidence in having a horse with that name? On a $5 bet made a few days before, he collected $500, so he should not be too unhappy. He is a lucky man, but he rarely gambles.

Love from us all, Joan, Marty, Charles & Greggie

While we were employed in Monaco, we were not allowed to gamble at the Casino – this was a good policy because it would be too tempting for employees to lose their hard-earned money, thus putting their families at risk. Monégasque citizens are forbidden to gamble or even to enter the premises, by a law ordained in the 1800s by Prince Charles III when the Casino was established. To my knowledge, Grace had never set foot inside, typically not wanting any more privileges than her countrymen, nor wanting to set a bad example. Of course, as sovereigns they could enter the Casino if they wished to. However, it was their custom that no one from the Princely Family would ever do so.

When we lived in Nice before Martin was employed by the Prince, we occasionally went to the famed Casino of Monte Carlo. Most visitors only see the outer rooms, familiarly called the "Kitchen," so dubbed because that was the area where the servants used to go while their patrons gambled in the *Salons Privés*. The public areas are ornately decorated with gold-leafed columns, crystal chandeliers, silk draperies and silk-lined walls. As opulent as they are, the public rooms pale beside the sumptuous old-world elegance of the inner salons, which are far more expansive, filled with exquisite artwork and sculptures in marble. The private part of the Casino has bay windows overlooking the sea with an exclusive bar, and its own entrance.

It is perhaps the most magnificent casino in the world, with ladies wearing beautiful gowns adorned with exquisite jewels, and men in black tie. The Russian aristocracy and their retinues of the past were no longer there, having been replaced mainly by wealthy Italians and Middle Eastern oil magnates. At the gaming tables, they would have large stacks of oblong plaques in front of them as "chips," usually of very high denominations. We saw fortunes won and lost in a matter of minutes.

Rainier and Grace often wrote letters and postcards to us while they were away, although I can't imagine when they found the time to do so, as their schedules were usually filled with official engagements. On May 18, Rainier wrote: "… We had a pleasant dinner with Onassis on board the *CHRISTINA*, moored on the Hudson off 79th street [in New York City]. The view from the ship was really fantastic! We are lunching at the White House on the 24th invited very nicely by the President…"

Both Grace and Rainier were thrilled to go to the White House to have a private luncheon with President and Mrs. Kennedy, and just seven other guests. Grace was seated next to President Kennedy, and found him to be an attentive listener, who was interested in everything (much like Grace herself).

Grace spoke to him of her concerns as President of the Red Cross in Monaco, and as a member of the International Red Cross Organization in Geneva. She had been receiving documents from their organizations all over the world, and many of those from eastern countries had anti-American sentiments. She had just received a document from the Red Cross in Korea that accused American soldiers of atrocities, which made her so upset that she had to raise these concerns with the President. He was shocked, and asked her several questions, indicating that he was going to look into the situation.

After lunch, the Kennedys gave their guests a personal tour of the White House, including the Lincoln bedroom and the rooms that Jackie had redecorated. The President had been very excited to show them some of his collection of Americana, being very proud of everything that had been part of the history of his country. Grace spoke with Jackie for some time about the challenges of raising a family in the public eye and trying to keep the relentlessly prying photographers away from the children.

Grace and Rainier both loved America, and very much enjoyed their time with the Kennedys. She kept the menu from the luncheon as a souvenir. (She had a tendency to keep everything, which was yet another thing that we shared in common.) For that occasion, she wore a green Givenchy dress, and a very unique white-feathered "turban" that looked absolutely stunning on her, but only Grace could have made this look so elegant.

This was not the first time that Grace had met Jack Kennedy. Years before he became President, when she was an actress, Kennedy had been in the hospital in New York for quite some time because of his back, and Jackie wanted to cheer him up. Jackie and her sister, Lee Bouvier, convinced Grace to put on a nurse's uniform and pretend to be the new night nurse, but Jack Kennedy recognized who she was right away, and they all laughed.

Grace was always concerned about people's well-being and wanted to do everything she could to make someone feel better. Both she and Rainier were very caring with Martin and me. One evening, Prince Rainier drove us in his beautiful Jaguar to a famous Provençal restaurant on the Middle Corniche Road above Monaco, known for serving meat roasted on a spit over a wood fire. We had a wonderful time and stayed until quite late.

As we stepped outside into the cold night air, I had a sudden attack of deep bronchial coughing. Grace was worried, but the Prince looked truly alarmed, saying that I sounded as if I were almost at death's door. Then he said, "I have just the thing." They bundled me up in the car, and we raced back to the Palace. He dashed inside and emerged with his own special cough syrup, which he insisted on giving to me. I was very touched by his consideration and concern. Grace called me the next day to ask how I was – thanks to the Prince's medicine, I felt much better.

When Grace and Rainier were with us, they could really be themselves, and we often saw how much affection they had for each other. You could see the love in their eyes as they looked and smiled at one another. They giggled and laughed a lot, and enjoyed teasing each other. However, they were highly aware that public displays of affection were unseemly for a royal couple, and the Prince was rather shy in public.

They were also both very affectionate toward the children, especially when they were young. The Prince and Princess always made time for their children, no matter how busy their days were. At the Palace, they all had breakfast together every day – Grace made sure that breakfast was healthy, because she was concerned about her weight and the health of the Prince. She wanted to keep their private meals light because they had so many luncheons, banquets and official dinners at which they had no choice but to eat everything offered to them, in order not to offend anyone. They had lunch with the children most days, when there weren't official luncheons, or if the Prince didn't have meetings with his Ministers.

I invited Grace for lunch in Nice on several occasions, but she usually enjoyed the European tradition of having lunch with her family at home, so we would go shopping in Nice afterwards and chat over tea in the late afternoon. Grace felt that having meals together brought the family closer together, reinforced family values and respect, and fostered communication. Whenever their schedules allowed it, they also had dinner with the children in the small dining room of their private apartments. If they had other engagements to attend at night, Grace would rush home to spend time with the children before they went to bed, then she would get ready for official functions, such as formal dinners at the Palace at 8 o'clock, or galas that usually began at 10 p.m.

We were often invited to spend time with them in their private apartments, which were located on the ground floor of the Palace, beneath the formal apartments. The rest of the more than two hundred rooms in the Palace were used mostly for formal receptions in the State Rooms, for guests, for administrative offices, and for the Palace staff. The Palace of Monaco was far too vast and grand to be truly comfortable to live in. It was a little ironic that many people dream of living in a Palace, yet the Prince and Princess chose to live in an apartment the size of a regular home.

The rooms of their private apartments were arranged in a line, with a corridor running alongside; you could pass from one room to the next, railroad style. There was a living room, dining room, a library/den, a separate bar, a bedroom, bathroom, dressing room, small kitchen, and the children's nursery across a small outdoor corridor, which led to the garden. Their apartments had a warm and cozy atmosphere, quite modest, but elegant in an understated way.

The living room had comfortable armchairs and sofas, interspersed with cloth-draped round tables with silver-framed photographs on them. In the middle of the living room was Grace's favorite piece of furniture: an antique gilt French sofa with three seats back-to-back shaped like a pinwheel, covered in beautiful blue silk with the words "I Love You" subtly patterned all over the material. It was called an *indiscret* (indiscreet), probably because it seated three people in a round, and one person could listen to the conversation of the other two. This was one of Grace's treasures that she had brought from her New York apartment, when she had some of her furniture shipped to Monaco after her wedding to make their apartments in the Palace more homelike.

We spent many quiet times at Rainier's bar in their apartment, where there were various plaques, one of which read, "Don't put off until tomorrow what you can do the day after tomorrow." Rainier had a great sense of humor. He was really a very modest man who could talk easily to anyone, regardless of rank or background. He had an uncanny gift of being able to tell many stories and jokes in different languages, without ever repeating them. Whenever we were all together, we always laughed a lot.

One of the Prince's favorite things was his pet parrot, Coco, who could whistle and make the sound of a cork being popped from a champagne bottle. The parrot said "Hello" when the phone rang and also imitated laughing voices. The Prince especially loved that it could whistle the Monégasque national anthem. Coco had once belonged to an old sailor, so it also had some pretty salty language at times. I had never known Grace not to like an animal, except for this parrot. We would be sitting in their small private dining room, when suddenly from the next room we would hear the parrot spewing obscenities in French. Grace was somewhat embarrassed by these incidents, but the parrot was very clever, and the Prince thought it was funny.

Coco the parrot could call all of the dogs by name. There were all kinds of dogs around at any given time, including Grace's adored black poodle, Oliver. Cary Grant had given Oliver to Grace as a gift when she was in Hollywood. The treasured pet became world-famous when Grace arrived in Monaco for her wedding, descending the gangplank of the SS *CONSTITUTION*, carrying Oliver under her arm. He was lively company, and Grace was heartbroken when Oliver was attacked and killed by another dog during one of our skiing vacations in Switzerland. We were all so sad to see Grace's grief, and although she tried not to let it show because she did not want to ruin everyone's vacation, her sense of deep loss was evident. In many ways, the death of her cherished pet severed the last link to her life as an actress. Although the Prince immediately presented her with another poodle in a compassionate effort to console her, none of her many subsequent dogs could ever take the place of dear Oliver.

Prince Rainier loved all animals, and created an animal garden below the Palace. This private zoo had a wide variety of monkeys, apes, exotic birds, and a menagerie of wild animals, including tigers, a hippo, and several types of wild cats. As a wedding gift, the King of Morocco had given him a pair of lions that later produced four cubs. Rainier particularly admired primates because of their intelligence, and had a favorite chimpanzee, which was occasionally allowed in the Palace. Although there was a zoo staff, the Prince enjoyed feeding the animals and fearlessly entered their cages, which made Grace very nervous.

Monaco – July 4, 1961

Dearest Mum and Dad,

The Prince and Grace invited us to luncheon at the Palace and for a swim in their new pool. It is gorgeous! What fun we had with water games in the fresh water. We had a delicious lunch afterwards and left about 4 p.m. That evening we had cocktails with the Maharani of Baroda on board Onassis's yacht.

Must dash – All love to you both, Joan, Marty, Charles, Greg

Grace and Rainier decided to add a pool at the Palace in the rear of the garden, which Prince Rainier designed himself. It was a large, asymmetrical swimming pool, surrounded by lawns, and beautifully landscaped with exotic trees. The pool was tiled in aqua blue mosaic and provided many happy hours of fun for the children and guests. With the lovely weather in Monaco, they often had parties and events around the pool, and many of their guests enjoyed going for a swim, from Hollywood royalty to the crowned heads of the world.

During the summer, we took the children to the Monte Carlo Beach Club, where we had a little cabana. The boys swam in the sea or in the Olympic-size swimming pool. When Grace came to the beach with Albert and Caroline, they would go to their large cabin to change and then come down to our cabana.

The children played together, digging in the sand, running around, and swimming. They loved to race each other, and entered competitions. Albert was a very strong swimmer, but Charles was often distracted before a race, so when they said, "Go," he was usually looking the other way, thus getting a late start.

Our children were invited regularly to the Palace to play with young Albert and Caroline. The nursery, which had been transformed from a storeroom, was large and airy with extremely high ceilings. It was decorated in soft yellow and white, with animals like rabbits and birds painted on the walls by a famous French cartoonist. The nursery consisted of a very large playroom, the children's bedrooms with a sliding partition down the middle, a small kitchen where food could be prepared for the children, and a room for the nurse. It had its own private entrance and stairs leading to the Palace gardens overlooking the Mediterranean, where the children could romp and play.

Albert and Caroline were not really aware of their privileged position, and behaved for the most part like regular children. They played "blind man's bluff" and all sorts of games. They climbed on the jungle gym, where Caroline would hang from the top, imitating a monkey. Charles and Albert dueled with swords, played cowboys, and had countless pillow fights. From an early age, Albert loved to roughhouse with his father and with our son.

Even within the confines of the Palace, the children were given a certain sense of independence, always under the watchful eye of Nanny Maureen. However, they were never allowed to run wild. Grace insisted that her children be courteous, polite and respectful; she wanted them to play and enjoy a normal childhood, but they had to have good manners. Caroline's curtsy was very graceful, and young Albert's bow was courtly. It was sweet to watch them.

Monaco – July 31, 1961

Dearest Mum and Dad,

We go to the Beach almost every day, picnic there, swim and do nothing. We are enjoying it while we may. Grace and the Prince and the children came down the other day, and they all had great fun with Charles and Greggie. We had been up to the pool at the Palace last week and had a delightful time, playing water games, having lunch. The children enjoyed the water, and Albie and Charles are really great pals. They invent games together, play on the swings, wrestle, etc. Charles still has many fears, I am sorry to say, but Albie gives him courage. Greg, on the other hand, is fearless, daring, destructive, egotist – but we adore him. The Prince said he looked like a little Swedish boy – his hair is so fair – he does!

I have at last found an excellent dressmaker to alter my clothes. She has remade several already, and I am very pleased. All for now.

Loads of love from us all, Always, Joan

When we first arrived for our consular posts in France, I was only twenty-four years old and could not really afford the wardrobe necessary for all of the official functions that we had to attend. At first, I made a lot of my own clothing or altered pieces from my mother or my aunt. I remade pieces as the seasons changed, and laughed when people would compliment me and ask where I got my suits. My biggest challenge was that for the first year, I only had one long gown to wear to all the formal events!

After a lot of searching, I was fortunate to find an incredibly gifted seamstress in Beaulieu, just on the border of Monaco. This talented lady, Madame Antoinette, produced the most extraordinary copies of designs from the great couturiers, which I could not otherwise have afforded. Even once we moved to Monaco and Martin was working for the Prince, I was on a very limited budget for clothing. Yet I had to look elegant and well-dressed for all of the functions we attended, including numerous black tie galas, among people who had unlimited resources and frequented the salons of Parisian designers.

Madame Antoinette managed to find original Chanel material and buttons, to recreate very authentic looking suits, and I am most grateful to her for her expertise and ingenuity. She was even able to reproduce Madame Grès's technique of delicately fine pleating, to create three long, Grecian-style evening gowns for me: one in purplish blue, one in emerald green, and one in white silk chiffon. They were beautiful and exquisitely made.

In September 1961, we attended the Second Annual Festival of Amateur Theatre with Grace and Rainier, which Rainier's father presided over. The multinational committee members were an illustrious and diverse group that only Prince Pierre could have garnered. The glittering galaxy of stars included Yul Brynner, David Niven, Noel Coward, Dino de Laurentiis, famous Italian actress Silvana Mangano, and Marcel Pagnol, among others.

Rainier and Grace both greatly loved and supported the arts. Inside the program for the evening was a quote from H.S.H. Prince Rainier III: *"You are 'amateurs' of the theater. But you do not merely content yourselves with loving it, you serve it faithfully with a full heart. While the hectic pace of our life today leaves us with little leisure, and to some the theater is just a means of amusement and relaxation, you are among those who have found in the theater a form of artistic self-expression. This is greatly to your credit, since the hours you devote to the practice of this art are not only drawn from your leisure time, but are freely and enthusiastically given with no thought of reward."*

This statement could be said of the Prince himself. As Head of State, he devoted himself and his life completely to his duty without thought of reward or recognition. He was born to it, destined to be the Sovereign Prince, and always served his people loyally and wholeheartedly, trying to make decisions that would fulfill the best interests of his country in the present and for the future.

Grace also shared the Prince's dedication to duty, and together they were a phenomenal team. Few people really knew how hard they both worked, how many hours they spent in their offices, answering correspondence, agreeing to represent a certain cause or solve a particular problem. They were running a country, and they had diplomatic relations with heads of state and other crowned heads from around the globe. Of course, Grace's role was different from that of the Prince; hers was more the position of "First Lady" while Prince Rainier was the Sovereign, but he would often speak with her about important matters and seek her wise counsel. They both wanted to do their best for the greatest good of their country, and to better the world whenever and wherever possible.

Although there certainly were perks to their job, and they definitely enjoyed it for the most part, Grace and Rainier really worked day and night, even when on vacation. They would be out at official functions until 2 a.m. or later, and then Rainier would be in his office around 9:00 the next morning. Even with all the servants and secretaries, there were never enough hours in the day for all of the duties and responsibilities of the Prince and Princess, and their engagement books were scheduled months ahead. Grace often said, "I know where I am going to be every minute of every day for the rest of my life." It was Grace's nature to be more relaxed and spontaneous, so it took a while for her to get used to the hectic and regimented schedule of being Princess of Monaco, but she took these duties and responsibilities very seriously and was committed to doing the best job she could – and it was indeed a job.

After breakfast with the family, Rainier would go to his office in the Palace to conduct state business, running the Principality like the CEO of a mega-corporation. Grace usually spent her mornings managing issues related to the many intricacies of the Palace household and dealing with the mail. Then there were all of the organizations within Monaco that required her attention.

It amazed me how Grace always made sure to keep in contact with her friends and family no matter how busy she was. She even addressed her packages and envelopes in her beautiful handwriting. Grace liked to choose her own gifts for people and wrap them herself, often with simple yet lovely little ornaments on the packages. (I usually kept these ornaments and used them for decorations on our Christmas tree.) Grace once asked me to help her wrap Christmas presents, and although I tried my best, I never managed to make them look as elegant as she did.

I treasure the things that Grace has given me over the years, such as a royal blue linen wallet with beige leather trim, a pretty blue necklace from Majorca, a light blue hanging bag for purses, and a dark blue angora sweater. (Grace obviously knew that my favorite color was blue, which she also favored.)

I never knew how Grace could keep up with all her correspondence, even with the help of the staff. Hundreds of people wrote to her, constantly seeking her assistance or advice on all sorts of matters. She was besieged with pleas for her patronage for various charities and events, for public appearances and speaking engagements, for interviews and photo shoots from publications all over the world. There were countless requests for autographed photographs, for money, and for help of all kinds. Grace never wanted to disappoint others, so she always tried to meet people's requests where she could, and although she had a secretary, she did her best to answer everyone personally. She had trouble saying "no," and would find herself making many personal sacrifices because of it.

Having been an actress, Grace received lots of fan letters, some of which would ask her for various things. One girl wrote to say that she was not working, and asked if Grace would send an item of her clothing. Grace was very pragmatic and considerate, so she thought to herself, "Well, what could the young girl wear?" She decided to part with her favorite suit, thinking that the girl could use it to go on job interviews or wear it to work. Much to Grace's surprise, the girl promptly returned the suit! Apparently, she had been expecting something more glamorous, but Grace was ultimately thrilled to have her suit back. She became very attached to her things and kept them forever. She especially loved to keep her old clothes, and was careful to watch her figure, so she could continue to wear them over and over again – she was not one to be concerned about being seen wearing the same outfit on numerous occasions.

To accommodate all of the various activities that demanded her presence, Grace would often have to change her clothes four or five times in one day, but she was masterful at it. During the daytime, Grace dressed very conservatively in skirts, blouses, and sweaters that were typical of the late 1950s. For public appearances, she wore suits in tweed, flannel or silk, depending on the season. She loved to wear shades of pink or blue, and rarely wore flowered or patterned clothes, except for the now-famous flowered dress that she wore to meet Prince Rainier for the first time. (She went to the Palace on very short notice for a photo shoot during the 1955 Cannes Film Festival, and it was the only dress that didn't need ironing, as a French labor strike had turned off all the power in the city of Cannes – she told me that she never really liked that dress!) When it came to formal events, Grace was stunningly elegant and so regal that she did not need to wear a tiara to look every bit like a princess. She was remarkable in how quickly she could completely transform her appearance.

Grace's daily schedule was such that she had little time to herself, but she enjoyed taking walks in the gardens with the children or the dogs, and swimming in the Palace pool. In the late morning, Rainier played squash or tennis to keep fit. The Prince and Princess would often have lunch together *en famille*, as is the European tradition, before going back to work. At every meal, the Prince always kept a small pad of paper and a pencil next to his place setting, so he could make discreet notes and reminders as things came up – Rainier had innumerable things on his mind and constant issues to attend to.

After lunch, Grace's afternoons were devoted to her charity work, and to all of the commitments that increased over time as she took on more and more philanthropic causes and responsibilities. Grace was never one to be idle; soon after they were married, she devoted her time and energy to doing what she could to help others. She immediately embraced the opportunity to work with the Red Cross, and took her position of President very seriously, both in Monaco, and as part of the International Committee.

The Red Cross in Monaco operated differently at that time from some of its counterparts in other countries. In Monaco, most of the social service organizations fell under the umbrella of the Red Cross. As President, Grace supervised all departments, all the planning and events, including the big annual fundraising galas. She personally reviewed every case treated. She went to the orphanage, and arranged for outings for the children. She visited people in the hospital, and in homes for the elderly. As her children grew older, Grace would take them along to train them for their future duties, and to give them compassion for those less fortunate.

When Princess Grace and Prince Rainier traveled, they were expected to make public appearances and state visits, to attend official functions, do press conferences, personal interviews and photo shoots for magazines. It was good for Grace and Rainier to have breaks where they could get away and relax for a few days – but they could rarely get away from the ever-present paparazzi.

In September of 1961, Grace and Rainier took Albert and Caroline on a cruise to Greece aboard Onassis's yacht *CHRISTINA*. Nanny Maureen had been ill, so Grace looked after the children by herself, which she loved to do. Others thought this was strange for a Princess, but Grace and Rainier wanted to be hands-on parents whenever possible. They often took the children with them on any trips that exceeded four days' duration. The family was relentlessly followed by reporters wherever they went, but Albert usually took it in stride and, at the age of three and a half, liked to monkey around for the photographers.

All of the tabloids were abuzz at that time, spreading false rumors that Maria Callas was enamored of Rainier. The tabloids claimed that divorce was imminent for the Prince and Princess. Grace was rumored to have delivered an ultimatum to Rainier, "Me or la Callas – either Maria Callas leaves Monaco, or I return to Hollywood." These stories were just ridiculous, as Grace was actually very friendly with Maria.

Grace and Rainier were both loyal Catholics, and their shared faith gave them a bond of strength that supported them through life's challenges. Their love of each other and their children also gave them a powerful partnership that the world could not defile, despite unrelenting efforts by the media to taint their marriage and their family with false rumors, innuendoes, and baseless gossip.

Over the years of knowing Grace, I got to witness first-hand how the tabloid press played with people's lives. Innocent situations would be distorted and perverted, or complete lies would be utterly fabricated. I certainly learned never to believe what I read in the tabloids, but these stories and falsehoods can be really hurtful and damaging to those involved, and one cannot imagine the pain that this caused to the entire family. At one time, they implied that there were kidnapping threats made toward Albert and Caroline, which though untrue, could have given some crazy person terrible ideas. It was appalling.

Monaco – September 24, 1961

Dearest Mum and Dad,

Yesterday, we had lunch at Rocagel with Grace and Rainier and the children. Grace made some American specialties herself, and we really enjoyed ourselves. Albie and Charles laugh continually, and Caroline feels a little out of it, so she busies herself by mothering Greggie. They are so sweet together. Grace has invited Charles to the circus tomorrow, and Grace and Rainier are coming in to dinner tomorrow night.

Loads of love from us all, Joan, Marty, Charles, Greg

Grace and Rainier loved going to Rocagel on weekends when their presence was not required in Monaco. Saturdays were reserved for the children and for family activities, so they tried not to have appointments then. The ranch was their tranquil place, where they could just relax and be themselves with the children and with friends in complete privacy, without all the servants and footmen that were always around them at the Palace. At Rocagel, they just had Maria and Quinto who cooked and served, along with one or two other maids, a gardener and guards at the gate. Grace sometimes enjoyed cooking for the family in the modern "American" kitchen that she had designed. She seemed to like everything, but she had a great penchant for peanut butter sandwiches. They both took great pleasure in gardening; Grace loved her flowers, and Rainier enjoyed planting trees and riding around the property on his tractor.

At Rocagel, Grace could more or less dress as she wished. I never knew her to pamper herself, and at the ranch, she often went without makeup, with her hair pulled back in a ponytail. In summer, she always wore a large hat to protect her delicate fair skin from the sun's rays. As a rule, Grace did not wear trousers at the Palace because the Prince frowned upon them at Court, but at Rocagel she liked to wear slacks or capri pants, or evening pantsuits for dinner. Grace rarely wore jeans, but loved flat shoes – her favorites were rope-soled canvas espadrilles. Even as a "country girl" she was absolutely beautiful.

Grace always did her own hair and makeup, unless it was a very elegant evening, in which case Alexandre would fly in from Paris to coif her. She was very gifted with her hair, which like many blondes was extremely fine and wispy, but that never showed because of the way she wore it. I was lucky that my naturally blonde hair was quite thick, which she envied, sometimes asking if she could play with it and dress it for me. At that time, I wore my hair in a French twist or chignon. Grace kept saying that I had lovely hair, and she wished that hers were fuller. She had a lot of hairpieces, such as chignons and braids that she added to her hairdos very skillfully. One would never have known that a professional hairdresser had not done it for her. She was also a master at doing her own makeup, which she probably learned during her days as a model and actress. I'd seen her look really tired at the end of the day, but by the time she finished doing her hair, putting on her makeup and a glamorous dress, she looked stunning.

Monaco – November 6, 1961

Dearest Mum and Dad,

We have been extremely busy the last few weeks, as we have been going to the Palace about three times a week for the movies and for the children to play.

We have also gone to Rocagel on Sundays, and this Friday Grace dropped in at our apartment with Albie to see Charles – we spent a delightful afternoon. The Prince is fond of us and plays golf three times a week with Marty. I am going to begin golf lessons, or else I shall never be able to play well enough to have Marty play with me. He is really becoming a good golfer.

I am taking ballet lessons twice a week with Grace. They give us a real workout, which certainly will do us good. I feel slimmer and better already. I wonder if we shall stay here another two years – I hope so, as life is just beginning to run smoothly. We shall soon know, as Marty is going to discuss it with the Prince in December.

Charles is really bright – he never ceases to ask questions. The other day he made me laugh when he heard I was taking ballet lessons. He said "Did Princess Grace lift you up like the man on television?" He had seen a Pas de Deux where the man carried the dancer on his shoulder! Isn't that funny?

Charles and Greg send loads of love to Grammy and Grandpa.

Love from Marty too, and Joan

Grace was quite gifted as a dancer (as was Caroline, who probably could have become an outstanding ballerina). During our biweekly ballet classes, Madame Ardant (Grace's future Lady-in-Waiting) and I struggled to keep up with Grace. She would often giggle at us in her inimitable way, which would make us laugh as well. Grace's laugh was infectious, endearing and soft. Her eyes would crinkle, and she got lovely laugh lines around her mouth.

It was also rather comical whenever Grace and I tried to play golf – we weren't very good and spent much of the time laughing at each other and ourselves. However, we enjoyed walking along the golf course at Mont Agel, which was spectacular, looking out over the snow-capped peaks on one side, with the Mediterranean on the other. One day, Grace and I were attempting to play golf when lightning suddenly started to strike in the mountains all around us. We immediately threw down our metal clubs and ran for shelter under a tree, but then we thought that wasn't safe either, so we ran out into open space and stood in the rain, waiting out the storm. Fortunately, it did not last long.

The boys and I were often invited to Rocagel while Martin and Rainier played golf. The children would ride ponies and play, while Grace and I walked around the property, sometimes gardening together, picking flowers or planting bulbs. After their golf game, the men would join us for a lovely brunch or supper, and Rainier would occasionally barbecue. Meals at Rocagel were casual and relaxed, with home cooked dishes like meatloaf, noodles, vegetables from their garden, eggs from their own chickens, and American favorites like cinnamon rolls, hot dogs or hamburgers.

Monaco – November 16, 1961

Dearest Mum and Dad,

Hope all is well. The little ones send their love. Charles is becoming so grown up, and you should see him play with Albie, who is in the rough stage of pushing, and with Caroline, who is very sweet and thoughtful. She adores Greggie and has even named one of her baby dolls "Gregory."

All our love, Joan

Caroline really loved Charles and Greg, and it was so sweet to hear her calling her beloved doll "Gregory." All the children got along surprisingly well, and there were rarely any arguments. However, one day I remember Albert at the age of four turning to Charles and rather imperiously saying, "You can't do that. I am *Albert de Monaco*." Charles looked him straight in the eye and said, "*Albert de* what?"

When Albert was about four, he donned the uniform of the *Carabinier*, the same one that Prince Rainier had worn at around the same age. The winter dress uniform of the Palace Guard consists of a dark tunic, blue trousers with a red stripe down the side, and a blue helmet – on official occasions, the blue helmet has layers of red and white plumes. (In the Mediterranean heat of summer, the *Carabiniers* wear white trousers, a white shirt with epaulettes denoting rank, and a white helmet – with red plumes for official occasions) The changing of the Palace Guard takes place every day at 11:55 a.m., and during special events such as the *Fête Nationale de Monaco*, the *Carabiniers* parade in the *Place du Palais* directly in front of the Palace.

On these official occasions, Prince Rainier wore his dress uniform in black with gold embroidery, which he designed. Across his uniform, he wore the red and white sash of the National Order of Monaco, along with the medals that he had been awarded over the years for merit, distinction, bravery, and military service. Grace also wore a red and white sash across her gown, with a large jewel-encrusted emblem denoting the Grand Cross of the Order of St. Charles, the highest order in the Principality, which the Prince had conferred on her.

Monaco's National Day celebrates the sovereign on the day of his patron saint – Prince Rainier chose November 19 to honor the feast day of Saint Rainier of Arezzo. This was the anniversary of Prince Rainier's accession ceremony, which took place on November 19, 1949. Festivities for the *Fête Nationale* usually began on November 18 with a large cocktail reception in the Throne Room. After dark, there were spectacular fireworks, with a buffet supper at the Palace followed by dancing late into the night. On the morning of November 19, a *Te Deum* Mass was held at the Cathedral, after which we would all walk a few blocks to the Palace where the Prince conferred honorary titles, medals and awards, and reviewed the troops while the Princely Family greeted the Monégasque people from the Palace balcony. This was followed by a huge banquet in the Throne Room, with selected Monégasque officials as guests. We would then go home and change into black tie for a gala at the Opera in the Prince's Box.

As a gift to commemorate Monaco's National Day, Prince Pierre sent me a charming photograph with a handwritten note on the back. He was wearing a dramatic black cape decorated with his medals, standing with young Albert in his *Carabinier* uniform and Caroline dressed in the traditional Monégasque costume, including a red and white striped skirt with an apron and a white blouse. It was very sweet.

On this special day for Monaco, Albert was very proud to be in his uniform as he appeared on the Palace balcony with his parents to review the soldiers. Martin and I were inside the *Salon des Glaces*, watching the family greet the Monégasque citizens gathered in the square below. Later, Albert suddenly went running towards the buffet table, and Grace, worrying about what he was going to do, said, "Don't do that, Albert." At which point Albert drew himself up and said in a firm voice, "Soldiers don't have mothers!" You never know what children are going to say when they are young!

Grace believed in a certain amount of strictness tempered with love and affection, feeling that children really wanted discipline, even when protesting against it. They needed boundaries and limits in order to feel safe and loved. Princess Caroline and Prince Albert were extremely polite and well behaved. Grace also taught them respect, believing that without this, one cannot be a whole human being.

Monaco – December 7 to 9, 1961

Dearest Mum and Dad,

Grace has been adorable recently, and we have seen a great deal of each other, either with the children, or at our biweekly ballet lessons. We spent last Sunday with them up at the Villa and had a delightful time. Albie is Charles's best friend, and they play together two or three times a week. This afternoon the Prince is showing cartoons for them at the Palace, and our two are invited. Albie comes here to our apartment with Grace once a week while Caroline takes ballet – and Caroline is so jealous that she has to come here, too, as soon as her class is over!

Saturday – We have been so busy taking ballet lessons with Grace and finally golf lessons (Grace is waiting to play with me so I must hurry). Tomorrow is Charlesie's party – Grace is bringing Albie and Caroline, and eight other friends are coming. I hope we survive!

Grace gave a small gathering to show "The Country Girl" – her Academy Award film. She was very good in it.

Loads of love from us all, Joan, Marty, Charles, Greg

To my knowledge, this was the only time that one of Grace's films was shown while I lived in Monaco, perhaps because it was not acceptable for a Princess to be a movie star. *The Country Girl* was the motion picture for which Grace won her Oscar, but after we watched it together, she commented, "My acting could have been better." I think the thing that she missed the most about acting was no longer having the opportunity to truly prove to herself, more than to anyone else, that she really was a good actress.

Grace began her professional acting career in New York and was among the first to do live dramatic television performances. Her uncle was the famous playwright, George Kelly, who wrote several plays that were adapted into films in the 1920s and 1930s, including *Craig's Wife*, for which he won the Pulitzer Prize. However, Grace wanted to succeed on her own merit as an actress, and not because of her uncle's acclaim or her father's power. She made her Broadway debut in *The Father*, playing Raymond Massey's daughter, and never lost her interest in theater, even after she went to Hollywood.

In just five short years, from age twenty-two to twenty-seven, Grace captivated the world in her meteoric rise to movie stardom. She was in the right place at the right time, and the world was ready for her gentleness backed with hidden strength, her refinement, her charm and her radiant beauty. Grace was cast with the top leading men of that era: Clark Gable, Bing Crosby, Cary Grant, Ray Milland, William Holden, Frank Sinatra, Jimmy Stewart, and Gary Cooper (remaining lifelong friends with many of them). It was absolutely amazing that she made so many wonderful films at such a young age – movies that have become classics loved by generations.

Grace starred in eleven major motion pictures from 1951-1956, including *Mogambo*, for which she won a Golden Globe for Best Supporting Actress, culminating in her winning the Oscar for Best Actress for her portrayal of the unglamorous wife of an alcoholic in *The Country Girl.* Her famous acceptance speech at the Academy Awards is often replayed on television, because of her extraordinary beauty and endearing humility.

When she married Prince Rainier, Grace was just getting into her stride in her craft. She was aware that she was on the threshold of becoming really good at acting, and I think it rather saddened her that she could not continue with her career. She wanted a family more than anything, and she had fallen in love with the Prince, who was a wonderful man, so in many ways she had no regrets. However, we were soon to find out that Alfred Hitchcock had recently approached her to return to Hollywood as his leading lady – perhaps this is why Grace wanted to watch and assess her performance in *The Country Girl.*

Monaco – December 26, 1961

Dearest Mum and Dad,

Charles's birthday was a great success, and the mothers enjoyed themselves, too. Charles received a gorgeous Indian outfit from Grace. I made a cake, and we made ice cream faces topped with rice krispie cones to look like clowns. (Greg and Charles are wrestling at the moment, and Charles says, "Shall we fight?" Greg says softly "Oui," and begins to pummel his brother. Then Charles falls, and Greg says "Mammie, Cha mort" (dead) – that is what comes of seeing Westerns on TV.)

For Christmas, Charles received a lovely Western suede cowboy jacket with fringes from Grace and Albie. Greg received a post box with different shaped pieces, and from Rainier a trading post with indians, which he adores, and Charles was given a scooter, which he is learning to ride slowly. The best things of all were the two pairs of cowboy boots sent by the Dales (plus Grace's jacket in which Charles is literally living). They are adorable, stomping around going "pow-pow," and the boots are even worn over pajamas!

Saturday, Grace and Rainier showed "Bambi" to the children. It was so lovely and was a great success. Sunday, we went to the Royal Opera of London Ballet to see Margot Fonteyn in "Sleeping Beauty" – marvelous. That evening at midnight, we donned long gowns to attend Mass in the Palace Chapel, followed by distribution of gifts (a golf ball sighter for Marty and a hanging bag with pockets for putting in purses from Grace), then there was a buffet supper with caviar, foie gras, salmon, ham flown in from Virginia, champagne and Bûche de Noël (Christmas log cake). It was fun, and we left at 4 a.m., to be awakened at 8:30 a.m. by two eager little boys.

Last evening we had a movie at the Palace. Thursday, Marty plays golf with the Prince, the Admiral of the 6th Fleet, and Father O'Connell. Friday, I have my ballet lesson, followed by luncheon at the Palace and a distribution of toys by G & R in the afternoon.

Tuesday is a movie, Wednesday G & R are coming here for a Chinese dinner on Marty's birthday. Thursday is another movie, Friday is Mrs. Joy's dinner for G & R, and Saturday is a Gala for the Foreign Colonies – whew. Luckily, most of these affairs are at night, so we see the children and leave after they are in bed.

Oh – the best news of all – the Prince has renewed Marty's contract for two years starting this January with a raise to $30,000. We are so pleased! He really almost loves Marty, and he was very generous to us!

Loads of love from us all and many thanks, Marty, Joan, Charles, Greg

Grace loved to have a Nativity play at Christmastime, which was held in the Throne Room of the Palace. Charles played Joseph, Caroline was the Angel, Albert was one of the Three Kings, and the staff's children also joined in the play. Everyone had beautiful costumes, which I'm sure Grace designed herself. She directed the plays, of course, which was yet another of her great talents.

We spent New Year's Eve with Grace, Rainier, and Onassis at the Sporting Club and the *Hôtel de Paris*, arriving home at 5 a.m. It was great fun dancing our way into 1962, oblivious to the fact that the events that were about to unfold in the month of January would trigger a year-long crisis for Monaco... Prince Rainier would risk losing his country, the French would demand Martin's head, Grace's life would feel more like a nightmare than a fairy tale, and I would have to decline the honor of a lifetime.

DAYS OF CRISIS

In January 1962, Grace and Rainier, Martin and I were all gathered together in their private apartment at the Palace, when Grace thought it would be fun to read everyone's horoscope aloud. Grace was very interested in people's birth signs, and she was almost an amateur astrologer. If she liked someone, she would subtly find a way of asking what that person's birth sign was. She was most interested in people's tendencies, and the various qualities that are characteristic of each sign of the zodiac. There are certain traits that people born under the same sign have in common, although some people remain skeptical of this.

Grace had just gotten a new book of horoscopes for the year 1962 and was eager see what was in store for us all. She read her own horoscope that said: "You are inclined to like lampshades with plastic covers on them," to which she laughed and said, "How did they know?" This was one trait that Grace had that one would not suspect of her, that of being very practical, almost to the point of being frugal. Of course, they did not have plastic covers in the Palace, but she was the kind of person who would preserve everything. When she looked up Rainier's birth sign of Gemini, she read, "You will soon be changing jobs"! We all laughed, but little did we know at that moment how this prediction was almost about to come true!

The year started off innocently enough, with Grace and Rainier coming to our apartment for Chinese dinner to celebrate Martin's birthday on January 3. We had fun playing gin rummy after dinner, and they stayed until 2:30 a.m. For the next two weeks, we were with Grace and Rainier almost every day, going to dinners, movies and galas. We went to Rocagel for Sunday brunch, where

Charles got to ride their new Irish pony "Babbling Brook," while Grace and I walked around the property and talked. On January 5, we went to the *Hôtel de Paris* for dinner, after which Grace and I walked home at midnight – it was a beautiful night, and we enjoyed walking, talking and laughing together. Grace loved to walk, and it was helpful after our copious dinner.

On the morning of January 6, Charles and Greg went to the Palace to play with Albie and Caroline. They brought their Sir Lancelot costumes, complete with plastic swords! They were not the only ones going to battle on that day. For some reason, during dinner at the *Gala des Colonies Étrangères*, Madame Tivey-Faucon got very upset. As Grace's Lady-in-Waiting, it was her duty to attend such functions in a way that served the Prince and Princess without drawing attention to herself. I never knew what happened, but the Prince got very annoyed. Her dismissal from their service followed very soon thereafter, and she later retaliated with what I believe to have been spite and betrayal.

A few days later, we attended the International Television Festival Gala, after which we were invited back to the Prince's private apartments for drinks and dancing. Prince Rainier did not like dancing in public with everyone watching him, but Grace loved to dance, so they often enjoyed listening to music and dancing together at home.

After formal dinners at the Palace, or when a gala event ended in the early morning hours, the Prince sometimes continued the evening's festivities by inviting Martin and me to their private apartments for a nightcap. On one such occasion a couple of weeks prior, we were joined by Margot Fonteyn, the world-famous English prima ballerina. She was a very outgoing and elegant lady with a sparkle in her eye. We were playing some records, and Margot tried to teach us all how to do "The Twist," which was a new dance craze at the time. None of us could quite get the hang of twisting our bodies correctly, because it was very different from any other dance step that we had ever learned. In her British accent, Margot said, "It's easy, just pretend that you're stomping out a cigarette with one foot, and drying your back with a towel at the same time. So you twist your foot and twist your body with the towel." We tried it and were amazed that it was so easy. The five of us all had a great time doing the Twist in Grace and Rainier's apartment. It seemed incredible that we would learn such a dance from one of the greatest classical ballet dancers of all time! From then on, we all enjoyed many late nights of dancing the Twist.

On January 23, we went to the Palace for Caroline's fifth birthday party. It was a wonderful masquerade party that took place in the formal apartments with marble floors, huge tables, giant chandeliers and footmen everywhere. Charles went as an Indian chief, wearing the costume that Rainier and Grace had given him. Tea was served in the Napoleonic Room, with mothers watching from the sidelines. It was amazing to see the children playing party games in these massive formal State Rooms filled with priceless antiques, and in the stately white and gold *Salon des Glaces.*

I must say that I was always a little worried that the children might accidentally break something, and I watched over my boys like a hawk. I think most of the small children were a little intimidated because of the enormity and imposing quality of these rooms. At one point, little Gregory was sitting in his costume, crying, because being in such an immense place terrified him. Gradually, these formal parties were eliminated to make way for more intimate children's parties in their own private apartments.

We returned home exhausted and were just going to bed that night when the phone rang at 11:30 p.m. It was Prince Rainier, asking Martin to come to the Palace immediately. Martin was not told the reason, but when one is summoned by the Prince, no matter what the hour, one does not ask questions. Martin dressed quickly and rushed to the Palace, which was just moments away. When he arrived, Martin was told to wait for the Prince in the small antechamber. He was surprised to see the French Minister of State for Monaco, Émile Pelletier, who had obviously shaved in a terribly nervous hurry, as evidenced by all the bits of bloody toilet paper stuck to his face.

The two of them waited together in anxious silence while the Prince held an emergency meeting with his Cabinet. Apparently, Mr. Pelletier had not been summoned but had shown up at the Palace demanding an audience with Prince Rainier. Mr. Pelletier grew increasingly upset, particularly at having to wait in the same room as "the American." He was furious because it was now after midnight, and he had to go to a clinic for prostate surgery the following day. He was so affronted by the situation that his agitation kept growing by the minute. As soon as the Prince was ready to receive him, Mr. Pelletier entered the room and immediately began arguing with Prince Rainier and insulting him. A shouting match ensued the likes of which Martin had never witnessed before, particularly not with a sovereign prince! Some said it could be heard throughout the Palace!

That night, Prince Rainier had received a very serious ultimatum from the French government that would eventually threaten him with being deposed, which made him absolutely outraged. Mr. Pelletier accused the Prince of being anti-French, to which Rainier angrily responded, "I went through Alsace as a junior officer, and now you dare to say that I am anti-French when you shit in my boots!" Mr. Pelletier rose up and shouted, "You cannot speak with me that way. I was Minister of the Interior for General de Gaulle, and I am Minister of State for Monaco through French appointment and your agreement, and you cannot speak to me that way." The Prince retorted, "You are right. You're fired!" Mr. Pelletier turned and stormed out, with Prince Rainier yelling after him, "It is not you who are leaving, it's me that puts you at the door!"

And then came the deluge...

Monaco – January 24, 1962

Dearest Mum and Dad,

We have been going through a crisis in Monaco between conflicting interests of the French and the Prince, which culminated in a sizzling all-night session last night. Heads were falling everywhere, but it all seems to be smoothed out for a while at least. Marty is still surviving and offered excellent advice to R., for which he is grateful. We have been on tenterhooks!

The children are well – yesterday they donned masquerade costumes to go to the Palace for Caroline's 5th birthday party. They had a lovely time. Charles went in his Indian costume and Greg as the littlest cowboy. He won a prize for being the cutest with his western swagger and serious face. He stole the show! They played musical chairs, pin the tail on the donkey and then had a wonderful feast of ice cream and cake in the gorgeous State Rooms. There were about 15 children there, and really, it was beautifully organized by Grace. She is an extraordinary girl. Caroline was a real Princess in her Sardinian costume and Albie complemented her perfectly. He and Charles are still great pals, and both G & R love him (Greg too, but he is so silent when he is away from home that no one knows what a lively, devilish, stubborn, strong-willed person he really is). Last Sunday we spent the day at the Villa Rocagel, and Charles rode Caroline's big, new Irish pony with Prince Rainier holding the bit. Charles was a real horseman, sitting tall in the saddle and moving easily with the horse and singing as he rode. He really was our pride and joy. Albie, who for once was afraid to ride, was forced out of pride to show Charles that he, too, could ride without fear. They were adorable.

Last week we attended the Television Festival Gala with G & R and were besieged by photographers who banged our heads with their cameras while we were seated, and had flash wires in front of Onassis's eyes – it was quite a sight! Callas and Onassis, the Marcel Pagnols (of "Fanny" fame) and the Vittorio de

Sicas (a most distinguished gentleman) were also at the table. It was a gay evening, which ended at the Palace at 3 a.m. after having danced the Twist.

We have two more Galas and then the Princes leave for Gstaad, where we shall join them for three weeks on February 19th. We shall have a breather for a while.

All love from us all, Joan

The night of January 23, 1962, sparked a crisis between France and Monaco during which Prince Rainier would almost lose his throne. President Charles de Gaulle was fierce about protecting French ways and ideals. He was a French purist who maintained supreme power over French broadcasting companies, censoring all the information that was aired in France. He even controlled and regulated the media and had all news broadcasts edited. He was disturbed that Radio Monte Carlo and Radio Luxembourg beamed their commercial programs into France without content control, and wanted to take over the parent company of these radio stations, which was based in Monaco.

The trouble originally began in the mid-1950s over Tele-Saar, a popular and powerful broadcasting station located in the Saarland (a territory along the Franco-German border occupied by the French after WWII, which France eventually had to return to Germany). Tele-Saar was one of the first private television and radio stations in Europe. Its broadcasts could be seen and heard in France, which created the threat of German propaganda and the advertising of German products that were potentially detrimental to French interests.

France's state television and radio stations were fully under government control, and were "their master's voice." De Gaulle recognized that radio and television made it possible to directly reach large groups of people, and thereby influence attitudes, beliefs and opinions on a mass scale. He realized the immense power of the media and used it to great advantage. He was a masterful and mesmerizing speaker whose popularity knew no bounds.

In France, commercial and private broadcasting was forbidden by legislation enacted in 1944, and De Gaulle wanted Tele-Saar and its very successful radio station, "Europe Number One," to be under France's control. This station, along with Radio Monte Carlo and Tele Monte Carlo, surrounded France and belonged to a Monégasque holding company called *Images et Son*, which was largely owned by the Monégasque Bank of Precious Metals. It was the largest privately owned broadcasting group in Europe.

A subsidiary of *Images et Son* was also building transmitters and a network of radio and television stations that would increase their broadcasting range into France. However, the French had no intention of letting that power escape their grasp, especially as television was a relatively new and rapidly expanding medium at that time. Ultimately, hundreds of millions of dollars of advertising and other revenues were at stake in the value of these peripheral radio and television stations.

In 1955, creditors had been worried about Tele-Saar's future in Germany, and had demanded immediate repayment of debts from *Images et Son*, plummeting the share value of the company. This caused the Monégasque Bank of Precious Metals to go bankrupt, which almost bankrupted Monaco itself. Through a third party, the French government bought shares of *Images et Son* from the Monégasque government, which had acquired them from the failed bank. Another 40,000 shares went to a private individual who had not fully paid for them. In January 1962, this individual proposed to sell these shares through the *Paris Bourse* (stock exchange) so France could acquire them. When Prince Rainier found out about this, he signed a Sovereign Ordinance forbidding the resale of the shares and recalling them for "default of price." The ordinance was countersigned by his French Minister of State, Émile Pelletier, on January 14, 1962.

Consumed by his love of France and intent on having what he wanted, President de Gaulle was increasingly annoyed that a small Principality within the confines of France was standing in his way – daring to defy him. Thus ensued the fateful night of January 23, when De Gaulle sent an ultimatum to Prince Rainier: "Annul your ordinance by 6 p.m. tomorrow or face reprisals." The Prince offered to send a delegation to Paris to explain what was at stake for Monaco but received the answer, "You may send representatives, but only to learn what shape the reprisals will take."

That night, Émile Pelletier (whom De Gaulle had personally proposed as Minister of State for Monaco) accused Prince Rainier of having coerced him into signing the ordinance forbidding the sale of the shares. In *The Saturday Evening Post* of July 1962, Prince Rainier recounted: "I said I was fed up with France's interventions. I admit I was over-aggravated. I said it was about time we found out what were our servitudes and where we had liberty of action." When Pelletier responded that he would tell General de Gaulle that Rainier was anti-French, the Prince fired him in a fit of Mediterranean temper, and sent word to Paris that his French Minister of State would be leaving his employ immediately. Rumors flew throughout the French press that Prince Rainier had actually slapped Pelletier in his fury, but Pelletier himself denied this in his own memoirs.

Prince Rainier rescinded his ordinance the next day, allowing the sale of the shares of *Images et Son*, but it was too late. He had awakened the ire of General de Gaulle, who felt that France had been humiliated and insulted by Prince Rainier's dismissal of the French Minister. De Gaulle was willing to fight for retribution and to demonstrate his might in a clash of power and wills.

In Émile Pelletier's memoirs, *Traversée d'une Époque*, he wrote that upon leaving the Palace, he went directly to Paris to tell De Gaulle his version of what had happened that night of January 23 (inaccurately recording the date in his book as 1961). De Gaulle responded, "*C'est encore une histoire d'Américains. Ils se foutent partout...*" (This is again a story of Americans. They meddle everywhere...) The gauntlet had been thrown down, and it seemed that somehow Martin, "the American," was being blamed.

After Pelletier left, Prince Rainier and Martin continued to have an all-night discussion until 5:30 a.m. regarding what course to take in response to France's intense criticism of Monaco's development. Prince Rainier employed Martin as his economic advisor because he realized that Monaco's future depended upon a broader-based economy, and the country could no longer solely derive its livelihood from the casino, or from philatelic and other similar revenues.

During that era, Monaco's approximately twenty-three thousand residents did not pay income tax, did not serve in the military, and were more or less looked after from the proverbial "cradle to the grave" through various social programs. There was no property tax or direct inheritance tax, and the Principality had no debt. Monaco had to find ways to increase revenues in order to thrive in a newly growing world economy. It was necessary for the Prince to be the visionary leader that he was in order to modernize his country.

As head of the Monaco Economic Development Corporation, Martin was very successful in attracting new foreign businesses to Monaco. In 1961, forty-six firms had been approved, drawn by the brochure that Martin had created. MEDEC's goal had been to attract fifty companies within three years, and Martin had virtually reached that goal in his first year.

At that time, gaming revenues represented only four percent of Monaco's income, thirty-one percent came from tourism, and the rest came from non-polluting light industries, such as chocolate, beer, plastics, cosmetics, and from executive offices of mostly international firms. (Long before Prince Rainier took the throne in 1949, gambling had at one time accounted for as much as ninety percent of Monaco's revenues, for lack of other sources of income.)

President de Gaulle became enraged because he felt that Monaco was taking businesses away from France, thus depriving his country of taxes. France had always frowned on Monaco's tax-free privileges, especially as less than twenty percent of Monaco's population were true Monégasque citizens; others were residents, many of whom were French, enjoying the benefits of tax-free living. De Gaulle was trying to rebuild his beloved country to pre-war eminence and had plans to make France one of the great post-war powers. To this end, he needed investment and reliable tax collection. Thus, the stage was set for one of the gloomier periods in Monaco's history.

Monaco – February 2, 1962

Dearest Mum and Dad,

It has been a stormy two weeks, and it is not over yet – the French might also be after Marty's head – but at least we have the new contract. Something will be arranged, I am sure. The Press can really turn a story the way it wishes by giving only one side – it goes to show one can't believe all one reads. The Prince should have left last week for Switzerland, but he does not dare. Grace has gone with the children.

Marty is leaving today for five days for business in Geneva and Paris – and fortunately it is a good time for him to be absent from here, for all he can do is get into trouble. The Daily Mail or Express of London had a wretched article blaming Grace (aided by her American friend, Martin) for the recent mess with the French. There is nothing that could be more untrue! There is no honor in the Press anymore. Marty's reputation is being smeared and for no cause – anyway he will come out of it with flying colors.

Charles will start school in March at the Palace with Albie and Caroline and with our former nanny teaching them for three months. It will be good for them all to be together and challenged in a classroom. It will be in the mornings only from 9 to 12. All for now – All love from us all and big hugs and kisses from Charles and Greg.

Love, Joan

The French were afraid of "Americanization," just as Americans were afraid of Communism. America and Russia were the great superpowers after the war, and everything was being westernized all over the world. The French were starting to speak "Franglais," and De Gaulle was a French purist trying to eliminate words like "hot dog," "drugstore" and "weekend," along with all the other American words that had crept into the French language.

With Grace being American, the French rag presses were all proclaiming that Princess Grace was Americanizing Monaco. Of course, this was total nonsense because Grace was old-fashioned and was committed to preserving Monaco's heritage and character, trying to save landmarks and historic sites. Although she did not have much support for this, she wanted to maintain as much of Monaco's history as possible, preferring her new country to remain picturesque, with the whole quarter around the Palace being protected as a historic monument.

When one of the tallest apartment buildings was finished and named the "Schuylkill," after the river in her home city of Philadelphia, Grace remarked, "I hope there won't be too many buildings of this size erected to spoil the lovely landscape." There have indeed been many more built since then, but in my own opinion they have been interspersed with the old buildings to form a harmonious whole in a more modern country. It was Rainier, "the Builder Prince," who had a vision of modernizing Monaco, which he certainly did. In many ways he didn't have much choice, because the only way that the tiny Principality could grow was up!

Prince Rainier was very "American-minded" – he loved the United States and liked having Americans around him, because he found them much more relaxed and open than the French. During that era, one could be friends with French people for decades without ever going to their house, and even after years of knowing someone, one would still call them "Monsieur" or "Madame."

Being an American in France was not easy at that time. Today, it is perhaps difficult to envision the climate of that period, but there was rampant fear of the American superpower taking over everything, or at the very least, foisting its ways on other countries. World War II had ended, leaving vast destruction behind. Europe was trying to rebuild itself after five years of deprivation and devastation. In France, people had been starving, eating anything they could find and subsisting on turnips to survive.

During the war, the United States provided its allies with $50 billion in supplies and munitions under the Lend-Lease program, and afterwards, through the Marshall Plan, the U.S. spent $15 billion to rebuild European economies and modernize industry. People are not always grateful for help, and the feeling in Europe was still one of mistrust and fear. France had recently been invaded by the Germans, and the people almost lost their country. Now as they were recovering, they were concerned that they would lose their cultural identity to the American invasion.

American soldiers were posted throughout Europe after WWII, some of whom were not used to being out of their own country, and although many were kind and good-hearted, others brandished money about and were rather inconsiderate. In Europe, the PX's on the U.S. Army bases were stocked with dreams. Americans could purchase anything imaginable for low prices, such as clothing and food of all kinds, even electric washers and dryers – everything the French could not acquire. I imagine they felt deprived and angry seeing luxuries in front of their eyes that they could not afford, and resented the wealth and spending power of Americans.

Many French people considered General de Gaulle to be a hero and savior of France. He had preferred to risk being convicted rather than give in to the Nazis. When France wanted to surrender to the Germans in 1940, he refused to capitulate, and lived in exile in Great Britain, where he established the Free French Forces. (During his exile, the French Vichy government court-martialed him twice, sentencing him to death for treason.) With the aid of Winston Churchill, De Gaulle gave radio addresses from England that were broadcast into France, encouraging the French to resist the German occupation. He urged his countrymen to never give up and to continue to fight in the resistance, which they did until they finally won the war (with the help of the British and the Americans, of course!). Thus, De Gaulle knew how powerful the medium of radio (and eventually television) was for reaching and influencing the people.

Eight days after the Allies landed at Normandy, General de Gaulle returned to France. He took office in Paris as Prime Minister three months later, and led the remaining French troops to advance with the Allies, liberating French towns as they forced the retreat of the Nazis. To resist counter-attacks from Germany, De Gaulle insisted on holding the defensive line in the newly liberated Strasbourg, along the German border (where Prince Rainier served in the French military at the age of twenty-one before being posted to Berlin). Once the war ended, De Gaulle became Chairman of the Provisional Government of France until January 1946, after which he retired from politics.

Twelve years later, in May of 1958, war in Algeria unleashed a political crisis in France, between those who wanted Algeria to remain a French colony versus those who wanted it to become independent. De Gaulle was brought back into power to put down the Algerian rebellion, and at his urging, the French people voted in huge majority to create a new constitution that gave the President more power than ever, in order to restore unity. De Gaulle founded the Fifth Republic of France and became its first President from 1959-1969. By the time an agreement was reached for Algerian independence on March 18, 1962, the former General had already set his sights on his next battle... with the tiny Principality of Monaco.

On February 6, the day before Prince Rainier left for Switzerland, President de Gaulle sent notice that he would be renouncing the "Good Neighbor" Administration and Mutual Assistance Convention of December 23, 1951. De Gaulle stated that the entire Franco-Monégasque agreement would have to be re-examined and renegotiated regarding economic, financial and commercial affairs, including tax and customs issues. Furthermore, if an agreement could not be reached by October of that year, Monaco would be treated like a foreign country and would face customs and immigration controls, as well as international tariffs and taxes.

Rainier wrote to Martin from Switzerland: "I am at complete peace of mind with myself and my actions... The disgraceful pressures and actions taken against me and my country, and the surprising and inadmissible threats and menaces made toward the Principality cannot be maintained. I really don't believe in the application of those threats! In poker you call a bluff! And I think that we must do so. I am, dear Martin, quite disgusted and quite discouraged by all this – honestly, it has been a shock to me. I love a fight, but a regular open and equal one! This is not the case!! To fight injustice, there are no means or methods when this injustice is served by ill faith, lies and brutal force. And in final is this all worthwhile! For what? For whom! Except my son!!"

Monaco – February 12, 1962

Dearest Mum and Dad,

We shall be off on Sunday morning for Switzerland. We received a letter from R., who is so discouraged about this whole mess with France. They have not even given him a chance to explain the situation to them – I feel sorry for him.

Enclosed is a clipping from France's most-read weekly paper – a scandal sheet. In which it says, "Dale, The Gray Cardinal" (like Richelieu was to Louis XIII). The opposition thinks that the Prince was wrong to have made the American Martin Dale his Privy Counselor. "He lives too much in his shadow." Inside it talks about "the affair Dale" and says "that we both live too much in the shadow of G & R. Dale's job is to attract AMERICAN (not true) capital to Monaco." "Says Dale, 'It is for the good of the Monégasques, but it is normal that certain among them will fear a loss of independence.'" Enough said! All for now —

Loads of love from us all, Joan

The French reported that Martin, as head of MEDEC, was a mysterious person who was nearly impossible to meet. Martin Dale was described in the French press as "*L'Éminence Grise*," a term that has come to mean "the power behind the throne" in reference to the tremendous influence that Cardinal Richelieu had during the reign of King Louis XIII. Richelieu, and his chief advisor (*L'Éminence Grise* or "Gray Cardinal"), are often painted as villains because their reach was feared and dreaded throughout France in the 1600s.

As Privy Counselor for economic affairs, Martin's proximity to the Prince upset a lot of people. He was his closest advisor, and Prince Rainier sought his opinion and advice on all manner of things. He appreciated Martin's frankness and honesty, even if he didn't always like what he had to say. Martin was one of the few people who was not afraid to speak up to the Prince, of course with the utmost respect, but with absolute candor. This is why Prince Rainier wanted Martin to work with him and for him in the first place.

On February 21, while we were all vacationing together in Switzerland, France issued a series of ultimatums to Prince Rainier, ordering Monaco to align its tax structure with the French system, and to stop being a tax haven for French citizens and businesses. De Gaulle even wanted the Monégasques, who had lived tax-free for centuries, to start paying taxes to France. The French were demanding taxation without allowing the people of Monaco to have any representation in the government of France (the same issue that had precipitated the American Revolution against England).

Rainier wanted to go back to Monaco immediately upon hearing this news, but he did not want his early return to signal panic in the Principality. Instead Rainier and Martin left Schönried to go to a hotel in Gstaad for round-the-clock meetings. Those who work for a sovereign are on call day and night, even while on holiday. As Privy Counselor, Martin could be summoned at any time, and often was, especially during the crisis that loomed throughout 1962. My letters told my parents the lighter side of things so they would not worry about us, but Martin bore a heavy burden, as did the Prince, who had no choice but to fight for his country and for his people.

Before the ultimatums arrived from France, we had all been enjoying a much-needed vacation, after the Pelletier incident in January. We were having fun together, unaware of how serious this whole crisis with France was about to become for Monaco and for the Prince, and ultimately for Martin as well. At that time, my biggest concern was whether the dish I was making would turn out well enough to serve to a Prince and Princess!

Over dinner at our chalet, Grace laughed as she told us the story about the famous car scene in *To Catch A Thief*. Alfred Hitchcock had insisted that Grace drive the car on the treacherous road above Monaco. Grace tried to protest, as she did not like to drive, and was a notoriously slow and careful driver. The movie was a thriller, requiring her to drive fast and recklessly. Cary Grant did not have to do much acting to play a nervous passenger, because he had been genuinely terrified. Grace could not wear her prescription glasses in the movie, and she could barely see the road without them, so it had been a harrowing experience for them both.

Grace casually mentioned that "Hitch" had recently asked her to play the lead in his upcoming film, *Marnie*. He had bought the movie rights to the book specifically for her to play the title role. Hitchcock was very taken with Grace after her roles in *Dial M for Murder* and *Rear Window*, and she had become one of his favorite leading ladies.

Prince Rainier was very supportive of Grace making the movie, because he knew how much she loved being an actress. He was excited to rent a house on location in the U.S. and make it a family summer vacation. He thought he could play golf and enjoy himself away from all his cares in Monaco. Grace said it wasn't exactly going to be a vacation for her, with the early morning call times and long hours on the set, but she was happy at the thought of returning to her craft, and thrilled that Rainier was keen to join her with the children.

Grace missed Hollywood, but many of her movie star friends frequently visited her in Monaco, including Bing Crosby and Frank Sinatra, who were both sparkling and fun-loving individuals. David Niven was one of Grace's dear friends; he and his wife Hjordis were often invited to the Palace and joined us on vacations in Switzerland, where they had a home. Martin and I were also invited to lunch at their house in St. Jean Cap Ferrat with Grace and Rainier. The Nivens were very warm, and we had a good time with them.

David was the same in person as he was on screen, witty, charming and debonair, with a twinkle in his eye. He was an attractive man who was fun to be around. Hjordis was his second wife, a very pleasant Swedish woman and former model. His first wife died tragically in 1946, while attending a party at the Hollywood home of actor Tyrone Power. The guests had been playing a game of hide-and-seek, when she stepped into a darkened doorway without realizing that it was the door to the basement; she fell down the stairs and died from her injuries. Sadly, she was only twenty-eight years old, with two young sons. It was a devastating loss for David, who loved her dearly.

Monaco – March 13, 1962

Dearest Mum and Dad,

Our vacation was lovely, and we had great fun with G & R. Rainier was somewhat upset by the events recently, and it is still to be straightened out. The General is trying to reduce this to a tourist attraction, which of course would ruin all of Marty's hard and magnificent work. They have not had so much progress in years since he has been here. They just had another huge article in the same paper I sent you with a large photo of Marty, Pelletier, and G & R – they chose the glummest pictures they could find and called Marty the "Pocket Richelieu." What meanness!

All love from all of us, Joan

The French have a saying: *pour vivre heureux, vivons cachés*, which means that in order to live happily, we must live hidden. Martin's work in the Principality was getting him a great deal of attention in the worldwide press. We were seen everywhere with the Prince and Princess, as we accompanied them frequently on both social and official occasions, although we tried to stay in the background and were rarely photographed with them. Neither Martin nor I sought public attention, but we were standing out and getting noticed nonetheless.

The allusion to Martin as a "Pocket Richelieu" referred to the fact that he was building and expanding the economic power of Monaco to the highest level it had ever been, and in the process had become a conspicuously close friend and advisor to Prince Rainier. The French believed that France and Monaco were being infiltrated by the CIA, and because Martin had been a U.S. Diplomat, they thought that he was a spy. It all seems so ridiculous, but there was quite a firestorm in the newspapers about all this at the time.

De Gaulle had demanded that the "Good Neighbor" Convention of 1951 be renegotiated, but he refused to sit down and speak directly with Prince Rainier until after the crisis was over. Instead, he insisted that Monaco send a delegation to Paris to negotiate with a French delegation. After Martin's successful part in the negotiation of the FCN Treaty of Establishment between the United States and France in 1959, President de Gaulle made sure that Martin would be nowhere near the negotiating table for Monaco.

Meanwhile, Martin had been trying to resolve the issues by working with the French Consul-General in Monaco, who was a good friend, and who was sympathetic to Prince Rainier's cause. But when the French Consul-General tried to plead the Prince's case to the French government, he was given one month's notice that he would be replaced in the Principality!

On March 13, 1962, the first official negotiations began in Paris between Monaco and France, but the French government refused arbitration and insisted on being the arbitrator in these treaty matters. The major issue was that no one living in the Principality paid any taxes. The French delegation wanted French officials to collect taxes from all Monégasque residents, including Monégasque citizens; Monaco would receive nine percent of the total amount collected, and France would keep the rest. When Monaco objected to this, the French said this was because Monégasques used French roads, but France did not impose this kind of toll on any other bordering countries, such as Belgium.

The French delegation was also objecting to their citizens living in Monaco to avoid paying taxes, who were considered to be defrauding the French government. However, before a French citizen or business could move to Monaco, they had to receive permission from the French Minister of Finance. Therefore, France should have been able to detect and identify any fraudulent intentions during that pre-approval process. The talks between the French and Monégasque delegations broke down repeatedly for months.

De Gaulle presented nineteen demands regarding taxes, customs, utilities, and... the dismissal of Martin Dale was number sixteen. The tiny country was under siege, so Martin offered his resignation to the Prince in order to appease the French. Of course, Prince Rainier, being the man he was said, "You can't go, and we can't give in." Rainier insisted that he should carry out the renewed contract that they had both recently agreed to, but suggested that perhaps it would be an ideal time for Martin to take an early and extended "vacation." They decided that our family would leave the Principality unannounced, which would give the impression that Martin had been dismissed.

Rainier did not want Martin to resign for several reasons, one of which was that he did not want to let France dictate whom he could or could not employ. The Prince had established Martin's position so that he was Privy Counselor and Economic Advisor to the Prince himself, and as such, he was actually considered to be a private employee of the Prince's household, not a public official.

Therefore, the Prince refused to allow the government of another country to tell him whom he could hire and fire in his own house. He felt that it would completely undermine his sovereignty to give in to this demand. He was adamant on this point, and would not permit Martin to resign just because the French were demanding it.

Prince Rainier was one of the last sovereigns on Earth to rule by Divine Right, and his ordinances were made by the Grace of God. Under the doctrine of the divine right of kings, a monarch derives the right to rule directly from the will of God, and is not subject to any earthly authority. The monarch is not bound by any other laws in the realm, including those imposed by church or state. Ruling by Divine Right also means that any attempt to depose the sovereign, or to restrict his powers, goes against the will of God and may be considered a sacrilegious act. Unfortunately, this did not seem to make any impression on General de Gaulle, who was determined to demonstrate his power as "might makes right."

The second reason that Prince Rainier did not want Martin to leave the Principality is the same reason that the French wanted him out: he was attracting an enormous amount of business and prosperity to Monaco. Between 1960 and 1961, bank deposits in the Principality increased about fifty percent. Within two years, more than 260 commercial licenses were authorized and 103 companies incorporated. Many of these were large American corporations, such as Allied Chemical, Chris Craft boats, and a large New York bank. This was exactly what was triggering the problems with France, but Martin was far too valuable to Prince Rainier as an economic advisor to let him go.

Above all else, Prince Rainier trusted Martin, valuing his counsel, his ideas and opinions. This is why Rainier was doing everything in his power to fight for him to stay. When the Prince thought that he would be going to the United States for three months in the summer so Grace could film *Marnie*, he wanted to make sure that Martin would be back in Monaco before July to look after everything while the Prince was away.

Monaco – March 20, 1962

Dearest Mum and Dad,

Marty offered his resignation to ease the French-Monégasque negotiations, but the Prince refused it and showed himself to be very warm towards Martin. He suggested that we should be here during July - August - September when he and Grace will be in the U.S. so that we can keep an eye on things, and he has given us two months' vacation starting in two weeks!! So you will be seeing us very soon.

What a hectic time we shall have in the next few weeks! Anyway, it seems that Marty has managed to turn this adversity into a triumph in his usual way.

In haste – Joan

On March 19, 1962, the Palace released an official announcement that Princess Grace would be making a motion picture with Alfred Hitchcock during her summer vacation. She was due to receive one million dollars for the film, which was unheard of for an actress in those days. She said she would donate the money to charity, because she really just wanted to act again.

Unfortunately, *Marnie* was a story about a kleptomaniac, with several aspects to the plot that did not really make it an appropriate role for the Princess to play. The idea of Grace making the film caused a tremendous uproar in Monaco; the Monégasques protested vehemently against it, saying that a movie star might become a princess, but it was not becoming for a princess to be a movie star!

It was the worst possible timing for Grace to consider returning to America to make an American movie. This would be viewed as tantamount to deserting the Monégasque people during their time of need and giving more fuel to De Gaulle to further attack their small and weakened country. Grace also did not want to be away from Rainier and the children for weeks of filming, and there was no way that Rainier could have gone to America during the crisis, which was only just beginning. Grace told Hitchcock that she was withdrawing from the film, reportedly without giving an explanation; on April 24, Hitchcock announced that the making of the film would be postponed for technical reasons.

It has often been said that the Prince refused to let her act again, but this is absolutely not true. He encouraged her to make the film because he knew how happy it would make her. Grace resolved that as much as she loved acting, she loved her husband and her adopted country more, so she again chose being Princess of Monaco over being an actress. She was very sad not to return to acting, but was even sadder at the terrible reaction that it had gotten from the Monégasques. To my knowledge, Grace never spoke about the movie again.

This was yet another bitter blow to Grace and Rainier, in a year that would see nothing but painful challenges and profound disappointments for them. To make matters even worse, throughout the 1962 crisis, they were also losing many of the people closest to them whom they counted on for support, who were leaving under various circumstances. Madge Tivey-Faucon, or "Tiv" as Grace called her, had been Grace's Lady-in-Waiting for six years. She had been somewhat judgmental of Princess Grace, and they did not always get along well, but as Lady-in-Waiting, she had been the closest person to Grace in the Principality from the beginning. Shortly after "Tiv" was dismissed, Grace's personal secretary, Phyllis Blum, left to marry Julian Earl, the nephew of Somerset Maugham. Princess Grace was a witness at their civil wedding on March 24, and while she was happy for Phyllis, she was sad to lose her trusted secretary and friend. Phyllis was a young American woman who spoke fluent French and was very close to Grace.

I am sure the Prince was worried that if Martin left, it would mean that I would have to leave Monaco also, and Grace needed people around her that she could trust, and with whom she could relax and speak English. This is probably one of the reasons why Prince Rainier suggested that I take the place of Madame Tivey-Faucon as Grace's Lady-in-Waiting in March of 1962. However, this proposal caused such an uproar in the press, that it became impossible for me to accept the honor. The idea that yet another American would hold such a close and official position in the Prince's household was like fanning the flames of the Franco-Monégasque crisis, and it created a furor the likes of which I could never have imagined.

While Prince Rainier was concerned about Grace's happiness and well-being, he also had to worry about the threat of losing his throne. De Gaulle had issued another ultimatum stating that if Rainier did not back down on his stance of remaining an independent and absolute ruler, he would depose the Prince! In January 1959, Prince Rainier had suspended the constitution of Monaco, and dissolved his National Council because they did not share his vision for his country.

Finally, in March 1962, Prince Rainier announced that a new constitution would soon be implemented. This appeased De Gaulle somewhat, but he still insisted that Martin Dale would have to leave. On March 29, Prince Rainier wrote to Martin: "...As for yourself, you can say that you did offer to the Prince your resignation so as to ease the situation between the French and Monégasque government, but that the Prince refused this resignation. Considering that a question of nationality could not interfere in technical fiscal difficulties. You have for personal reasons asked to take your yearly vacation earlier than in the summer, and this will be probably granted. On returning from this vacation, you may occupy some other function, maybe even in the private sector, this depending on the Prince's decision."

The French were extremely irritated over the success of MEDEC, so Prince Rainier chose to end the program earlier than originally intended. Even the name "Monaco Economic Development Corporation" upset the French, because it was in English! MEDEC would have to be disbanded, but it had already reached its three-year goal within the first year of operation.

In *The Saturday Evening Post* of July 1962, Prince Rainier said: "When De Gaulle was here in 1960, he asked me about Martin Dale..." He continued: "If Martin Dale had been a Frenchman, it would probably have been all right. The French say it's in violation of our treaty to hire an American in a government position. But the treaty covers civil servants, which Dale is not. He is a member of my household. If I want a doctor who is a Turk, or an economic advisor who is an Israeli, this is my personal home, and I have a right to decide for myself. When the crisis arose, Dale offered his resignation. I said, 'I won't accept it.' But I did suggest that he take his vacation then. 'Your physical absence', I told him, 'would be a good thing.'"

In April, we packed up our family to get out of the Principality, while Pierre Notari, the Prince's Minister of Finance, tried to negotiate a calm-down of the situation with the French. Shortly before we left, we went to Rocagel for dinner and talked with Grace and Rainier about the crisis for hours, with Grace in tears. I was so sad to leave her under these circumstances, but we had little choice. During our two-month banishment from Monaco, I took the children to Canada to visit my parents, while Martin pursued business interests for the Prince in the United States.

Monaco - April 2, 1962

Dearest Mum and Dad,

Saw G & R until 4 a.m. this morning and had a long talk with them. They are very fond of us, and we shall be coming back certainly unless he becomes just plain R. Grimaldi, which is unlikely. See you soon!!

All love from us all – Joan

After negotiations in Paris broke down on April 3, France publicly denounced the "Good Neighbor" convention of 1951. Prince Rainier was given exactly six months' notice before treaties covering customs, postal, telegraph and telephone services would end. If an agreement could not be reached within that time, a customs blockade would be implemented around Monaco at the stroke of midnight on October 12th, the day after the treaties would expire.

Upon hearing this announcement, the Prince was willing to make as many concessions as were necessary without undermining Monaco's authority. In the March 23 edition of the French newspaper, *France Soir*, Prince Rainier had said: "We cannot accept direct taxation. We are perfectly eager to have an understanding with the French on many issues, but direct taxation would be an infringement on the very roots of our sovereignty." The one thing the Prince could not do was to integrate into France's fiscal system, because this would jeopardize the very existence of his country that he had sworn to serve.

Later in April, France fired another shot, announcing that it would end its treaty with Monaco on pharmaceutical products, when it expired in three months. This would effectively strangle a multi-million-dollar a year industry. A French government permit would soon be necessary for each product sold on French territory that was made or even imported through Monaco. At the time, there were four large laboratories there, which sold their products almost exclusively to France.

An article in the *Sunday Times* of April 15, 1962, addressed France's unsporting attack on tiny Monaco as a battle of "Goliath against little David." The writers asked, "Does the David of the Principality still have a pebble in his slingshot?" A Swiss newspaper remarked that "a great power does not always give a good impression by using measures of coercion against a minuscule neighbor, whose only force consists of fifty *carabiniers* and a few cannons dating from Louis XIV." The rest of the world stood by and did nothing but scoff at the situation, as if it were a political farce. But this was a very real battle for the Principality, whose livelihood and future were at stake.

General de Gaulle had declared war on Monaco, but it was essentially a war that was being fought on paper, using treaties as his weapons – it was a strategic tactic designed to cripple Monaco and Prince Rainier, one treaty at a time. De Gaulle also wanted to make sure that Martin Dale would be a casualty in his war against "Americanization" in Europe, if not a direct target. The only thing that Martin could do to help the Prince was to leave. However, they were in frequent communication while Martin was in exile, and he continued to provide advice and support to the Prince during his absence. Prince Rainier had been a soldier during the war, distinguishing himself for bravery in the line of fire, so he was not going to give up without a fight.

The French were able to exert pressure on Monaco because of a treaty that was signed in 1918 as part of the Treaty of Versailles, in which France had agreed to provide Monaco with water, power, and other amenities. As the second smallest country in the world, after the Vatican, Monaco was dependent on France's infrastructure to support it in all ways. This treaty guaranteed France's protection of Monaco's sovereignty in return for the Principality conducting itself "in perfect conformity with the political, military, naval and economic interests of France."

De Gaulle claimed that the Treaty of Versailles made Monaco a protectorate of France, while Rainier insisted that Monaco was a sovereign country, with over a hundred consuls in about thirty nations at that time (including twelve Monégasque consulates in the United States alone in the 1960s). For centuries the Principality's sovereignty had been acknowledged in many international treaties, and Monaco had Foreign Ministers in several European countries, including France and the Vatican.

King Louis XII of France recognized Monaco's independence in 1512, signing a document of perpetual alliance. Then in 1641, King Louis XIII signed the Treaty of Péronne, which confirmed the sovereignty of the Principality. The Franco-Monégasque Treaty of 1861 also guaranteed the total independence of Monaco from French political influence, under the Prince's sole authority. At that time, Prince Charles III of Monaco ceded the neighboring towns of Menton and Roquebrune to France, which reduced Monaco's territory to one-twentieth of its previous size. In exchange, he received 4 million francs as compensation for the land and gained the formal recognition of the independence of Monaco. However, De Gaulle didn't deem it necessary to honor these treaties.

The French were now demanding: "*Monaco doit céder d'abord! Acceptez le principe de l'alignement et puis nous serons très libéral dans ses arrangements et applications*"! (Monaco must first concede! Accept the principal of the alignment, and then we will be very liberal in its arrangements and applications.) Imagine if your neighboring country was demanding to collect taxes directly from you, insisting that your government must surrender its fiscal sovereignty and concede to aligning its tax structure with theirs, while refusing to define the terms of that taxation until after the agreement was made. How could Prince Rainier agree to subject his people to that?

Fiscal alignment with France would ruin the Principality of Monaco economically, and would destroy its sovereignty and independence since the right to tax is one of the essential attributes of sovereignty. Moreover, by committing itself to automatically accept all subsequent changes in French fiscal policy, Monaco would no longer have autonomous control over its own budget, and would cease to exist as a sovereign State.

Monaco began as a tax-free walled city dating back to 1215, when the Genoese built a fortress known as "The Rock of Monaco." While most kingdoms and principalities throughout Europe heavily taxed their subjects at that time, Monaco attracted permanent residents by granting land and tax exemptions. Monaco's tax-free status was part of its heritage.

Rainier could not concede to these demands, and wrote in a letter to Martin, "...But actually how can you negotiate with people who refuse to do so with you!! No discussion is alas possible." Prince Rainier urged Martin to find a way to get some support from the United States, either politically or at least in the court of public opinion, to apply pressure on France so it would stop preying on the Principality. Essentially, France was trying to take over Monaco and impose its laws on Monégasque citizens and residents.

The Monégasques did not want to become French citizens, and not just because they did not want to pay taxes; they had survived for hundreds of years as a minority, even within Monaco, and they did not want to lose their cultural identity. Less than twenty percent of the population of Monaco claimed direct Monégasque descent and spoke their own language that was derived from both French and Italian. In the 1960s, there were many Monégasque subjects who had never gone outside their borders, or who had never ventured further away than the nearby French city of Nice. They were proud of their culture and their heritage, and they did not want to lose their Prince, or their country.

The next major blow came when France threatened to cut off Monaco's water, gas and electricity. Monaco was completely dependent on France for all of its vital supplies, so Prince Rainier was obliged to examine all of the potential consequences of the crisis. He wrote to Martin in the United States, asking him to investigate options for Monaco to become energy independent:

"I must ask you to carry out for me a very special mission, which I can only ask you as I trust you, to carry it out for me in complete impartiality and devotion... I want you to find out the firms in the States that could supply us with equipment to produce our electricity and fresh water... As for the production of the electricity, there exist thermo production ships. I heard that two of [these] ships had been stationed at Lisbon after the war, and supplied electricity to the entire city during about a year, during the reconversion of the electrical system there. Would you please look into this matter *without delay*, and send me some information on the subject... I could *only* ask you, whom I trust, to explore such a domain and get me something sure and solid, that I can in some eventuality count upon!"

We were terribly concerned about Grace and Rainier, and about Monaco's future, as well as our own. In the April 21 issue of the popular French magazine, *Paris Match,* it was written that the Prince had sent Martin packing back to the United States, as he was supposed to have been "the Trojan horse of Wall Street!" Prince Rainier kept insisting that he must fight on Martin's behalf, and for his own sovereignty. He wrote: "...As for you, dear Martin, I quite understand that you cannot have any final and definite arrangement as to your private situation here... My wish is that you come back of course, and that you continue to work for me... I insist that you have a title and stay a member of my household. This is, as you know, a very strong and very firm stand of mine, of my complete and absolute liberty of action as to who is in my private service."

Prince Rainier corresponded often with Martin while we were in exile stateside for a two-month "vacation." He poured out his hopes and fears, his anger and frustrations, and his envy of us being in North America. He had been looking forward to spending time with the family in the U.S. so Grace could film *Marnie*, and was quite disappointed when the Monégasques would not allow it: "Many thanks for your letter, but as there is no film scheduled, our plans may be changed as to the trip over and the stay in the States. There is the crisis... and this will command any of our moves. A sure thing is that I will not leave the spot until all is over or going to a satisfactory issue. Then and only then shall I yearn to get a breath of fresh air of true liberty in your country!!"

These were very difficult times for Prince Rainier, as the French were trying to strangle the Principality in red tape, with the requirements of visas, tariffs and permits for practically everything. On May 7, France announced that within one year, Monégasque trucking companies would need special permits to operate on French highways. There were ten trucking firms in Monaco moving 200 tons of payload daily from the surrounding areas; since the Principality was so small that it could grow no food, everything had to be trucked in.

Four days later, Monégasques were declared foreigners in France. Any Monégasque citizens who were living or working in France were ordered to report to local police stations to apply for residence and work permits like other foreigners.

Although Prince Rainier felt that he did not dare to leave Monaco during the crisis, it was his duty to attend the wedding of Prince Juan Carlos of Spain and Princess Sophia of Greece on May 14. More than one hundred and fifty members of Europe's royal families went to Athens to witness the eldest daughter of the King of Greece being married to the future King of Spain. Grace wrote from

Athens, "...it is all very exciting – The Greek royal family is so charming & the Queen is so much prettier than her photographs."

In one day, the royal couple had three ceremonies in three different locations, to satisfy Catholic, Greek Orthodox, and civil requirements of the religious and political leaders in both Spain and Greece. Juan Carlos would only be crowned King of Spain thirteen years later, upon the death of the Spanish dictator, General Franco.

At the royal wedding, Prince Rainier and Princess Grace received a lot of support regarding the crisis with France. Rainier wrote to Martin; "...We had a nice time and met a lot of the crowned and uncrowned heads of Europe... All were very strong in telling me to fight and keep a firm attitude towards what they called: 'a mean and unjust action on behalf of the French government...'" It was unfortunate that many of these royals no longer had enough political power or diplomatic influence to be able to assist Grace and Rainier at that time.

After the wedding in Greece, Prince Rainier and Princess Grace took the children to Madrid. It was good for the family to have a few days away from the crisis in Monaco. It gave them a bit of rest, and some much-needed normalcy. We received a sweet postcard from Spain with a bull on the front. It was written to Charles in French in young Caroline's careful handwriting, with four-year-old Albert's valiant effort at making a signature: "Dear Charles, this is a bull. I embrace you as does Albert."

Grace took care to personally teach her children how to count and how to write, and always encouraged them to learn, to study and to do their best. Albert was quiet, but determined; you could almost see the wheels turning in his head. Caroline was like a sponge, eager to learn, engrossed in picture books, and showing a touching enthusiasm for everything and everyone around her. She was a very thoughtful, brilliant and observant young girl. One day she said to her mother, "There must be many Gods," to which Grace responded, "No, there is only one God." Caroline then replied, "There must be many Gods, because there are so many churches." She was not yet five!

No matter where they were, Grace always made sure that the family went to Mass on Sundays. Although Rainier was somewhat less devout than Grace, he took comfort in the spiritual guidance of Father Tucker, who had been his personal chaplain for eleven years, and was like a father to him. During the crisis with France, Rainier needed all the encouragement he could get, especially while Martin was away. He wrote again on May 21: "...I have no support and no real help, genuine and sincere!... I am in fact completely and entirely

ALONE and well isolated!! I am sick to death with this situation and I really do not know what to do and who to turn to."

Rainier spent many sleepless nights worrying about the fate of his country and its citizens, even more than he worried about the possibility of losing his throne. He confided to Martin: "...I cannot really tell you all that is happening here and around, as I have not the time or space... and also I am tired and weary!" The constant barrage from France was wearing Rainier down, just as it was designed to do. But the most profound bombshell was not delivered by General de Gaulle, but by the Prince's closest spiritual advisor, Father Tucker.

On June 1, the day after Rainier's 39th birthday, Father Tucker left Monaco without saying goodbye. He had sent a letter a month earlier, asking the Prince for permission to resign, because he believed that he was becoming too old to serve him properly. The Grand Chaplain of the Sovereign House of Monaco was expected to accompany the Princely Family on their travels. Father Tucker was in his seventies and had only been able to do that occasionally, so he felt that a younger chaplain would serve them better. However, his love and attachment to Princess Grace and Prince Rainier was so profound that he could not bear saying goodbye to them, so he left unannounced.

Grace and Rainier were away from the Palace, and the suddenness of his departure came as a terrible shock to them. Prince Rainier was truly devastated. He became very depressed and distraught at the loss of their beloved Father Tucker, as did Grace, particularly at such a difficult time.

However, it was precisely because of the crisis with De Gaulle that Father Tucker decided to leave. He was concerned because the closest people to Prince Rainier were all Americans, from his wife, to his chaplain, to his Privy Counselor. This was contributing to the ongoing crisis with France, so he believed that his leaving would make it better for Rainier, by having one less American around.

We returned to Monaco to give moral support to Rainier and Grace shortly after Father Tucker left. We quietly slipped back into the Principality on June 19 and tried to keep a low profile for a while. We were invited to the Palace several times, spending long evenings in their private apartment, discussing all that had gone on while we were away. They kept the conversation light at first, telling us about the wonderful gala that we had just missed in June, attended by the royal newlyweds, Princess Sophia and Prince Juan Carlos of Spain, with an appearance by Frank Sinatra. We could feel the burden that they were both carrying and tried to lighten it as much as we could. We had Grace and Rainier over to our apartment for dinner, playing gin rummy and laughing together, until the Prince and I lost... he hated to lose at anything!

Monaco – June 24, 1962

Dearest Mum and Dad,

We are more or less settled now – but for how long, I wonder? The offensive will begin soon, I fear. However, all we can do is to hang on, for to give in would mean disgrace. Anyway, we are enjoying the summer season here to the fullest, for it may be our last one in this paradise. We would be very sorry to leave. Grace and Rainier had us up for a nightcap the day we arrived, which was very nice, and we have seen them several times since. They have been very gay and relaxed with us, which makes us rather happy.

Charles started school the day after we arrived. Most of the shopkeepers etc. are pleased to see us back, but the members of the Government look at us as if we were lepers. Their hatred of "the American" is only too evident. They are jealous of Martin's position and are ready to stab him in the back. All will turn out for the best, I am sure, so do not worry.

Loads of love, Joan and Marty

By July 1962, the crisis in Monaco had reached such a fever pitch in the media that even *Ladies' Home Journal* wanted to report on the story. Princess Grace had appeared on the cover of the magazine and done an interview for them the year before the crisis began, so they wanted to return to Monaco to do a feature article on Martin, and his work as Privy Counselor and Economic Advisor to the Prince. With the worldwide press talking about "the American" at the center of the firestorm with France, journalists often tried to get his side of the story. Martin felt that he had to decline all requests for personal interviews out of loyalty to the Prince, unless Prince Rainier himself specifically asked him to speak to the press.

However, in order to help the world understand Monaco's situation, Prince Rainier agreed to do a comprehensive interview for *The Saturday Evening Post* in July of 1962. When asked whether Monaco could survive if De Gaulle carried out his threat to cut Monaco off completely in October, Prince Rainier replied: "We're examining all the possibilities of converting to full independence. My finance minister is looking into the economic side, and we're doing many technical studies – such as how to convert seawater into fresh water. Our food could come by sea... We might have two or five or even ten hard years before we reached the golden age. But I can only say what General De Gaulle himself once said: 'It is preferable to die standing up than flat out on your belly!'"

When asked, "Since your frontiers wind through the streets, could the French really set up boundary controls – customs and so forth?" Prince Rainier responded, "It's completely impossible. Of course, the French could copy Berlin and build a wall. But then they would really look ridiculous." He continued: "You know that our accord with France is embodied in the Treaty of Versailles. So any breach could be challenged by every one of the Versailles signatories. I think, myself, that the French are perhaps embarrassed, now that they've got themselves in deeper than they intended. France is stuck with this idea of fiscal alignment. They have offered me an unofficial proposition. If I accept the principle, they say, then they'll see how to work it out. But we can't bottle ourselves up by agreeing to a principle without knowing what it entails."

The question arose in the interview as to whether Monaco could bring this issue to the World Court in The Hague. However, under the terms of the treaty with France, Monaco could not take the case to the World Court without French authorization! The situation was, as the French would say, *impossible!*

Monaco – July 8, 1962

Dearest Mum and Dad,

We had a nice luncheon with G & R and the Admiral of the 6th Fleet on board the carrier "INDEPENDENCE" the other day. The water was rough, and we had quite a time boarding the ship from the little Chris-craft – but we managed, with a dousing. It was fun.

Last week they had "Prize Day" at the pool at the Palace, which was enjoyed by the children and parents. The Prince took special interest in it and awarded prizes with sweet little notes attached.

All is well, but we are still not sure what will happen – time will tell. There are those who are working against us, but I am sure that we will manage. Shall write soon.

All love from us all, Marty, Joan, Charles, Greg

Despite the continuing crisis with France, Rainier and Grace wanted to make sure that life remained as normal as possible for the children. Charles went to school at the Palace with Caroline and Albert, where they were all privately tutored with a couple of other children whose parents were close to the Prince. Having their early schooling at the Palace allowed Albert and Caroline flexibility in their studies, because classes would be suspended whenever they were away with their parents.

One of the highlights for the children was the graduation and prize-giving ceremony at the end of the school year. It was warm in Monaco at that time, so it was held outside, by the swimming pool at the Palace. On this particular day in 1962, Grace was dressed in pink from head to toe, and served "Pink Lady" drinks before lunch. I joked with her that she was entirely coordinated to the last detail, including her choice of cocktail! The young ones played, after which we were all served lunch by white-gloved servants wearing white summer uniforms.

The Prince then called the children one by one to receive their prizes for scholastic achievement, while Grace filmed the event with her movie camera, as did Martin and I. It was great fun to see the delight on the little ones' faces. They thoroughly enjoyed it. Gregory was too young to attend school at the Palace, but Grace and Rainier very thoughtfully invited him to the graduation and gave him a special little prize, which made him feel included.

Monaco – July 26, 1962

Dearest Mum and Dad,

Albert comes to the pool twice a week for lessons, and the children have a grand time together. In fact they were photographed by "Paris Match" and "Oggi" – two of the largest magazines in France, and Italy and by the newspaper "Nice-Matin." In "Match" they gave a full-page portrait of Caroline and Charles, calling him Prince Albert!

Tonight we are going to "Rocagel," G & R's house on the hill, for dinner. Jester [our poodle] will be mated to Gamma, Grace's poodle, next week. They are having quite a time keeping all their other dogs away from Gamma, and it will be a miracle if the puppies turn out to be Jester's.

There have been a series of concerts in the courtyard of the Palace. The setting is fairy-like with the frescoes under the arcades lighted in pink, and the white marble double staircase lighted in brilliant white. We have heard Brailovsky, Rubenstein and Bernstein, and will hear Van Cliburn next week.

Bernstein was extraordinary. He really is a genius. He conducted his own "Overture to Candide" and then conducted and played the piano at the same time doing Mozart's "Concert in F." He brought down the house. Last evening after the concert there was a reception in the Palace gardens around the exquisitely lighted pool. The Maharani of Baroda was there, wearing an incredible necklace of rubies and emeralds in three tiers – each stone looking the size of a rock. It was a very elegant evening, and it lasted until 2 a.m.

The boys send XXXXOOOO, and Marty and I send all our love, Joan

For centuries, the Grimaldi Princes were known for their patronage of the arts, and especially for music. Prince Antoine I of Monaco grew up in the French court of Versailles in the 17th Century and studied with Lully. He developed such a love for music that he created his own orchestra and an opera company. Prince Rainier carried on this tradition of the arts by offering concerts at the Palace, with the renowned National Opera Orchestra of Monte-Carlo (now called the Monte-Carlo Philharmonic Orchestra), which is one of the oldest permanently established orchestras in the French-speaking world.

Originally, only official events took place in the courtyard of the Palace, the *Cour d'Honneur*, which was rarely open to the public. In 1959, Prince Rainier started a tradition of offering outdoor summer concerts in the courtyard that the public could attend, and that were also recorded and broadcast on the radio. But first, he had to undertake extensive repairs and renovations.

At the time of the French Revolution, the French occupied the Palace of Monaco from 1793-1814. The rooms of the Palace were turned into a poorhouse, the Grand Apartments into a military hospital, and the Throne Room became a kitchen. The Palace was looted of most of its art and treasures, and part of the south wing was so badly damaged that it had to be demolished.

Prince Rainier and Princess Grace painstakingly restored much of the Palace to its current splendor, bringing in artisans and specialists, and searching all over France to retrieve items that had once belonged to the Grimaldis. The 16th Century frescoes on the courtyard walls had to be repaired by experts from the Louvre's School of Restoration. Prince Rainier also had the Palace courtyard repaved, with thousands of pebbles and stones laid in a geometric pattern forming pathways leading from the grand marble staircase.

For concerts and outdoor ballets, the colonnaded courtyard of the Palace would be dramatically illuminated, as would the Gallery of Hercules and the stained-glass windows of the Palatine Chapel. The orchestra played in the center of the horseshoe-shaped staircase, reminiscent of the one at the royal Château of Fontainebleau in France. The acoustics in the courtyard were wonderful, apparently because the walls from the different wings of the Palace were not actually parallel, so the "trapezoid" shape of the courtyard eliminated undesirable echoes, providing exquisitely clear sound. It was a magical setting.

Monaco – August 20, 1962

Dearest Mum and Dad,

After having been to so many parties in the last two months, where people only think of new, extravagant ways of amusing themselves, Marty and I have come to the conclusion that when we make our fortune we shall not live an empty existence like these "poor," unhappy, bored people. This experience here has really opened our eyes.

Last week we had dinner with the Maharani of Baroda at the Hôtel de Paris with G & R and had a very good time. It is all interesting, but we could never spend our lives doing this.

Two weeks ago we received a wonderful break! "Life" Magazine came to Marty to take his photograph for their issue on the "100 Most Successful Young Americans," which will be published soon. I am so proud of Marty, and it comes at the perfect time because we cannot stay here forever in this job, although the French are not at all unhappy that Marty is here, for they realize his stabilizing influence. His counsel has saved the day many times, if the truth were known. After the "Life" article there will be many offers, perhaps. So far our luck is holding out.

I have played golf with Grace several times. It has been fun, but we both play quite badly. Afterwards we go to "Rocagel" for a drink or dinner and have a good time. Marty still plays golf with R. twice a week, and Marty's game is excellent. Grace is very sweet, and we get along well together. We had an hysterically funny time when we tried to mate Jester with her dog, Gamma. It was a fiasco – poor Jester was a greenhorn, but now he looks everywhere for Gamma – poor thing. Charles and Greg send loads of love to Grammy and Grandpa.

All our love, Joan and Marty

During and after the crisis with France, Prince Rainier and Martin often played golf together. This was not just for exercise or to blow off steam, but it was also the only place that they could really talk in privacy. At over 2,500 feet above sea level, the Monte-Carlo Golf Club was high in the hills near Rocagel, away from the prying eyes and ears in Monaco. However, according to Martin, "The Prince and I played golf a couple of times a week, mainly because the Prince's office was bugged, and my apartment was bugged, and he thought that we could talk on the golf course. But, of course, his caddie, who was an Algerian, also was bugged! We knew all of this because we brought in one of the security companies to find out where all the bugs were, and then we decided that we would leave the bugs, because it was easier to leave them and to be careful. But the Prince just couldn't refrain; knowing that the bugs were there, he would say some of the most incredibly impolitic things."

After several months of demanding the dismissal of Martin Dale, the French finally gave up asking for him to leave the Principality. It seems that at some point while we had been away in "exile," Charles de Chambrun, Martin's counterpart in the negotiations for the Franco-American FCN Treaty of Establishment in 1959, came to Martin's defense. He remembered Martin well from that experience and came forward to convince the French government that Monaco was more amenable with Martin there than without him. De Chambrun succeeded in getting the French to remove that demand from their list. This allowed Martin to continue to fulfill his contract with the Prince.

All of the tension in Monaco did not really concern the super rich, who traveled between their palatial mansions, massive estates and sumptuous villas around the world, and would simply choose another tax-free country to claim as their main domicile if Monaco's tax-free status were to end. Many of the grandest mansions were actually located in France, so life would not change for them, and the Franco-Monégasque crisis was simply light conversation while they sipped champagne. The most important thing to the world's elite was that the summer months were the social season for them on the Côte d'Azur, and we were often invited to the most beautiful mansions I have ever seen, located in and around the Principality.

One afternoon, Grace and I were asked to lunch at the home of a wealthy American heiress. As we sat down at the table, there was a veritable arsenal of sterling silver utensils lined up at my place setting, including one that was a sterling silver tube. I had never seen anything like it before, and had no idea what to do with it, so I waited and watched our hostess. I looked over at Grace and noticed that she also seemed to be unfamiliar with this apparatus, which was not used at the Palace. We both observed our hostess as she slid this silver tube onto the base of an asparagus spear and then nibbled on the asparagus. We both followed suit. It was a bit awkward using this contraption, but we managed! Grace and I laughed about it on the way home.

The official season for Monaco took place every year from November to February, after the tourist season. This was when many of the wonderful annual charity balls and galas were planned, as well as the fabulous ballets and operas. It was also the time when the Monégasque National Day and the *Fête de Sainte Dévote* took place. However, in 1962, everyone was holding their breath, wondering what was going to happen when France's six-month deadline expired in October. Would France cut off the electricity, gas and water to Monaco? Would there be customs barriers around the Principality? Would anyone still come to Monte Carlo?

Throughout the summer, General de Gaulle continued to apply unrelenting pressure on the Prince. Apparently, De Gaulle did not take off for the month of August, as all of his countrymen traditionally did, at least not where sanctions against Monaco were concerned. On August 21, France signed a decree providing for fines or imprisonment for anyone acting as an intermediary for operations between French and Monégasque banks, and for financiers not registered with the National Credit Council. This was France's way of trying to keep track of the money flowing in and out of Monaco, especially from French citizens.

On August 22, 1962, everyone was shocked to see the news that Charles de Gaulle had narrowly escaped a violent assassination attempt. A group of militants, who were upset that De Gaulle had given Algeria independence from France, opened fire on the General and his wife as their Citroen drove through the streets of Paris, killing two of his bodyguards in a hail of bullets. This was one of several attempts that were made on the French President's life (later depicted in the book and the film, *The Day of the Jackal)*.

Monaco – August 28, 1962

Dearest Mum and Dad,

Tension is mounting slightly as the October 12th deadline in the Monaco-France tussle draws near, but I am sure that all will work out well.

Our life is just as hectic as before, but everyone will be leaving here in a few days to move on to Rome, Paris or New York. I must say we have been going to the best hotels and restaurants and to the most lovely, impossible-to-live-in mansions. It is exciting and fun.

We went up to "Rocagel" with the children this Sunday and had a wonderful time. The children rode horseback. Greg had his first ride and loved it – he kept repeating "Me ride horsy."

Loads of love from us all, Joan and Marty

In the summer months, the Côte d'Azur is overrun by tourists, including the idle rich and socialites of the world. Many businesses close in August throughout Europe, and it seems that everyone takes their month-long holiday on the French Riviera. During this time, the Princely Family often retreats to their hilltop ranch.

There was an intimate private chapel at Rocagel for celebration of Sunday Mass. One of the Prince's chaplains would come up the winding roads from Monaco on weekends, when the family was in residence. Afterwards, he was invariably invited to stay for lunch and often supper, which was a delight for us all, as the chaplains were sparkling company, very human and amusing. They were of the Order of the Oblate Fathers of St. Francis de Sales. Over the years, this trusted position was occupied by Father Tucker, Father O'Connell and Father Boston.

Father Tucker had been well loved, and it took Prince Rainier many weeks to recover from him leaving. Father O'Connell was another personal chaplain to Their Serene Highnesses, and he often joined Rainier and Martin to make up a foursome for golf. Just before he was to leave Monaco, I saw a man outside the Casino, perfectly attired in a gray suit and tie. He looked very familiar, but it took me a moment to recognize that it was Father O'Connell, as he was not in his usual black suit with white clerical collar. I walked up to him and said, "Father O'Connell, is that you?" He looked from side to side, then with a twinkle and a smile, he quietly said, "Shhh, I've just got to get in to see that Casino before I leave!"

Prince Rainier often said, "*La vie doit continuer* – life must go on, for each and for all of us." Despite the constant stress, he always tried to maintain a positive demeanor and a normal lifestyle, for the sake of his well-being and those around him. On September 13, we went to Rocagel to have lunch with Grace's brother, Kell, and with Bing Crosby and his wife, Kathryn. Rainier cooked hamburgers on a barbecue they had imported from the U.S., then the men went to Mont Agel to play golf. (Bing scored a 68 on a par 71 course!)

The next day, we saw Grace and the children at the Monte Carlo Beach Club – Grace and I swam together in the sea, talked and relaxed while the children played. Then we ran into Grace and Rainier again the following night at a restaurant in the hills outside Monaco. Martin and I were dining with the owner of the famous gambling club in London called Crockfords. He told us that the Earl of Sandwich famously invented the "sandwich" at the club, because he did not want to get up from the gambling table for dinner, so he asked for cold meat to be brought to him between two slices of bread!

Grace and Rainier were having dinner with the symphony conductor and his wife. They said goodnight and left the restaurant, as we were finishing our meal of roast suckling pig. Martin and I were returning to Monaco late at night, when we were shocked to see Grace and Rainier standing on the roadside. Apparently, the conductor had had an accident driving on this dangerous road, but fortunately, no one had been hurt. Grace and Rainier were a little shaken, so Martin and I drove them to Rocagel. We stayed and had a nightcap with them to calm their nerves, then went home at 2:30 a.m. (This was September 15, 1962, almost twenty years to the day before Grace would have her fatal car accident on these treacherous roads.) We were very relieved that tragedy was avoided that night in 1962, and that we could be there to help.

On September 19, talks resumed in Paris, but things started to look grim for the Principality when negotiations between the French and Monégasque delegations seemed to be failing once again. The deadline was looming, and the French were stonewalling Prince Rainier's three Ministers, with one member of the French delegation in particular who would not budge.

Princess Grace and Prince Rainier went to Paris on October 1, but the Prince was still not allowed to negotiate directly with the French on his own behalf. Martin and I joined them in Paris on October 11 to lend moral support, visiting with them at their new apartment on the Avenue Foch, where Prince Rainier was constantly being updated regarding the ongoing discussions.

As the sands of time dwindled in the hourglass, the treaty with France was due to expire at midnight at the start of October 12, 1962. However, on October 11, France gave a slight reprieve, extending the deadline for continuing negotiations by 24 hours, but it was no use. Mr. Valéry Giscard d'Estaing, the French Minister of Finance (who would later become President of France), gave a press conference in which he said that the conversations between the French and Monégasque delegations could not reach an accord regarding the fiscal questions, so the French government would implement consequences, with the first series of measures being customs controls.

These customs barriers would create a huge problem for those living on the Côte d'Azur. The Riviera's main Basse Corniche road runs directly through Monaco, as a major artery through the South of France. The tiny Principality is situated between the French cities of Nice and Menton, so anyone driving from one city to another would have to go through two customs barriers in just 3km (2 miles). Monaco's population was about 23,000 people, but saw a daily influx of 16,000 workers commuting from France and Italy into the Principality, which would be a nightmare to manage with border controls.

A customs barrier would certainly be an inconvenience for the thousands of tourists who went to Monaco each year, especially in the summer, when this could amount to upwards of two thousand tourists per day. Would it impede those who were determined to catch a glimpse of the beautiful Princess Grace? De Gaulle was counting on the border controls to force Prince Rainier to capitulate.

On October 12, Prince Rainier hurried back to Monaco, where he received word from Paris that the Franco-Monégasque convention had been officially renounced, and customs barriers would be instituted at the border immediately, beginning at midnight. The Prince rushed back to the Palace, with crowds of Monégasques standing in the pouring rain, applauding him with encouragement. As the clock struck twelve that night, everyone in the Principality hung their heads. General de Gaulle declared the blockade of Monaco.

However, the customs agents that were set up on the border between the two countries did not seem to really know how to handle the situation. When people driving from Monaco were asked what they had to declare as they entered France, it was rumored that most of those crossing the "border" gave the same stock answer: "a box of matches, a handkerchief, and a beer." There were hundreds of cars, and only a few customs agents with a stop sign, causing such a long line that many of the cars were abandoned, creating gridlock. Reportedly, some cars were proudly waving the red and white flag of Monaco, while others simply waved a white flag of ceasefire. It was absolute chaos in the pouring rain in the middle of the night – but it only lasted for forty minutes before the French customs agents gave up their posts. There were hundreds of members of the worldwide press there to report on the whole debacle, along with crowds laughing and commenting on the farce from both sides of the border.

De Gaulle had not really taken into account the logistics of this strategy, and what it would mean for France. It was virtually impossible to completely enforce the border between France and Monaco, because many streets are divided between the two countries, where one side of the street is in Monaco, while the other side of the street is in France – some houses and shops have their front door in one country, and the back door in the other! The only way to truly establish customs controls, considering this circuitous and irregular border with Monaco, would be to build a wall like the one in Berlin.

Before WWII, France had implemented customs controls at the small Spanish enclave of Llivia, which cost the French $250,000 per year to maintain, for negligible income. France would have spent a fortune to establish and maintain customs barriers with Monaco, requiring customs posts on almost every bordering street! The sporadic customs checks that ensued were more of a nuisance and a hassle for everyone on both sides of the border.

Monaco – October 19, 1962

Dearest Mum and Dad,

We have seen G & R lately and visited their new Paris apartment, which is gorgeous. They are hoping all will go well. The General's vanity was wounded, and the Prince has made all the concessions he can without betraying his people and the French living here. My opinion is that Monaco is being made a scapegoat for France's other problems – but I hope that a settlement will be made soon. It would be such a shame if Monaco were to become another Cannes or Nice, but I am sure that it will not.

Besides all of this, the former Lady-in-Waiting of Grace's has written a series of six articles in the largest scandal sheet in France, exposing the private lives of G & R. What a dirty thing to do and at a very bad time.

Loads of love from us all and XXOO from the boys. All my love, Joan

In the midst of all of the stress, turmoil, pain and disappointment that had relentlessly battered their lives that year, Princess Grace and Prince Rainier experienced another shock when they read a series of articles by a seemingly disgruntled former employee. Grace's Lady-in-Waiting, Madame Madge Tivey-Faucon had been let go by the Prince at the beginning of 1962, after serving them for several years. An Australian, Tiv had been in the Prince's employ for about six years as his English-speaking secretary before he married Grace, and she was very devoted to him. Prince Rainier thought she would make a good secretary and later Lady-in Waiting for Grace because she spoke French and English and could help her learn to speak French. He also hoped that she would be able to help Grace become familiar with all of the unspoken rules of protocol that govern being a princess. However, Tiv often seemed to me to be rather snobbish and judgmental with Grace, and with everyone around her except, of course, the Prince.

A few months after her dismissal from the Palace, Madame Tivey-Faucon sold a tell-all story about Grace that appeared in several installments in *France Dimanche* (the French equivalent of *The National Enquirer*), revealing very personal details of her private life. Each article seemed to me to make statements that had the potential to malign the reputation of the Princess. These articles were full of criticisms about Grace's taste in American furnishings, about her importing specialty foods from America like turkey and ham for holiday meals rather than buying food in France, about her ordering American fashions from New York instead of Parisian couture – in essence, there were many statements that would fan the flames of anti-Americanism in Europe. Tiv said that the Monegasques called Princess Grace an "iceberg," and that the reason for their supposed lack of love for her was that she stayed true to who she was after her marriage, and remained too American.

One of these articles was entirely focused on Grace's tendency to be practical. Tiv criticized her thriftiness, being horrified that Princess Grace had kept and worn the same maternity dresses for both of her pregnancies. She stated that Grace's motto was "Don't throw things away, don't waste anything: everything can be used again." Rather than finding this an admirable trait, she made it sound like it was a terrible thing for a princess to be conscientious. She said that Grace brought back gifts for all her staff whenever she traveled, but Tiv complained that they were ordinary gifts, like boxed soaps. Week after week, the affronts went on and on...

This was all extremely hurtful and embarrassing to Grace, who was always loyal and trusting with those around her. She was deeply wounded by the betrayal of someone that she had allowed to be so close to her, saying, "Joan, I have been so kind to Mrs. Tivey. Why would she do this to us?" Grace never understood what could make people act unkindly or dishonestly.

Earlier that year, when it was proposed that I should succeed Madame Tivey-Faucon as Grace's Lady-in-Waiting, the press emblazoned headlines such as "Grace comes to the aid of her husband by defying France in naming an American as Dame D'Honneur." It was actually the Prince who wanted me to be Grace's Lady-in-Waiting, because I was such a close and trusted confidante. A Lady-in-Waiting accompanies the Princess at all times, and after Madame

Tivey-Faucon's behavior, the Prince wanted to make sure that they had someone they could really rely on in such an important position.

The Lady-in-Waiting tends to the Princess's needs personally, as well as during social and official functions; she has to constantly be aware of everything that is going on, and anticipate the needs of the Princess, as well as the Prince. For instance, at a reception, if someone is monopolizing the conversation with the Princess, the Lady-in-Waiting discreetly moves in and politely interrupts, introducing that person to someone else, so the Princess is not left in an uncomfortable or awkward situation. Even though I was never employed by them, there were times when Prince Rainier would subtly signal me across the room to rescue him from conversations during receptions – it took me a little while to figure out that I was expected to watch for his signals, and respond to them.

One of the jobs of the Lady-in-Waiting was to essentially make sure that everyone was comfortable. For example, for formal dinners at the Palace, if they thought that one of the invited guests might not have a long gown to wear, then the Lady-in-Waiting would wear a short cocktail dress so the guest in question would not feel underdressed and out of place. The Lady-in-Waiting had to be present at all times, but stayed in the background like a shadow; I was exceptionally good at remaining invisible, as evidenced by the lack of photos of me with Grace, even though I was often right beside her!

I had always managed to avoid being in the public eye until that time, but it was in all the papers about Grace choosing an American to be her Lady-in-Waiting. Earlier that year, in the *Samedi Soir* issue of *France Dimanche,* it said: "In place of Mme. Tivey-Faucon, she has named Mrs. Dale as her Lady-in-Waiting. Mrs. Joan Dale is the wife of the American Privy Counselor of Prince Rainier, his 'Eminence Grise' they say, and the man who will push him to oppose the decisions of the French government." With all that was going on, it was the worst possible time for me to accept such a position – one more American in a prominent post in Monaco would have just been the very last straw for the French.

Although it was a great honor, I could not accept, as much as I would have liked to. That was one of the few times that my photo was in the newspapers with Grace. At first I was a little flattered to be receiving attention from the media, but then it became intrusive and deceitful. I began to really empathize with Grace as to what it was like to be constantly under public scrutiny, and to have people saying things that were not true.

Madame Jacqueline Ardant was named in my place. Her husband, Colonel Jean Ardant, was a long-time friend and Chief of Protocol for Prince Rainier, who oversaw everything at the Palace (*Gouverneur de la Maison Princière* – governor of the Prince's household). Madame Ardant was a lovely person who served as Princess Grace's Lady-in-Waiting for many years. Her daughter, Fanny Ardant, is one of the greatest French actresses.

France was humiliated after the abysmal failure of the customs barriers, but the new Franco-Monégasque "Good Neighbor" convention was yet to be resolved, and would still take several months to negotiate. In the meantime, Prince Rainier made a bid for U.S. military tourism, proposing Monaco as an ideal place for U.S. servicemen posted in Europe to meet for a vacation with their families, as an "everyman's paradise." At the time, there were over 300,000 U.S. troops and airmen stationed in West Germany, England, Italy and France (although De Gaulle would later close American bases). Having served in the French military, Prince Rainier had a great respect for those in uniform. He welcomed the U.S. naval ships in Monaco and even invited U.S. sailors to the Palace at Christmastime, due to Grace's inspiration. The Prince had always been well received by the U.S. Naval Admirals and Commanders, and wanted to return the hospitality in his beautiful country.

Monaco – November 3, 1962

Dearest Mum and Dad,

All is quiet here. Negotiations will begin again soon, and I am sure that a satisfactory settlement will be made. Marty is still keeping busy with large and difficult projects, which he is handling well, against overwhelming odds. I wonder how long we shall stay here, and where we shall go from here.

Charles is starting school at the Palace on Monday. It will do him good to do some work as he is ready for it. He has become a real little gentleman with a very polished hand-kiss, an easy, charming manner, and a tremendous sense of humor. We can tease him now, and he takes the joke with laughter. Greg is a minx and gives Grace a hard time – not speaking to her, which is embarrassing – because she once teased him, and he has never forgotten it! He is still very shy, but once he really conquers it, he will be a charmer.

Loads of love from us all, always, Joan

Grace had a tremendous sense of humor, but never at anyone else's expense; she loved to tease playfully, as did Prince Rainier. Our son Greg was sensitive and could be quite serious and stubborn. I don't recall what exactly Grace had teased Gregory about, but he refused to speak to her again for the longest time, which was very awkward for us all. He was not quite three years old, and there was simply no reasoning with him. He was quiet and observant, and one never knew what he was thinking. Grace loved Greg, perhaps identifying with his quiet character and being overwhelmed by an active older sibling, as she had been. She always made sure that Greg received special gifts so as not to feel overlooked, as his older brother was far more in the limelight.

Charles was eleven months younger than Caroline, and three months older than Albie. When Grace started schooling at the Palace for Albert and Caroline, she kindly invited Charles to join them. Gregory was unfortunately too young, and had to attend nursery school at the *Dames de St. Maur* convent. The Palace school had a charming young French schoolmistress who gave the children lessons and encouraged them to play. During breaks between studies, they played hide-and-seek, cowboys and indians, and climbed the jungle gym on the Palace grounds.

Monaco – December 6, 1962

Dearest Mum and Dad,

Monday is Charles's birthday, and we are having 15 children! Heaven help me – I will really need a rest afterwards. They are looking forward to it so much.
Tonight we are having G & R in to dinner, and then we shall go bowling afterwards. Hope it is fun! We enjoy being with them very much. All for now.
Loads of love from us all – Joan, Charles, Greg, Jester [the dog]

Negotiations were still not finalized with France, but after everything that we had all been through, the celebrations for Monaco's National Day felt extra special in 1962. Somehow, everyone seemed to parade in their dress uniforms with a little more pride, and the Prince was very grateful to have the love and support of his people as the Princely Family greeted the Monégasques from the Palace balcony, while Martin and I looked on from the *Salon des Glaces*. Later at the Stade Louis II, we cheered with Grace and Rainier as Monaco even won the soccer game that day against the French, to the great delight of everyone in the Principality. That night Grace enchanted attendees at the Opera gala, looking breathtaking in a white beaded Lanvin gown, adorned with the jeweled emblem of the Order of St. Charles with the red and white sash across her bodice. Howell Conant's photos of her that day have endured as a quintessential portrait of the regal Princess Grace. She beamed with joy all day long, delighting in the celebrations of her family, and of her people.

On December 17, 1962, a new Constitution was established in Monaco, replacing the old constitution of 1911 that had been suspended by Prince Rainier in 1959. The New Constitution proclaimed:

Art. 1. – The Principality of Monaco is a sovereign and independent State within the framework of the general principles of international law and the particular conventions with France. The territory of the Principality is unalienable.

Art. 2. – The principle of government is a hereditary and constitutional monarchy. The Principality is a State under the rule of law, committed to fundamental freedoms and rights.

Art. 3. – The executive power is exercised by the highest authority of the Prince. The Prince's persona is inviolable.

Art. 4. – The legislative power is jointly exercised by the Prince and the National Council.

Art. 5. – The judiciary power is exercised by the courts and tribunals.

The new Monégasque Constitution was intended to improve the institutions of the Principality, and also to establish trusting relationships with its neighbors. It reinstated the National Council, which approves the Principality's budget that the Prince proposes, as well as a Municipal Council that addresses municipal affairs. A Minister of State (chosen by the Prince from a list of French candidates) presides over a Council of Government Ministers, who all report to the Prince. The Prince has power of legislative initiative, but the Assembly can deny his suggestions. The new constitution gave women the right to vote, and also abolished capital punishment; as a final concession, the Prince gave up his absolute right of justice, an antiquated law that allowed the Prince of Monaco to pass sentence and condemn someone to death!

Monaco – December 29, 1962

Dearest Mum and Dad,

We have been rushing since Charles's birthday, and it seems we have not stopped. Albie and Caroline were sweet, and they played well with everyone. Charles felt very grown up being five now, and Greg can hardly wait for his "anniversaire," which will take place in Switzerland at Villars where we shall be with G & R.

Christmas Eve we spent at the Palace. We were in long gowns for Mass, and afterwards we had caviar and vodka while G & R gave out their gifts – a book on foreign policy for Marty (!) and a lovely blue angora sweater for me. Rainier said he did not dare put Marty's real gift under the tree so we were all anxious to see it. We opened it at home – it is a lovely portable tape recorder! It runs silently and magnifies very well – perfect for a spy! It is a very generous gift.

After the tree we had a delicious buffet supper of ham, cold salmon and jellied chicken in white sauce. We came home about 4 a.m. Since then we have been going to children's parties and films, to dinners at the Palace and others, etc. It is a gay season here, but Marty is beginning to tire and is getting anti-social, which comes over him every once in a while after much effort.

He has been to London on business and has been working very hard on numerous big "deals," which are made harder by the lack of co-operation here. The Prince is beside himself with the number of his government men who try to torpedo anything that is good for the country. It is a real Italian city-state in the old style (1500s).

All our love – Joan, Marty, Charles, Greg

We were all happy to see the year come to an end, especially Grace and Rainier. Martin kept his job... and his head! Rainier had managed to keep his throne, and his country... And we were all relieved that Prince Rainier's horoscope for 1962, "You will soon be changing jobs," did not come to pass.

Despite the crisis with France, Martin still did extraordinarily well in his work, helping to increase the economic revenues in Monaco by sixty-five percent over what they had been the previous year. The business volume for 1962 was estimated at around $200 million, while in 1961 it was $128 million, and ten years earlier, it had been only $30 million. Additionally, tourist business doubled since Grace and Rainier's wedding, to 100,000 visitors per year at Monaco hotels. Almost two thousand visitors a day stood outside the Palace, hoping to catch a glimpse of Princess Grace. I guess they are right when they say that there is no such thing as bad publicity, but what had ultimately turned out well for Monaco certainly had been painful for everyone involved.

There were still terms of a new treaty with France that were yet to be finalized, and many months of negotiations ahead before France and Monaco would eventually manage to agree. Grace encouraged Rainier the whole time, advising him to keep a dialog going, and to avoid pushing too hard or too fast. She reminded him to be patient, knowing that his Mediterranean temperament might cause him to be somewhat impetuous. The 1962 crisis had been a stressful experience to say the least, particularly for dear Grace, but she stood by her husband and remained Her Serene Highness in every way.

The De Gaulle crisis had left the Principality badly shaken. Prince Rainier had to give a certain amount of power back to the Ministers in the Monégasque government, who were now taking full advantage. At that time, there were few people surrounding the Prince who could be trusted. Monaco in the 1960s was a hotbed of intrigue – betrayal and gossip were rife. There was a game of obstruction being played, a power trip by those who were trying to thwart the Prince's vision of progress for his country, even by some of those closest to him...

DAYS OF DISTRESS

With the Franco-Monégasque crisis almost behind us, we thought we could all breathe a sigh of relief as we entered 1963, but unfortunately, more trouble was on the horizon. Monaco had just withstood repeated attacks from the General threatening to overtake the Principality and depose the Prince. However, another formidable man had already taken over the essential heart of Monaco and had the power to destroy it from within. Although this man had been a trusted friend to Prince Rainier for a decade, he would soon sadly become an adversary. This man was Aristotle Socrates Onassis, one of the wealthiest and most powerful men in the world.

Onassis put money ahead of everything, including his wives, lovers, and friends. He wanted Monaco to remain a playground for the world's elite, while Rainer realized that those in high society could be fickle and fleeting, going to any place that was "fashionable" at the moment; for these wealthy socialites, places and homes went in and out of style, and could be tossed away like clothing. Monaco had already suffered the economic effects when the Russian aristocracy of the old-world stopped frequenting Monte Carlo as their winter getaway. Rainier believed that Monaco could not maintain a stable or growing economy based only on the "seasonal" visits of the ultra-rich. He hoped to encourage a younger clientele by offering amenities that were more affordable.

Prince Rainier wanted to attract captains of industry and the U.S. military, whose presence was more stable in the region. Aristotle Onassis did not really seem to care about the future of Monaco or its economy; he simply wanted a tax haven for his companies, and a thriving customer base for his investments. He also loved to "collect" famous people – the wealthier and more famous the better, and he wanted to keep Monaco exclusive.

Onassis had managed to acquire a majority interest in the SBM, which owned a large percentage of the Principality's prime real estate, with as much as twenty-five percent of its waterfront, and many of its most important landmarks and exclusive properties. The SBM's holdings consisted of the Casino, the five biggest hotels, including the *Hôtel de Paris* and the Hermitage Hotel, along with the two Sporting Clubs where the galas were held, the Monte-Carlo Beach Club, the tennis club and the Monte-Carlo Golf Club, as well as many restaurants, bars, cabarets and night clubs. It was the cornerstone of Monaco's economy, and the largest employer in the Principality.

Originally named the *Société des Bains de Mer et du Cercle des Étrangers à Monaco* (The Society of Sea Bathing and Foreigners Circle in Monaco), the SBM was founded in 1863 by Prince Charles III. He wanted to establish Monte Carlo as a resort destination, with a world-class casino, and a spa with mineral baths and bathing cures, which were very popular and successful in Germany at the time. He set out to create something substantial that would bring an influx of people and revenues to his seaside Principality.

The SBM was a publicly traded company, and Onassis started acquiring shares in 1952, owning 300,000 shares within a year. He kept quietly buying until he was the majority stockholder with 520,000 of the million outstanding shares, gaining more and more control over the Principality by acquiring an ownership stake in its most important asset. Onassis then set up the headquarters of his companies, Olympic Maritime and Olympic Airways, in the magnificent offices of the SBM. Monaco became his personal kingdom, and the *CHRISTINA*, the largest yacht in the world at that time, was his floating castle.

In the beginning, Prince Rainier welcomed Onassis as a man whose money could help Monaco. The Prince always had a vision of bringing his Thirteenth Century Principality into the modern age. He needed an infusion of wealth into the country, because it had almost gone bankrupt in 1955 after the fall of the Monégasque Bank of Precious Metals and the *Images et Son* debacle.

Onassis initially brought many improvements to Monaco and the SBM, including building a spectacular restaurant on top of the *Hôtel de Paris*, with windows all around creating a panoramic view of the sea, and a ceiling that slid back to reveal the sky. He also created an exclusive and luxurious indoor pool at the hotel that was inaugurated in July 1961.

However, Aristotle kept a stranglehold on what he would allow the SBM to invest in. His main interest was in the real estate value of the land of the SBM holdings, which he wanted to develop for his own personal gain, regardless of their historic merit. This included a plan to build on the land of the Casino, which is one of the most beautiful and picturesque gems on the French Riviera. Fortunately, Onassis could not undertake any construction without government approval, which prevented him from destroying this historic landmark.

Prince Rainier was also hurt that Onassis had a habit of being a fair-weather friend. He had been conspicuously absent during the crisis with France, and many people suspected that he was secretly moving his assets out of Monaco in case the Principality fell. He did not lend his considerable power or his wealth to support the Prince, and as usual, was only concerned with his own financial interests.

Right after the October 1962 deadline passed, Onassis offered to sell his fifty-two percent ownership in the SBM to the Prince, but the price that he demanded was way too high; the proposal also came with several conditions, which included a clause that Rainier would not be able to sell the shares to anyone else. In London's *Daily Express* newspaper of February 21, 1963, Onassis gave an interview in which he said that he had offered his shares of the SBM to "help" Rainier. He said, "I gave Prince Rainier and his government a 90-day option on my shares. I did so because of his difficulties with the French government. I wanted to help him if possible." He said he was relieved that the Prince did not take him up on his offer because "I never want to lose my interest in the Casino." It was a huge and very lucrative business.

The Prince recognized that whoever controlled the SBM essentially controlled Monaco, and he had to have a majority of shares in order to realize his vision for his country. Since he could not force Onassis out, he tried on several occasions to buy him out. They met frequently, but Onassis would repeatedly renege on their agreements. Rainier incredulously said to me, "Onassis gave me his word, and I trusted him!"

Aristotle Onassis was a master at manipulating people and situations to his own benefit. He would smile and agree to things amiably, telling people what they wanted to hear, but then find excuses and ways to avoid following through. Onassis would say that Monaco was another one of his toys to play with, and often joked that he owned the Principality and was its king. Prince Rainier was outraged.

It got to the point where the Prince and Onassis could rarely even meet anymore, so Martin got thrown into the middle of the situation as an intermediary. His mission from the Prince was to find a successor purchaser of the SBM from Onassis. First, Martin wisely got an option in writing from

Onassis, stating that he would sell his shares at a particular price. Then he found a group in London who were interested, and made several trips there to verify that the various backers involved were all legitimate. Once they had reached an agreement, Martin went to Onassis with the deal, ready to exercise the option.

Martin asked when the purchasers' accountants could look at the books and do all the due diligence. Onassis replied, "Well, you have an option, and you can put down your money, but you cannot come in and look at our books. We are a highly confidential gaming establishment, and we have an obligation to our clients." As Onassis had correctly surmised, the English couldn't do business that way, so the deal collapsed. The Prince got angrier, and would not speak to him for many months, and Martin was no longer able to speak to Onassis for him, either. Onassis had Prince Rainier in check, and the stalemate went on until Rainier would later find a brilliant way to beat him at his own game.

Monaco – January 10, 1963

Dearest Mum and Dad,

At the moment Marty is in London again on a 4-day business trip. I am sorry I could not go along, but – another time. Rainier had asked all of us to accompany them to London, but the timing was not right so we could not go. We shall be in Switzerland with them, however, and I hope we all like Villars and its accommodations. We shall be there from February 1 until March 1.

All love from us all, always, Joan

Socially, the year 1963 had started with a bang. New Year's day, Martin played golf with the Prince, and then we all had a wonderful time together with the children at Rocagel. The next day, we had dinner at the Palace, and then on January 3 there was a charity tea and fashion show to benefit the Red Cross. I was seated at Princess Grace's table, watching models present designs by Lanvin, Nina Ricci, Guy Laroche, Louis Feraud, Hermès, Balmain, and many others, all incorporating astrakhan or ostrich feathers. Afterwards, we celebrated Martin's birthday at the Palace with dinner and a movie.

January 6 was the *Fête des Rois*, or festival of the Three Wise Men, which was celebrated with a gala to benefit refugees from all over the world who were now living in France. We were again seated at Grace and Rainier's table. This gala was held at the *Hôtel de Paris* in Monte Carlo, under the patronage of Prince

Rainier and Princess Grace, and Prince Sadruddin Aga Khan, High Commissioner for Refugees at the United Nations and also an Executive Secretary for UNESCO.

The program for the gala had a cover designed by artist Jean Cocteau, and a touching foreword written in French by Princess Grace, roughly translated: "*In this world that is said to be well organized, that there are still hundreds of thousands of refugees in camps, aging and awaiting the end of their existence, seems inconceivable, inhuman and unjust! And yet this exists, and we must wake up in order to act and remedy it. In 1949, the United Nations created the High Commission for Refugees. It made it possible to give all these unfortunates status and protection. But this is not enough, because while we live happy and free... others, men, women, children, live without a country, without a home, without work, thus without hope! ...250,000 refugees live in France, several thousand of them are handicapped. They need to be helped. They need us to help them find work and a future. All of the profits from this event will be devoted to this simple yet essential gesture of aid to one's fellow man.*" She signed it simply in her bold handwriting: Grace de Monaco.

Grace knew what it was like to work for a living, as she had insisted on making it on her own in New York without the help of her family. She was not a socialite who approached charity as a pastime, but wholeheartedly cared for others and tried to help as many people as possible in any way she could.

In 1963, Princess Grace's love of children inspired her to found AMADE (*Association Mondiale des Amis de l'Enfance*), which operates today in association with UNICEF, UNESCO and the United Nations Economic and Social Council. AMADE helps children worldwide by defending their essential rights and bringing access to healthcare, as well as promoting self-sufficiency for communities in developing nations, by focusing on education and vocational training.

Through various galas and events, Princess Grace was always trying to think of ways to raise money for charity. In this milieu of people who had everything, the offerings had to be exceptional. For the gala event to benefit refugees, there was a charitable auction for which the jeweler Mauboussin donated exquisite jewelry. Princess Grace herself offered a beautiful piece of jewelry in gold with rubies and emeralds, which raised 12,500 francs at auction. There was also a charity raffle of a lovely ivory statue, and a gold and silver compact from Cartier. I was thrilled that Martin won the compact, which was simple and elegant. There were three hundred attendees that evening, raising money to better the conditions of the refugees.

The next day, Martin went to London with Grace and Rainier for business. Upon their return, they invited us to dinner at the Palace, followed by the Gregory Peck film, *To Kill a Mockingbird*. Gregory Peck and his lovely wife, Veronique, were frequent guests at the Palace. He was a very impressive person, who radiated peace that was born of inner strength. Fondly referred to as the "gentle giant," he was a quiet, charming man of great depth and honesty. He loved his job and said that he went to work happy every morning because it was a delight for him to act, so he put his whole heart into it. He was a sincere and dedicated man of conviction, who did a lot of good work for Hollywood and for greater causes. I found him to be exceptional, as did Grace.

Princess Grace felt that the arts were essential to society, as they had been for centuries. She was aware that people in the arts devoted their lives to their craft; most receive little reward or recognition for their hard work and are lucky if they can earn a living by expressing their talent and doing what they love. Grace wanted to promote the arts in any way she could, lending support to artists, actors, filmmakers, etc., not just in Hollywood, but all over the world.

Grace was instrumental in creating the International Television Festival, which was held annually at the Winter Sporting Club in Monaco. Countries from around the globe would submit their best television programs in such categories as comedies, dramas, documentaries, children's programs, best actor, best actress, etc. That year, one hundred television programs from sixteen nations vied for the Golden Nymph statuette. Expert judges sat comfortably in armchairs around a television set in order to view the entries, somewhat as it would be in your own living room.

Television was a relatively new and growing medium at that time, and both Prince Rainier and Princess Grace were aware of its potential influence. Thus, the Prince wrote a French introduction in the program for this event: "...*For my part, I have believed and continue to believe, more than ever, that television is not yet an art, but it can and must become one; we must then help it to evolve and find its true artistic form in its true vocation. We must therefore encourage and reward its efforts in the field of artistic expression, as well as in its role as an agent of understanding and connection between the populations of the world... That is what I hope and await from this Festival, and I have great confidence that it will contribute to this new industry, for it to find its artistic voice in service to truth and good taste in information, education and the relaxation of free men on all continents.*" Prince Rainier recognized the power of television to reach the masses. That is one of the reasons why he had fought for the shares of *Images et Son*, which controlled independent radio and television stations in Monaco and its surrounding areas.

For the gala of the International Television Festival, we were seated at Grace and Rainier's table with Italian actress Gina Lollobrigida, George Hamilton, and others. Grace looked lovely in a pale blue satin gown, with a beaded bolero top. After dinner, there was a mesmerizing performance by the incomparable Marlene Dietrich, who stepped out on stage wearing a full-length white mink coat, which trailed behind her in a long regal train. She dramatically threw off the coat, and you could hear the entire audience gasp as she revealed every curve of her exquisite figure in a skin-tight, skin-colored, see-through sequined gown that she had actually been sewn into – it looked like she was wearing nothing but carefully placed gold sequins! She was absolutely breathtaking, and dazzled everyone in the audience. When she began to sing, it was simply magical. The Prince turned to me and said, "What a pity that our sons cannot see somebody like this. They would never be able to imagine it."

Marlene Dietrich was truly a living legend, and was one of the first entertainers to have her legs insured for a million dollars – an outrageous amount at that time. After the show, the Prince and Princess invited Ms. Dietrich to join us for a drink at the Cabaret of the Casino. It took her a while to be unsewn from her gown, but when she appeared, she looked absolutely magnificent. She was a fascinating person, a good conversationalist, and one of the most outstanding people I ever met.

We all enjoyed dancing into the early morning hours. Grace loved to dance, and although the Prince was rather reluctant to do so in public, he was a fantastic dancer with great rhythm. In fact, he was very gifted in all the arts – a true Renaissance man. He and Grace were a great combination together, and they made a good team in every way.

Martin, too, was a wonderful dancer, and we flowed so well together that people would often stop and watch us dance at the exquisite balls. Martin and I were also an excellent team, which served us well as diplomats and in service to Prince Rainier. Martin was extremely intelligent with a good sense of humor, and men particularly enjoyed speaking with him, as he could converse brilliantly on a wide range of topics. I was more social, inquisitive and a very good listener. It helped that we were both fluent in English and French, and we very much enjoyed meeting new people, especially the fascinating luminaries that we encountered in Monaco.

On my birthday, Martin had to leave again for business in London. Grace sent me beautiful flowers, then she and I went shopping and for a swim at the

Hôtel de Paris pool. Grace loved to go shopping in her black London taxicab that had been converted into a chauffeured limousine – it was roomy and comfortable, with ample space for purchases! Afterwards, Grace and Rainier invited me for a simple and intimate dinner at the Palace. Caroline's birthday party was three days later, then we all went to Switzerland for a month.

Villars, Switzerland – February 18, 1963

Dearest Mum and Dad,

We see Grace and Rainier almost every day. They are relaxed and full of fun here, where they are farther away from their troubles. We have had some very gay evenings with them for dinner and dancing. Marty had to return to Monaco for a week and they were so nice to invite me to their chalet alone with them for dinner, after which we played scrabble (I had to be careful not to win too often – nor at gin rummy). We have been skating together (Grace and myself) while Marty and the Prince ski. Charles skates beautifully and runs all around the rink with Caroline. They are sweet together.

Love from us all, always, Joan

Charles and Gregory were among Albert and Caroline's first playmates, so they developed a very special relationship, even accompanying them on vacation so the children would have someone to play with while they were away from Monaco for a month. In Switzerland, we always rented a place close to Grace and Rainier's chalet, whether they were in Gstaad, Schönried, or Villars. Sometimes, the boys were invited to lunch at the Prince's chalet, or Albert and Caroline would come to our place for lunch.

Following their afternoon nap, we all went to the ice skating rink. Caroline was quite good on ice, even at a young age. She would take Charles and Greg by the hand and encourage them. Greg was very little and stood clinging to the side of the rink wearing his snow boots. He was quite afraid to step onto the ice, so Grace and I took turns leading him around. I am not a good skater, but Grace managed to keep on her feet and do some backward skating rather elegantly. Mostly, we all laughed a lot, as we enjoyed spending time together with our little ones doing things that were healthy and rather "ordinary."

In Switzerland, we had lots of casual dinners with Grace and Rainier. We usually played games at night, including blackjack, or passing an orange from person to person under one's chin, which always erupted in gales of laughter. We listened to records, danced, talked and relaxed. Grace loved to film the children, as did Martin, so there were times when we set up the movie projector and delighted in watching our home movies together.

There were many parties where Grace and Rainier invited friends from Monaco and from the U.S. to join in the festivities. We had parties at the top of the mountain, which we had to access by funicular. Sometimes when we went out, there might be a band playing, and after much encouragement, Rainier would occasionally go on stage and take over the drums – he was an excellent musician. There were also parties for the children, and we often celebrated Albert's birthday there, and sometimes Greg's as well.

Villars, Switzerland – March 9, 1963

Dearest Mum and Dad –

Our vacation is almost over, and it has been a pleasant one. We shall leave the 15th – the day after Albert's 5th birthday and shall drive to Monaco. Greg is speaking fluent French and English now and offers information to people instead of remaining silent. He adores Prince Rainier and runs to see him, and even Grace has won him over after a long struggle. He is a stubborn little boy who loves to make scenes – but he is lovable.

I wonder how long we shall stay in Monaco? Marty has to go to Philadelphia and New York for a month in April on business for the Prince. I am sorry not to go along, but it would be too expensive and at a bad time.

Recently, a Communist was elected to the National Assembly in Monaco, and he has been attacking Marty's work – even to the extent of putting a long article panning Marty in the "Patriote" – the Parisian Communist newspaper. This could influence how long we shall be staying!

Also Cholly Knickerbocker, the famous American gossip columnist, wrote about Marty, Rainier and Onassis, saying that Marty would take over the running of the Casino – nonsense! That is not his type of work, and I wonder who could have given out such a story! Life is never dull! (Cholly was the brother of designer Oleg Cassini, whom Grace almost married, but her parents did not approve.)

Loads of love from us all, Marty, Joan, Charles, Greg

The rumors of Martin's involvement in Monaco's gambling casinos were completely false, and were partly fueled by Onassis himself. Martin had no part in any of the gambling, neither personally nor professionally. He was responsible for attracting businesses to Monaco that, for the most part, would not create much pollution, like perfume, cosmetics, and small plastics manufacturing, and had nothing to do with the SBM.

An article then appeared in the French Communist newspaper, *Le Patriote*, insinuating that Martin was engaging in quiet back room deals with large American companies, which was utterly untrue: "Martin Dale, Privy Counselor, and Mr. Schmidt, European Director of Pan American Airlines, left for Switzerland where Prince Rainier is vacationing." There ensued a long article decrying alleged corruption and further "Americanization" of Monaco.

Monaco – March 22, 1963

Dearest Mum and Dad,

We are at last home in Monaco, and it is wonderful to be back in the warm climate. Unfortunately, we had bad news. The day we left Villars I broke out in a rash and thought it was from some salmon I had eaten. It got worse and worse, so we stopped in Lausanne and found I had German Measles in the second month of pregnancy... I lost the baby because of the illness... The doctor says that in two months we can start another little one. Let us hope so, as we want a third child so much.

Hope you are well. Sorry to give you bad news... I am feeling very well – so do not be anxious. Grace was adorable and came to see me, plus sending a lovely azalea plant.

Loads of love from all of us, Joan

Soon after we returned from Switzerland, Martin had to go to the United States to spend a month meeting with prospective companies and banks who were interested in opening European branches, offices or headquarters in Monaco. These companies included Continental Illinois Bank, Mellon Bank, and Hertz Car Rental. He also had several meetings with executives and lawyers from Pan Am Airlines, who were in discussions regarding a large hotel that they wanted to build there.

During that time, Martin went to Philadelphia for the first Travel and Vacation Show, which Grace's brother, Kell, presided over. Two hundred exhibitors were slated to participate in the ten-day show from April 19-28, and Monaco was presenting a booth for the first time to court American tourism. Martin wanted to make sure that the presentation would meet the Prince's high standards and reflect the desired image of Monaco as a world-class resort destination. He was also there to make preparations for Monaco's participation in the World's Fair, which would take place in New York the following year.

Martin was in charge of making the official arrangements for Grace and Rainier's six-week trip to the United States with their children. On April 17, Martin met the Princely Family at Idlewild Airport (now JFK), and found himself transporting a car full of their luggage to Philadelphia. Prince Rainier arrived on a Pan Am flight with Princess Caroline and Nanny Maureen; Princess Grace arrived a bit later on a separate Pan Am flight with Prince Albert. They took precautions of traveling separately to avoid the risk of an airline disaster wiping out the Grimaldi dynasty.

Princess Grace and Prince Rainier were going to Philadelphia for an official visit, including opening the Travel Show on April 19, and several other official engagements that were organized in their honor by the City of Philadelphia. It was also a visit to Grace's hometown, which involved lots of family events at the various Kelly households. The Kelly clan very nicely welcomed Martin and entertained him constantly, including him in their family celebrations.

Monaco – Tuesday, April 16, 1963

Dearest Marty –

We spent a lonely Easter without you but managed to enjoy it somewhat. R. said he did not envy you your job and wondered how many bottles of Aspirin you had consumed while dealing with the Mayor, and all the others. I told him to tell you I missed you, and with a twinkle in his eye he said that he would tell you what a naughty girl I am being! Knowing how he teased me when you were on other trips, I expect he will really enjoy pulling your leg! I have been exemplary in my conduct and have not gotten into any compromising situations! Last night I did go with G & R in their cavalcade to the British-American Hospital Ball at the Hotel. We were home and in bed by 1 a.m. – a record for a gala evening!

Grace has been very tired lately, and I hope she can stand up to the trip, although she is really looking forward to it. We all send loads and loads of love. Have a good time and please write.

Always your, Joanie

FROM THE DESK OF
MARTIN A. DALE

Philadelphia – April 17, 1963

My Darling,

Although it is well after midnight, and I am really dead tired from having spent the entire day at Idlewild, greeting our friends upon their arrival, fighting off newspapermen and photographers, and driving back to Philadelphia in a Ford station wagon loaded to the rafters with luggage, I do want to write this brief note to tell you how very much I love and miss you.

I was again in New York bright and early for a meeting with Hertz, whom I have brought into Monaco in a fairly big way. Then to the airport for the long wait.

The Prince's plane came in half an hour ahead of time, and since they wouldn't listen to me and press to have the car admitted to the runway, the journalists practically swamped him and Caroline. They had him tangled up in microphone wires, etc. The crush was terrific, but he kept his chin up and remained in fairly good humor. I got my way for the Princess's arrival, and it went off without a snag. The car was right at the gangway; she posed for a few photos and then into the car and away.

Grace was very sweet and told me how much you missed me, but I also learned that you were the belle of the B.A. Ball and are really wowing them as the gay party girl. I'll have to put you in a convent when I return. All kidding aside, though, I want you to go easy. I don't want you to jeopardize your health for a few evenings out.

All my love, my sweetheart,
Devotedly, Marty

Monaco – Thursday, April 18, 1963

My Dearest Marty –

I was so happy to receive your newsy letter today. It is very lonely here now that G & R are gone – even the atmosphere is not the same. Grace phoned me just before she left for the airport, which was very sweet of her, and Albert wanted to say goodbye to Charles. I was very touched.

I am feeling very well now – all mended. I just wonder if the opportunity will ever be right to have another baby? I do hope so!

Do have a good time with G & R – they are very pleased with the job you are doing – they said so. Give my love to everyone – enjoy yourself.

Your ever loving & adoring Joanie

FROM THE DESK OF
MARTIN A. DALE

Philadelphia – April 21, 1963

My Darling,

Last evening, at six I got a call inviting me to Mrs. Kelly's for dinner with Grace and Rainier and a few family friends. I got home fairly late and with too much alcohol in me for my own good. I have finally had to risk ridicule by claiming that I can't drink more than two scotches without falling asleep.

The official part of the visit is now over. It went fairly smoothly. On Thursday, we had dinner at the Sheraton Hotel for the whole family and me. On Friday, we started in the morning with the City Hall welcome ceremony, then the motorcade to Convention Hall for the walk through the various exhibits of the Travel Show. The photographers were thick as flies and made it really unpleasant for everyone. Fortunately, our exhibit was completed on time and was truly magnificent – by far the best of the Show, and Grace and Rainier were very proud.

Friday night, I was invited to Mrs. Kelly's for dinner and a family party for G & R's anniversary. It was pretty good fun, and G & R were in good spirits, despite a family drama. Saturday, I was up at 6:00 a.m. and looking after the various details of the day's events, luncheon at the Ben Franklin Hotel, motorcade to the

Travel Show. Then last night the surprise invitation to return to the Kellys. I fear I am getting too involved. Today, I played golf with R., and Don Levine [Grace's brother-in-law]. After golf, we all went to Don's for another party with all the clan. The dinner was great, steaks cooked on the barbecue, but the party was marred by a really strained relationship between G & R (who had obviously had a fight that morning) and several other members of the family. Grace had been crying, and R. had just about reached the end of his rope. Father Tucker was there also, and I was delighted to see him and he me. I hated to have him witness the discord.

Tomorrow is a tough day. The press will be legion, and I fear that the Prince will blow his stack. I'm going to lie low to escape the fireworks.

I love you with all my heart
Devotedly, Marty

Monaco – April 25, 1963

My Dearest Marty –

I received your letter in record time and am glad to hear you are well, despite all your running. They all must like you, or they would not bother inviting you, so do not feel you are getting too involved. It is too bad G & R had a tiff, but in the family atmosphere it does not surprise me. There are so many of them, and they are so different from Europeans.

Loads of love from your adoring Charles, Greg and Joanie

Grace and Rainier were only human, just like everyone else. They were not perfect, nor did they profess to be – it is the rest of the world that wanted to put them on a pedestal and make them the perfect couple. All couples experience stress and strain from time to time, especially when faced with extended visits with family and in-laws, which usually involve the challenges of family dynamics. For Grace and Rainier, this was further complicated by all of the demands of their official obligations and the press whenever they visited the United States.

As much as Prince Rainier loved America and Americans, he was raised in Europe with a different sensibility. He was sent off to a rigorous boarding school in England at a young age and never experienced the type of American family gatherings that the Kellys enjoyed, particularly with such a large and outspoken family. It could be overwhelming for anyone, even for Martin, who was raised in America!

The Prince had a rather wicked sense of humor and loved to tease people. Whenever Martin was away, Rainier joked with me about him "playing the field," which I would laugh about. But Martin was very jealous, and when the Prince teased him about me being the "gay party girl" while he was away, it planted a seed of doubt in his mind that created suspicion and paranoia, which actually ended up affecting our marriage. Nothing could have been further from the truth, as I was always a very faithful wife, but when one hears such things repeatedly, even as a joke, one does not always know what to believe, unfortunately.

It did not help that Monaco had a very small town mentality, where everyone watched everyone else and knew everyone else's business. An innocent "hello" in the street between a man and a woman would have people whispering. It was rumored that I was having affairs with other men, which was absolutely ridiculous. I was a young American woman, and American women had a reputation in Europe of being "free." I was friendly, open, and smiled a lot, which the French sometimes mistook for flirting, because French women were quite reserved.

In any case, Martin and I both suffered with all of his business traveling, and I also suffered his jealousy when he returned. Whenever Martin was away, I had to be particularly careful regarding what invitations I accepted, and whom I spoke to, or was seen with. He was very controlling and would repeatedly interrogate and admonish me about my behavior. However, he was also very sweet and thoughtful, writing to me constantly, and often bringing back lovely presents for me.

Martin traveled quite a lot on business for the Prince, particularly to Paris, London and the United States. Sometimes the children and I could go with him, but at other times it was not possible. Grace and Rainier were very thoughtful when Martin was away, and often invited me to join them so I would not be lonely.

Grace was a good friend, who was unquestionably loyal to the core to everyone she loved and cared about. She always defended me to Martin, who would sometimes believe some of the absurd rumors that circulated in the Principality. Grace was also a thoroughly faithful person, so whenever I read reports of her alleged liaisons, I always shook my head, knowing how unfounded and outrageous all these rumors were. Everything made news – things were distorted or entirely untrue, as gossip was practically a national pastime in Monaco.

Monaco was nicknamed *le pays de la peau de banane* (country of the banana peel), referring to the care needed not to slip up, in a place where every move is being watched. Living in an atmosphere of suspicion was not easy, and it put added strain on daily life. Grace was exemplary in her behavior, always upright; she had to constantly be aware of her image and of the people around her.

Grace was a very intelligent woman, particularly in the practical sense. She was incredibly astute in sizing people up, and was usually uncannily correct! Grace had an exceptional intuition that served her well. She was also an amateur graphologist, who tried to examine people's handwriting to get a sense of their true character, especially if they were writing to ask her for something.

Occasionally Grace would say to me, "Somehow, I don't trust so-and-so. I get an uneasy feeling." She would mention this to the Prince, who learned over time to heed her concerns and consider them carefully, while formulating his own opinions and decisions. Rainier believed that women had a keener insight in analyzing personalities, while men, although they had similar instincts, had been forced to subjugate them because it might be seen badly in business.

People were constantly trying to curry favor with the Prince and Princess. Some were extremely artful at insinuating themselves wherever they felt they could gain something. Behind the scenes, Grace supported her often-beleaguered husband with wise counsel and a calming influence, always there to soothe and smooth the ruffled feathers.

Monaco – April 1963

Dearest Mum and Dad,

Grace and Rainier were terribly kind to me and invited me to dinner and to the movies [before they left for Philadelphia to meet Martin], and also to the Opera to hear "Il Trovatore" with the world famous tenor Corelli, which was extraordinary. Grace was ill that evening, and I was seated on Rainier's left in the Box so that people thought they had seen the Princess. That is fine – why disappoint them? However, the resemblance is only valid from a very great distance.

Marty is scouting around while he is in the U.S. for something else, with hopes it would be here or in Paris, or London. We shall see what happens. If he could keep on being advisor here, it would be good.

We all send loads of love, Joan

Grace and I looked quite alike, and we had many characteristics in common. We were of the same height, similar build, moved in the same manner, and were both blue-eyed, fair-skinned blondes. (We even had the same middle name, Patricia!) I sometimes looked more like Grace than her own sisters did. However, Grace's beauty far outshone mine, and she was remarkably photogenic – unlike me.

One day I saw Grace looking extremely tired. She had circles under her eyes and redness around her nose caused by her allergies, and in general she looked rather unglamorous. She said, "I look and feel so terrible today, and I have a very important photography sitting with Howell (Conant). What am I going to do, Joan?" When I later saw the results, the un-retouched photographs were excellent, including one that has often been reprinted all over the world. Perhaps it was her inner radiance shining through that made her so miraculously photogenic!

I was often chauffeured from the Palace in the official car, and the *Carabiniers* saluted when they saw the license plate, as we held a position of importance in Monaco. In the square in front of the Palace, there was usually a throng of people, hoping to catch a glimpse of the Princely Family. When the crowd saw the car emerge from the gates, they rushed over and peered in the windows. They all cheered and waved when they saw a young blonde woman seated within. I thought, "My goodness, they think I'm Princess Grace! What should I do? If I don't smile, they will think that Grace is an 'ice princess.' Should I just smile and enjoy it?" I thought to myself, "Why not?" so I smiled and waved. I'm sure they went home thinking, "Gosh, she didn't quite look like her pictures," but perhaps some of them who were standing further back thought they had seen the person they had come all the way to Monaco to see. I had brief moments in the sun, so to speak, upholding Grace's image – but I did feel a little like a fraud, albeit a happy one.

Monaco – May 13, 1963

Dearest Mum and Dad,

It is wonderful to have Marty home again – we really missed him so much. Home was not the same without him! Marty has decided definitely to look for another position. It has been a wonderful experience here, and I am very sad to think of it coming to an end, but when we came, we knew it was only temporary. The climate is so marvelous and the life so interesting that I shall regret it immensely. Although December is a long way off, it seems very close. Rainier wants Marty to continue as a consultant for him, which would be nice, but we cannot make our lives here as there is no future in it.

Loads of love from us all, Joan, Marty, Charles, Greg

Martin returned to Monaco on May 7. After completing his business on the East Coast, he had taken a few extra days to fly out to La Jolla, California, to see his parents. Then he flew up to Vancouver Island in Canada to visit my parents, which was very sweet. Our little boys were thrilled to see their daddy when he finally came home; they had grown and changed so much in the month that he was away.

Grace and the children stayed on in the U.S. and then went to Paris. Albert and Caroline enjoyed spending time with all of their cousins in America, but still missed their friends Charles and Gregory. They sent a postcard of Independence Hall in Philadelphia, written in Caroline's handwriting: "At the moment we are at Ocean City but cannot go outside because we have colds."

After Martin's trip to the United States, he had many interesting job prospects for when his contract expired at the end of the year. However, the Prince did not want Martin to resign and insisted that he stay on as Privy Counselor, despite ongoing pressure from the Monégasque government and from President de Gaulle, who was still unhappy with Martin's presence.

The De Gaulle affair continued to haunt us, even after we left the Principality. An article in the *Washington Post* of June 20, 1965, said: "Apparently the work of a young American had much to do with encouraging French ire during 'La Crise' [the 1962 crisis]. Martin Dale, now thirty-three, met Prince Rainier when he was American Vice Consul in Nice. They became fast friends, and Dale was appointed Privy Counselor to the Crown for economic affairs. His principal duty was to attract business to Monaco. It is said that Dale's unrestrained advertisements of the tax benefits were most offensive to French eyes and ears.

It was widely rumored at the time of the resolution of the crisis, in the spring of 1963, that the French had demanded – and Rainier had agreed – that Dale leave the country. The young American (whose wife is said to bear a strong resemblance to Princess Grace) did not leave until last December, however."

On May 18, 1963, after months of ongoing negotiations, France and Monaco finally reached a new accord, signing a Tax Treaty and a new Customs Convention. In all, six different treaties were negotiated, including regulation of insurance, pharmaceuticals, postal and telephone services, and tariffs. A new "Good Neighbor" convention also defined the scope of commitments between France and the Principality. The essential terms of the treaties included these concessions from Monaco:

- *French citizens residing in Monaco had to pay taxes, unless they had lived in Monaco for more than five years before October 13, 1962.*
- *There would be no tax imposed on Monégasque citizens.*
- *Companies earning more than twenty-five percent of their income from outside of Monaco would be taxed in France, and companies below that threshold would continue with tax exemptions.*
- *New and future residents in Monaco would be taxed like the French.*

Prince Rainier had ultimately stood his ground and successfully defended his country and his people against the mighty French General and the threat of a takeover by France. In the end, after the unrelenting attacks against Monaco, and all of the turmoil in a yearlong battle, the French government merely managed to punish French citizens residing in the Principality, taxing those who had sought to escape from their grasp. Monaco could no longer be promoted as a tax haven for individuals or companies, but there were still many benefits and attractions for living and doing business there.

Rainier came back to Monaco on May 25 to attend the twenty-first annual Grand Prix of Monaco the next day, which was also the Grand Prix of Europe that year. After the race, there was a gala banquet at the *Hôtel de Paris*. British racecar driver, Graham Hill, signed Martin's program from the gala, as the winner of the Monaco Grand Prix of 1963. He was a dashing and witty Englishman, who was the only driver to win Le Mans, the Indy 500, and a Formula One World Championship.

Monaco – June 6, 1963

Dearest Mum and Dad,

We have been out every night attending dinners for the Grand Prix de Monaco. The Prince came in specially from the U.S. to attend it, but we did not see him – I think he is upset that Marty is leaving, but we cannot stay here forever. It is sad to think of leaving in six months. The anti-Americanism here and in France is at a peak, for just this week there have been many nasty cracks at Americans in the magazines, and they have renewed the offensive against Marty in "Paris-Match," the widest read French magazine, where they wrote a full-page article blaming him for the Franco-Monégasque crisis, for wanting to turn Monaco into a Las Vegas (nothing could be farther from the truth) with Grace as his accomplice (another American). This seems like a put-up job, especially as the Franco-Monégasque Treaty was just signed – no one knows Marty is leaving, but they still need a scapegoat. He can hold his own anyway. We still do not know what we shall be doing – we may even return to the Foreign Service.

I think our friend on the rock is expecting in January. She has not yet returned, so we have no confirmation. We all send loads of love.

Always devotedly, Joan, Greg & Charles

The Communist Party was extremely active in France. They were upset that Monaco was becoming wealthier, with Martin as Economic Advisor to the Prince. The Communists were basically anti-rich, and anti-American because the United States represented the height of capitalism, so Martin was viewed as an American "Capitalist Pig." Just as the Americans were vehemently anti-Communist, the Communists were passionately anti-American.

Grace was also the target of anti-Americanism, as the limelight was always on her. When she became Princess of Monaco, suddenly all the world was focused on the tiny Principality. Monaco experienced an economic boom after her arrival, tourism more than doubled, and many things began to change. Grace came to Monaco with many fresh ideas, in a country where things had more or less always been done the same way, and by the same people – for years, for generations, and in some cases, for centuries.

Princess Grace restored the national ballet company, inaugurated the Monaco Flora Festival, the International Television Festival, and the Garden Club. She ended the live pigeon shoot, and encouraged many of her husband's ideas and innovations. Grace appreciated the charm of old Europe and did not always personally agree with the modernization of Monaco, but she supported the Prince and his vision for his country. Grace was old-fashioned and conservative in many ways, and most of the projects that she championed reflected these values.

After the Grand Prix, Prince Rainier left on May 30 to join Grace and the children in Paris, where he would celebrate his fortieth birthday the following day. They then went to England to stay at Broadlands, the home of Lord Louis Mountbatten, Prince Charles's beloved great-uncle. Grace and Rainier were very fond of Lord Mountbatten, as he was of them, and they visited him quite often over the years. (He died as an unfortunate victim of an IRA bombing in 1979, and all of Britain mourned his loss.)

Grace sent me a postcard of the stately 60-room manor of Broadlands, where Queen Elizabeth had honeymooned: "We are spending a lovely week-end in this most beautiful setting - Our travels soon come to a close & I look forward to seeing you soon." I missed Grace terribly when she was away. Things were just not the same without her; it seemed like everything stood still, as if nothing were happening until she returned. Of course, there were always all kinds of events taking place in Monaco, but Grace brought life to everything with her glorious light. When she was gone, it was like days without sunshine. I could not wait to see her after she had been away for eight weeks.

Monaco – June 1963

Dearest Mum and Dad,

We had G & R in to dinner. G just went through the same thing that I did. It really laid her low as she had been trying for years. She is in good spirits though, as I think it happened for the best as she had the same scare as we did.

R. is going to pick up his new yacht soon (140 ft.), and we are waiting until he goes before leaving on vacation. Marty is so discouraged now as he is being attacked underhandedly again by the Monégasques and the Communists. He has put in three years here of hitting his head against a stone wall. Marty is looking around now and has had several offers – we shall see.

All our love from us all - Joan, Marty, Charles, Greg

Grace was about two months pregnant when she miscarried. I knew exactly how she felt, as I was still somewhat depressed and recovering from the loss of our third baby in March. We would both have been pregnant again at the same time, and we were both grieving at the same time. Although in those days, we just put on a brave face for the world and carried on as soon as we were physically strong enough. No one talked about such things, and we felt very blessed to have each other to confide in. We were both shaken, but very hopeful that we would be able to become pregnant again. We shared a great deal together, joys and sorrows, and I was grateful to have Grace there with me as a friend, and happy that I could be there for her when she needed the support, compassion, love and understanding that she gave to everyone else.

Several events at the Palace were canceled as Grace laid low for weeks while she recovered. I visited Grace at the Palace to play cards and sat by the pool with her. Of course, life went on as usual for the children, who were not aware that she was not feeling well. Rainier proceeded with their wonderful prize-giving by the Palace pool, marking the end of the school year. Charles received an underwater mask from the Prince for excellence in school, and a Waterman pen as an award for writing and application. The children were thrilled to receive their prizes, while Grace looked at her two beautiful children with love, pride and gratitude. Afterwards, we all swam and had a delightful lunch in the garden.

Monaco – August 5, 1963

Dear Mum and Dad,

Saturday evening we went to the Menuhin concert at the Palace. It was fairy-like in setting, and the music was beautiful. Afterwards G & R gave a reception in the Palace garden around the lighted swimming pool. The guests were interesting: Dame Margot Fonteyn, Maharani of Baroda and eighteen-year-old son – both wearing fantastic jewels, the Princess of Bourbon-Bavière, the Duchess of Acquarone, etc. It was a truly memorable evening. Grace wore a filmy, blue flowered chiffon long gown with floating kimono sleeves – she looked gorgeous. We shall be going to the Red Cross Ball – the most glittering one of the season. It should be fun.

All for now and all our love, Joan, Charles and Greg

We met outstanding people during our time in Monaco – many celebrities, heads of state, famous and infamous people. Over the years, we encountered a veritable parade of the world's royalty who visited the Palace. One of the most extraordinary people we had the opportunity of knowing was the Maharani of Baroda, whom I often mentioned in my letters.

The Maharani Sita Devi of Baroda, second wife of the Maharaja Pratap Singh Gaekwad, had a passion for jewelry, and an extraordinary collection of over three hundred priceless pieces, some dating back centuries to the Mughal Empire. These treasures included a famous "pearl carpet" measuring approximately 5 feet by 8 feet, made with over one million natural seed pearls and encrusted with 2,500 diamonds, as well as hundreds of rubies, sapphires and emeralds. (Sotheby's sold the Baroda Pearl Carpet in 2009 for $5.5 million.) There was a seven-strand necklace of enormous pearls (two strands of which were sold at Christies in 2007 for $7.1 million), and a three-tiered diamond necklace with the famous 128.48-carat Star of the South diamond, with the 76.5-carat English Dresden diamond as the pendant! (In 2005, the value of these two diamonds was estimated at $736,000 per carat!)

When they married in 1943, the Maharaja of Baroda was reported to be the eighth richest man in the world, and the second wealthiest Prince in India. (His fortune in 1939 was estimated to be $300 million – the equivalent of about $5 billion today.) The Maharani was known to have brought hundreds of magnificent gems from her husband's Crown Jewels to Paris and New York, in order to have Van Cleef & Arpels reset them into contemporary designs. The Maharaja bought a mansion for the Maharani in Monaco and moved many of the great treasures of Baroda there. In 1956, she became a citizen of Monaco after her marriage dissolved, and she was a lively part of the social scene.

In August of 1963, we went to the outdoor Sporting Club to attend the Gala of the Red Cross, which Grace presided over. The gala was honoring the one hundredth anniversary of the International Committee of the Red Cross, created by the Swiss, Jean Henri Dunant. The Geneva Convention of 1864 was also based on Dunant's ideals, and he was awarded the first Nobel Peace Prize in 1901.

The crème de la crème of society were at the Red Cross Ball in haute couture gowns, wearing exquisite jewels that surpassed anything that one could imagine. There were over nine hundred guests, who dined on lobster and caviar. It was a lovely summer night, but it became so warm dancing in long gowns and black tie that Grace and Rainier invited us afterward for a swim in the Palace pool, at two o'clock in the morning!

At the gala, Martin and I were seated at Grace and Rainier's table, with David Niven to my right, and the elegant Maharani of Baroda seated across from me. She always looked stunning in all of her brilliantly colored saris with exquisite designs woven with golden threads (she told me she had over four hundred of them), each worn with matching sets of elaborate jewels from the legendary Baroda collection, with the gemstones usually coordinating with the color of her sari.

David was always a spirited conversationalist, very charming and debonair, just as he was on screen. Over dinner, he and I were both admiring the shimmering necklace that the Maharani was wearing, which looked like an Egyptian collar, about eight inches wide – with matching earrings, bracelets and rings. Intrigued, David and I mused over the unusual cut of the large stones, which were sheared flat, giving them the appearance of mirrors. I wondered what kind of stones they were.

I turned to David and said, "What do you think that necklace is made of?" He said, "I don't know, but I'm not shy, I'm going to ask." Truly, he was never shy, and said, "Your Highness, might I comment on your exquisite necklace, and ask its history?" To which the Maharani replied, "Oh, yes, my dear, these are sheared diamonds. They are from the Fifteenth Century and have been in the Baroda collection since that time." There were three tiers of rectangular-shaped, highly polished diamonds, each about one inch long. They were smooth, flat and dazzling. David and I were utterly amazed; we had never seen anything like it before, and never would again.

On my left sat Maharajkumar Sayajirao Gaekwad, or "Princie," as he was called, the Maharani's handsome and somewhat spoiled son. For her, the sun rose and set on him. That evening, he was wearing a long Indian silver brocade tunic, studded down its entire length with real diamond "buttons." Princie was explaining to me that he had a blue one with sapphires, a red one with rubies, a green one with emeralds, etc. He told me that his mother was going to give him a huge diamond ring for his upcoming nineteenth birthday. He also said that he wished that earrings were in fashion for men as they had been in his grandfather's day. (If he were alive today, he would have had his wish – he died tragically on May 8, 1985, soon after his fortieth birthday. The Maharani was devastated and died four years later in Paris.) I remember the Maharani asking Prince Rainier if he could help Princie to become responsible and have a worthwhile goal in life. She must have realized what damage her over-indulgence had caused her precious boy, whom I last saw sitting alone aimlessly at the bar of the *Hôtel de Paris* in 1983.

The Maharani often invited us to her sumptuous dinners at the Empire Room or the Grill of the *Hôtel de Paris* in Monte Carlo. She seemed to like "the young American couple," and surprised us with gifts of jewelry: for me, earrings of gold set with diamonds, emeralds and rubies from Van Cleef & Arpels, and for Martin, platinum and diamond double-sided cufflinks from Cartier. Rumors were heard that in order to support her extravagant lifestyle, the Maharani was slowly selling her phenomenal jewelry collection.

Grace and Rainier decided to take a long holiday in Ireland for most of September, so Grace could really recuperate from her miscarriage. She wrote: "...We are staying on the most beautiful property outside of Dublin, and I am having the first good rest since Switzerland - It is marvelous - Everything is so green and lush, and even though it rains nearly every day we do not mind - The rain here of course is like a soft mist compared to our downfalls... The children are riding, and the Prince plays golf every day - I do a little of both - Today however I am off to Dublin for some shopping... Fondest thoughts to all - Love - Grace –"

According to Rainier, "When the Princess and I are away together, we try to behave as much like ordinary people as possible." Grace and Rainier both enjoyed going shopping as a couple, but it was so difficult with the paparazzi following them everywhere. They could really only go out together when they were in very big cities, like London, Paris or New York, where they could be a little more incognito amongst the crowds of people. If the Prince and Princess were together, everyone recognized them. However, when they were apart, people often came up to them, saying, "You look just like Prince Rayneer," or "You remind me of Grace Kelly," but no one ever thought it was really them!

Grace told me that she had casually invited the Maharani of Baroda to stop in and visit them at the house they had rented in Ireland for their holiday. The Maharani arrived with her maid, bodyguard and chauffeur, who were not expected. Grace said she was beside herself because the house was not very large, so they had to do quite a lot of shuffling around in order to accommodate not one, but four people. In fact, Albert and Caroline had to give up their own bedrooms for the entourage! The Maharajas of old were used to traveling with hundreds of servants, so I imagine the Maharani thought nothing of bringing only three!

Monaco – September 6, 1963

Dearest Mum and Dad,

Happily, Marty and I are getting along better than ever after almost ten years of marriage, which is hard to believe. Marty just showed me last night the beautiful diamond he brought back. He has been keeping it a secret, and I am thrilled with it. He really is sweet to me, bringing the gorgeous mink wrap (even Grace thought it beautiful).

R. wants Marty to stay on – he will be lost without him. We received a lovely card from him from Ireland, where they are vacationing peacefully after their cruise was thwarted with the burning of the engine room in his new yacht. Luckily he had not taken possession of it, but they are disappointed as they cannot have it for five months. If I were they, I do not think I would be too happy to own it after such a disaster had transpired. One would be uneasy.

I shall let you know our future plans as soon as we have decided what to do. We feel a little uncertain, but I know that Marty always comes through.

Loads of love from us all, Joan, Marty, Charles, Gregory

Rainier was looking forward to picking up his new 140-foot yacht in August, but it caught fire in the shipyard in Holland where it was being built. I don't think Grace was too unhappy not to have the yacht right away, as she easily became seasick. I'm sure that she was quite relieved to spend her holiday on terra firma, in her lovely ancestral homeland of Ireland. Grace visited the cottage of her ancestors there (which she later purchased in 1973). She felt very proud of her heritage, and the Emerald Isle was always close to her heart.

The Irish people also loved Grace. Everyone stared at the Princess wherever she went – both men and women admired her beauty and radiance. On the street, she was so revered that there would often be an absolute horde of admirers surrounding her car, but rather than being concerned for her own welfare, she was always worried about those who might be injured in the throng. This happened everywhere she went in the world, but was particularly frightening in Ireland where the adoring crowd of thousands swarmed her motorcade, and began to rock her official car. While it was evident that they were doing so out of love for her, Grace was very claustrophobic and found this to be quite terrifying.

On a trip to Genoa, Italy, the crush of the crowd was so intense that they actually pushed the side of her car in! People would touch her and rip buttons off her clothing as souvenirs! This kind of attention from the public and the media only seemed to get worse as the years passed, and Grace became more frightened in crowds over time, but she never let it show. She was far more concerned about the dangers that this posed for her children than for herself.

Monaco – October 1, 1963

Dearest Mum and Dad,

Well, we have some news now about where we shall be. When Marty told the Prince that he was really leaving, the Prince absolutely blanched and begged Marty to stay on here for one year or two. We did not need much persuading, I must say, as we love it here and are very fond of G & R, and we were very happy to accept. Also, the salary here with apartment provided is about double what private industry is offering. Anyway, we are delighted and shall plan to come to see you in February while G & R are in Switzerland.

We have seen G & R often since their return. I played golf with Grace – badly, but it was great fun and we enjoyed it. Then we all had dinner together at Rocagel. Marty plays golf with R. three times a week. He will never again have a job like this one! They have been very sweet to us, and we do enjoy their company. They will be leaving for Paris soon for the month of October, and Charles will begin school at the Palace in November. Greg went to the Palace last week and adored Albie and Caroline, which is quite a change, as he used to cry and hang onto my skirt from the moment we arrived.

All for now – Loads of love, Joan, Marty, Charles, Greg

Martin worked in the long wing of the Palace, close to the separate offices belonging to Princess Grace and Prince Rainier. If Martin did not have a meeting at lunchtime, he would leave his office and pick up Charles, who was at school at the Palace, to bring him home for lunch every day. In France, lunch is a family affair and is the big meal of the day, often lasting two hours. After eating, the children would have a nap, and then Charles would return to the Palace with his father for the afternoon.

Princess Grace enjoyed this European custom of long lunches with the family, which she spoke about in the book *Another Way of Living*. On the day that she was being interviewed for the book, I had been having tea with Grace in her private apartment, when she suddenly remembered something important that she had to do. As we both got up to leave, she said, "Joan, at 5 p.m. I'm expecting an author, John Bainbridge, who is writing about Americans living abroad. If I should be delayed, would you please entertain him until I return?"

I stayed in their apartment and waited, as Grace had requested. After a while, one of the footmen knocked on the door, and escorted Mr. Bainbridge into the sitting room. We chatted amiably about the Prince's extensive menagerie, as he was fixated on a floor-to-ceiling cage housing a very active monkey with large bug-eyes and a very long tail. Grace soon returned, apologizing for being late. With her quiet elegance and easy manner, she immediately put her guest at ease. I withdrew at this point, leaving Grace to do the two-hour interview about living in Europe, in which she said, "One thing I enjoy is that people here take the time to live in a pleasant way. They are not as rushed, not as hurried, as they are in the United States. For example, there is the midday meal, which the family takes together. This is a custom that I think is very pleasant. It is one part of taking time to enjoy the days."

There is a beautiful rhythm to life in Europe that focuses on the important things: family, friends and food! Every morning in Monaco, I walked along the Port to the open-air market to buy fresh food for the day's meal, as is the custom in France, and in many parts of Europe. Even though I had help, I enjoyed getting out and talking to people, finding it to be a cheery way to start the day. The Condamine market has been in existence since 1880, and you can still hear the locals speak in their unique Monégasque language. Over the years, I developed a very good rapport with the merchants. I had my favorites, and they would always greet me enthusiastically with a smile, saying, "*Ah, Bonjour Madame*," making sure to give me the best produce. They knew who I was, and whom Martin was, and I'm sure that they thought I was little crazy doing my own shopping, but they chalked it up to me being "American."

Monaco – November 15, 1963

Dearest Mum and Dad,

Grace has been very sweet since she returned [from Paris], and we have had nice talks together. I gave her a history of the theater for her birthday – a lovely volume – which mentions her uncle, George Kelly, the playwright.

Monday evening, the "season" began with dinner and a movie at the Palace. King Michael of Romania and the Queen were there, as well as the Princess Royal of Denmark. We saw the film "The V.I.P.s" with Liz Taylor and Burton.

Tuesday was Grace's birthday, which we celebrated at Madame Banac's apartment – as we do every year. She has a fantastic spread with caviar and vodka, smoked salmon, pheasant in gelée, the "loup" fish and mayonnaise, cake, champagne, etc. We always play "charades" or another game, and it really is not bad. She has a knack of finding amusing things. It was great fun.

Always, Joan

The November celebrations for Monaco's National Holiday were festive as always, especially since everyone was in a wonderful mood, because Monaco had won the soccer game against Bordeaux. Everyone was filled with pride and joy for the Monégasques and their Sovereigns. It was quite romantic and picturesque, and I was so glad to have the opportunity to experience it again.

However, that joy vanished three days later when John F. Kennedy was assassinated on that fateful day of November 22, 1963. We were all devastated, along with the rest of the world. Earlier that day, Grace and I had taken Caroline, Albert, and Charles to an outdoor traveling carnival located at the Port. It was a rare occasion, and the children were so excited with the various games. They were too young for the rifle shoot, so Grace picked up one of the rifles, attempting to win stuffed animals for the young ones. I cannot remember if she won anything, but a photographer took her picture with the rifle, and the following day headlines in the paper blazed, "Grace having fun after learning about assassination."

Needless to say, Grace was hurt and horrified when she saw the photo and its appalling caption. Innocent fun was being twisted to sell papers, without concern for her feelings. In fact, with the time difference between Europe and the U.S., the photo was taken hours before the tragic incident occurred. When we all heard about it, we were in deep shock. Grace, who knew him personally, took the news very badly. She was in mourning for several days, saying that it felt as though she had lost a member of her own family. On the day of his funeral in Washington, November 25, Grace held a funeral service at the Cathedral of Monaco in JFK's memory. A few months later, Avenue President J. F. Kennedy was named in his honor along the Port Hercule.

After several weeks of global mourning for the loss of one of history's greatest leaders, life started to get back to normal, although the world had profoundly changed. The children were too young to fully understand what had happened, and life had to continue for them, preserving their innocence.

We had a birthday party for Charles at our apartment, which included a few other children from Monaco, and mothers who came in for tea. Grace was very attentive to all the children, making sure that napkins were tucked under chins, so ice cream would not get on their clothes. Grace recorded everything for posterity with her movie camera, and I took photographs.

Grace and I continued our autumn routine of ballet classes twice a week and went Christmas shopping together in Nice. We enjoyed the annual traditions, including Midnight Mass in the Palatine Chapel on Christmas Eve followed by *Réveillon* with Grace and Rainier, and Christmas Day with the U.S. sailors at the Palace, where we all played foosball! Then on December 26, Grace took me in her Rolls Royce to the *Hôtel de Paris* for a relaxing sauna and swim in the luxurious hotel pool, followed by dinner at the Palace.

The end of 1963 came with much relief for all of us, as it had been a year filled with tremendous joys and sorrows personally and globally. It also finally marked the end of the Franco-Monégasque imbroglio, making it possible for Martin to salvage most of the economic development program, which had been his major responsibility as Privy Counselor. This would eventually allow us to leave with a feeling of satisfaction and accomplishment.

During the eighteen months of crisis, we drank deeply from the cup of disappointments and frustrations. It is ironic that De Gaulle, whom Martin had admired so much, had twice caused him distress: once when his Princeton professor dismissed his thesis predicting that De Gaulle would return to power; and the second time when De Gaulle wielded that power to repeatedly demand Martin's dismissal.

I was so happy that Martin renewed his contract to work with the Prince for one more year. I knew our time in the Principality was limited. However, I loved every minute of living in Monaco and treasured my dear friendship with Grace. I was very much looking forward to all the wonderful times we would still have together in the year ahead.

DAYS OF GRATITUDE

Monaco – January 3, 1964

Dearest Mum and Dad,

We had a delightful Christmas Eve at the Palace, starting at midnight with Mass, followed by a distribution of gifts (Martin received some golf balls in a leather cigarette case from R., and Grace gave me an Irish linen luncheon set. The boys received a play school desk set, and Greg, a marvelous cowboy costume). Then we had a buffet supper consisting of cold salmon, ham stuffed with a foie gras mousse, jellied eggs, roast beef, champagne, caviar and vodka, cake (Christmas log). We talked and then went home at about 4 a.m.

We have entertained 6 sailors who were in port here on the U.S. submarines, and they really appreciated a taste of home. We had Christmas lunch, and I had no help that day. It was fun, and after, we went to the Palace – this is something that the sailors will never forget. They were thrilled and awed by the grandeur of the building, for some of them had never been away from their farms before joining the Navy.

New Year's we went to the Metropole Hotel and afterwards joined G & R to wish them a happy New Year. They were very gay and sweet to us.

Last night for Marty's birthday we went to Rocagel for dinner with G & R and stayed until 3:30 a.m. playing a game called "Diplomacy." Grace had made a cake for Marty – something she would not do for everyone! It was a lovely evening. Must dash – shall write in a few days.

Loads of love, Joan

Every year, a ceremony called *Réveillon* took place at the Palace, celebrating Christmas Eve. It was an intimate gathering that began with midnight Mass in the private chapel of Saint Jean-Baptiste at the Palace, followed by a buffet in the large formal dining rooms at 1 a.m. Then we would be presented with gifts. It was a warm, friendly, and delightful occasion that usually lasted until about four o'clock in the morning.

At Christmastime, the ships of the U.S. Sixth Fleet stationed in the Mediterranean would pull into port for shore leave. After Grace came to Monaco, she began a yearly tradition of inviting several of the sailors to the Palace for Christmas dinner. We followed her lead and also invited a few sailors to our apartment, which they really appreciated. We took some of them bowling at the *Café de Paris* in Monte Carlo on the *Place du Casino*, and then offered them a traditional home-cooked holiday meal. After dinner, we all gathered at the Palace for gift-giving. Thinking of others was second nature to Grace, and I am sure she empathized with the sailors' homesickness, being so far away from the United States.

We spent Martin's birthday at Rocagel, and my birthday at the Palace for dinner and a movie. Winter was the season for many of the major balls and gala events. We again attended the annual *Gala des Colonies Étrangères* at the Sporting Club, and the fourth annual International Television Festival. There were also several dinners at the Palace throughout the month of January. Then Grace came over to our apartment with her dog, Gamma, so they could say goodbye to us (and our dog, Jester), as we would not be seeing each other for two months.

While Grace and her family went to Switzerland, we took our boys on a whirlwind tour from February 2 to March 30, scouting for places to move to at the end of the year. We went to Spain, Portugal, Guadeloupe, Jamaica, Miami, Mexico City, Acapulco, La Jolla to see Martin's parents, Las Vegas, San Francisco, then to Victoria to visit my parents. We sent postcards to Grace and Rainier along our journey, and they wrote letters and cards to us at my parents' home. I stayed in Victoria for three weeks, enrolling the boys in school there so they could keep up with their studies, while Martin went to Chicago and New York on business.

When Martin left the United States Foreign Service in 1960, he had been assured that he would be welcomed back to the U.S. Diplomatic Corps. During our trip to North America, Martin applied to be reinstated for the beginning of 1965, after his new contract with the Prince would expire. He had to go through security clearance again, and then he was called to Washington, D.C., for an interview in March of 1964.

At that time, Henry Cabot Lodge Jr. was U.S. Ambassador to the Republic of Vietnam; he wanted to avoid war, establish an economic prosperity program, and create stability in the region. Ambassador Lodge had somehow seen Martin's file and was intrigued because Martin spoke Chinese and French, was economic advisor to the Prince of Monaco, and he had taken part in negotiating the Franco-American Treaty of Establishment. Ambassador Lodge wanted Martin, but he wanted him to be posted to South Vietnam right away.

Martin was told that because of the growing unrest in the region, dependents were being withdrawn from Vietnam, so he would not be able to take his family with him to Saigon, as it was considered a "danger post." The head of personnel at the State Department told Martin that his orders were written, and that he could either go to Vietnam immediately, or there would be little chance of him ever being reinstated in the Foreign Service again. He was also told that he would be returning to the same rank and pay grade as when he left, without taking into account the work that he had been doing for Prince Rainier for three and a half years. The State Department had backed Martin into a corner, giving him an unfair ultimatum, as he had already committed to fulfill his contract with the Prince for nine more months. We returned to Monaco wondering what the future would hold for our family.

Monaco – April 3, 1964

Dearest Mum and Dad,

The night we arrived was the British-American Hospital Ball, and we were at Grace and Rainier's table. They were pleased to see me, and I managed to hold up well but collapsed the next day and slept most of the time.

Charles is in advance in school, and in his examination today he did very well. There will be no school for three more weeks (too bad) as G & R are going to Lisbon on their yacht with the children and governess. It is a good thing that Charles is bright! I shall continue his English reading in the meantime.

All our love from all of us, Joan, Marty, Charles, Gregory

We arrived back in Monaco on March 30, just in time to attend a gala ball that was held at the *Hôtel de Paris* to raise funds for the British-American Hospital Queen Victoria Memorial in Nice. The hospital was opened in 1906 for

English speaking patients – British and American – who were living on the Côte d'Azur. The hospital did not receive any government subsidies and was funded entirely by charitable donations. Wc were seated at the head table with Their Serene Highnesses. Princess Grace lent her support to this charity because there were many expats living in the South of France who benefitted from medical services provided in English. Winston Churchill, who had spent a great deal of time in Monaco (in a magnificent suite named after him at the *Hôtel de Paris*), sent a message in honor of the event: "The work done by the British-American Hospital is most worthy of our support, and I send the Annual Ball Committee my very good wishes in their commendable endeavors to raise funds. I hope you all have a happy evening."

The next night we went to the Palace for dinner and to see the Marlon Brando movie, *The Ugly American* (which, considering the rampant anti-Americanism that surrounded us, was a rather unfortunate title!). I gave Grace a memorial Kennedy half-dollar that I got for her in the U.S., and she was very touched. Rainier left the following day to finally pick up his new yacht in Holland after the engine fire delayed its completion by several months.

Grace invited us to the Palace while Rainier was away, and we enjoyed catching up as we had missed each other very much. I was sad to let her know that Martin had made up his mind that he would definitely be leaving at the end of the year, which he had already told the Prince. The constant attacks from the press and from the Monégasque government were making it too difficult to continue living in such a small place, even though we still did not know where we would go.

On April 3, Martin and I celebrated our tenth anniversary by going to the Cabaret at the Casino, where we enjoyed a romantic evening of dinner and dancing. He gave me red roses, and a wonderful surprise: a magnificent large diamond marguerite ring, by the prestigious Monte Carlo jeweler, Balanche, designed from the diamond cufflinks that the Maharani of Baroda had given him. I wore it every day thereafter.

Princess Grace flew to Lisbon on April 10 with the children and their nanny to meet Prince Rainier aboard his new yacht. On April 19, they celebrated their eighth wedding anniversary, but had to be back in the Principality for that day in order to welcome the U.S. Ambassador to France, who was making his first official visit to Nice and to Monaco. The Ambassador enjoyed a luncheon at the Palace in his honor, followed by a tour of the Grand Apartments, then a game of golf with Prince Rainier and Martin. Rainier returned to the yacht soon afterward, and on April 30, the Prince proudly sailed into Monaco's harbor aboard the *ALBECARO II*, named for their children.

Monaco – May 4, 1964

Dearest Mum and Dad,

I have not written for a while, I guess – Please do excuse me as we have been unbelievably busy with social obligations...

I have also had to teach Charles every morning for three weeks, which takes much time. Fortunately G & R have just arrived with the lovely new yacht, so school will begin again. Then I have had many sick calls on older people, Prince Pierre, Marquise de Polignac, etc., who are getting a bit better, plus the American Ambassador's visit, the Cannes Film Festival. Our heads are spinning! Marty is beginning to chafe, as he suddenly becomes anti-social after he has gone out too much. I rarely get tired of it!

Yesterday, we went to Rocagel and had a delightful picnic-style lunch. R. is a little upset at Marty's decision but is warm to us. Tonight we go to the Palace to dinner and a movie "Irma la Douce." At the end of the week we leave for the weekend at Dijon in Burgundy to have Marty made a Chevalier of the Tastevin Society – a great honor in France. One drinks and tastes fabulous wines and dines extraordinarily, it seems.

Loads of love from us all, Joan, Charles & Greg

We had a delightful picnic lunch at Rocagel with Grace and Rainier, Mrs. Kelly, and a few friends. We had hot dogs, pizza, baked beans, and potato salad – a real "American" picnic. Lunch also included the Monégasque specialty *pissaladière*, which was reminiscent of our first picnic at Rocagel, when it was nothing but a barren rocky landscape.

The road to Rocagel high above Monaco was a treacherous one with few guardrails. It was very steep and fraught with seemingly unending hairpin curves. When I drove alone, I was sometimes harassed by impatient truck drivers, who would tailgate and repeatedly honk at me. They were in a hurry to deliver soil for the Monaco land fills, coming from the tunnels that were being dug out in the hills above. I suppose they must have been paid by the load, because they often drove very fast and rather recklessly. I always had trepidations when I drove my children up to Rocagel to play with Albert and

Caroline, and was grateful to regain our cozy apartment after having negotiated the tortuous route. Grace also disliked driving on this road.

Grace was always thoughtful to include us in many of their family activities. On May 27, seven-year-old Princess Caroline had her First Communion at the Palace Chapel, which was beautifully ornate, yet simple and peaceful. It was a moving ceremony attended by all of the Prince's family, as well as nannies and valets. Caroline wore a short white organdy dress with a veil. She handed out cards and *dragées* (candy coated almonds) in a white box with her double-C monogram under a golden crown, with the date commemorating the occasion. Grace was so proud of Caroline, who handled herself like a true Princess and a very poised young lady.

After the ceremony, there was a champagne reception in the garden with hors d'oeuvres. Quinto and Maria, the Italian couple who looked after Rocagel, had been invited as guests but looked somewhat uncomfortable, standing by themselves way in the background. Caroline rushed up to them and said, "Oh, you can't stand here by yourselves, you must come and have something to eat," so she took them both by the hand and led them to the buffet.

I'm very touched every time I think of Caroline's sensitivity at such a tender age. She was the true daughter of both her parents and remains so today, having blossomed into an enchanting woman who is her own person at all times, whether at social occasions, in intellectual discussions, or with her gorgeous children. Grace imbued Caroline and Albert with her sense of caring and kindness, and Rainier instilled thoughtfulness and strength in them.

May 31 marked Prince Rainier's forty-first birthday, which we celebrated together the night before. There was a wonderful buffet supper at the Palace, with caviar canapés in the shape of hearts, smoked salmon canapés, cold lamb, chicken salad, cheese, strawberries and ice cream. It was a warm, casual and fun evening with a screening of the hilarious Peter Sellers film, *The Pink Panther*. Martin gave the Prince a handsome crocodile cigar case, which he loved. He sent a thank-you note in which he had drawn amusing cartoon characters with cigars, holding the cigar case. I usually gave him birthday cards that were quite cheeky, knowing that he appreciated this sort of humor. He wrote to Martin: "Please tell your dear wife how much I did laugh when opening her birthday card."

The day after Rainier's birthday, Grace and Rainier left for Paris. We were seeing a little less of them at that time, partly because of our mutual travel schedules, but also because Rainier was a bit hurt that Martin was leaving him. He kept trying to devise new incentives and opportunities for Martin to stay, raising his salary significantly, but there was little more for Martin to do, as they had far surpassed all their goals. Rainier wrote from Paris: "Now as to the future!! You are, or have the intention of leaving my service... I quite understand that... the French and this local 'Anti-American' feeling making it difficult, if not unbearable for you... Then there is your career which is very important, and I am sure that it will be more brilliant on your own than tied up with and in my service in the 'lousy' atmosphere that is heated in Monaco..."

No one had ever left the Prince's service of his or her own accord, and it took Prince Rainier a long time to finally accept that Martin would be leaving at the end of the year (sadly, I had to accept it as well). The Prince considered Martin a friend. Grace understood that Martin was still very young and ambitious at just thirty-three years of age, and there was nowhere for him to go in his career in the Principality – he was second only to the Prince! We had many wonderful friends in diplomatic and aristocratic circles and enjoyed meeting so many fascinating people in Monaco. Life could not possibly ever be the same for us anywhere else.

However, Martin was still being blamed for everything, and the widespread resentment continued to escalate after the crisis with France was over. Even though MEDEC had been a phenomenal economic success for Monaco, it was called a fiasco by the press because the very idea of it triggered the ire of De Gaulle. Martin was often facetiously called the "Boy Scout," with caricatures appearing in the press of him in a Boy Scout uniform, wearing his distinctive glasses. Martin had, in fact, been a proud Eagle Scout as a young boy. In America, being called a "Boy Scout" meant that you were a good and honest person; the French meant it to be anything but that. Fortunately, we had Grace and Rainier standing by our side as loyal friends.

For this very reason, Martin did not want to trouble the Prince anymore, because Prince Rainier continued to take a lot of heat from the French, and from his own people, for keeping him in the Principality. Martin felt that he and the Prince were still on very good terms, both in friendship and in their working relationship, but he really could not continue his career in Monaco.

The question still remained, where would we go? I tried not to think about it, because the idea of leaving Grace made me terribly sad and depressed. I could not bear the thought that I would no longer be near her. I just focused on trying to enjoy our last six months in Monaco as much as possible.

Once Rainier finally accepted Martin's resignation, he put his hurt feelings aside and made the most of our friendship. We were invited to the Palace very often from then on, and we had lots of long talks and casual evenings as friends with Grace and Rainier, in their private apartments, and in ours. We had cocktails on Rainier's yacht, lounged by the Palace pool and dined at Rocagel. We went bowling with them and watched wonderful movies at the Palace, such as Peter Sellers in *Dr. Strangelove*, and the James Bond film, *To Russia with Love*. Even our meals at the Palace became more relaxed, with tomato soup, fried eggs on toast, cheese, and strawberries with cream. Our friendship felt like family. We were invited to the Palace to celebrate the wedding anniversary of Grace's sister, Lizanne, and her husband Don. Then, we had them all over to dinner at our home – with "Uncle Rainier" entertaining our children.

Monaco – June 19, 1964

Dearest Mum and Dad,

Last night we had Grace and Rainier in to dinner with Grace's sister and brother-in-law, Don and Lizanne Levine. Greg got up enough courage to ask the Prince to play clown for him by banging his nose into the door and pretending to be hurt. He is so good with children, and they seemed to enjoy themselves, although Grace had a terrible attack of hay fever. She was exhausted from having sneezed for two hours that afternoon! R. is pleased with Martin again so all is well.

We are still wondering what we shall be doing come December. There is a freeze on governmental hiring – Johnson's economy drive – but Marty is looking into business offers as well, so he will not be left holding the bag.

Charles is having instruction in swimming at the Palace, and soon he will be able to dive. In the last week, Charles has been reading fluently and so well that he can read bedtime stories to Greg! All for now. Charles and Greg send loads and loads of love to Grammy and Grandpa.

All our love, Joan and Marty

The Prince was wonderful with children and was a very loving and caring father. Albert and Caroline learned English and French simultaneously, speaking French to their father and English to their mother. The Prince spoke beautiful English, having had an English nanny and being educated at Stowe and Summer Fields in England, but French was his true language, and one had to speak French with him to know his real charm and personality. Grace worked diligently to learn to speak French fluently, which she spoke to dignitaries and to the staff, but she was most comfortable in English, which she spoke with friends, with her children, and with the Prince. In later years, the children also became fluent in Spanish, Italian and German. Multilingualism is so important in their position of entertaining foreign leaders and royalty.

It was amusing to hear our children playing with Albert and Caroline, as their conversations would alternate between French and English, often within the same sentence! I found this amazing, as I was raised uniquely speaking English, with a smattering of French, growing up in Canada; however, I ultimately became fluent in French to the point of earning a teaching certificate when I was in Strasbourg. Charles was totally bilingual and to this day is often taken for a Frenchman. Gregory spoke French first, which turned into an amusing mixture of both French and English, until he finally sorted both languages out individually.

Our boys took swimming lessons with Albert and Caroline at the Palace pool, and the Prince played with the children as they all splashed around. For the school prize-giving that year, Prince Rainier gave the boys plastic swords, so there was no end of dueling going on that summer. It was going to be very difficult to tell the boys that they would soon be leaving their dear friends Albie and Caroline, and I was not looking forward to the heartbreak.

Returning from Bahamas – August 4, 1964

Dearest Mum and Dad,

I am writing this on board the Pan Am plane. Marty left for the Bahamas a week before and then telephoned me to fly out immediately, as he wanted my opinion and could not explain adequately from a distance about Freeport and the Grand Bahama Island. So off I dashed, leaving the boys with cousin Penelope, who had arrived the day before. I took her to the Hôtel de Paris for a delicious dinner, which thrilled her, and then we went to the concert at the Palace in the Courtyard and were invited afterwards by G & R to a reception in the Palace Gardens around the pool. Penelope was so pleased, and Grace said she would ask her and the boys up to Rocagel while I was gone, which was sweet of her.

Grand Bahama Island is in full development and was the dream of a man named Wallace Groves, a charming man, to build a city out of nothing. There is the most luxurious hotel I have ever seen there, plus a golf course, casino (the only one near Florida) and four new 500-room hotels being built. Mr. Groves,

the President of the Bahama Port Authority, the holding company in charge of
the development of the Island ($200 million has already been invested!), liked
Marty and offered him the job of Vice President and Assistant to the President
of this company at $36,000 a year plus transportation of effects and passage (he
also paid Marty's and my trip this time, $2500 – so he must be pleased with
Marty's potential, and I am sure he will do a wonderful job). It is a great
challenge in any case, and island life with wonderful swimming, sandy beaches,
tennis, boating, and an excellent private English school will do the boys good
and give them a chance to develop and be less confined. The people there –
mostly English, Canadians and Trinidadians, are pioneer-minded and are fired
with a desire to create. We shall be building our own house, which will be great
fun and we hope it will be ready by January 15th when we arrive.

Loads of love from us all, Joan

The Freeport Grand Bahama Port Authority had written to Martin to get a
copy of the brochure, "Monaco Can Help Your Company." They were so
impressed with it that they sent a man over to Monaco to meet Martin, wanting
him to help promote the expansion, development and economic growth of Grand
Bahama Island, as he had done for Monaco. Martin decided to go to Freeport in
July to look into the opportunity, and he liked the prospects so much that he
called and asked me to get on a plane immediately to see Freeport for myself.
The President of the Port Authority, Wallace Groves, offered us two lots of land
to build a house on, and provided numerous incentives, including a very high
salary at that time.

Wallace Groves had acquired over 100,000 acres on Grand Bahama Island
in the late 1940s, and was the major stakeholder in the Grand Bahama Port
Authority. He also received large land grants from the Bahamian government in
1955, and agreed to build schools, roads, hospitals and utilities, as well as
develop commercial and industrial enterprises on the island, in exchange for tax
concessions. Freeport is a free trade zone where businesses pay no taxes, helping
it to become the second major city in the Bahamas after Nassau.

Martin accepted the position of Vice President, Assistant to the President,
and Director of the Grand Bahama Port Authority, Ltd. We would be moving to
Grand Bahama Island, the fourth largest island of the Bahamas, about sixty miles
due east of Palm Beach, Florida. This island was enjoying an economic boom
that defied description, and the Grand Bahama Port Authority was both a quasi-
governmental body and an active business organization, with a controlling or

financial interest in most of the major business ventures. The Port Authority owned the "airport" (which at that time was nothing more than a thatch roof hut!) and the exclusive gambling rights on the island. Just nine years previously, there were only four fishing villages and a lumber camp there; by 1964, with over $200 million already invested, Freeport was becoming a thriving community with excellent schools and medical facilities, and was developing into an important resort area.

Finally, we could relax and enjoy the rest of our time in Monaco, knowing where we would be moving to at the end of the year. It was a relief to have all of the uncertainty coming to an end, and we were determined to make the most of the time that we had left. There were still many galas and social functions to attend, and many wonderful moments to look forward to spending with Grace and Rainier before we were to depart in December.

We arrived back in Monaco in time to attend an excellent concert of Brahms and Strauss in the Palace courtyard on August 4. The National Opera Orchestra of Monte-Carlo played on a stage surrounded by the horseshoe-shaped staircase, and was superbly conducted by the world-renowned Zubin Mehta, who was quite young at that time. The outstanding soloist was one of the top Spanish guitarists, Narciso Yepes, who created the 10-string guitar.

The next day, we witnessed a very poised young Caroline carrying out her first official function for the Monégasque Red Cross, while her mother beamed with pride. With a crowd of officials and dignitaries looking on, Princess Caroline, in a dainty white dress and matching hairband, gracefully unveiled a plaque inaugurating the Avenue Henri Dunant, named for the founder of the Red Cross.

The following day was the Red Cross Gala, *the* Ball of the year, which attracted the well-known and well-heeled people of the world under the auspices of its famous President, Princess Grace of Monaco. The decor on the outdoor terrace of the Summer Sporting Club was breathtaking in its splendor, with a double tier of twenty Corinthian columns that were somehow superimposed on the front of the building by designer André Levasseur. These elegant columns were draped with a gauze-like glittering material, forming arabesque arches invoking the theme of *A Thousand and One Nights*. Twenty tons of water was re-circulated among various fountains, with jets of water and cascades adding to the harmonious ambiance.

At 10 p.m., the Prince and Princess arrived and were presented with an antique box and a miniature sedan chair containing large bottles of Christian Dior perfume and eau de toilette. Grace was elegant in a formal gown of embroidery and white lace, with her beautiful blonde hair in an upsweep entwined with jewels. We were seated at the table of the head of the SBM. Also seated with us was the much in-vogue Spanish portraitist, Alejo Vidal-Quadras; Howell Conant, official photographer for the Prince and Princess; Marie Bell of the Comédie Française; Danielle Fugère, prima ballerina of the Paris Opera; and the Jahlans.

Monsieur Jahlan bought several tickets to the charity raffle and put a stack of them in my hand. After a sumptuous dinner, the floorshow was scheduled to commence with the famous "Bluebell Girls" – like the showgirls at the Lido, in stunning costumes with outstanding headdresses. Suddenly, it began to pour, and hundreds of guests rushed inside to save their haute couture eveningwear. (The Summer Sporting Club has since been rebuilt on land reclaimed from the sea, with a retractable roof to combat the unpredictability of the weather.)

The Prince's table, plus other official tables including ours, remained seated outside on the terrace in the rain. We stayed to watch the feature presentation: Eleanor Powell, who was sometimes dubbed the female Fred Astaire. Partnered that night with Rip Taylor, she gamely carried on with a mesmerizing tap-dancing performance in the torrential rain, despite the hazards of slipping on the wet floor. Her tap-dancing mat and costume were ruined, but she received a standing ovation. As it continued to rain even harder, the remaining guests on the outdoor terrace finally dashed inside, with tablecloths covering their heads and dresses.

Once inside, we heard numbers being called for the raffle; I peeled apart the sodden tickets in my hand, and much to my surprise, I had a winning ticket! I won a sitting for a charcoal portrait by Vidal-Quadras! He was a very charming and attractive gentleman, who immortalized some of the most illustrious people on the planet. His clients have included the royal families of Spain, Denmark, Italy, Greece, Luxembourg, Austria, Jordan, Iran, along with the Monégasque sovereigns and their children, exalting the "incomparable beauty of the Princess of Monaco." He was quoted as saying, "I consider Grace Kelly as one of the purest faces I have ever studied." He also did portraits of iconic celebrities such as Marilyn Monroe, Audrey Hepburn, Maria Callas, and Yul Brynner. I was thrilled with the portrait he did of me, which only required two sittings. It has always hung in my living room, serving as a constant reminder of this extraordinary and marvelous time in my life.

The dazzling necklace and bracelet in gold, set with rubies and diamonds (red and white are the colors of Monaco, and the Red Cross) that was donated by Van Cleef & Arpels, was won by the enormously wealthy Duchess of Arenberg.

She had some of the most exquisite jewels I had ever seen, and she generously donated this jeweled set that she had won back to the Monégasque Red Cross, to raise money for humanitarian causes in a future raffle.

Monaco – August 24, 1964

Dearest Mum and Dad,

The new job sounds fabulous. We shall be leaving here on December 22nd on board the CONSTITUTION for New York. The thought of leaving Monaco is a sad one, and G & R are so sorry to see us go. They have promised to visit us on Grand Bahama Island, and Rainier said that we might never get rid of him!

We attended the famous Red Cross Gala Ball, where I have never seen such gorgeous dresses and jewels in my life! We have met fascinating people lately – Greta Garbo, Begum Aga Khan, Greer Garson, Zsa Zsa Gabor, John Spencer Churchill, Prince Orsini, Princess Rachevsky, Princess Chervachidzé, Zubin Mehta, etc. The Maharani of Baroda invited us to a gala last week, where she wore the most extraordinary pearls with diamonds the size of matchboxes.

Grace is expecting in February, and she is delighted. I am keeping Caroline's adored poodle "Lindy" for the six weeks they will be on board their yacht. The other night Lindy ran away from our nurse, which caused us to spend a tormented, wretched night and day until she was found. [Even the police were out in a frenzy looking for the royal poodle!] It is a terrible responsibility to keep someone's pet, but all's well...

We all send loads of love, Marty, Joan, Charles, Greg

The following week, we attended the "Tropical Ball," with six hundred elegant guests. André Levasseur designed the wondrous décor that carried you into the tropics, with an oasis of palm trees thirty-feet-high, tropical ferns, banana trees complete with live perching parrots, and other colorfully plumed exotic birds. Martin and I joked that this seemed a fitting preview of the scenery we would soon have in the Bahamas! An immense red drapery covered in ferns and roses in various shades descended the outer facade of the Sporting Club, while blazing torches danced in the sea breeze, and fountains with changing colors played gracefully. It was amazing.

The Maharani of Baroda hosted two tables of twelve people; I was seated at one of them with her son Princie, Princess Chervachidzé of Russia, and Prince

Orsini of Italy. There were gorgeous centerpieces of exotic flowers on each table. The orchestra of Aimé Barelli wore flower leis and played the rhythms of mambos, sambas, rhumbas and cha chas. This was followed by Latin dancing performed by the statuesque Bluebell Girls, wearing multi-colored tiered costumes, with the feature entertainment provided by the Spanish singer, Carmen Sevilla. A magnificent fireworks display closed the evening, while "Calypso" perfume by Robert Piguet was distributed to all the female guests.

André Levasseur designed and decorated many of the extraordinary galas in Monaco, creating a vision that transported one into a world of fantasy, glamour and the exotic. He had been a fashion designer and assistant to Christian Dior, then went on to become a set and costume designer for the Comédie Française, and for numerous ballets and plays throughout France and Monaco. He had designed the set and costumes for a special ballet created for the wedding of Princess Grace and Prince Rainier. Levasseur was a master of staging, and his creations were elaborately detailed and exquisitely beautiful. Grace loved to work with him on themes for the galas; she got very excited about his ideas, which were masterfully executed and stunning to behold.

One year, the guests at the International Summer Sporting Club gala were amazed to see an astonishing transformation from a barren land fill in front of the club into a large lagoon. There were clusters of palm trees with three lit fountains, whose waters cascaded in waterfalls. It was a gorgeous sight that vastly enhanced the already fairy-like open-air setting. The gala had a circus theme, with caged lions, tigers, bears and other wild animals. The evening climaxed with an aerial trapeze act called the "Sky Show," with a daredevil aerialist dangling from a helicopter that was hovering over the large lagoon.

Monaco has always been renowned for its incomparable galas, with entertainment provided by the top stars of the day, such as Frank Sinatra, Sammy Davis Jr., Eddie Fisher, Marlene Dietrich, and Gene Kelly, to name a few. The decor and floorshows were extravagant, with dancers wearing extremely lavish costumes with plumes, sequins and jewels. Everything was of the highest quality, the food and wines were exquisite, the guest lists read like "Who's Who in the World," and the closing fireworks were breathtaking.

Events in Monaco were always sublime and impeccable. Nothing ever went amiss; the planning was perfect for every dance, every fireworks, every ball. Only in Monaco have I seen such harmony and beauty in décor, combined with outstanding performers, elegant guests, extraordinary cuisine, and stylish service. Monaco is a rare and brilliant jewel. It spoiled us because nothing would ever compare to it again, not even galas in New York or Paris.

Over the summer, Grace and I enjoyed spending time alone together, and with our children. We went shopping, swam at the Palace pool, went up to Rocagel for intimate dinners, and cheered our children in swimming races at the Monte-Carlo Beach Club. We had tea at my apartment, lunched together casually at the Palace, and spent as much time as possible enjoying our friendship, knowing that we would soon be separated by miles of ocean.

Martin was asked to join the Prince and three mutual friends, including race car driver Louis Chiron, on a two-week cruise to Athens aboard Prince Rainier's magnificent new yacht, the *ALBECARO II*. Grace and Rainier had been invited to attend the wedding of King Constantine of Greece with Princess Anne-Marie of Denmark. Originally, Grace had left for Athens on the yacht with Rainier and the children – they were to have been gone for six weeks, while we looked after Caroline's dog. However, Grace was about three months pregnant and felt so seasick that they had to turn around and come back to Monaco. Rainier still wanted to go to Greece by boat, so it turned into a men's cruise instead.

"ALBECARO II"
Elba, September 1st, 1964

My Dearest Love,

It is now 10:45 p.m., and we are all in the salon, chatting easily about everything and nothing in particular. We sailed last evening just after midnight, and I have never in my life seen anything so beautiful as the view of Monaco at night from the sea. It was breathtaking, and I imagine that the spectacle of the shimmering lights fading in the distance was rendered even more lovely than the reality, because of the thrill of leaving on this cruise. You must pardon me and try to comprehend my joy at being invited on this memorable trip. It is like the fulfillment of an incredible dream. At the same time, however, I miss you and wish it had been possible for you to share this with me. Like love, moving experiences should be shared to be fully appreciated.

I adore you, Marty

Monaco – September 4, 1964

Dearest Darling Marty,

Tuesday I went to the Beach and saw Grace, then I sat for the final touches of my portrait by Alejo Vidal-Quadras, a charcoal drawing which makes me look regal. Wednesday I went to lunch at the Palace.

This morning I rushed up to the Palace with the boys for a review of the English Fife and Drum Band. We watched from the Palace Balcony, which was thrilling. Tomorrow the boys are invited to the Palace. See you soon.

With boundless love, Your, Joanie, Charles, Greg

"ALBECARO II"
September 10th, 1964, 9:00 A.M.

My Darling Sweetheart,

We arrived in Greece this morning at about 7:30 after a 37-hour run from Malta through really rough seas. The yacht was bobbing like a cork despite the stabilizers. We passed the time playing gin rummy.

Malta was interesting but not much fun. We visited all the points of tourist or historic interest with the Monaco Consul. We went on shopping excursions in quest of illusory bargains (and there is no better definition of chaos than 4 or 5 men trying to shop together as a group with different desires and tastes). The best part of Malta was that I found the perfect gift for the Prince, and he is delighted with it. Although it took me hours of searching and $3 in taxi fares, I located a beautiful parrot (a double-yellow headed Mexican parakeet) and gave him to Rainier, complete with cage and two weeks of parrot food. Although he doesn't speak yet, he is a gay, noisy fellow, who has been amusing us all.

Love to the boys, devotedly,
Marty

Monaco – September 10, 1964

Dearest Darling Marty,

Sunday, Greg had a slight cold, so Charles and I went to Grace for tea. Tuesday, Grace, Father Boston and I had lunch at the Woods. Wednesday,

Grace asked me up for a swim and lunch. There was just the two of us and the children, and we had a delightful, gay, relaxed time, talking, swimming twice, shopping. We got on like sisters.

Love, Joan

Monaco – September 12, 1964

Dearest Mum and Dad,

Grace has been so sweet to us since Marty has been gone. She has invited us to the Palace for lunch and a swim several times, and I have had long, relaxed talks with her – better than any we have ever had. She will miss us, I am sure, and I certainly shall miss her, poor dear. It is harder to live in this fairy tale country than one would imagine. We shall look forward to visiting here, though, as we leave a great deal of our hearts behind.

We all send loads of love, always, Joanie

Grace and I spent almost every day together while our husbands sailed to Greece. She always managed to find time for me, despite her busy schedule. I would call her at nine o'clock in the morning, which was the best time to get in touch with her. Even if she were about to run off to an appointment, she would give me her time and attention. She had great patience and never rushed one off the phone with "Got to go now," and all the hurried actions that most busy modern people do. She had a way of taking everything with such ease.

There was only one time I remember Grace being slightly disorganized, when I was with her in their private apartment as she was preparing for a trip. She could not find her passport and was getting very upset. This was the only time I really saw her lose her cool. She just stood there saying, "I don't know what I'm going to do because I can't find it. I have looked everywhere, and we have to leave pretty soon. I just have to find it." I presume that she finally found it because she did go on the trip after all, but she probably could have gone without a passport, as everyone in the world knew who she was!

Grace felt that she should be treated like everybody else, and she certainly was never "high and mighty"; I never saw her put on airs. Other people in lofty positions can become unbearably entitled, arrogant, demanding, and difficult to be around. She always carried herself with a natural dignity and treated everyone with respect, which inspired others to treat her with respect and reverence.

We flew to Greece to join our husbands on September 15. Grace and Rainier stayed in a hotel in Athens, while Martin and I were invited to stay with our longtime friends, Mary and Angelos, who had a vast apartment on Herodou Attikou Street, right next door to the Greek Royal Palace. We could clearly see the palace guard – the famous Evzones, known for wearing layered, short white skirts in the ancient style, and white shoes with red pompoms. They are also known for having a Beefeater-like demeanor, whereby they do not flinch while on guard duty, no matter what the distraction.

Athens – Friday, September 18, 1964

Dearest Mum and Dad,

Cannot believe we are here in this fabulous, ancient land! Our hosts have been so wonderful and gracious that we shall always remember our visit. The Royal Wedding was a glittering affair with more crowned heads than one has seen in many a year – we saw them all from a distance, and it was exciting. I leave Sunday by plane, and Marty goes back by yacht with Rainier on an eight-day trip back to Monaco.

Loads of love, Joan, Marty

Martin and I did not attend the Greek Royal Wedding, but we had a close-up view of the procession from the balcony as it passed directly below us. The morning of September 18 began with a twenty-one-gun salute. At 9:45 a.m., the royal cortège departed from the Palace, with thirteen horse-drawn carriages and motor vehicles transporting the royal families of the bride and groom, and all of the reigning sovereigns from around the world. Queen Elizabeth II of England was the only European monarch who was not present; in her place, she sent Prince Philip and her two teenage children, Prince Charles, and Princess Anne, who was part of the wedding party as one of the Princesses of Honor. Although the newspapers reported that Princess Grace was present, she had been overcome by the heat and nearly had a miscarriage, so she was confined to bed and could not attend the wedding itself, although she had attended the Royal Ball two nights before.

Cavalry mounted on white horses preceded the open Victorian carriage, drawn by four horses, in which sat the young King in full white-dress uniform, and his mother, Queen Frederika. The crowd roared as the young King passed, and he waved and smiled. Slowly coming into view was an open landau drawn by six white horses, in which sat the King of Denmark in the full-dress uniform of an Admiral, and his lovely eighteen-year-old daughter, Anne-Marie, wearing an ancient Grecian-style wedding gown with flowers, and a diamond tiara holding her veil. She was radiant as the growing swell of voices shouted, "Long live our Queen!" and "How beautiful is our Queen!"

At the age of 24, King Constantine was the youngest monarch in the world at that time, and at 18, his bride would become the youngest queen. The elaborate Greek Orthodox ceremony took place in the Cathedral with sixteen hundred guests in the sweltering heat. As the long ceremony ended, they left the Cathedral, and all the bells in Athens (and in all of Greece) rang out the happiness of this radiant young couple.

They traversed the city back to the Royal Palace, with exuberant crowds throwing a blizzard of confetti with thunderous shouts of congratulations. The day had been declared a national holiday in Greece, so one million Greeks lined the streets. It was a jubilant crowd under our balcony as the newlyweds re-entered the Palace, where a garden luncheon for eighty fellow royals awaited them. We were most fortunate to be outside on a shady balcony, because the heat was unbearable, and many people were fainting, especially inside the Cathedral. I was very concerned about Grace when I found out that she had succumbed to the heat, especially considering she was expecting the baby in February; I contacted her immediately to see if there was anything I could do while she was on doctor-ordered bed rest.

Athens, 1964

My Dear Grace,

I am so very sorry to hear that you are not feeling well and hope with all my heart that there is no danger. If you feel up to having visitors, I should be very happy to come to see you for a short while. I shall be staying here until Wednesday morning, and please do not hesitate to ask if there is anything I can do for you here or in Monaco – see how the children are, for example.

Please do take good care of yourself, dear Grace. We shall be thinking of you.

Affectionately, Joan

The return trip on Prince Rainier's yacht was delayed because of Grace's condition, and I also stayed in Athens for several days to make sure that she was safe. Our hosts were due to leave for New York but insisted that Martin and I remain in their palatial apartment after they left. When we returned from accompanying them to the airport, we were touched to find that the servants had moved us from the comfortable guest quarters into the sumptuous master suite. Our Greek friends demonstrated that hospitality has a very special meaning in Greece, looking after us with extraordinary warmth and generosity.

I visited Grace each day at her hotel and sat by her side – I was terribly worried, as she did not look at all well. I could tell that she was afraid for her unborn baby, and for her own health, and I tried my best to keep her mind off it so she could rest and recover. Rainier was beside himself with concern, helplessly pacing in front of the hotel while I visited with her. After five days, Grace sent for Albert and Caroline to come to Athens. When I knew that she felt well enough, I flew back to Monaco, and Grace finally flew home on September 26. Martin and Rainier resumed their journey on the yacht, returning on October 4 (after delays of losing an engine and the radar system en route).

On their way back, Rainier had arranged to meet with Aristotle Onassis in an effort to put all of the unpleasantness of the past two years behind them regarding the shares of the SBM. Although they had once been friends, they had barely had any contact since the last time Onassis reneged on an agreement at the beginning of 1963. Onassis consented to a meeting, inviting the Prince to bring his yacht alongside the *CHRISTINA* off his private island of Skorpios. Martin and Prince Rainier went aboard and were delighted that Ari and Maria Callas were exceptionally warm and friendly. After long talks, Rainier and Martin finally reached a total agreement with him over a whole list of things, including the SBM. (However, six months later, Onassis repeated his pattern of going back on his word, after which Rainier would hardly speak with him again. Rainier was forced to find a very clever, unorthodox, and perhaps somewhat shocking solution to this ongoing battle, which would not be resolved until 1966.)

"ALBECARO II"
September 30, 1964, 11:30 A.M.
Off the Adriatic Coast of Italy approaching Sicily

My Dearest Darling Joanie,

The return trip has been an eventful one thus far and very memorable. We spent the night at anchor off Corinth, and on Sunday we sailed to Onassis's small (10 sq. miles!) island called Skorpios. The Prince had arranged a meeting with O. to iron out their differences. We arrived at Skorpios at about 3:00 p.m., and it was an extraordinary sight – a lovely, Greek Ionian island – with clear blue water and abundant foliage, the bleak Greek coastal mountains rising in the distance and the CHRISTINA at anchor in the protected bay. I took lots of film footage, which I hope will give a true impression to the imposing beauty of it all. Callas was sitting on the aft deck when we came in. Then O. arrived, and he and Callas came to the ALBECARO for cocktails and invited us on the CHRISTINA for dinner – a sumptuous affair (blinis and caviar, filet, and an ice cream peach cake for dessert). On Monday, O. took us on his speedboat all around the nearby islands, and we watched the local fishermen go after the day's catch. Then lunch on the CHRISTINA – copious – and "le tour de propriétaire" [guided tour by owner] of the island. Then Ms. Callas and O. came over for dinner, and I had an interesting talk with O. about the Bahamas deal and other things. We left Skorpios yesterday morning. However, last night we ran into a violent storm, and one motor went out. I slept through the excitement. I am told that we were really in danger, being tossed about by a rough sea and unable to steer or make headway with only one motor. We are now 2 hours from Sicily, and the Prince has ordered a stop of half a day in Messina to regain the motor.

Adoringly, Marty

Grace rested for several days upon her return. I continued to be very worried each time that I went to see her at the Palace, because she still did not look well at all. She finally regained her strength after a very long and frightening two weeks. She was so excited to be pregnant again, but after she had lost a baby the year before, this was a terrible scare for everyone. This pregnancy was difficult for her and left her quite weak, but she had several more months to go before the baby was due.

She carried on with her duties throughout the rest of her term and tended to Albert and Caroline as much as possible. In October, Caroline started school at the *Dames de St. Maur*, where she was registered as Caroline Grimaldi. Grace enjoyed walking her to and from school whenever her schedule allowed it.

  Grace introduced art classes and soccer lessons for Albert and Charles at the Palace, and professional soccer players from Monaco's winning soccer team also coached them in the stadium! Grace and I watched with a mixture of pride and amusement, as they had more enthusiasm than coordination during their first soccer lesson. She turned to me and said, "They look as if they know what they are doing, anyway!" It was thrilling for them to be coached by pros in the huge stadium, if not a little intimidating, particularly as members of the press were photographing their every move!

  After the cruise to Greece, Rainier was much more relaxed and warmer with us than ever. We had many intimate evenings at the Palace with late night conversations, movies, bowling, etc. During a buffet dinner at the Palace, Rainier served some apple pie to us himself, which was fine at Rocagel, but unheard of at the Palace with all of the servants around. Rainier was in a surprisingly good mood when he told us that he had sold his yacht, which he had only just picked up in April. It was beautiful, but it had quite a few problems in the six months that he had owned it, and he wanted something more manageable – at least he had gotten to enjoy his cruise to Greece with Martin and the others. They all had a wonderful time, and as we were soon to leave for the Bahamas, it was a memory that Martin would treasure forever.

Monaco – Monday, November 2, 1964

Dearest Mum and Dad,

  Maureen [my best friend from childhood] just left yesterday after a week's stay in which we did more things than anyone could imagine. Grace was terribly sweet and invited her to the Palace four times, including a children's Halloween party and a large dinner of 18 in the large official dining room (the first one of the winter season).

  We are so busy now as there are many people to see before we leave and with the season beginning at the Palace, plus sorting, packing, selling and giving away – Christmas, gifts, etc. Please forgive me if I do not write often.

Loads of love, Joan

Grace was always warm and welcoming, and enjoyed meeting new people. When my cousin Penelope visited me earlier in the year, Grace went out of her way to make her feel comfortable, inviting her to Rocagel when I had to go to the Bahamas unexpectedly. My childhood friend, Maureen, did not want to miss the opportunity to come see me in Monaco, knowing that we only had two months left. Maureen was a bubbly Irish Catholic girl, and Grace was happy to have her come to all of the events taking place at the Palace, including movies and formal dinners with European royalty.

Grace loved to have fun, and enjoyed planning and attending parties. She got very excited in anticipation, like a little girl; she would get a radiant sparkle in her eyes and a gleam in her smile when preparing for a party, and smiled ear to ear when attending them. She was a lot of fun to be with, and life was never dull when she was around.

For Halloween, there was a fabulous costume party for the children in the afternoon, while the mothers sipped champagne in the evening. Grace created a terrific Chamber of Horrors at the Palace, to the delight and trepidation of the children and guests. Although Halloween was not celebrated outside America, Grace did not want her children to miss out on the thrills of this experience. She delighted in the joys of her children – in fact, her greatest joy was giving joy to others.

One evening, Martin and I were invited by Grace and Rainier to a small party at the Palace held in the *Salon des Glaces*. We were among a select group of their close friends, including Colonel Ardant, Chief of Protocol, and Madame Ardant, Grace's Lady-in-Waiting. We were expecting the arrival of the Prince and Princess, when Prince Rainier appeared with a stunning, dark-haired woman on his arm. We all turned to look at each other in astonishment, wondering who this lady was and what had happened to Grace. Suddenly, there was a burst of laughter and a familiar giggle. It was Grace wearing a dark wig! She was a truly sublime actress who fooled us all – we had no idea who she was. Rainier also pulled it off without a glint of a smile until after Grace was revealed. We all laughed and joined in the joke. We might have expected something like this in their private apartment, as they both loved practical jokes, but never in the large formal reception rooms at the Palace! Grace looked equally beautiful as a brunette, but I never saw her in disguise again.

Grace had a delightful sense of humor and could always laugh at herself, which is a rare quality. We had been together at a buffet luncheon when Grace was expecting Stephanie. She had served herself a rather large plateful, which she could not finish. She was about seven months pregnant at the time, and she looked at me and said, "Oh, I guess my eyes are bigger than my tummy," then she looked down and laughed, saying, "Well, not exactly."

As we were packing and getting ready to leave Monaco, we were looking forward to celebrating Grace's birthday on November 12, and all of the events surrounding Monaco's National Day for the last time. On November 2, we were invited to a wonderful dinner with Princess Antoinette, Prince Rainier's sister, whom we had grown quite close to and who continued to write to us for years after we left Monaco. Two days later, Princess Antoinette and Prince Rainier were suddenly called to Paris where their father had been dealing with a prolonged illness. Sadly, Prince Pierre passed away a week later on November 10 at the age of sixty-nine. Prince Rainier and Princess Grace were devastated, as was Princess Antoinette; all of Monaco was in profound mourning with flags at half-mast throughout the Principality.

Monaco – November 18, 1964

Dearest Mum and Dad,

We have had a sad time here as Prince Pierre, Rainier's father, died last week. He was a fine man, a true aristocrat, and the end of an era has come with his death. A beautiful funeral service was held yesterday, followed by a buffet lunch for those relatives and friends who came and who are staying at the Palace. It was a sad time, but we feel closer to G & R, having shared in their sorrow as well as their joys. G is standing it well, thank goodness. We all feared for the baby as she had not been in good health recently. We have a month's mourning, and the family 3-6 months. Loads of love from us all,

Always, Joan

Prince Pierre's body was returned to Monaco, where he lay in state. On November 15, there was a Mass for Prince Pierre in the Palace Chapel, filled with beautiful wreaths and flowers. The funeral took place on November 17, and all shops, schools and businesses in Monaco were closed in observance of this great man.

Prince Rainier was in full military dress uniform with only a few of his medals, a sword at his side, and carrying his cap as a sign of respect. Grace was dressed in mourning with a long black veil, holding the hand of young Caroline, while Albert held the hand of his father. Martin was also in full mourning attire with a black waistcoat, top hat, black gloves, and "unshiny" shoes, while I wore a black dress with gray stockings. The princes of the De Polignac family, including Prince Louis, wore the military uniform of the sovereign order of Malta.

Martin was part of the cortège, arriving at the Chapel at 8:45 a.m. for the *levée du corps*. After prayer in the chapel, the cortège gathered in the Palace courtyard, and the procession made its way through the ancient streets of the old town toward the Cathedral of Monaco. The coffin was draped in the flag of the Prince's coat of arms, with a cross of red and white roses upon it.

It was a beautiful and emotional service, with musical selections from Bach and Mozart that Prince Pierre had personally requested before his death. The service was followed by a reception at the Palace with a buffet luncheon. Prince Pierre was laid to rest later that afternoon in the *Chapelle de la Paix*. We had Albert and Caroline come to our apartment to be with Charles and Greg, so their parents could have some quiet moments of reflection and peace. It was a very sad day for everyone, as were the days that followed.

Monaco was in official mourning for a month, and all of the ceremonies and events of the Monaco National Day were cancelled, except for morning Mass at the Cathedral. It was a terrible loss, and it took Grace and Rainier quite some time to recover. Rainier wrote to Martin: "Many thanks for all your words of sympathy in these cruel moments. It is a great comfort for me to feel how my dear father was liked and admired by all. Please share with Joan all my most sincere appreciation for your sharing of my sorrow and grief... Thus now for ever... The chapter is closed, and the memories lost into the past! Regrets of perhaps not having given in return to him what he gave to me... remain and will linger on. Death is something so terribly strong and definite!"

Prince Pierre's passing in 1964 brought an end to one of the last remaining old-world aristocrats. He was a great man who loved and supported the arts and everything beautiful in this world. He founded literary and arts councils, and was President of the National Commission for UNESCO and the Monégasque Olympic Committee (perhaps influencing his grandson, Prince Albert).

We were privileged to know such a man, and I missed his elegant manner very much. He was very fond of Martin and me, and had invited us on many occasions for dinner and drinks at his beautifully furnished home, Clos St. Pierre, not far from the Palace on the *Rocher de Monaco*. He had specially requested that we be invited to his small birthday party at Maxim's in Paris. We had last seen him in April when he invited us to his home for cocktails, but he was already unwell at that time, coughing frequently. He went to Paris shortly thereafter for medical care. Prince Pierre was always very kind to me, writing notes in English in his inimitable style on stationery with an embossed crown, which he mailed to whatever parts of the world I found myself in.

I was most flattered in my young years to be thus addressed by such a regal member of the aristocracy. Prince Pierre was a true gentleman in every sense, and to be around him was to know that chivalry was indeed alive. He was the most courtly and dashing nobleman I had ever known. He was a commanding figure who inspired awe and respect, yet at the same time, he was not intimidating but was warm, gracious and welcoming, making everyone feel equally important and at ease in his presence.

Grace very much loved her father-in-law, and he was tremendously fond of her right from the beginning. They grew very close, and his death was quite devastating to her. Grace was always mindful of Prince Pierre's devotion to the arts, which were also dear to her own heart. Before Prince Rainier married, Prince Pierre had been the major patron and supporter of perpetuating the arts in Monaco. He was responsible for the founding of many awards for art, music, drama and literature. After his passing, Grace took over many of these responsibilities.

Monaco – November 26, 1964

Dearest Mum and Dad,

For the first time since the funeral, we are invited today by G & R to a small Thanksgiving luncheon at the Palace, followed by a Walt Disney film for the children. They are not accepting any invitations, which is perhaps good for Grace, who is feeling better now.

Loads of love from us all, Always, Joan

Grace and Rainier slowly started to emerge from their grief. They celebrated American Thanksgiving quietly at the Palace with a luncheon of Maltese turkey with chestnuts and sausage stuffing, followed by *Mary Poppins* for the children. A couple of days later, Grace and I went Christmas shopping to get her mind off things, then we had tea together at the Palace, where Rainier and Albie joined us. Everyone was very warm but subdued under the circumstances.

Before we left for the Bahamas, we had a slew of farewell parties, luncheons and dinners. We had made many wonderful friends in Monaco, who gave us lovely parting gifts and hospitality; it was hard to say goodbye. Even the government Ministers held dinners in our honor, although I know some of them were not really sad to see us go.

We arrived at one of our going-away parties in formal dinner dress to find a big surprise: our friends, who had gathered to wish us well, were all wearing tropical attire, such as sarongs, shorts, and straw hats! The place was decorated with pineapples and bananas, with a banner saying, "Welcome to the Bahamas." We danced to Caribbean rhythms, and even did the limbo (which was not easy in a tight silk cocktail dress!). It was great fun and a wonderful send-off.

The children had a farewell party at our apartment. Albert and Caroline gave our boys a beautiful accordion and some boats for the Bahamas. Then Grace and I went to Nice in their Rolls Royce, and the two of us had a lovely picnic along the Riviera.

We invited Grace and Rainier to our apartment for dinner one last time, and I made a chicken curry that the Prince had enjoyed during one of our vacations in Switzerland. Suddenly the lights went out (due to a French gas and electric strike!), so we dined and talked cozily by candlelight. Grace gave me a beautiful pendant: a round gold medallion with turquoise flowers on the front, and her double-G monogram on the back, which I cherish. Rainier gave Martin an underwater diving watch, which he would make great use of in the Bahamas.

On December 13, Martin got to enjoy his last official act as Privy Counselor at the inauguration of the new railway tunnel that diverted the unsightly train tracks from the seaside, freeing up huge tracts of prime land in Monaco for expansion and development. A $3.2 million railroad tunnel was constructed, and the rock that was dug out of the mountains for the tunnel created land fill along the coastline. This was one of the masterpieces of city planning that Rainier and Martin had worked on to fulfill the Prince's vision for his country. Martin had the honor of being one of the first people through the tunnel, followed by the inaugural celebration luncheon at the *Hôtel de Paris*.

Monaco – December 18, 1964

Dearest Mum and Dad,

We are in the hotel now after five days of packing – what a ghastly job it was! G & R are giving us a farewell party on Monday night, and we sail Tuesday the 22nd on board the INDEPENDENCE from Cannes.

In haste – we all send loads of love, Joan

The night before we left Monaco, Grace and Rainier gave us a quiet farewell party at the Palace with friends. It was subdued as they were still in mourning, which suited the sad occasion for us, as we had been so happy there. The Prince was a superb employer, and Martin had very much enjoyed working with him. There was a buffet dinner of champagne, caviar, smoked salmon, and chicken, followed by bowling for the last time. Grace and Rainier then invited the two of us for a farewell drink in their private apartments.

Grace was very empathetic, and although I put on a brave face when it came time to leave Monaco, I knew that she felt my sadness, especially at leaving her. She really did not want me to go, both for her sake and mine. She felt tremendous compassion for me moving to an essentially deserted island, and we joked that it would be like Robinson Crusoe. I laughed and cried at the same time. We said a tearful farewell, hugging each other, knowing we would remain friends even from afar, but life would never be the same again.

After we said goodbye, I cried in the car all the way back to the *Hôtel de Paris*, where we were staying before boarding our ship. The following day, I phoned Grace to thank her for everything. Rainier and Grace sent the Palace cars to take us to our ship, with thirty-three pieces of luggage! They had sent along a lovely bouquet of flowers, a wonderful bottle of Veuve Clicquot champagne, an etching of the Palace, and a delightful handwritten note from the Prince: "Happy sailing! …See you soon, à las Grande Bahamas or in piccolo Monaco." They were dear and loving friends, and we would miss them terribly.

Prince Rainier gave us one final wonderful surprise. Among his many talents, Rainier loved architectural design and had asked to see the drawings of the house we were planning to build in the Bahamas. He gave us some excellent ideas and advice, and ultimately helped us design our dream home. To our utter astonishment, Rainier offered us a fireplace and mantelpiece that had come from a Fifteenth Century château in France, which he had originally bought for Rocagel but never used. This wonderful housewarming gift became a treasured memory of our dear friends, and the centerpiece of our new home

Grace's annual Christmas tradition at the Palace of Monaco with U.S. Navy sailors (L to R) Greg seated with Albert playing with a new fort, Charles on Grace's lap, Joan standing with Rainier

Prince Pierre (Prince Rainier's father) with Prince Albert in the uniform of the *Carabinier* (Palace Guard) and Princess Caroline in the Monégasque national costume

At work while at play
Martin and Rainier at the Monte-Carlo Golf Club at Mont Agel

Martin bringing Charles to school
on the way to his office
at the Palace of Monaco

Birthday party for Charles at our apartment in the Ruscino
(L to R) Caroline, Charles, Greg, Albert

December 10, 1961 birthday party for Charles at our Monaco apartment (L to R)
Seated: Fabrice, Caroline, Charles
Standing: parent, Joan, Grace, our nanny Jacqueline

Greg's birthday party in Villars, Switzerland
(L to R) Standing: Joan, Grace (giving Albert a napkin)
Seated: Caroline, Greg, Albert, May, Charles

Villars, Switzerland, February 1963
(L to R) Back row: Albert, Isabelle, May, Caroline. Front row: Greg, Charles, Fabrice

February 1963, Villars, Switzerland
Caroline looking after 3-year-old Greg
on the ice

Switzerland 1963, Greg, Charles and Albert hanging around on the ice rink

Albert's inspiration for Monaco's
Olympic Bobsleigh team?
Albert and Charles sitting on
Caroline, lying on a sled
Schönried, Switzerland
February 1962

Princess Caroline hosting a tea party in her
playhouse at Rocagel 1962 (L to R) Albert,
Caroline, Greg, and Charles

Charles and Albert practicing their salutes at the Palace of Monaco

Summer 1964, Palace of Monaco
Young soldiers at attention: Greg, Charles and Albert

Summer 1964, monkeying around on the jungle gym outside the Palace: Caroline, Greg, Albert, Charles

Caroline and Greg in the sandbox on the children's playground at the Palace, summer 1964

July 1964, prize-giving at the Palace
Charles bowing as Prince Rainier gives him
an award for excellence in school

July 1964 luncheon after prize-giving at the Palace pool
Lunch served to the children by white-gloved servants
Greg on the left, Caroline in foreground on the left, Charles and Albert in background

1962 at Monte-Carlo Beach Club
Charles, Greg, Grace, and Albert in front of our cabana

Albert and Charles playing in the sand at Monte-Carlo Beach Club
(Greg in background)

August 1964
Grace at Palace pool age 35

August 1964
Greg, Charles, Albert, Caroline
in the gardens at the Palace of Monaco

September 1964 – Prince Rainier's yacht, *ALBECARO II* leaving Monaco harbor (view from our apartment)

Rainier and Martin on board the *ALBECARO II* cruising to Greece September 1964

September 1964 at Skorpios, the private Greek island of Aristotle Onassis (L to R) Onassis, Rainier, Martin, race car driver Louis Chiron

PART THREE:
THE CORRESPONDING DAYS

DAYS OF PARADISE

We set sail from Monaco on December 22, 1964, and spent Christmas on board the SS *INDEPENDENCE* en route to New York and then to the Bahamas. Charles and Greg were worried that Santa Claus would not know where to find them at sea! Although we left our friends and the wonderful social whirl of the Mediterranean with great regret and considerable reluctance, it was to embark on an exciting and challenging new adventure in the Caribbean. We had endured all manner of political storms in Europe, now we would have to survive real ones...

While we were singing "Auld Lang Syne" on New Year's Eve, our ship suddenly sailed into a terrible storm on the Atlantic Ocean. People were being knocked to the floor, and it was not because of too much celebrating! We encountered a hurricane the likes of which the Captain of our ship had never seen in his forty years at sea. The waves were unbelievable, and we were bobbing like a cork in the middle of the Atlantic Ocean. One minute we were sinking, looking up at the waves looming above us like a wall of water, and then we would be thrust to the top again, like a huge roller coaster – it was terrifying! Seventy-foot waves crashed over the decks, breaking everything on the ship, including portholes. A gigantic wave smashed into one of the cabins on the uppermost deck and broke through the windows; fortunately, the people had been sitting on either side, or they would have been killed and washed out to sea.

The storm lasted for twenty-four hours while the ship was at a standstill, simply rising and falling over and over again. I seemed to be the only one still walking around, clinging to the rails, and even climbing to the upper deck to film the angry surf! The giant waves were black, with green spray and white foam – it was an extraordinary sight. I was not seasick and was one of the few people eating in the dining room, but I do love being on the water. Charles was ill, Martin was horizontal, but Greg and I were fine. I somehow managed to bring tea to our cabin for everyone, despite the undulating passageways. Charles, who had just turned seven, looked out at the sea and said, "I'm a pretty good swimmer, but I don't think I could last a minute in that."

We finally arrived in New York City in a snowstorm on January 3. We were more than a day late, because the Captain had to put the ship in reverse in order to keep it steadily afloat. The ship was in all the newspaper headlines around the world, and everyone was worried about us. It had been quite a distressing journey, but somehow we made it. We had everything we owned on board, but our only concern was for the children's safety.

Upon our arrival, I went by train with Charles and Greg to visit my parents for one month on the west coast of Canada. Martin went directly to the Bahamas to get us settled in our temporary new home, as our "dream house" would not be built for months to come.

Martin bought a Ford Mustang in New York and loaded it to the rafters with our belongings, driving down to Fort Lauderdale to take a ferry to Freeport, Bahamas, in order to start his new job. As Vice-President of the Grand Bahama Port Authority, he was in charge of tourism, business and industrial development. He also served as President and Chief Executive of the passenger shipping companies. It was quite a change from the life we had in Monaco, but everything that Martin had learned from Prince Rainier would prove very helpful in the economic development of this small island in the Caribbean.

Our departure from Monaco was terribly sad for me. It was as if I had been wrenched away from my home. The only thing that gave me comfort was knowing that I would maintain my dear friendship with Grace, and we would correspond with each other frequently.

When Grace heard about our ship being delayed by the terrible hurricane, she wrote: "Am glad to know that you were not injured during the big storm - We were so anxious when we heard about the size of the waves..." She said that the family had gone up to Rocagel after the Christmas party for the Monégasque children, and wrote about entertaining the American sailors on Christmas Day and taking them bowling – I felt terribly nostalgic for Grace's wonderful annual traditions.

For Christmas, I had given Albert and Caroline beach robes, which Grace thanked me for, saying, "The Dales will not seem so far from Monte Carlo beach." She finished her letter by writing, "May 1965 be the beginning of a new & fulfilling period of your lives with many joys and blessings – Love, Grace." It made me so happy and so very sad at the same time.

Grace was in her final month of pregnancy and was finding it hard to stand for any length of time. In the letter she wrote on my birthday, she joked, "Am under the hair dryer at present, trying to write on my knees, but there is so little lap left!" She was setting up the nursery and hiring another nurse, as Nanny Maureen was leaving but would stay until the end of March to care for the baby, and to "help the children to adjust to the new intruder," as Grace put it.

With all the preparations for the baby's arrival, Grace was still organizing several events for January, including the International Television Festival, celebrations for Monaco's patron saint, Sainte Dévote, and Caroline's eighth birthday party. They also had a Cardinal staying at the Palace, which meant a great deal to them as a Catholic family. Even with all of this going on, Grace still took the time to send me a telegram on my birthday, and write a chatty letter, in which she apologized for not thanking me for my Christmas gift (a silver-framed photograph of Charles and Greg, sitting on a chaise lounge with Albert and Caroline): "In my letter to you I did not mention how much I love the photograph of the four children – It is really so sweet of them all & the frame sets it off beautifully."

Victoria, BC, Canada – Feb. 1, 1965

Dearest darling Marty -

I have just heard the news of Princess Stephanie's birth – two weeks ahead of schedule & I have just dashed off a note to Grace sending our best wishes and love. Poor Albie being sandwiched in between two lively girls!

Loads of love. Your adoring, Joan

Stephanie Marie Elisabeth Grimaldi, Countess of Polignac, was born on February 1, 1965. Grace wrote that "The baby is divine," and said she would send me photos of her christening taken by Howell Conant. She was so happy that Stephanie had come early, as she had been experiencing a great deal of pain and exhaustion. She said that she had gone to lunch with her mother, and then went to rest, as she was not feeling well. By 5 p.m., the baby had arrived, which was such a relief to Grace after a very difficult pregnancy. Thankfully, the doctor had come from Paris ahead of schedule, because he had been very worried about her symptoms.

Grace wrote of the delivery, "There is a wonderful book written by an Englishwoman that gave me a few hints that were most helpful in perfecting my system – all went so easily, except of course for the last ten minutes, which always seem an eternity & is a real son-of-a-bitch - no matter how you look at it - But with no anesthetics, I was sipping champagne right afterwards & back at the lunch table a week later - My only problem is lack of sleep - nursing the baby is very tiring & of course takes up so much of the day - I haven't been able to do anything but feed her & myself - and, naturally, I am the size of a horse! …Much love from all – Grace."

I was so happy for Grace that she and the baby were well after the close call in Greece. It felt strange that I would not be there for the christening of one of her children, and the distance was becoming palpable. When the boys and I arrived in the Bahamas, I felt like a castaway on a barren island. I was far away from everything, even from civilization itself. Grand Bahama Island was in its infancy, and its only "city" of Freeport was just being developed. It was worlds apart from the sparkling jewel of Monaco – it was a beautiful place, but very isolated from the cultural events and fascinating people that we had known. The boys loved it, although they dearly missed their friends, Albie and Caroline.

Freeport, Bahamas – April 8, 1965

Dearest Mum and Dad,

Grace was terribly sweet & sent us a beautiful satin box of candy-coated almonds in honor of Stephanie's baptism. She is a dear person to have remembered us. As yet we have not heard from R. He is perhaps angry that Marty left him to stand alone; however, in his heart he knows it was the right thing to do. I guess he will get over it. Marty is the only person to have left his service of his own accord, so he is naturally feeling unhappy.

Loads & loads of love, Joan, Marty, Charles, Greg

Martin soon received a very long, wistful, and philosophical letter typed by Prince Rainier, dated April 3rd to 9th! Martin had written to Rainier, sending newspaper clippings from the Bahamas, to which the Prince responded, "...I get nostalgic about knowing these far away lands... but it does not seem in the reality of the things possible for me to think about leaving and discovering these new lands... of hope and glory! Troubles and worries seem to be my lot for the time being, more so than usual."

Rainier was very upset once again with Aristotle Onassis, who had broken another agreement that he made in 1964. He wrote: "I have put a complete stop to any contacts or talks between myself and Onassis. The last a month ago was dreadful. He produced a paper as a base for agreement that was a complete retraction on the main points to which he had agreed to in February 1964!" Onassis would now have to deal directly with the Monégasque government. However, Rainier had managed to make peace with President de Gaulle, who expressed his condolences over the death of Prince Pierre. Rainier was looking forward to being received in Paris on April 27 by De Gaulle, who had invited the Prince and Princess to an intimate luncheon.

The Prince apologized for taking so long to write, knowing that Martin would understand how terribly busy his schedule was, and trusting that we would not attribute his silence to anything else. In the end, Rainier understood that Martin felt his job there was done, as it would take years before the economic development that he had brought to Monaco would be fully established, once the land fill at Fontvieille was complete. In many ways, Martin had been too successful at his job, and it would take some time for Monaco to catch up with its growth.

Rainier was gushing over his new baby princess, telling us how sweet and pretty Stephanie was. He expressed how frantic he was that his other two children were growing up so fast, and worried that children grow away from their parents. It made him feel that he was aging.

He must have been in a place of deep thought when he wrote in that same letter: "...The world seems in a nice mess, does it not, or is it less noticeable where you are. If only one could awake the universal conscience (or is there now none left anywhere??) to the urge and the necessity, for LIFE in peace! All this money going into war or aggression preparation... instead of it being devoted to doing away with hunger, and thus regaining peace throughout the world... Suddenly, sometimes... one stops in one's work, to wonder WHY?! What good is all this trouble spending time and energy... and life, and health... for what?...

a grain of sand to be washed away any minute, by an overflowing wave of discontent and anarchy!... We are but a lower form of ants, I believe!"

People do not realize how heavy a burden a crown can be, especially for a man who cares deeply about the planet, the oceans, and the animals on this Earth. As the leader of even such a small country, he often thought about the plight of the world, and how he might improve it. He once wrote: "Men are mad, so nature is following suit!" I think he was very sad not having Martin to talk to anymore, and he poured out his heart and soul in many letters. He ended this one by saying, "Well, so as not to let you feel 'let down' by your friend in Monaco, I will send this letter off. I just cannot find time to get even with my personal mail!!"

As the years wore on, he had more demands and responsibilities as Sovereign Prince, and less and less time for himself. Most of Rainier's letters would begin with profuse apologies for taking so long to write, begging for Martin's understanding of his prolonged silence. What is most remarkable is that the Prince found the time to write at all, because most of his letters were very long, many handwritten or personally typed by Rainier himself (with lots of hand-corrected typos).

Rainier was getting increasingly frustrated and expressed that he was losing his enthusiasm, especially after his forty-second birthday. The Prince told Martin that he envied him going undersea diving in the Bahamas, but he had long given up diving himself, which he used to love to do. He wrote: "...I suppose it is the age and this job of mine that takes all enthusiasm out of me! ...Your job seems exciting and productive. How wonderful it must be to be able to decide and ACHIEVE projects!! Here it is always the same thing (Blablabla lots of it) and nothing comes out of it! I am sick and tired of it all. Happily I have the family and the wonderful children..."

Grace wrote to me in May that she had gone to Philadelphia for the wedding of her niece, Meg, daughter of her eldest sister, Peggy. Caroline had been thrilled to be in the wedding party with all of her cousins. This was a rare typed letter from Grace, as she usually wrote all of her letters in her bold handwriting, but she was in a hurry to send it to me, and she typed quite fast. (She handwrote at the end "Please forgive the many typing errors," but there were hardly any, other than a lot of hyphens, and instead of one period, she repeatedly ended sentences with two, three and even four periods!) She couldn't wait to tell me that Albert had his First Communion the day before, and she was so proud: "It was sweet and touching....The boys were very serious and took the occasion very much to heart."

Grace confided that she was exhausted and was quite concerned that she had not fully regained her strength, since giving birth to Stephanie. However, it had been very difficult for her to be away from the baby while she traveled overseas: "Now about Miss Stephanie.. who is just the dream of the world... It broke my heart to leave her to go to Paris before New York... I cried all the [way] up on the train.. And as happy as I was to be in the States, it was bliss to return to my wee one.... The Prince is mad about her, and the two of us are dribbling idiots in her presence.. I guess the older one gets, the more one appreciates babies..."

Grace also adored animals and was crushed to hear the sad news of the death of our pet poodle, "dear little Jester," who had been so in love with her poodle, Gamma. "They are such wonderful little friends.. It is like losing a member of the family...." She ended her letter by lamenting: "I cannot tell you how much I miss you... And the birthday circuit was certainly lacking Dale participation... Hope all is going well for you... Stay well and give my love to the boys... Love, Grace."

Freeport, Bahamas – July 15, 1965

Dearest Mum and Dad,

I received a lovely letter from Grace before she left for Ireland, enclosing some beautiful photographs of Stephanie, & Albert's first communion. They are treasures. Rainier wrote Martin a long, friendly letter telling his troubles & showing an envy of our type of free life. Someone recently sent us a clipping from the Washington D.C. Post (Newspaper) dated June 20, 1965, about Monaco and Martin, in which they say I bear a striking resemblance to Grace! It is a good article and says how successful Martin was in Monaco.

Your loving, Joan

In August, Martin had to go to Hamburg, Germany, on business, so he invited me to join him and suggested that we go to Monaco beforehand. I was so excited to see Grace and Rainier, to meet baby Stephanie, and to visit with all our friends. Grace sent a lovely letter, saying "Am thrilled that you will soon be here – Please come and stay with us here at Rocagel – But if you prefer being in Monaco, I quite understand..." Only their closest friends and family were invited to stay with them at Rocagel, so we felt very honored. When we lived in

Monaco, we had been there many times, but this was the first time that we would actually stay there as guests.

We arrived in Monaco on August 24 and phoned Grace right away; it was lovely to hear her voice again. We had a gorgeous room at the *Hôtel de Paris* for the first four days, overlooking the Monaco harbor, and it felt like we had come home. We were invited to the Palace for a drink with Grace and Rainier, and they welcomed us warmly – it was as if we had never left. We had a lively conversation, catching up on everything with them in their private apartments, and it was hard to believe that eight months had passed since we were there last. We went to the Summer Sporting Club and had a sumptuous dinner, laughed, danced, and saw an extraordinary floorshow. Exhausted, Martin and I went back to the hotel after midnight and went to sleep, grinning blissfully. It was wonderful to be back!

The next day, we went up to Rocagel for a party. Grace greeted us, looking radiant as always, wearing a lovely Provençal print skirt and a peacock blue silk blouse. Many of our friends were there, and it was delightful to see them again. We met baby Stephanie for the first time; she was indeed beautiful and her parents' pride and joy – they lit up whenever they looked at her. We gave gifts to Albert and Caroline from Charles and Greg, who missed them very much. Grace's brother, Kell, was also visiting from Philadelphia.

We had cocktails and a fabulous Chinese dinner, with shark's fin soup, egg rolls, sweet and sour shrimp and spare ribs, fried rice, lamb moo shu, jasmine tea, and champagne! I sat next to the Prince and enjoyed his brilliant sense of humor, which I had truly missed. After dinner we talked, listened to records, and played foosball. We left at 1 a.m. to go dancing at a club in Monaco, where we saw the Maharani of Baroda. Before returning to our hotel at 4 a.m., we went to have spaghetti Bolognese at Tip Top, just like old times.

The next day, we had cocktails with the Maharani of Baroda in her enormous and lavish suite at the *Hôtel de Paris*. She looked absolutely stunning in a lovely green embroidered sari, with a matching set of exquisite emerald jewelry, of course. She enjoyed filling us in on all the gossip and events that had transpired in Monaco since we left.

On Friday, we went to lunch at the Palace with Grace and Rainier, Albert, Caroline and baby Stephanie, the David Nivens, the Louis Chirons, and Kell. It was a buffet lunch, given for the swimming teams from the USA and France, and it disappeared very quickly. I got to enjoy tasting the Monégasque specialties that I had been longing for, including *pissaladière, tarte aux blettes* (Swiss chard tart), stuffed zucchini flowers, stuffed eggplant, etc. It was delicious and easy to understand why the athletes would devour it so fast. They did us a favor, really, as we had plans for dinner on the terrace at the *Hôtel de Paris*, with Grace and Kell. After dinner, we dashed in Grace's car to go to the swim meet of the athletes from the luncheon, and then we drove up to Rocagel to spend the weekend. Rainier was waiting there for us, and we sat up talking and drinking champagne until very late.

In the morning, we played with the children, then walked all around the beautiful property and gardens of Rocagel, with Grace showing us all of her lovely flowers, which she was so passionate about. It was a marvelous and relaxing day. Rainier, Martin, and David Niven went to play golf, leaving Grace and me to talk. Grace told me about the terrible brush fire that had recently threatened Rocagel. Fire brigades from all the surrounding districts were called in to fight the blaze on Mont Agel, and for a while it seemed they were losing the battle. Everyone was frantic to save precious items, by removing them from Rocagel as urgently as possible. They quickly packed up works of art, family photographs, home movies, paintings, and Grace's Oscar (which later remained in their private apartments at the Palace). Fortunately, the house had been spared, much to everyone's relief.

Later that evening, I accompanied Grace to a spectacular outdoor ballet, which took place overlooking the *Baie des Anges* (Bay of Angels) in Nice. Margot Fonteyn and Rudolf Nureyev were performing, and they were magnificent. They were "the" ballet couple of that era, renowned all over the world. Grace was the guest of honor that evening, and I basked in her reflected glory, as she always made sure that those around her received the light that shone upon her.

After the performance, Grace and I went backstage to congratulate the stars, finding them in extremely cramped makeshift dressing rooms hurriedly assembled in the park. Dame Margot Fonteyn was gracious as always, but Nureyev was like a Russian prima donna, complaining about the dressing rooms and how difficult it had been to dance on the temporary stage, where the planking bent and groaned at every step. They were exquisite dancing partners, although he was extremely egotistical and temperamental.

Margot danced with grace and fluidity, and a dramatic presence that made her the Prima Ballerina of the world – she is often regarded as the standard of perfection for a ballerina. Margot Fonteyn was such a star of the Royal Ballet that Queen Elizabeth made her a Dame of the Order of the British Empire in 1956, six years before she was partnered with Nureyev. They began dancing together after he defected from Russia in 1961 at the age of 22. She was 42 and was considering retiring at that time, but they went on to dance together for seventeen years. She finally retired at the extraordinary age of 60.

We returned to Rocagel and again talked and drank champagne until long after midnight. They were so warm and welcoming, we regretted having to leave the next day. The four of us played foosball after breakfast, and Rainier and I won! After lunch, the whole family stood in front of the house, singing to give us a touching send off. It was a marvelous time!

Martin and I went to Hamburg for business, then on to Sussex, England, to the estate of Sir Charles Hayward. He was one of the key investors in Freeport, and his son, Sir Jack Hayward (known as "Union Jack"), was a major shareholder in the Grand Bahama Port Authority. Jack had a home on Grand Bahama Island and became a close friend of ours.

On our return to the Bahamas, we were stranded in New York by another hurricane, which stopped all flights, with 126 mph winds and rain battering the Caribbean. Fortunately, we were able to arrange for the boys to meet us in New York before the storm hit. Hurricane Betsy reached Category 4 and caused over $1 billion in damage – it was one of the deadliest and costliest storms in history. I was relieved that we were not in the Bahamas during the worst of the storm, but we were worried about what we would find when we got home. We were very grateful that our property was not damaged, but this was one of the drawbacks of living in a tropical "paradise."

It was difficult for me to return to the isolation I felt in the Bahamas. We had so enjoyed our time in Monaco, and seeing our dear friends again made me feel rather homesick for our old life, although I tried not to let it show. Grace's correspondence always lifted my spirits and made me feel close to her, despite the miles between us.

In October, I received a letter that she had begun writing on September 27: "Dear Joanie - It was so nice to receive your nice letter at the end of a tiring day - It has cheered me - So happy you missed the hurricane - but I thought it had come before you had the time to get home - I was in one once in New Jersey in '44 & it was terrifying - The force of the sea & wind is unimaginable - and one learns a great respect for nature - Your pictures are darling - Thanks so much - It was just wonderful seeing you both again & you both looked marvelously well."

Her letter continued on October 18 from Paris, stating that her duties as head of the Monaco Red Cross had taken her to Vienna for ten days, interrupting her letter writing. She was there for an international meeting to discuss the various issues that the organization was involved with all over the world. "The Red

Cross meetings went very well - It was most impressive & a tremendous satisfaction when one works in a small way with every day Red Cross problems to see 106 countries gathered together who do the same things & there to see how much can be agreed upon by so varied & large a group - It was fascinating - Vienna of course is a dream & I loved it so - although had not nearly enough free time to see everything - Rainier joined me for my last few days there which made it nice."

The Red Cross valiantly steps in to help people deal with the aftermath of devastation from wars and disasters of all kinds, providing relief efforts and other services, such as blood drives, etc. It was an organization that Grace was very proud to be a part of, and she made great efforts to raise a lot of money and to enhance awareness to benefit the Red Cross over many years.

Grace wrote to me in November that she had taken on even more work, as head of the Girl Guides in Monaco. (Caroline was a Girl Guide, and enjoyed participating in many of their activities together with her mother.) She had recently established the Princess Grace Foundation, funding it herself to assist those in immediate need. She also decided to create the *Boutique du Rocher* (in the old part of Monaco near the Palace), to support local artisans by giving them a place in which they could sell their handcrafted items. Grace loved to make things with her hands and greatly admired the work of others. She particularly wanted to create an outlet where elderly citizens could derive a small income from their craft, while also preserving these potentially dying art forms. Grace enjoyed supporting the arts in all ways, and her foundation later established the Princess Grace Dance Academy.

On November 23, she wrote: "Excuse the typewriter but I am up to my neck in unanswered mail, and I see no way out before Christmas... I seem to get more and more work... If only I were better organized, it wouldn't take up so much time..." I knew Grace to be extremely well organized, but she was always demanding more of herself. I believe that she took on far too much for one person, but she was absolutely driven to help as many people as she possibly could. In that same letter, she said that she was creating a day nursery, Monaco's first daycare center, which would allow women with young children to support themselves, while their children were well cared for. Grace often brought armloads of toys to this nursery and spent time reading, singing and playing with the children.

While she believed that it was best for a mother to stay home with her children, she was also aware of the need for a woman's independence. For her, it was very important to be as present as possible with her children as a hands-on mother, and to be really involved with their day-to-day activities. This was the role that she most enjoyed and valued in life. She was always worried about them, and wrote that she had a terrible scare with baby Stephanie, who experienced a bad reaction to a vaccination that caused terrifyingly high fevers, which fortunately subsided. Above all, Grace was committed to putting her family first, while also serving the Principality and the world as head of many organizations and charities.

I think one of the things that fueled Grace and kept her going is that she loved to have fun, and she wanted everyone else to have fun as well. This is one reason why it was so important for her to be involved with planning all the galas and charity events, because she wanted them to be successful, and she often measured that success by people's enjoyment. If people enjoyed themselves, they would give more and want to come back; they would talk about the event and make others want to attend in the future, which would increase the awareness and support for the organization.

There were many events that Prince Rainier and Princess Grace had to attend as guests of honor – some of these were more enjoyable than others. In December, Martin and I made a brief 48-hour stopover in Monaco after a business trip to Rome. Over dinner at Grace and Rainier's private apartments, we discussed the festivities for Martin's induction into the *Chevaliers du Tastevin* the year before. He had proposed that Grace and Rainier also be inducted, and they were due to have their ceremony at the *Château du Clos de Vougeot* later that month. Focused on promoting the enjoyment of the wines and cuisine of the Burgundy region of France, the *Tastevin* is a private society whose members include statesmen, diplomats, artists, intellectuals, and prominent individuals from many diverse areas of interest.

After we returned home to the Bahamas, Grace wrote, "We loved our dinner at Dijon with the Tastevin - What an evening! It set my liver back ten years, or ahead I should say - I never said no to anything & our menu was colossal - & wines superb - Tremendous fun." The photos from that ceremony show the *Chevaliers* (knights) looking at Grace with adoration. She was indeed beautiful that evening in a Givenchy satin two-piece suit, her eyes shining with happiness, and the Prince looking at her with obvious love and devotion. The toast made that night was, "Wines from Burgundy must be drunk by Princes while standing, by ladies seated, and by us, kneeling before you, Princess."

Grace had a wonderful sense of humor, and could always find a way to laugh at herself and at situations that others might find frustrating. After returning from Switzerland in January 1966, she wrote: "We got off to Schönried somehow -

the day after Christmas - A bit of a rush to say the least - My departure with children, dogs & Christmas toys that just couldn't be left behind was really something - James Bond's secret case spilled out all contents on the train platform (naturally) & the whole *mise en train* [start of the trip] had a Charlie Chaplin aspect about it." Before they left, she was thrilled to have had "a real live baby Jesus" (Stephanie!) for their nativity play, which took place in the Throne Room of the Palace, but she said that she only had time for one rehearsal, "so it did not run as smoothly as one would wish!!"

Never wanting anyone to feel bad about anything, Grace had a way of making everything okay. For Christmas, I had sent her a hand-made, straw sun hat from the Bahamas, trimmed in one of Grace's favorite colors – pink. She looked especially lovely whenever she wore pink, and the hat was rather chic with pink flowers all around the wide brim. I did not have much experience in packing and shipping a hat, and, although Grace's letter was ever so polite and tactful, the hat had obviously arrived somewhat crushed: "I found your cute hat on my return from Switzerland - It was a little squashed but with loving care & a little steam it will re-bloom very shortly." I sent her another straw hat from the Bahamas as a replacement, which Grace wore in a photo printed in her book, *My Book of Flowers*, where she is picking wildflowers perched on the edge of the property at Rocagel, overlooking Monaco in the distance below. I was thrilled to see that she actually wore it!

Martin had sent Rainier a Bahamian steel drum, as we had enjoyed the Prince's skill at drumming when he performed for us on several occasions at Rocagel. The Prince wrote with his usual humor: "I received with delight a piece of an oil drum! Noticed it was sent by you… understood that you know that I love drumming… by pure frustration of not being able to beat on people around me! And thus I took up the pen as soon as I could to write and thank you most sincerely for your thought and your wonderful-sounding gift. The children join in thanks, as they also are delighted by this noise-producing 'thing' from the far-away Bahamas. It was thoughtful of you, and I do appreciate your thought."

After we left Monaco, Prince Rainier appointed Martin to be Consul of Monaco at Freeport. The Bahamas was a British colony ruled by Queen Elizabeth II (until 1973, when it became part of the British Commonwealth). In May of 1965, the Secretary of State for the Colonies reported that Her Majesty had signed the exequatur approving Martin's appointment as Consul of Monaco.

On February 28, 1966, Queen Elizabeth and Prince Philip visited Nassau in the Bahamas on their tour of the Caribbean. As part of Martin's official post, we were invited to be presented to Her Majesty aboard her yacht, *BRITANNIA*. It was a huge, imposing, and impressive ship. I curtsied as we met the Queen, and Martin bowed. Martin was announced to the Queen as being the Consul of Monaco to the Bahamas, to which she responded with her inimitable British humor, "Oh... and what else do you do?" Martin was a little taken aback, but said, "Your Majesty, we do have *one* Monégasque subject in the Bahamas."

Later that evening there was a reception at the Governor's mansion, where we spoke briefly with Prince Philip, who was very interesting and amusing, but rather quick and to the point. The Queen was wearing a flowing white chiffon gown, and an emerald and diamond tiara with matching necklace, bracelets and drop earrings. At age 39, she looked regal and stunning, and the whole experience was absolutely marvelous. We spoke to Her Majesty about Freeport and Monaco, and laughed about our "one" subject living in the Bahamas. The Queen was fantastically witty and charming, despite the fact that she had a toothache that day and had to visit a Bahamian dentist!

The year 1966 marked the hundredth anniversary of the founding of Monte Carlo. To commemorate this centennial, Grace sent me a gorgeous, round pendant in gold from the jeweler Balanche, featuring a gold sun with blue enamel, and a Monégasque shield in red and white enamel with a gold crown in the center. In gold around the medallion it said: "*MONTE CARLO 1866-1966.*" Although many people think that Monte Carlo and Monaco are the same, Monte Carlo is actually an area within the Principality of Monaco. The district was named after Prince Charles III (Monte Carlo means "Mount Charles"), who founded it in 1866. He built the Casino and founded the *Société des Bains de Mer* as a way to entice people to come to Monaco as an upscale resort, which included the grand *Hôtel de Paris*.

On top of all the usual annual events that Grace was responsible for, she had taken on the role of President of Monte Carlo's Centenary, which meant that she was planning and organizing all of the special events that would be taking place throughout 1966. These included a clay pigeon shooting championship, a Star Class regatta, an international tennis tournament, and a stamp exposition in honor of Monaco's philatelic renown. In addition to all of the annual balls and galas, there would also be a *Bal du Centenaire* in May and a charity ball called the *Bal des Petits Lits Blancs* (Ball of the Little White Beds), to benefit children under the patronage of Princess Grace, plus several other cultural and festive events and activities. There would be special weeklong events, such as "United States Week" in July, in which Grace would participate in playing baseball! I could not imagine how she would manage to take it all on. She wrote, "Am busy with my Centenaire & don't have enough time for my three angels."

Grace took her job as Princess of Monaco very seriously, and it was indeed a full-time job. No one realized how much Grace did for Monaco, both as its representative when she was abroad, and in Monaco itself. There were endless functions that she was expected to attend, and she recognized it as her duty as the wife of the Head of State. People counted on the Princess of Monaco to be there, and she could not say no. She did enjoy it, but it became exhausting, with late nights followed by meetings and luncheons, over and over again. Her schedule required someone with Herculean abilities, but she was determined to do it all.

Grace felt fortunate that they had their private ranch of Rocagel that she could retreat to, so she could rest and relax, but then there were always the regular demands of being a mother of three young children. In the middle of the onslaught of Centenary events, all three of Grace's children came down with whooping cough, including baby Stephanie, who was just over a year old. Grace wrote that it had been a "terrifying experience" that just went on and on: "Stephanie had not had all of the necessary shots, so her case was quite serious - She scared us to death on several occasions - it was just awful – 'As if I didn't have enough on my hands...!' –"

She managed to write a letter to me in May: "Joan dear - Have been wanting to write for so long - In fact, I had a letter half-written on my desk since the middle of March - I have never been so busy & never tried to do so many things at one time - and when we did take off a few days for our tenth anniversary - we went to Seville!! A place where no one sleeps & it is considered practically a mortal sin to even want to - We were on the go every minute there, but it was fun..."

She wrote about all the events that she had just completed, and how satisfied she had been with the success and beauty of the Flower Show, attracting seven thousand visitors in four days. Then she told me about all the events coming up, including a major costume ball (worrying about how she was going to get there wearing a huge hoop skirt), and going to Ascot in England, among many other engagements. She wrote, "At the end of the year when I am a hundred years old and in a nursing home – will you visit me?"

With everything that she had going on that year, Grace shocked me with this invitation: "My brother is either bringing or sending with someone two of his daughters (10 & 11) to stay with us for a month - Will you still consider sending us Charles? We would love to have him & Albert would be so happy - I will ask my brother to contact you & perhaps they could all come together - Around the fourth or fifth of July would be best - Then I can take them all directly to

Rocagel." Charles was thrilled that he would be seeing his dear friend, Albert, whom he really missed.

It always amazed me that no matter how hectic Grace's life was, she somehow managed to include friends and their children's friends, even on their vacations. At eight years old, this was Charles's first big trip by himself, and it was so thoughtful of Grace to take the time to send me a reassuring telegram as soon as he got there; "Charles safely arrived. All is well. Love Grace." (Even royalty did not make long distance phone calls in those days!)

Grace wrote from Rocagel, keeping me informed of what was happening: "...Albie & Charles were so happy to see each other again, and we are really delighted that he could come over and be with us... I put all three children to bed after lunch & they had a good nap and now are ready for anything." Charles participated in all the events, even when the family visited Rainier's sister, Princess Antoinette. Grace looked after Charles when he had a cold and although I never asked this of her, she profusely apologized for not finding the time to take Charles to see his former dentist! She was simply amazing. She had Charles write to us on Rocagel stationery:

ROCAGEL

Dear Mommy and Daddy,

I met Mister Kelly and he put us on the New York flight to Paris. I arrived there and the plane was a smooth one. I am now safely arrived at Rocagel and I gave everybody their presents and Albert already had a James Bond can but he does not have one at Rocagel so he wanted it.

Love From, Charles

Upon Charles's return, both Grace and Rainier sent letters saying how wonderful he was, and Rainier added, "Thank you so much for sending over such a nice little ambassador!" He even wrote in a subsequent letter, "Charles is a wonderful boy. I have pleasure in repeating it. He was perfect and handled himself so well during his stay with us." This was such a relief for us, because one never knows what could happen with young children over three weeks. Grace wrote: "...He was sweet & we loved having him – He seemed fascinated by Stephanie & when I asked him if he wouldn't like a baby sister like that, he said no, that he had changed his mind & would rather have an older sister instead." She finished her letter, "The house is so quiet today that it seems very strange - Only three children after six seems nothing at all."

Freeport, Bahamas – August 1966

Dear Aunt Grace,

I had a wonderful time at Rocagel and the Palace and liked staying with you very much. I liked playing with Albie very much and Stephanie is so cute, I adore her. I had a safe return but the twelve hours were pretty dull because there was nothing to do on the plane. But the meals were very good. Although the plane swayed a bit only Susan got airsick. Please give my love to Uncle Rainier, Albie, Caroline, and Stephanie.

Love From, Charles

Freeport, Bahamas – Aug. 18, 1966

Dearest Mum & Dad -

Charles had a fabulous time in Monaco. They were wonderful to him, and Rainier sent a note with Charles for Martin – addressed "To Martin Dale, father of Charles, by special messenger." It was a lovely letter saying what a good houseguest Charles was, that he got on so well with Albie, and what remarkable French he spoke. He ended up by saying that they were coming to Phila. & N.Y. in early September & could we possibly meet. We are trying to get them here or will go to N.Y. or Bermuda to see them. It should be fun! Grace wrote to say how good Charles had been. They went to the Hôtel de Paris for a film, to the Palace for swims, to the Monte-Carlo Beach Club, to the baseball game & American Barbecue at Mont Agel (you saw pictures on television of Charles with Albie & Caroline at the Palace pool – we saw it, too, very good interview – Grace was very beautiful, poised & intelligent), to David Niven's for a birthday party, to Princess Antoinette's for lunch. Rainier's sister, Princess Antoinette, wrote us saying "What a darling your Charles is! How intelligent, and sweet and fun and.... 'bien élevé' [well brought up]. We enjoyed having him so much and I wanted to tell you we all love him and congratulate you on such an adorable boy! Thought of you and wished you were here too! Best wishes from us all & a kiss for Charles. Antoinette de Monaco." Is that not a glowing report?

Much, much love from us all, Devotedly, Joan

We had waited eighteen months for our dream home to be built on "Bahamian time," and we moved our belongings in at the end of June. With Charles in Monaco, it was a relief for me to only have one child around in the chaos, while I got us settled during the month of July. After living in the house for just three months, we got hit with yet another storm! Hurricane Inez's horrendous winds battered our house and property for three days, making a mess of everything, destroying our new landscaping, ponds, etc. We didn't even know if the house would stay standing, but we had nowhere else to go on a low-lying island in the Caribbean! The eye of the hurricane came directly over our house, and we soon found out that the flashing on the roof was not done properly, as we watched water pour down the walls of our brand new home. The power went out, and we had a large tin of caviar (a gift from Charles Revson of Revlon cosmetics), which would spoil without refrigeration. Martin and I decided to sit on the floor in our living room and enjoy it by candlelight, as we watched it rain inside and out!

Martin was once again gaining a great deal of attention for the work he was doing – this time regarding the economic expansion of Freeport. He was being interviewed by *Life* Magazine, *Time* Magazine and even *Parade*, among other publications. Martin caught the attention of Charles Revson, who had established a Caribbean distribution center for Revlon in Freeport. Revson began to court Martin to come to work for him in New York, and kept giving him extravagant gifts like caviar in larger and larger quantities!

Prince Rainier wrote to Martin in December 1966: "What a wonderful thing to be able to *do* things and get them done and on the way. You are certainly lucky. A true and honest challenge is always worthwhile." Rainier was still experiencing frustrations in Monaco, especially with Onassis as the major shareholder in the SBM. Onassis had been playing games for years, making formal agreements on several occasions to sell his 520,000 shares to Prince Rainier, only to repeatedly renege. But this was not a game for the Prince, who had to find a way for the Principality to gain control of its largest company and greatest asset, because the future of Monaco depended on it.

Onassis had been refusing to make improvements on the properties of the SBM, seemingly allowing operations to become rundown so he could then capitalize on redeveloping the land. The National Council and members of the Monégasque government were becoming concerned about the condition of the SBM under the control of Onassis. The State only owned a very small amount of its shares, so it had little power or influence over the organization.

Onassis was famous for saying, "The rules are: there are no rules." The Prince was so fed up with Onassis after years of trying to do business with him, that Rainier finally decided the only way he could win would be to change the rules. He urged the National Council to pass a law that would force the SBM to create 600,000 additional shares of stock to be sold exclusively to the government of Monaco, thereby trumping Onassis. It was a brilliant move!

On June 25, 1966, the National Council of Monaco, backed by the French government, approved a bill to increase the number of shares from 1 million to 1.6 million, with the government of Monaco buying the new shares for around $9 million, and becoming the majority shareholder in the company. Furious at being outmaneuvered, Onassis ended up contesting this with the Supreme Court on January 27, 1967, but Rainier would be the ultimate winner in this very real game of Monopoly!

Rainier wrote: "Many thanks for your appreciation on the finalizing of the Onassis affair... Only then really will we be able to go ahead with all the cleaning up and the projects for the SBM." After this, Onassis reluctantly agreed to sell his shares, reportedly receiving well below market value for them, although he still gained a profit of several million dollars on his original investment. He sailed away on the *CHRISTINA*, and thus ended an era in Monaco.

Freeport, Bahamas – Dec. 28, 1966

Dearest Mum & Dad

I am feeling well, though indigested & sleepy most of the time & I tire easily. We have the Charles Revsons (Revlon) here (they gave us 4 lbs. of the most exquisite caviar I have ever tasted!) Grace & Rainier are at Montego Bay, Jamaica, and have asked us to come to see them – I hope we can go down for a few days!

Loads of love from us all. Your loving, Joanie

1966 had been tremendously busy for Grace, right up to the end. In December, she wrote: "I am struggling to survive until Christmas – This has been an exhausting year & it is not finished yet – We have just had a 24-hour visit of Prince Philip, but the festivities of the British week continue until Fri." Grace also wrote that she and Rainier were taking the children to Jamaica after

Christmas for a much-needed vacation: "It would be wonderful to see you all -
Any chance of you getting over to Jamaica while we are there? I am looking
forward so much to relaxing in the sun & swimming every day…" Charles even
received a personal invitation: "We are en route for Jamaica, I hope you can
come to see us… your friend Albert."

When Grace and Rainier asked us to join them on their family vacation in
Jamaica, and to bring the boys along, I was thrilled. I was quite starved for
culture in the isolation of the Bahamian islands, and I always kept a bag packed
in case anyone invited me to the mainland! Unfortunately, the timing was
terrible, as I was newly pregnant and experiencing quite a bit of sickness. Also,
we were hosting Charles and Lyn Revson, who were preparing for the opening
of a Freeport branch of Revlon International in early January, and it was
impossible for Martin to leave. I was terribly sad and disappointed.

Freeport, Bahamas – January 1967

Grace Dear,

*I tried to telephone you Saturday morning but found the line was under
repair, and when I finally got through, the operator asked for the Prince instead
of you. I shall try later in the week and shall hope to talk to you. How are you
enjoying Jamaica? It is a lovely island, tropical with luxuriant growth – so
different from the Bahamas and other West Indies Islands. I am so glad that at
last you are able to enjoy a well-deserved rest after a most busy but fruitful year.
We have read all about the Centennial Festivities with pangs of regret that we
could not share in some of them, but also with joy at their obvious success,
thanks to your diligent work.*

*We should like nothing better than to see you, and it is hard to believe that
you are so near to us. Unfortunately, Martin has very important business
meetings with people from New York at odd intervals this week, and it is too late
to cancel them. Could you possibly spare even one day to stop by unofficially to
see us in Freeport? (Martin is so proud of the development here that he would
love to show it to you and the Prince.) There is a BOAC jet flight direct from
Montego Bay nonstop to Freeport every Monday, Wednesday, and Friday,
leaving around noon and arriving here at 2:45 p.m. The plane continues to New
York and London. We miss you very much and it would give us such pleasure to
see you again. The Prince asked us when we would next be coming to Europe,*

but I fear it will not be during 1967, as we are expecting a new addition to the family in July – we are thrilled! However, we shall be tied down for a while.

The boys were so happy with the flashlight and the jumping shoes, and I adore the gorgeous Pucci scarf. It is absolutely beautiful – many, many thanks for remembering me.

If there is any chance of your coming, dear Grace, please let us know. We would be so very happy to see you.

Love, Joan

We were thrilled to receive a telegram from Rainier on January 9: "Arriving Freeport 2:45 p.m. January 10. Hope to see you. Prince Monaco." Although we would not get to see Grace and the children, it was a wonderful surprise that the Prince would be arriving the following day. Of course, it meant that I was in a bit of a frenzy to get everything ready with such short notice!

For months, Prince Rainier had wanted to visit us in the Bahamas; he was especially eager to see the house that he had helped design. At the beginning of December, he had written: "My Dear Martin, I would love to see your island and I must do so with first occasion. I will try and talk about it to the government (= my wife!!). And as soon as I see a light of possibility I will write to you to organize things." When he ended his letter with, "Love to all. See you soon I hope!!" we never imagined it would be this soon... On the morning of January 10, we eagerly checked on the flight to make sure everything was on time, only to discover to our great chagrin that someone had booked Prince Rainier on the flight through Nassau instead of through Freeport – which were on two different islands! Martin had to phone the Prince in Jamaica to give him the upsetting news. So near, and yet...

Freeport, Bahamas – Jan. 22, 1967

Dearest Mum and Dad -

We did not go to Jamaica, but the Prince telegrammed us to say he would stop here briefly on his way to N.Y. Unfortunately, his travel agent booked him on the Nassau flight. It was a disappointment. However, Martin flew to N.Y. on business & had dinner, saw a show & went to Sardi's with Grace & Rainier. I was very unhappy not to go but I guess it would have been silly to put the baby in jeopardy. Grace sent me a sweet birthday wire & they promised to send Albert here in the summer of 1968.

Loads of love, Joan

When Lynden Pindling came to power in the Bahamas on January 10, 1967, things started to change rapidly, and one could feel the simmering unrest. It became more and more evident to us that it was time to leave the Bahamas, especially when I heard Pindling speaking at a school rally, inciting the children by passionately repeating "down with whites." The situation grew more and more tense, culminating in an angry mob throwing stones at Martin as Vice President of the Port Authority during a bus strike. Martin decided to take Charles Revson's offer of a job at Revlon in New York, and we would move right after the baby was born.

Pindling actually liked Martin and me, inviting us to one of his inaugural events, where we were conspicuously the only white people. (This was not an issue for us, but it obviously was an issue for others, judging by some of the hateful looks we were getting, which made us quite uncomfortable.) Pindling was a very interesting and well-educated man, who had gotten his law degree from King's College in London and was ultimately knighted by Queen Elizabeth. After he was elected the first black premier of the Colony of the Bahama Islands at the beginning of 1967, it triggered a growing revolution that would lead him to achieve independence from England, with the Bahamian people calling him the "Father of the Nation." But it was a very scary time for us.

Shortly before we moved to New York, I received a phone call from a man who asked, "Is this Mrs. Dale?" When I said yes, he menacingly proclaimed, "I am going to kill you!" A chill went down my spine, but I managed to remain calm and sweetly responded, "Oh, really, when and how are you going to do that?" He hung up immediately, and I went weak in the knees and dissolved in tears. We never found out who made that call, but from the sound of his voice, he was *not* Bahamian. For the rest of my time there, I was constantly looking over my shoulder, living in fear and dread.

I never told Grace about the death threat that I received, but I felt a sense of comfort from her words whenever one of her letters arrived. Those letters always meant far more to me than she ever knew. In February, Grace wrote: "...We were so sorry to miss seeing you, but it was nice to get a glimpse of Martin in New York - Getting back to normal after our trip was very difficult - I think it is a mistake to try to go away just after Christmas - Everything is so hectic…"

She wrote of many things that were on her schedule: "I just made a hurried trip to Paris - Took Wed. night train & flew back this noon… We did get to see Yves St. Laurent collection - It is quite fantastic but I do not know who can or will wear most of the things - many trousers & jackets à la Al Capone - very masculine, all but some zany African inspired evening clothes - I need a few things for our summer trip to Canada & for a TV program that I will comment here in May - But I can not quite see myself as a 1930 Marlene Dietrich…"

In July, Prince Rainier and Princess Grace would be officially attending Expo 67, the world's fair in Montreal, which was slated to be a colossal affair. In June, she wrote to me about their upcoming trip to Canada, and couldn't wait to tell me her wonderful news: "We too are expecting again - It is just two months - Haven't seen my doctor as yet, but I think it will be for the first part of January - I am pleased, but would have preferred waiting until after our big trip this summer - I haven't told the children as yet because it makes such a long wait for them - We have been very excited about our trip - We will go by boat to Montreal - We have three official days in Ottawa - Montreal & Quebec & then we cross Canada by train - & after a couple of days in Vancouver we fly to Alaska & visit several towns there before going down to San Francisco & L.A. We plan to return around the 21st of August…"

Grace and I had shared so much together, and I was excited to think that we were once again pregnant at the same time. It made me feel so much closer to her across the miles. She wrote to me with motherly advice: "No salt the last 2 or 3 months." She also expressed her loving care and compassion for me having my baby in the Bahamas: "Have been thinking of you often these days as your time draws near - I just hope you are not too uncomfortable & that these last weeks will go quickly - It must be getting quite warm there now - but how wonderful that you have your own home to bring the baby to right away." She ended with, "Many loving thoughts to you all - & I hope it's a girl. Love, Grace."

Several weeks later, we were shocked and horrified to receive the terrible news that Grace had suffered a devastating miscarriage while at the Expo in Montreal, and would ultimately not be able to have any more children. Both Rainier and Grace were absolutely stricken. They loved babies, they loved their children, and they loved each other.

The stress and strain of all the events at the Expo had been too much for her. Over 8,000 people crowded around Prince Rainier and Princess Grace at the Monaco Pavilion, with everybody wanting something from them. People were chanting, "You are gorgeous, Grace!" and "You are lucky, Prince," showing their admiration and adoration. Everywhere they went, people flocked to see them. Grace always carried on with all her duties throughout her pregnancies, which was exhausting for her and resulted in two miscarriages. The first one occurred in June 1963, just after I had also lost a baby during pregnancy. When I was pregnant then, Grace had said that she would like to be godmother to my child, which had made losing that baby even sadder for me.

When our daughter, Pamela, was born in the Bahamas on August 1st, Grace very sweetly agreed to be her godmother, so she was named Pamela-Grace in her honor. Thinking back on it now, I realize what an act of true graciousness this was for her to share my joy in her time of sorrow. In her selfless generosity, Grace immediately sent baby Pamela a beautiful cup with a ballerina on it that said: "Tuesday's child is full of Grace," as both of them were born on a Tuesday.

After suffering her miscarriage, Grace spent ten days relaxing with her mother at the seashore in Ocean City, NJ, then went to the Beverly Hills Hotel and Bungalows to recover from her ordeal. She had not been there for twelve years, but found it heartwarming that people were inundating her with flowers and phone calls. She wrote me a very sweet letter from there: "Congratulations and best wishes on the safe arrival of Pamela Grace Elizabeth - I am so happy for you! Isn't it wonderful that you have a baby girl? She will be such a joy and delight for you - Girls always stay close to their mothers - Particularly after they grow up - It was very clever to save her for last! I would be delighted to be her godmother but will have to let you know about the christening… Thank you for all your sweet thoughts after our disappointment - that makes two boys we have lost - I never really regained my strength after the centenary - My love to you all & a special hug to my godchild – Grace."

I agonized over whether I should ask Grace to come to our baby's christening so soon after her devastating loss, but since she was going to be Pamela's godmother and was such a dear friend, how could I not? I decided to make the invitation, and let her choose.

Grace responded: "How I wish I could see little Pamela Grace - she must be just precious… Joanie - I really feel that it will be too difficult for me to get away to come for the Christening. I am very sorry not to be present for such an important day… I just hope it won't be too long before we can get to N.Y. and meet the newest Dale."

We had invited Rainier and Grace to visit us in the Bahamas many times, but it had never worked out, despite all our efforts and near misses. We were about to leave the Caribbean after only two and a half years, and it seemed like we were running out of time to host our friends. However, when Grace could not make it to the christening, Rainier agreed to come in her place. He came ostensibly for "MOD Sports Week," to determine the best shooting team in the finals of the Winchester Claybird Tournament.

FROM THE DESK OF
MARTIN A. DALE

Freeport, Bahamas – 23ʳᵈ August 1967

H.S.H. The Prince of Monaco
Monseigneur,

Although casual clothing will be in order during the week in Freeport, there will be one black tie dinner, at which the ladies will wear short cocktail dresses. We have planned a "Mod Party" on October 28ᵗʰ, and Carnaby Street dress will be worn. For the men this apparently means checked or loud striped trousers and outlandish shirts. For the ladies it will be miniskirts and the usual mod trimmings. We are bringing in a leading mod dance band from England for this party and I have been told that Twiggy will also be on hand.

We are truly delighted that Grace has accepted to be Pamela's godmother. Joan joins me in sending you our fondest regards and warmest thoughts from all of us to Grace, yourself, and the children.

Sincerely, Martin

Prince Rainier came to Freeport on October 22, and stayed in the "Sovereign Suite" at the Holiday Inn, which had been completely refurbished in honor of his visit. We enjoyed showing the Prince all that Martin had accomplished in the economic development of Freeport in under three years. He was intrigued that the casino in the Lucayan Beach Hotel was named the "Monte Carlo Room." The Prince enjoyed golfing, and skin-diving in the crystal clear blue waters. Martin also took him fishing, as Rainier had seen photos of the big fish that his cousin, King Simeon of Bulgaria, had caught when he had visited us twice before.

Finally, Rainier was able to see the house that he had helped design, but which we had only lived in for a year. Unfortunately we had already packed up our belongings for our move, so it was completely empty, but the beautiful antique stone fireplace that he had given us still remained. (Regrettably, we had to leave it behind, because the house had been built in such a way that we could not take it out without destroying it.)

Grace sent an elegant antique vermeil cup for her goddaughter's christening along with a touching handwritten note: "With much love to dear Pamela Grace – may her life be a long and happy one." At the ceremony, Mrs. Wallace Groves stood in for Princess Grace as her alternate godmother, and Sir Jack Hayward was Pamela's godfather. Prince Rainier enjoyed holding the baby, and he was very sweet with her.

It was an unofficial visit, but there were several parties and events in Prince Rainier's honor; although they weren't exactly the elegant affairs he was used to in Monaco, he seemed to have a good time. It was to be our last hurrah in the Bahamian Islands, which we were trading for the island of Manhattan. We would look forward to seeing Rainier and Grace much more often in New York on their many trips to the United States.

DAYS OF GRACE

Life in New York was a total change of pace from everything we had known before. Charles Revson provided us with a large apartment that he owned on Park Avenue, and Martin immediately became immersed in the workaholic schedule that being a corporate executive in New York demanded. We were back in "civilization" – if one can call New York City civilized!

Grace sent a letter on November 1, just after our move: "This must be a busy time for you getting settled in your new apt. I do hope that you will like it. I am sure that you will enjoy living in New York." Grace was so enamored with the city that she had stipulated in her MGM contract that she would maintain a residence in New York. She wrote to me sometime later when we moved to Fifth Avenue at 86th, "I know you will love that situation on Fifth Ave. I was at 988 on the 7th fl. & loved it – it broke my heart to give it up."

At first, Martin really enjoyed his stimulating and challenging job as Vice President and Assistant to the President of Revlon International. For 1968, Revlon launched a new advertising campaign for their premium Ultima II line of cosmetics. They created a special supplement for *Town & Country* Magazine, featuring over twenty famous international hostesses sharing their ideas for entertaining, including the Maharani of Baroda and Princess Grace of Monaco. This was one of the first big projects that Martin was involved with at Revlon, and he contacted many of the socialites, aristocrats and royals that we had met over the years in the diplomatic service and in the Principality.

Martin gave Princess Grace a gorgeous, limited edition large traveling case for jewels and cosmetics, which was handmade in Italy from black crocodile lined in quilted calfskin. It had beautiful black calfskin boxes inside that could be locked to hold jewels. It also contained a full assortment of Revlon's Ultima II line. It was spectacular, and Grace was thrilled with it: "Please tell Martin that I took my handsome Revlon case to London last month & really love it - I am enjoying the products too - They are excellent."

Grace and Rainier took the children to Villars for their annual holiday in Switzerland. She wrote to me in April: "We are here for two weeks catching the last few patches of snow & enjoying the skating rink - We miss you all - It is hard to believe it's five years since we were all here together..."

New York – June 18, 1968

Dearest Mum & Dad -

I had lunch with Grace and several friends today at Vera Maxwell's apartment. We had a very good time & it was nice to see her again. She is looking well. She is traveling alone with Stephanie. Tomorrow she will come to tea to see Pamela. It will be nice to see her quietly and alone. Then Martin & I will go to the Plaza for a farewell drink before she leaves tomorrow evening.

Loads of love from us all, Joan

Grace came to New York with three-year-old Stephanie to see Pamela-Grace for the first time, and we took wonderful photographs of her holding her godchild. She and Rainier had gone to Venice for a weekend for a charity ball, and Grace brought Pam a beautiful twelve-inch vanity mirror, elaborately decorated with gold Murano glass. It was so delicate and fragile that she had hand-carried it on the plane. Grace stayed and chatted for five hours, despite all her other engagements, and the little girls were so taken with one another that Stephanie did not want to leave at dinnertime. Six weeks later, she sent a darling telegram, remembering her goddaughter's first birthday: "Many loving wishes for a big birthday – Aunt Grace."

One of the highlights for me of living in New York was that I got to see Grace quite often. We had a wonderful time when Grace and Rainier visited New York for a few days in October. Grace looked gorgeous, as always, although she said that she was a "physical wreck" after all the events in the Principality. We went to see Marlene Dietrich perform at a gala; she had aged quite a bit since we had seen her in Monaco five years before, but she still managed to look stunning in another skintight, silver sequined dress, and her voice remained remarkable.

The next morning, Grace called at 10:20 a.m. to ask if I would like to go shopping with her, and said she would be over to see Pam in one hour. We took a taxi to Mark Cross, where Grace bought twenty photo albums in leather and five brown suitcases. We enjoyed window-shopping as we walked along Fifth Avenue, delighting in a beautiful, cool autumn day in New York.

It was October 4, her late father's birthday, so Grace went to St. Patrick's Cathedral to light a candle and say a prayer for him. Afterwards, we crossed the street to Saks Fifth Avenue, where Grace bought some simple white blouses, stockings and shoes for herself. We went upstairs to the children's department to buy three pairs of shoes, as well as some blouses, a leather vest, and a lovely formal gown in blue velvet for Caroline, who was now quite grown-up at almost twelve years of age. Grace told me that she and Caroline had gone camping in Italy with the Girl Guides, which had been great fun for them both.

We met Rainier for lunch at *La Grenouille*, after which he went to Abercrombie & Fitch, while Grace and I walked to the townhouse where they were staying. On our way, Grace bought an old milk jug and an antique painted sewing machine as we shopped for antiques until 4 p.m. Somehow a famous gossip columnist wrote about our outing, and the Chanel dress that Grace had been wearing. The following evening, we went for cocktails, dinner and a Broadway show with Grace and Rainier, who were joined by Mrs. Kelly, and Grace's sisters Lizanne and Peggy, including us like part of the family.

Martin's job at Revlon made it much easier for me to find gifts for Grace. She wrote to us from Rocagel in January 1969: "It was so kind and thoughtful of you to send us that carton-full of wonderful products. I am enjoying trying each one. They are beautifully presented and must surely have a great success. The perfume is interesting. I like Norell's very much. Thank you for thinking of me. I will have no excuse for wrinkles now!"

Despite how busy they both were, Rainier and Martin corresponded with each other very often throughout 1969, with both of them offering each other words of wisdom and encouragement. Rainier wrote, "…I am sorry to see that you seem in your last letter to be a little 'bored' by your actual job. Cheer up! There is a good part or side in any job… I suppose, so look for it if you have not yet found it? It is a shame that we were rushing through New York the last time but it is generally like this. Next time we must have a boys' lunch together. Nothing so new here. Always the same mentality to deal with, with the same worries, troubles and annoyances…" When Rainier found out that we would be visiting Monaco that summer, he wrote: "…We are expecting you all, in June. Grace tells me of your arrival to these shores. Wonderful. Looking forward to seeing the Dale tribe again…"

Hôtel de Paris
Principauté de Monaco
June 14, 1969

Dearest Mum & Dad -

The Hôtel de Paris has given us Winston Churchill's Suite!!! And it is beautiful! We have a huge entry & salon, three bedrooms with huge dressing rooms & baths. Also there is an enormous terrace from where we can see all of Monaco & the Palace.

Grace sent a gorgeous bouquet of flowers & we are to have lunch at the Palace tomorrow. It is really great being back! Hope all is well & do take care of yourselves & Pammie. Give her a huge kiss from us & tell her we miss her.

Loads of love, Joan

Thanks to my parents taking care of little Pamela, Martin and I were able to travel to Europe with the boys for three weeks in the summer of 1969. We were treated royally, staying in the lap of luxury in the Winston Churchill Suite at the *Hôtel de Paris*. We were invited to the Palace for lunches, dinners and garden receptions, and the fabulous Fourth International Festival of Ballet.

We were thrilled to go to the exquisite *Salle Garnier* on two occasions: the first was for the opening of the Ballet Festival with the New York City Ballet performing Balanchine's "Jewels," and the second time was for a gala concert. It felt magical to sit in the Prince's Box with Grace and Rainier again.

They were ecstatic to have recently moved into their brand new apartments in the Palace. (On January 30, 1969, Grace had written: "I am frantically trying to finish our new wing & just when we are on the point of moving in I have to go off to Canada for a few days as guest of the Quebec Carnaval.") With three growing children, Grace and Rainier's old apartments had become too small. They decided to rebuild part of the southwest corner of the Palace that had been destroyed after the French Revolution, extending it out to the edge of the garden. The exterior was built to complement the façade of the existing Palace.

Grace designed the new apartment with the latest conveniences and modern elegance, in neutral tones of white and beige – it looked like it came right out of *Architectural Digest*. The living room had breathtaking two-story-high windows modeled after those of New York's Lincoln Center; Grace told me that putting up the curtains was a real challenge because they were so enormous. It had a homey atmosphere, with a large fireplace and cozy little nooks to sit in, and silver framed family photos on almost every table. The apartment was very bright, with a beautiful view.

Off the living room, there was the dining room and kitchen, with a less formal sitting room or family room down the hall. The dining room had a silk drapery canopy on the ceiling, which made the room feel warm despite its large size. On the walls hung the Vidal Quadras portraits of the family. Off the dining room was a little sitting room facing the *Place du Palais*, which is where Grace and I often talked on subsequent visits while she did her needlework. It was a very sunny and cozy room, with rather formal yet comfortable furniture, including Grace's favorite *indiscret*.

The boys were invited to the Palace several times to have lunches and dinners with Albert and Caroline, and to swim in the Palace pool. Grace had them there for the entire day on several occasions, and the children very much enjoyed getting reacquainted. It was a wonderful trip, and we all enjoyed ourselves immensely and had great fun together. We were welcomed back into the fold as if we had never left! Upon our return home, we were delighted to receive a lovely note from Rainier with some photographs of our time together: "It was nice to see you all. Come back!"

FROM THE DESK OF
MARTIN A. DALE

New York – September 5, 1969

H.S.H. The Prince of Monaco
Monseigneur:

You were very thoughtful to send the photographs of Charles and Greg with Albie. The photographs are excellent of all three boys, and it is obvious that they were having a wonderful time together, as in days gone by. I hope that they will have many such reunions over the years to come, since childhood friendships have a very special meaning. And, of course, the snapshots which you so kindly took and sent to us are a cherished memento of a particularly happy summer vacation for all of us. Thank you again for your exceptional attentions while you and Grace were so otherwise preoccupied with official and social chores.

I think that by now Joan has written to Grace with the news that we will be adding to our family sometime next March. It has been a fairly difficult summer for Joan, being pregnant with the attendant physical discomforts, and with me away much of the time.

We have noted with great pleasure and anticipation that you plan to be in New York in early November, and we would love to arrange a theater evening with you. Is there any play in particular that you would care to see or should we just choose one of the new openings, which are very limited this year? As soon as you can give us a tentative date, I shall make the arrangements, and it will be grand to see you again.

Joan joins me in sending our warmest and most affectionate regards to Grace and yourself.

                Most Sincerely, Martin

When Rainier heard the news that we were expecting again, he sent a very touching letter to Martin on September 15: "What wonderful news for you and Joan; BRAVO! I do hope all will go well, and that your new addition will be a prize winner... So you are catching up with us and taking the lead even!... That is bratty! I am distressed when I think that because of obligations and official business, we lost two babies already these last years; we would be at five now, which would have been wonderful!"

For their upcoming visit to New York, we were trying to find a show to take them to, but "free love" seemed to have taken over Broadway. Rainier wrote, "...on no condition do I want to go to 'Oh Calcutta' or to 'Hair'... I am too old-fashioned for those productions!" We chose the musical "1776," about the American Revolution, which seemed sufficiently old-fashioned.

Grace sent a letter in October: "...We are so looking forward to our N.Y. visit even though it will be ever so brief – I am so happy that you are expecting again & pleased to know you are feeling better." When they visited us the following month, we celebrated Martin's promotion to Senior Vice President for Corporate

Planning and Administration for Revlon International, which meant extensive travel for him to Europe, Central America, and the Caribbean.

New York – Nov 12, 1969

Dearest Mum & Dad -

Last week was particularly busy while Grace & Rainier were here, although we only saw them twice, as everyone wanted to entertain them. We had a delightful evening with Grace & Rainier. They came for champagne to our apartment & we included Vera Maxwell & three of their friends. Then we went to see the new musical "1776," which was an intellectual & very well handled musical. Then we had supper at the Japanese restaurant & with the hibachis it was very warm & uncomfortable, but we all laughed & we shall remember it for a long time. The Prince sent me a lovely chrysanthemum plant with a sweet thank you note, saying how much they had enjoyed the evening & even lost weight from the "steam bath." They both have been dieting & look very trim & slim. There were television cameras as we entered the theater & a crush of people. One man in the crowd said how much I looked like Grace! Another lady mistook me for her & said what an added joy "I" had given her! I had a fleeting moment of glory, but enjoyed it – who doesn't?

We all send loads of love - Your loving, Joan

Grace and Rainier wrote to us from Gstaad in February, which brought back many wonderful memories of our winters together. In January, they went to a luncheon with French President Georges Pompidou and his wife, Claude at the Élysée Palace in Paris. Although the lunch was supposed to be informal, Grace said that there was much protocol. She was a very unpretentious person, but her role as Princess was often so fraught with the rules of protocol that even informal occasions were still governed by strict formalities, making it difficult for her to relax. She took it all in stride and always acted accordingly.

She said that she had been traveling so much that she felt as though she had been living out of a suitcase for four months! Back in Monaco, she had the usual events that she was responsible for organizing and attending. She was very pleased with the success of the International Television Festival, which was becoming more and more important every year, especially as the medium of television itself was growing in importance.

Grace's Garden Club also kept her very busy. She loved flowers and was touched to have had two special breeds named for her: a fragrant pink rose called "Grace de Monaco," and a yellow lily, "Lys Princess Grace." She founded the Garden Club of Monaco in 1968 and was always very deeply involved in organizing the club's big annual event, the International Flower Show, which took place in May each year. Grace wanted to help people in all ways, and she felt that flowers could brighten people's lives, so the Garden Club would decorate homes for the elderly at Christmas, put flowers in churches, and do charity bazaars, etc.

Many of the galas and international events in Monaco that were held to generate funds for charity or to stimulate tourism were inspired by Grace, although she never publicly took credit for them. Grace did not care about receiving recognition; she was gratified at the thought of doing as much as she could for Monaco, and to support causes that would help other people in the world. Despite all her increasing duties and responsibilities, she always took the time to remember birthdays and to acknowledge special occasions, like the birth of our fourth child, Eric. She sent a telegram four days after he was born: "Thrilled and delighted over wonderful news. Love to you and new baby boy."

Family was the most important thing in this world to Rainier and Grace. When Martin's father passed away in the fall of 1970, Rainier wrote him a very profound and compassionate letter: "I was so sorry about the sad news of the death of your father that occurred during your stay over in Europe, these events are always most trying and *éprouvant* [testing], as they have a deep significance in one's heart and mind... the great link of affection is broken, and the page of one's life is turned, when a father disappears. I hope that you got over the stress of all this, and that your dear family and the new addition have brought you many kinds of true joys."

It had been a terrible loss for Rainier when his own father died at the end of 1964, just before Martin and I left Monaco. Martin had been there to comfort him during that time, and we had all felt tremendously sad. Prince Rainier had grown very close to his father later in life, when Prince Pierre returned to live in Monaco to be near his son once he acceded to the throne. Prince Pierre was forced to leave Monaco after his separation from Princess Charlotte, when Rainier was just six years old.

Rainier's mother rarely set foot in Monaco and preferred to live at her *Château de Marchais*, not far from Paris. She would go to Paris to see Rainier, or the family would visit her at Marchais, especially during the fall. Built around 1540, the Château and the surrounding farmland (about seven hundred acres) were purchased in 1854 by Princess Antoinette of Monaco, wife of Prince Charles III, and have been in the Grimaldi family ever since. The Château grounds were larger than the Principality, with excellent woodlands for hunting. In November, Grace wrote to me from there: "It is a beautiful place & wonderful to get a taste of real autumn weather - Albert is learning to use a shot-gun & naturally delighted."

Grace and Rainier always wrote in their letters about their children's latest activities and accomplishments. They were both very proud of their three children. Albert was especially proficient in sports like judo, soccer and swimming. He also studied the guitar, while Caroline studied the flute, and Stephanie, the piano. Grace commented: "I am anxiously awaiting the interesting concerts they produce!"

They decided to send Albert and Caroline to summer camps in the United States, so the children could have "normal" childhood experiences of being in the great outdoors, which they thoroughly enjoyed. Grace also wanted them to be with kids from different backgrounds and learn camaraderie. She lamented: "It will be terrible for us but a wonderful experience for them." As a child, Grace loved summer camp, where she learned to ride horses, to play tennis, and to sail, among other things. In the fall, Rainier reported, "The two 'big ones,' Albert and Caroline, loved their summer camps, and there is one thought in their minds, go back next year, which they will do, as they still like camp life, which will not last!!!"

The following summer, Albert returned to his camp in New Hampshire, and Caroline went to her camp in Pennsylvania. Grace and Rainier decided to take a vacation in the U.S. themselves, after the demands of all their regular responsibilities and activities, including a record attendance for the Grand Prix of over 160,000 people (with 9000 cars and 500 buses descending on the tiny Principality for one day!). They rented a house at Bald Peak on Lake Winnipesaukee. Rainier was looking forward to it as much the children were, perhaps even more so: "I am very excited, as I do not know that part of the country at all."

Afterwards, Rainier wrote: "We have spent in this delightful spot of this great country a really wonderful month of vacation. I cannot tell you how lovely and relaxing it has been. I really did 'unwind'... I just brought Caroline to her camp in the Poconos; she also loves this camp life and was delighted to find all her old pals for a month! ...But we have had a GREAT time, with complete privacy in this lovely region, where the locals are so nice and kind. But alas, we have, Grace and I, been very lazy, and I have enjoyed life without calling or alerting the friends and pals!! ...I am sorry we were not able to meet, but it is all my fault!"

It was so important for Grace and Rainier to have private time to spend together, as they were a working couple who had less and less time off from their duties. In fact, even while on vacation in the United States that summer, Grace was still working. In June, she had gone to Los Angeles to make a special appearance at a charity benefit for the 50th Anniversary of the Motion Picture and Television Relief Fund, which offered health and retirement care to entertainment industry employees. Gregory Peck was chairman of the organization that year and served as producer of the gala, with performances by Barbra Streisand and Frank Sinatra.

Organizations all over the world constantly beseeched Princess Grace to speak or work on their behalf. Grace often lent her patronage to charities and championed causes that she believed in. In July 1971, Princess Grace gave a groundbreaking speech to La Leche League International in Chicago, Illinois, to a conference room filled with 1400 mothers and 800 children. She had joined the organization after the birth of Princess Stephanie in 1965.

Grace believed that it was best for mothers to nurse their babies in order to give them everything that they needed for optimal health and growth. Studies were being done that proved how important mother's milk was for the well-being of the child. This speech came at a significant time, when more and more women were using baby formula, being shamed out of nursing their babies (especially in public), or being too busy with their careers as working mothers. The *Chicago Tribune* of July 15, 1971, said that the switch to bottles and formula began in the early 1900s, with breast-feeding dropping in the United States to about 12 percent of mothers in 1956 and 18 percent in 1966. Princess Grace once again used the spotlight that was always upon her to bring awareness to the important role that mothers played in the health and well-being of their babies and children, perhaps affecting an entire generation.

Princess Grace believed that nursing a newborn baby was an essential experience of love and bonding between a mother and child that gave them a lasting sense of security. In her speech, she said: "*I have many duties and obligations of State along with my husband; but my family comes first... When they first needed me, and I them, there were no compromises; State had to wait upon mother. I had never considered anything but breastfeeding when I had children. And when these children came, two girls and a boy, I breastfed them as I always intended to do, simply as something which was to me wholly normal and right. I had never thought about it as anything extraordinary for me to be doing – neither as a working woman, which I had been in a so-called glamorous profession, nor as the wife of a ruling Prince."*

There were many facets to the brilliant gem that was Princess Grace. On the one hand, she considered herself to be a feminist, believing that women could do anything they set their mind to, and she certainly was a career woman. On the other hand, she had some rather old-fashioned ideals. One of the reasons that she wanted to speak at La Leche League was because she believed that babies, breastfeeding, and sexuality were all very wholesome and natural, and she was concerned about the growing decadence and depravity in society. She was very outspoken about issues of decency in popular culture, and she became the first female member of the Board of Directors for Twentieth Century Fox Film Corporation, in an effort to stem the proliferation of debasing topics in films that were emerging in the 1970s, which were marking the end of innocence in western society. At times, Grace took on controversial issues, but she had tremendous courage and conviction, and was not afraid to speak the truth about what she believed in.

Caroline also shared her mother's courage and conviction. When Caroline was in her late teens, she wanted to go to Israel to live on a kibbutz in order to experience a shared community lifestyle. One day while I was visiting, we all had a spirited conversation about it over lunch at the Palace. At the time, Grace felt that Caroline had never lived under hardship nor done manual labor, and worried that she would not be able to cope or stay with it. Years later, Grace felt that the experience might have enhanced her daughter's life, and maybe she ought to have encouraged it, but she was always trying to protect her children.

One of the ways Grace tried to shelter Caroline at age fourteen was to send her to St. Mary's boarding school in England, in order to get her away from the prying eyes of the paparazzi. When Grace and I managed to get together for a quick visit in London, she told me how much she missed her beloved daughter, and how difficult it was being apart from her. However, Caroline was extremely bright and needed the intellectual stimulation of being scholastically challenged.

Grace and Caroline were always very close and got along well, so it was a tremendous sacrifice for both of them. According to Grace: "Really - when one child leaves the nest - it is like losing an arm." She constantly wrote about how hard it was having Caroline so far away, especially around birthdays: "My birthday was lovely, only my Caroline was missing - It is hard to adjust to her absence - she is such company & I miss her terribly - I will pop over to see her next week again… so many other things I wanted to tell you during our brief visit - but just wasn't enough time - It was so good to see you, though & you look so well."

FROM THE DESK OF
MARTIN A. DALE

New York – January 27, 1972

H.S.H. The Prince of Monaco
Monseigneur:

The time has flown by, and I am more derelict than usual in my correspondence, for which I hope that you will forgive me. Fortunately, we have not been completely without news, since Joan managed to see Grace briefly in London at the end of October, and Joan has been consistently more reliable in corresponding with Grace than I have on our end. My only excuse is that I have been traveling extensively, and in recent months more to the Far East than to Europe. However, I am sure you know that you are frequently in our thoughts, and the long silence does not bespeak any change in our friendship from this end.

I fear that we are becoming more or less accustomed to this uncivilized and unsafe city, and we almost accept the anarchy, the rudeness, and the muggings as a normal condition of life, hoping that we will not be the victims. I know that it is crazy to put up with it when there are so many more pleasant places to live, but I guess that we have to be prepared to pay the price for "success" in this world of big business.

I have been considering leaving Revlon, and there have been several really tempting other offers, but each time Revlon has countered with a promotion potentially exciting and challenging, and I have come back to the ranks like a good soldier with a few scars and a bigger office to soothe the pain. Apparently, they want me to move up to Senior Vice President – Finance and Treasurer of the parent company, Revlon Inc., and this does offer a very appealing challenge. Que faire?[What to do?] Joan and I are spending many late hours talking it over, but the decision changes from day to day and week to week.

With luck, I may be making a trip to Europe in February, and I shall take the liberty of calling to find out whether you are in Monaco, in Switzerland, or wherever. I would love to see you, and perhaps I can work out a side trip or detour to wherever you may be.

Joan and the children join me in sending our fond regards and affectionate thoughts to Grace, the children and yourself.

Sincerely, Martin

In March, Martin decided to leave Revlon to work for W. R. Grace, a multinational conglomerate comprising some thirty-five businesses in the U.S. and Europe, with 66,000 employees and a total sales volume of over $2 billion at that time. Martin's principal responsibilities were planning and development, including acquisition and divestiture negotiations and "trouble shooting."

When Martin visited a company owned by W. R. Grace, the employees used to call him "the grim reaper," because when he showed up, it usually meant that the company was about to be sold off. The responsibilities of this job weighed heavily on Martin. He would be away from the family a great deal, and company policy did not allow me to travel with him.

Before Martin started his new position, we took a quick trip to Europe to see our friends. When we returned home to New York, we received a sweet letter from Grace: "Just a note to thank you for the lovely photographs... I want to take a bite out of Pamela – she is precious & so beautiful... It was wonderful seeing you both – sorry we had to rush off to Paris & didn't have more time to see you - Hope Martin will enjoy his new job - Love to you all – Grace."

Life got busier and more hectic for all of us during the 1970s. Martin was completely involved in his new position as Corporate Vice-President of W. R. Grace; he worked very hard, traveled a great deal, and had little free time. We did enjoy the ever-changing scene and cultural advantages of New York City, but sometimes the tensions of everyday city living and the general edginess over the mounting crime rate detracted from the pleasures.

Grace wrote in November, 1972: "...I never seem to sit still for very long these days - My autumn has been spent traveling back & forth on short trips here & there - I must go to Bern - Paris & London (twice) before Christmas & then we will take all the children up to Lürs in Austria over New Year's." Rainier was also traveling back and forth between Paris, London and Monaco.

We all continued to write to each other, but more sporadically. Rainier resorted to typing some of his letters for speed. He decided to rent a small hunting lodge not far from Paris, where he could get away from the world and get "back to the simple country life" that he craved.

FROM THE DESK OF
MARTIN A. DALE

New York – November 22, 1972

H.S.H. The Prince of Monaco
Monseigneur:

I must compliment you on your typing, which is becoming so professional that my only recourse is to use a secretary.

It is a great feeling to get back to nature, living a simple life in rustic surroundings. I really do envy you. The pace here in the New York area is inhuman and stupid. We are running all the time like sandpipers on the beach and letting life slip by.

We were very interested to learn that you have changed your mind about having Albert go away to school. I think that when we visited you in April, Grace had mentioned to Joan that you were thinking of one of the Jesuit colleges in France. There is always a great risk in sending a boy away to school, since most of the boarding schools are terrible, and you take the risk of bad influences, which are not discernible until too late.

We are thinking of a bold step with regard to Charles' education. We have applied to have him admitted to the Lycée Carnot in Cannes for one year beginning next September. He will be in Seconde [10th grade], and we think that that is a good time to get him re-immersed in French culture and thinking in French as a preparation for the baccalauréat exams one year later.

Sir, I do hope that you will excuse my not having written for so long. As usual, you have been in our thoughts and we have spoken often of you and Grace, but the pressure of my new job has really been quite extraordinary, with an unbelievable amount of homework. As a consequence, I have been neglectful, and even my family is reproaching me for being so preoccupied with work.

Joan and the children join me in sending all of you our affectionate thoughts and best wishes.

Sincerely, Martin

Martin had been made Executive Vice President for Strategic Planning and Development of the Consumer Products and Services Group of W. R. Grace, and the new assignment meant much more travel for him. Like many executives, he seemed to be away more than he was home, which was difficult for all of us.

The children were often a major topic of our letters back and forth. Grace and Rainier genuinely cared about our children, and of course, we were always interested to know what was happening in the lives of their extraordinary family. Martin and I were both horrified and relieved to read Grace's letter of February 10, 1973: "Caroline gave us a fright by falling off a horse, flat on her back - It happened at Rocagel & fortunately we were there at the time - She had to lie still for several days but is now back at school and quite well with no permanent damage." Their children were all so active in sports that one could not help but worry about accidents like this and the potential consequences, so we were very happy to know that Caroline was okay.

Grace continued: "We are delighted to know that Charles might be in Cannes next year - It will be fun to see him and have him near - We plan to keep Albert here at the Lycée and not send him away to school - He will go back to camp in New Hampshire for six weeks this summer - which he loves & it does give him the chance to be on his own - away from family & sisters!"

The children were all growing up so quickly, it was making our heads spin. Rainier finished one of his letters by saying, "All is well with the family. Albert is so tall, I look like a midget next to him! Very annoying! I am getting complexes!" To think that Charles, Caroline and Albert were already teenagers and starting to be on their own away from family was mind-boggling. Grace made sure that her children spent as much time together with them as possible, so they still took family vacations when school schedules allowed.

We tried to see Grace and Rainier whenever they were in New York, and I jumped at any opportunity to see them in Europe. It was wonderful to be back in Monaco, even for a short time. I enjoyed seeing the family and attending the opera with Prince Rainier and Princess Grace in the Prince's Box, which brought back many happy memories.

Monaco – March 18, 1973

Dearest Mum and Dad,

Had a delightful luncheon en famille with Grace, Rainier, Albert and Stephanie. They were so sweet to me, and we talked in their small den after lunch for several hours – even Albert and the Prince remained, so I was flattered. Albert is a talkative, engaging, thoughtful young man.

Much love from us all, Your Joan

The following month, Grace made a brief visit to New York, and we went to lunch at *Quo Vadis*. It was unexpectedly pouring with rain when we left the restaurant, and after waiting for twenty minutes, there were no available taxis in sight (which is always the case in New York when it rains!). It was absolutely teeming, causing the street drains to be backed up ankle deep with water as one stepped off the curb. Grace looked around and said, "I remember there used to be a bus that ran along Madison Avenue," so we made a dash for the corner, where there was an awning that could shelter us. As we had no umbrella, Grace was worried about my suit getting ruined, which was so characteristic of her to be more concerned about others than about herself.

As we ran through the downpour, Grace asked me what the fare was for the bus. When I told her how much, she exclaimed, "Thirty cents! I remember when it was a dime." I said, "Well, it has been a long time since you have been on a bus, Grace." We then made another dash through the puddles and got on the bus. Two men immediately stood up to give us their seats, which really showed how naturally regal she was, because that never happens in New York.

Grace was fairly incognito in her raincoat, with a scarf over her head in her usual fashion. A lady came up to her and said, "Has anybody ever told you how much you look like Grace Kelly?" Grace smiled broadly and said, "Yes, I have heard that on several occasions." In an interview in *Cosmopolitan* Magazine in April 1955, Grace had said, "I'm never recognized on the street. I am always somebody who looks like Grace Kelly." I wonder if the lady ever knew that it really was her. Who would believe that the Princess of Monaco would be taking a bus? But she loved it.

Amusingly, when Pam was around three years old, we got on a New York City bus, with her wearing a white rabbit fur hat and muff from Neiman Marcus that Grace had given her. The bus driver looked at Pam and said, "You look just like a little Princess Grace," and my daughter piped up and said, "Yes, she's my godmother." I think she gave the man quite a shock.

Grace and I got off the bus near our apartment and ran through the rain again, until we reached my building. Her visit to the apartment had been rather impromptu. I phoned ahead from the restaurant to tell Sylvia, our housekeeper, that the Princess was coming over and to please get the children ready. Sylvia had very thoughtfully dressed the children in clothes that Princess Grace had previously given to them as gifts: a fashionable dress in white and maroon for Pam, and lederhosen from Switzerland for my youngest son, Eric. Being a rather rambunctious three-year-old, Eric decided to hide his only pair of dress shoes; Sylvia frantically looked everywhere, only to find them moments before we walked in the door. Princess Grace stayed for quite a while and saw Gregory, Pamela, and met Eric for the first time. Eric seemed to idolize her – he could not take his eyes off her and sat there staring in absolute awe.

Grace's loveliness was disarming. Even though she was unassuming about her beauty, it was truly breathtaking for anyone in her presence. It was not just her elegance, but also her energy, her radiance, and her graciousness. She had a dazzling aura about her, and was absolutely enchanting in every way. It really brightened my life to see her.

Grace truly enjoyed seeing our children and always cared for them as if they were her own. She sent a telegram for Pam's sixth birthday: "Happy birthday love and kisses, Aunt Grace." When Charles went to Cannes to study for his baccalaureate, she was so sweet to invite him to be with her family soon after his arrival in September 1973: "Just a note to let you know that Charles was with us over the week-end - It was fun to see him again after so long - He is so grown up but still such a sweet boy - Albert enjoyed having him & I hope we will see him often"

In March of 1974, Princess Grace and Prince Rainier took their children to Rome to be presented to Pope Paul VI. Grace and Rainier had been to the Vatican on several occasions with the Sovereign Pontiff of the time. Prince Rainier had a private audience with Pope Pius XII in 1950. Then in 1957, both the Prince and the Princess were presented to Pius XII, when the Pope decorated Prince Rainier with a medallion denoting the Order of the Golden Spur, which was the second highest of Papal Orders. In 1959, they had a private audience with Pope John XXIII, who recognized their influence on the world, and appreciated their attachment to the Vatican. They carried on a long tradition of close relations between the Principality and the Holy See.

Prince Rainier and Princess Grace were also presented to Pope John Paul I and John Paul II on subsequent visits to Rome. Grace said that John Paul II was awe-inspiring. He radiated goodness and kindness, and was a giant among men, who led all faiths by his simplicity and sincerity.

Grace told me about the time that she was to be presented to Pope John Paul II at the Vatican. As she was walking in the customary long black dress and black veil, she suddenly stopped short. She was holding Rainier's arm, and he was forced to come to a halt as Grace whispered, "Rainier, back up!" He looked at her quizzically, and she smiled broadly so no one could see her whispering to him through her teeth without moving her lips, "I've stepped out of my shoe!" Gallantly, without missing a beat, he took a step backward with her so Grace could step back into her shoe. They then proceeded forward to be presented to the Pontiff, heads held high, as if nothing had happened!

Grace sent me a postcard from the Grand Hotel in Rome: "We are enjoying a wonderful week here in Rome with the children - We look forward to having Charles with us over Easter." Charles was living with a French family in Cannes while he went to school in France. We were pleased that he had renewed his friendship with Albert after so many years apart, and we were thrilled that he got to spend weekends and Easter with the family at the Palace and at Rocagel. However, as a teenager, Charles found it a little disconcerting to have everyone staring at him and taking photos when he was with the Princely Family, which was just a small taste of what Albert and his sisters went through on a daily basis.

Rainier and Grace invited Charles to the International Tennis Championships (after which Albert rekindled their competitive childhood rivalries by beating Charles in a few games), and he was a guest in the Prince's Box for the Monaco Grand Prix in May. Prince Rainier wrote: "...We had Charles with us for the Grand Prix weekend. I think that he enjoyed himself. We also had the two Giscard D'Estaing boys who are very nice boys [their father had just been elected President of France the week before, following the sudden death of President Georges Pompidou]. So we were quite rejuvenated this year! I must say that we need it! Charles looked well despite the demands of the end of the scholastic year."

New York – April 15, 1974

Dearest Mum and Dad,

We just returned from a lovely week in Cannes and Monte Carlo, where we saw Grace and Rainier, who had just returned from Pompidou's funeral. Charles looked great, and was very happy and full of enthusiasm. We had a lovely time together.

Pamela had a great time and really has become a little lady. Her behavior and table manners at the Palace were perfect. She sat next to Prince Albert, and she looked like a lovely little princess herself. We lunched in private with the family, which was nice. It was like old times, and it was very pleasant. Later, Pam had a private tour of the lovely State Rooms, and she was particularly impressed by the Prince's Throne Room. Pam's French improved very much, and she now speaks it to me during the day. She is trying to teach it to Eric, who will go to the Lycée next year.

We have great news, which arrived today. Charles has been accepted at Princeton! We are delighted, as it was terribly competitive.

All my love and devotion, Your, Joan

In the spring, Martin, Pamela and I visited Charles, staying at the Carlton Hotel in Cannes. During our visit, we attended the opera at the *Salle Garnier* in the Prince's Box with Grace and Rainier. It was all very exciting for Pamela, who was then six years old and had never been to Europe before. We were invited to the Palace for lunch, and Pamela was awestruck by the beauty of the *Galerie des Glaces*. We waited in the elegant living room of the private apartments, as Pam admired all the framed photographs of the family, then she became fixated on the exquisite portrait of Grace wearing a tiara that was done entirely with black pegs on a white background. It was an amazing likeness and a truly extraordinary work of art.

Grace and Rainier greeted us warmly, as did Albert and Stephanie. Prince Rainier was celebrating the twenty-fifth anniversary of his accession to the throne that year, and he looked wonderful; of course, Grace looked lovely as ever. We were led into the dining room, where footmen in livery served lunch on silver platters. Pam's eyes got very wide, as she was very nervous about doing everything properly, but she carried herself very well for one so young.

An imposing Palace and a formal luncheon could be quite daunting for a little one who had never seen someone use a knife and fork to peel and eat a banana!

Pamela wisely watched and copied everything that the Prince and her father did. After lunch, Stephanie took Pam to her playroom, where she was amazed by all the playthings, including an extraordinary walk-in dollhouse. It had been great fun for her and the memorable experience of a lifetime.

In 1975, I got to spend some wonderful time with Grace and Rainier in Monaco on my own while I was on "spring break." I had recently re-entered the academic world in New York, working toward a Master's Degree in Communications. It was demanding to be a student with two young children at home, but it was also gratifying.

Postcard – Monaco – March 13, 1975

Dearest Mum and Dad,

I have had a delightful time here, going to lunch at the Palace and to the opera in the Prince's Box with Prince Rainier and Princess Grace. I was their only guest, and we had many laughs together.

Much love, Joan

Later that year, I met with Grace in Paris in October. She had just moved into their lovely new home on the Avenue Foch, near the Bois de Boulogne. Grace was spending more time there with Caroline and Stephanie, who were both in school in Paris. Grace was very welcoming and happy to see me. We sat together and chatted over tea. She told me that when the children became teenagers, it was very tough for her, especially because every move they made was reported, and often distorted. It was difficult enough to be a teenager without being under scrutiny.

Grace managed to keep Caroline fairly sheltered until she attended school in Paris. Albert was very focused on sports and was not as much in the public eye as his older sister, who was relentlessly followed by paparazzi. At eighteen, she was one of the most photographed young women in the world, and was considered perhaps the most eligible royal beauty at that time. There was constant speculation about her social life, but a bodyguard always escorted her wherever she went, and she could not be alone with any young man.

Grace believed in allowing her children to make their own mistakes, so they could grow and learn from them, because she knew that she would not always be able to shelter them from the world, nor protect them from themselves. She thought it was important to let her children know that their parents were not perfect, and that they made mistakes like everyone else. Grace felt that a parent should not be afraid to show their weaknesses to their children, so they would know that their parents are human and learn to forgive them.

We shared our woes and concerns that day, confiding in each other about the challenges of life. When I told Grace that I was worried that my marriage was in trouble, she told me that all relationships have their ups and downs, and periods of drifting apart and coming back together. I told her that after twenty-one years of marriage, Martin and I had become like strangers, with him being away more than he was home. Grace was very empathetic, especially as she and Rainier both had to travel a great deal and spend time apart, because of their increasing duties and responsibilities.

Grace was quite lonely at that time, living in Paris with the children, while Rainier had to remain in Monaco to attend to the demands of being the Sovereign Prince. Grace traveled back and forth to Monaco to manage everything that was required of her, all the while fretting about what might happen to Caroline in her absence, even with ever-present bodyguards. These were trying times, but both Grace and Rainier were in agreement that it was best for her to be with the girls in Paris, despite the difficulty of them having to be apart.

That night, Grace invited me to stay for a very informal supper at her apartment with ten-year-old Stephanie. It was delightful and cozy, sitting at a small table in their den. Stephanie was very informed and spirited for her young years, and the love between mother and daughter was very evident. After Stephanie went to bed, Grace and I talked for hours, late into the night. Grace said that if Martin and I did split up, she would have suitors lined up around the block for me. I was surprised to hear her say that and asked her if she would like the same for herself, to which she replied, "I have enough problems. I don't need to add to them." She was very sweet and made me feel much better, although I was very sad to leave. Grace was such a good friend who seemed to have it "all together"; I valued her wise counsel and wished that I had lived closer to her.

I often wondered what our life and family would have been like if we had stayed in Monaco. We had all been so happy there, but alas, life takes us on its own journey. Living in New York was very stressful for me. Grace had written in an earlier letter: "You really have a beautiful family, and I know how proud you are of them - But I'm sure you need a lot of patience & stamina to raise four children in New York." It was not a safe place for the children, and I was worried about them all the time. Martin changed with the high stress and expectations of being an Executive Vice President at a multinational conglomerate; he worked late nights and traveled so much that he was rarely home. We became like two ships passing in the night, and we had drifted apart.

When Martin wanted to leave us that year just before Christmas, I begged him to stay through the holidays for the sake of the children, to let us have one last family Christmas together. I did not know what I was going to do as a single mother, with two young children in New York. (Pam was eight years old, and Eric was only five.) Charles was away at Princeton University, and Greg was at boarding school at Phillips Exeter Academy... I felt utterly alone.

I thought about moving back to Europe, and Grace said that she would help me get settled and introduce me to some new friends. I was so afraid to be on my own after more than twenty years, but Grace made me feel safe and almost excited about the possibilities of a new life. However, Martin continued to work for W.R. Grace in New York and would not allow me to take the children out of North America, even though he traveled to Europe all the time and would have seen them often. Again, I was devastated. I wasn't sure what I was going to do, but I knew we could not stay in New York for much longer. We put on a happy front for the sake of the children that Christmas and did not let anyone know that the Dale household was falling apart.

At the beginning of 1976, we broke the news to the children that their father was leaving; he was traveling so much already that he told them it was like he was going away on a very long business trip! Grace wrote me a loving and supportive letter from Schönried in Switzerland: "Needless to say, we are very sorry to know that you & Martin are separating - it is a difficult situation for you & as always the woman suffers more, I think - You have the responsibility of the children & the problem of being a woman alone - not easy & my heart goes out to you - If there is any thing I can do, or any way I can help - please ask me - you are such a wonderful girl - These things shouldn't happen to you - But who knows what is best - We must keep faith & most important, keep strong physically as well as mentally - (easy to say!)... We plan to be in N.Y. a few days around the 4th of July & I hope we can see you then - Meanwhile - Courage! And I hope all works out in the best possible way - Love – Grace."

As I was in the throes of being divorced, Grace told me, "Perhaps it is all for the best for all of you, and as I must choose one of you, I choose you as my friend, dear Joanie." This was typical of her to be very loyal. The Catholic faith frowns on divorce, so Grace and Rainier felt that they had to choose between Martin and me. Since Grace chose me, they severed their relationship with Martin, whom Rainier had frequently corresponded with over the years as a friend and confidant. It was a really sad loss for everyone.

When Grace came to New York with the family for the celebration of America's Bicentennial, they invited me to lunch on July 5 at the Regency Hotel on Park Avenue. It was lovely to see them all. At almost twenty, Caroline was stunningly beautiful and absolutely brilliant. Albert, eighteen, was charming, warm and very kind. Stephanie at age eleven was still the apple of her parents' eye. After lunch, Grace and I walked together arm-in-arm down Madison Avenue, talking and window-shopping. She was very sweet, compassionate and encouraging. Martin and I were officially separated, and it had taken a terrible toll on my children. The two young ones felt like they were in a pinball game, being bounced back and forth between Martin's Central Park South apartment on weekends and my Upper East Side townhouse during the school week.

On July 6, Grace invited me to her hotel room so she could see Pam. Albert, Caroline and Stephanie were there. Pam was almost nine and had been truly devastated by our separation. It cheered her to see her godmother, and Grace very thoughtfully remembered her birthday the following month, as she always did, which made Pam really happy. She gave her a lovely rag doll with blonde hair like hers, and a matching nightgown that Pam could wear – it gave her comfort at that time. On July 7, Grace and Rainier threw a lovely reception at the Regency at 5:30 p.m. and asked me to bring Charles and Greg. Afterwards, they invited us to dinner at *Le Lavandou* on East 61st Street, which was excellent. It was wonderful for the children to reconnect, and Grace had been so sweet to include us like family.

Because Grace had such a passion for flowers, and also for preserving things, two years earlier in 1974, I had given her a book on pressing flowers as a birthday gift. At that time, she wrote: "Your lovely book on pressed flowers finally arrived - Only took 4 months!! It is most interesting & I am delighted to have it." Grace began to press flowers as a hobby, and then she became inspired to make beautiful collages with them. Some of these designs were featured on Monaco's famous collectable postage stamps in 1976, which Grace enclosed in a letter to me as soon as they were issued: "Here are the new stamps made from my flower collages - the colors have been a bit too forced, but I am so pleased."

Princess Grace signed her floral creations "GPK" (Grace Patricia Kelly). I believe that she signed the works simply with her initials (and those of her maiden name) partly because she was humble and worried that her designs might not be appreciated. She also wanted to express her true self and creativity, and not have her art assessed based on her being Princess Grace of Monaco. Of course, she could not avoid people knowing who made them, but she wanted to explore her talent in her own right.

Grace was an extraordinarily creative and gifted person. She was an Oscar-winning actress, and she was also an excellent dancer and painter. She was always busy making things with her hands, from her constant needlepoint projects, to knitting and crocheting, embroidery, pottery and all kinds of handicrafts. It took her years to finish a needlepoint vest in maroon with petit point flowers that she made for Rainier, but by the time it was done, he had gained a little weight, so she had to let it out slightly. It was a labor of love, which I recall seeing him wear only once.

Even though she was multi-talented, it took great courage for Grace to actually exhibit the work that was so dear to her heart, because she really was worried whether anyone would like it: "I am also getting excited over my exhibit June 9 at Drouant Galleries - (The feet are getting colder by the minute!)" That first exhibit in 1977 at the gallery of Madame Drouant in Paris was a huge success, with her pressed flower collages selling for $400 to $1600 each. She exhibited forty-six pieces, which sold out immediately, and donated the proceeds to her charities. Her only intention was to share her artistic abilities in the hopes that she could bring joy to others.

New York – November 1977

My dear Grace -

Recently I have been thinking about you, & your birthday is a good occasion to write. I am sending a small remembrance, which should arrive shortly.

I was delighted to hear about Caroline's engagement. It hardly seems possible that she is old enough to marry when I look at the photographs of all the children together years ago in Monaco. You will be busy planning for the wedding – what a job!

Albert is at Amherst? That is a wonderful university & a good choice. I hope the boys can get together sometime. Charles graduates from Princeton next June & then will be out in the "real world." Greg is an enthusiastic freshman, starry-eyed & embarking on a new life. He just got the lead role in one of Princeton's principal plays – not bad for a green freshman! He is also trying out for Daniel Seltzer's "Hamlet," apparently giving an excellent performance. I am proud!

I do have news – moving again. My lease in New York expires in July '78 & for many reasons & with some trepidation I bought a lovely house with sea & mountain views in Victoria, British Columbia, Canada, where my parents live & where I was brought up. I have had many agonizing moments, but I am glad to have made the decision. It will be a healthier, happier environment for the young ones. Charles will be on his own anyway & Greg will come on holidays to visit. Leaving Greg in the East concerned me at first, but he really has a very level head & an insight into life that is unbelievably deep for one so young. I shall be happy to settle down at last, as I love to have roots.

It is up to me to provide a stable home for the children. Martin loves them deeply but seems incapable of really reaching them. I shall not remarry for a long time. I have a responsibility to fulfill. I guess women really are left "holding the bag." Anyway, I feel strong & capable at last of coping with the responsibilities, and I feel happy about myself.

I do hope to come to Europe before I move to the West Coast & I should love to see you, as you are very dear to me. You are a real & caring friend – so rare to find.

With much affection always, Joan
A special hug from Pam for your birthday –

As the Princess of Monaco, Grace was never able to return to her love of acting, but over the years she had found other ways to publicly express her artistic talents. She lent her distinctive voice to narrations: in February 1966, she had done a Canadian television program about the Red Cross called, "The View From Geneva," and in February 1967, she had narrated another TV program, "Monte Carlo: C'est La Rose," a musical tour of the Principality. On December 20, 1977, Grace invited me to a benefit for the historic Beacon Theater in New York City. She was there to introduce the Academy Award Nominated Documentary, *The Children of Theatre Street*, which she narrated under the official billing of Grace Kelly.

The film tells the story of Russia's famous ballet academy, the Kirov School, where the most elite ballet dancers were trained, including Nureyev, Baryshnikov, Nijinsky, Pavlova, and Balanchine. Each year thousands of children apply for admission, but few are accepted. The young dancers are separated from their families for months or sometimes years, dedicating their lives to the agony and the ecstasy of dance.

Charles and Greg joined me for the wonderful black tie event, and the film was deeply touching. Grace was beaming, and proud to be part of something so beautiful. She loved the ballet and the arts, and she was in her element in this milieu of artists. I was so happy for her. Her feet still had not touched the ground when she and Albert came to my townhouse for tea the next day. She was absolutely radiant and emanating an energy of joy and fulfillment – it was inspirational for me. Grace gave me courage to express myself and pursue my own fulfillment, which I was still in the process of discovering.

That was to be our last Christmas in New York before I would move to Canada, so Grace wanted to come to my home and see all of my children. Greg had decided to surprise his best friend from Exeter by inviting him over without telling him who else would be there. Jeff – now an extremely successful lawyer, who is never at a loss for words – walked into our living room, saw Princess Grace, and for the first time in his life was absolutely speechless. Even decades later, he still remembers the "beatific calm and glow that emanated from her." He managed to turn to Albert, and told him about a friend of his at Amherst who played on the soccer team with "a great guy named Al Grimaldi," never realizing who he was! I'm sure that Albert still treasures the years he spent at college in relative anonymity.

We spent a very nice time chatting and had a delightful afternoon together. Grace was even busier than usual at that time, doing a tour to several U.S. cities for "Birds, Beasts and Flowers: A Programme of Poetry and Prose" which was an evening of live poetry reading and recitation that would also benefit the work of the World Wildlife Fund. I saw her deliver this program at Princeton University in March 1978, and I was in awe of how beautifully she performed.

From the moment that she humbly yet regally walked out on stage, Grace knew how to command an audience. Her magnificent presence captured theatregoers and held them entranced. Her soft and dulcet tones, rising to a compelling crescendo, made an electrifying performance. She recited one of the poems with a marvelous southern accent, knowing just when to pause for dramatic effect. I had visited with her at the Nassau Inn in Princeton before the presentation, and she looked very tired; but she put on a stunning taffeta gown, did her hair in an elegant braided crown, and she instantly transformed into the gorgeous Princess Grace that everyone loved and admired so much.

Grace's poetry reading offered her a chance to be on stage, but in a refined way that would not bring criticism from Monégasques who felt that their Princess should not act again. She was very excited to have the opportunity to practice her beloved craft with British actor, Richard Pasco. They took turns dramatically reciting poems from such poets as William Blake, Walt Whitman, Shakespeare and others. Grace often carried a copy of Shakespeare's sonnets with her when she traveled, and knew many of them by heart. She was delighted that the tour was so well received, with large sold-out audiences, standing ovations, and favorable reviews. She and Richard Pasco later released an album of the same name in 1980, which she gave to me as a gift.

During our time together in Princeton, I told her about the enchanting city of Victoria, where I had grown up and where I had recently bought a house. I had been living in New York City for eleven years, and was ready to move to a healthier and more peaceful environment. The only things I would really miss about New York were Grace's frequent visits. I always thought that we would grow old together, and at least see each other a couple of times a year.

In the middle of packing for my move to Canada, I received a delightful invitation to attend Princess Caroline's wedding to Philippe Junot on June 29, 1978. After the movers cleared out my Upper East Side townhouse on June 23, I boarded a plane two days later for the long journey to Monaco via Paris and Nice. I was exhausted from the move and from the trip, but I was so happy to be back. A sweet note welcomed me: "Sorry I couldn't be here to greet you on your arrival. Love, Grace."

I arrived just in time to attend the pre-wedding Ball for Princess Caroline on June 27. I came alone to the wedding, and despite all that occupied Grace as hostess, she was as considerate of others as ever. At the Ball, she came up to me and said, "Joan, I want you to meet a lovely, charming couple." She brought me over and introduced me to several people, including the Count and Countess of Barcelona, and the Duke and Duchess of Cadiz, with whom I had a delightful conversation. Making everyone feel at home was one of Grace's great gifts; she made you feel warmly welcomed and drew you into whatever was happening.

When I unpacked my dress for Caroline's wedding, I was distraught to find that I had forgotten to bring a hat. Not only was it proper etiquette for women to wear a hat, it was also common sense, as the wedding was taking place outside, in the courtyard of the Palace under the Mediterranean sun. I didn't have time to go shopping and didn't know what I was going to do.

Grace was always very clever, creative and practical, so I sought her advice, although I hesitated to do so with all the details that she had to attend to. I was so glad I did, as she advised me to take the Hanae Mori scarf that matched my dress and wrap it into a turban, which ended up looking very chic and fashionable for that era. In fact, during the reception, a famous Parisian hat designer actually complimented me on it! This was even more extraordinary as many of the royals, celebrities and society ladies there were wearing his creations! Grace often wore a headscarf or turban, which looked lovely on her, but she looked beautiful no matter what she wore.

The religious ceremony of the wedding took place in the Palace courtyard at 11 a.m., with the wedding party coming down the elegant white marble staircase lined with gorgeous flowers. Princess Grace looked absolutely lovely as she descended the stairs on the arm of her dashing son, Prince Albert. She wore a flowing pale yellow chiffon Dior dress with a matching wide-brimmed yellow organza hat. (She later whispered to me that she had made the mistake of wearing new shoes, which were causing her terrible agony, but she carried on gamely with a smile throughout the day.) Prince Rainier appeared in full morning dress, gallantly descending the stairs with his beloved daughter, Princess Caroline, who was glowing with youthful joy and innocence at just twenty-one years of age. Caroline was beautiful in a simple long white Christian Dior dress with tiers of embroidered lace throughout the full skirt and long diaphanous sleeves. Garlands of delicate white flowers adorned her hair.

Lattice screens festooned with flowers partitioned the large courtyard to provide a more intimate setting. The guests were seated in rows around the outdoor altar. It was a beautiful day for a wedding, but quite hot sitting in the sun. Being in the courtyard of the Palace brought back many happy memories of glorious evenings, attending wonderful outdoor concerts and ballets under the stars in the "good old days."

The wedding ceremony was originally supposed to take place in the small and intimate Palatine Chapel, but as the guest list grew to over three hundred people, they had to move it outside. Guests included crowned heads like the Aga Khan and the Prince of Sweden, dignitaries from all over Europe, and many of Grace's dear friends like David Niven, Gregory Peck, Cary Grant, Frank Sinatra, and Ava Gardner. Marc Bohan, the designer for Dior who created the dresses for Grace and Caroline, was also present.

Thankfully, the Prince had ordered that helicopters could not fly over Monaco on that day, so the wedding was peaceful, without the noise and the intrusion of the press. However, during the ceremony I suddenly saw the shadow of a gigantic "bird" passing overhead... Looking up, I saw a man in a bright rainbow-colored hang-glider, swooping over the Palace with a huge telephoto lens trying to photograph the wedding, presumably for a Parisian magazine! Only Monte Carlo television was permitted press coverage, so others resorted to great lengths to try to get the scoop!

After congratulatory hugs, the newly married couple walked through orderly throngs of well-wishers, who lined the streets of Monaco-Ville, on their way to the *Chapelle de la Miséricorde* in the old town. According to custom, Princess

Caroline left her wedding bouquet as an offering to the Virgin Mary in a gesture of piety.

The outdoor luncheon in the Palace square featured small stuffed Monégasque specialties, ratatouille Provençale, fried filet of sole, celery remoulade, Waldorf salad, ham with pineapple, cold roast beef and turkey, *fougasse* bread, Monégasque pastries, and strawberries, all with Moët et Chandon, and 1964 Pommery rosé champagne. The bride and groom cut the exquisite wedding cake, topped with two white doves. Each guest at the tables of ten received *dragées* (white candy-coated almonds), in a lovely round Limoges box with an intertwined "C" and "P" and the date in gold, to commemorate the occasion.

After the cutting of the cake, the couple departed by helicopter to an unknown destination for their honeymoon, while we all waved from below. Prince Rainier stood on the Palace ramparts, waving his white handkerchief, until the helicopter carrying Caroline and Philippe completely disappeared. Rainier and Grace both wept during the ceremony; the Prince particularly felt the loss of his cherished first-born daughter, and he would miss her terribly.

Monaco – June 29, 1978

Dearest Mum and Dad,

Have enjoyed an unforgettable experience with the delightful wedding of Caroline. I was indeed privileged to have been included in all the festivities. Grace has a heart of gold.

Much Love, Joan

Having recently graduated from Princeton at the age of twenty, Charles came to Monaco to participate in a world-class backgammon tournament a few days after Caroline's wedding. He played the game very well, becoming the youngest New York State Backgammon Champion when he was sixteen. I was delighted to have Charles join me, returning to our old home after so many years.

Charles and I were invited to an intimate dinner in Grace and Rainier's private apartments, where they served a simple meal of melon, pesto spaghetti, mixed salad, cheese, and currant gelée for dessert. It was a fun evening. Grace and I enjoyed talking and finally getting to relax together after all her preparations for the wedding. I was touched that Grace would spend so much time with me, when she had many friends and guests who had come to visit.

Grace told me that she and Rainier had strong reservations about Caroline's marriage, feeling that she was too young to take such a step at just twenty-one. They were also concerned that she was marrying a man so much older, who was known to be a playboy. Grace later wrote: "Rainier went through a very difficult period during & after Caroline's wedding - He is a bit better now - happily - She & Philippe are doing well - They enjoy playing house - But she was much too young for such a step - but we can only wait & see..."

As life got more hectic over the years, birthdays always provided us with an opportunity to catch up with one another. Grace would send me a telegram on my birthday every year, with "Loving wishes for a Happy Birthday." In November of 1979, Grace wrote: "Thank you for your birthday wishes - 50 comes as a jolt - There are no two ways about it - But on we go & I am busier than ever but I prefer it that way..." She had been doing her poetry readings in Dublin and London, and was thrilled with the response: "...the Herald Tribune gave me such a beautiful review & rave that it lifted my spirits & I was able to face my half century with a light heart."

Grace told me that Caroline had been very successful as the head of the Monégasque Committee for the International Year of the Child, already following in her mother's footsteps. Albert was doing well at Amherst, and had toured Europe with the Glee Club, and Stephanie was enjoying being a teenager. She ended her letter by saying: "Last summer we visited the Springs Mills in N.C. It was such fun to watch my sheets being printed & made - I have a contract for three years with them..."

After reading about her exhibit of pressed flower collages, Springmaid approached Princess Grace to lend her floral designs to a line of linens, including tablecloths, napkins, and bed sheets. Springmaid was one of the first companies to introduce designer linens, and Grace agreed to create a line for them under three conditions: the proceeds would go to charity, the line would bear only her initials "GPK," and her likeness and image would never be used for promotion.

A news release quoted Grace as saying, "As an artist, I feel it is fulfilling to extend my art into practical and beautiful home furnishings. Through these designs, I hope to share with others the beauty that I've found in nature." Grace created five patterns for Springmaid that earned more than $1 million in royalties, which she donated to her charities. (Springmaid discontinued the line after her tragic death in 1982.)

In June of 1980, Princess Grace had a second exhibit of her pressed flower collages at the *Galerie Drouant* in Paris. She continued to modestly sign them "GPK" and was absolutely thrilled that they were being so well received, especially as they were creations that came from the essence of her heart and soul. Grace shared her secrets of flower pressing in *My Book of Flowers*, which she co-wrote with Gwen Robyns (interestingly, Princess Grace's name appears in the copyright simply as "Grace Grimaldi"). Later that year, Grace sent Pam her book, inscribed "To Pamela - with love from her god-mother - GRACE, Christmas 1980." It encompasses many aspects of the beauty and use of flowers, and I consider it a treasured work of art.

That summer, as a gift for my daughter's thirteenth birthday, I took her on a three-week tour of Europe. We called the whirlwind tour, "If It's Tuesday, This Must Be Belgium," after the famous movie, because we went practically everywhere – except Belgium. We started in London, then went to Amsterdam, toured Germany, Switzerland, Italy and France, saw the magnificent châteaux in the Loire Valley and spent several days in Paris. It was an absolute thrill for Pamela, who shared my sense of adventure, passion for travel and interest in art and history.

The pièce de résistance would be going to Monaco and staying at Rocagel as guests of her godmother: "Am delighted to know that you will be coming to Europe this summer - I would love to see you and Pam in fact I would love to have you both spend a few days with us at Rocagel..." I wrote Pam a little note as soon as I received Grace's invitation: "Can you believe that Aunt Grace has invited us to their private home at Rocagel for several days! What an honor – Your best birthday ever!" I usually kept a travel diary to help me recall places and events when I later revisited them in my memory:

Saturday, August 2, 1980

At 1:05 p.m., Pam and I took a flight to Nice from Paris. A gray-uniformed chauffeur from the Palace greeted us and carried our luggage in ghastly humidity to a new model Citroën. We drove up to Rocagel, arriving at 4:30. Grace greeted us warmly with hugs and kisses.

Soon after we arrived, Grace took us into the garden room, a type of sunroom with glass on three sides and a glass roof with thin blinds to prevent the sun's direct rays. There was an organized disorganization of telephone books with ancient irons sitting on top of them, pressing Grace's extensive collection of flowers and leaves for her unique collages. She demonstrated how she made her artistic arrangements, inspired by her love of beauty.

After some refreshments, Grace showed us to the guest suite on the ground floor of the house. It was Grecian in feeling, with white stucco vaulted ceilings, which made the room cool in the humid weather. The suite consisted of a living room, bedroom, bathroom and dressing room, with furnishings in rattan.

While Grace talked to an author who was writing a book on Legionnaires' disease, Pam and I toured Prince Rainier's fantastic collection of antique and exotic cars housed in an immense exhibition hall at Rocagel. It was an impressive collection spanning all eras, comprising the evolution of motor vehicles from the earliest models to the latest beauties. These included a Model T Ford from 1924, a Model A Ford from 1930, a 1921 Peugeot, a 1935 Packard, along with different vintages of Mercedes, Jaguar, Maserati, and of course, Rolls Royce and Bentley, among many others. He had military vehicles, sports cars, and even racing cars.

At 7:30, Rainier greeted us warmly in the living room, dressed casually in a pink shirt and nice trousers. Grace looked striking in a flowing hostess pants suit. Albert chatted while nibbling on the hors d'oeuvres – small, delicate pizzas – before he went to a restaurant where the waiters roller-skated!

Grace, Rainier, Pam and I had an intimate, casual dinner in the dining room at eight o'clock. We had a squash casserole, salad, fruit, and wine, followed by coffee in the living room, in the familiar surroundings of the past. The sofa and over-stuffed chairs had been re-covered, but with the same flowered chintz material that I had remembered from the 1960s. There were vases with beautiful flower arrangements everywhere, including in our rooms – all filled with flowers grown at Rocagel. Various dogs were underfoot, scuffling and jumping on the sofa, which seemed to annoy the Prince.

We joked for a while, and then spoke seriously about Legionnaires' disease, which is a deadly form of pneumonia caused by bacteria dispersed from air conditioning and showerheads. (It is called Legionnaires' disease because the first outbreak occurred in July 1976 at a convention of the American Legion at the Bellevue-Stratford Hotel in Philadelphia.) Grace and Rainier were staying at that same hotel when the outbreak occurred, and narrowly escaped infection. Grace was allergic to air-conditioning and had turned it off immediately upon entering their room, which may have saved their lives.

All of us were ready to retire by 11 p.m., so Grace came down to our guest rooms to make sure that all was as it should be and asked if we needed anything. She gave me Rory Cameron's book to read, *The Golden Riviera*. We said goodnight, and Pam went to sleep with a blissful smile.

Sunday, August 3, 1980

The morning was hot and hazy at Rocagel. Grace was already at the table in the cheery dining room when we arrived for breakfast at 8:30. We were served croissants, *pain de seigle* (rye bread) and *pain de campagne* (country-style bread). There was honey from Rocagel, along with fresh cherries and apricots from the trees that Rainier himself had planted many years before. Pam was thrilled when her godmother gave her a beautiful porcelain bird for her thirteenth birthday. The Prince promised to give Pam something later.

After breakfast, we went for a walk around the property. The weather was terribly hot! As we toured the ranch, we saw a variety of animals, including cows, ducks, chickens, flamingoes, and many of the bees that had produced our morning honey! We walked through the cow gate to admire the splendor of Monaco lying below us in the distance. We then went swimming in the gloriously cool swimming pool. It had a charming stone changing-hut nearby, with a trellis covered by vines that provided much-needed shade. Albert appeared after a late night, followed by Rainier, who also joined us for a swim.

Lunch was served at 1:30 on the lower terrace in front of our guest room. We had wine from Rocagel, freshly made potato chips, *pissaladière*, melon with prosciutto ham, zucchini stuffed with cream cheese, hard-boiled eggs surrounding carrots and lettuce, and cheese. For dessert, we had Grace's own plum whip that she had made herself, which was light and delicious. Coffee was served while Grace and I chatted, seated on chaise lounges.

Grace took a photo of me with her new Olympus camera, and Pam took a charmingly informal photo of Grace and myself. Afterwards, Grace and Albert went to Monaco to pick up Caroline, who had just arrived from London, where she had been studying creative writing for six weeks at Cambridge.

Pam and I took another peaceful swim in the pool, and then dressed for dinner. I wore a long Italian crepe gown with floating train, and Pam looked sweet in a long pink dress (Albert commented on it, which made her night!). At eight o'clock, we went up to the living room to find Rainier and Albert, along with Father Lo Penta, who had just said Mass for the family at their private chapel. Rainier served white wine while the other guests arrived, including Prince Alexander of Yugoslavia, and Caroline (who looked a bit fatigued after traveling). We had Dom Perignon pink champagne and *pissaladière* hors d'oeuvres out on the terrace. It was a lovely, warm evening. Grace arrived, apologizing for being late. She looked wonderful in a black satin Chinese tunic top and matching harem-style pants with tight anklets.

Dinner was served in the dining room. I was seated between Prince Alexander and Albert. We were served cold jellied consommé, tiny fresh green beans from the garden at Rocagel, lamb chops, small potatoes, cheese, and cassis sherbet with fresh fruit cocktail. Later, we had coffee in the living room, while Albert prepared his "special" after dinner drink: grappa and lemon – seemingly innocuous, but lethal. Caroline was very lively and amusing.

We talked until 11:15, then Prince Rainier drove Grace and me to Monaco in his Ford Ghia, while the young ones watched television. Grace and Rainier did not really want to leave Rocagel, but they were persuaded to attend a function given by the Di Portanovas, who spent a fortune in Monaco. Baron Enrico "Ricky" di Portanova was heir to the fortune of his grandfather, Texas oil magnate Hugh Roy Cullen. Ricky and his wife, Sandra, were "jet-setters" who were known for their parties and for their penchant for enormous amounts of caviar.

When we arrived at the *Hôtel de Paris* at 11:45, dignitaries at the hotel greeted us, along with Baroness Sandra di Portanova, who was wearing a frothy black and white tulle ball gown with musical notes embroidered on it. Grace whispered to me that she felt underdressed for this occasion after seeing our hostess. It was a "musical evening" as a theme, hence the musical notes on our hostess's gown – I couldn't help but wonder whether she had found the dress to match the theme, or whether she had set the theme to go with her dress. The music for the evening included violins, and a Dixieland band.

We were ushered into the party with ceremony by Prince Louis de Polignac (Prince Rainier's cousin and Albert's godfather). I spoke with Prince Louis at length while we were served from magnums of Pommery Champagne. We watched the human zoo and blissfully enjoyed blinis with large amounts of Beluga caviar. There were many familiar old faces... looking older.

We danced on an impossibly small dance floor in the hotel bar. Some very flamboyant show-offs were almost coming out of their dresses. These ladies were rather drunk, or as Rainier put it, "pissed." Overall, it was quite a display of decadence, with sycophants paying homage to Grace and Rainier. We left at 3 a.m., just as spaghetti with caviar was being served. It was a battle to follow Grace and Rainier through the crowd, but I managed to make it out of the hotel without stepping through our hostess's net gown.

As we got in the car, Grace said that maybe we should have stayed at the party for the caviar spaghetti! She then suggested that we go to the all-night restaurant Tip Top for spaghetti Bolognese, as we had done in the "old days," but Rainier did not think that was seemly after leaving the party, especially because the restaurant was just down the street. The Prince skillfully handled the treacherous drive back to Rocagel.

When we arrived home, we found ourselves slightly hungry, so we raided the refrigerator. We giggled as we had a little "chickie" (Grace's name for chicken; she called presents "prezzies" and dinner "din-din," champagne was sometimes "champy"). Grace loved to have endearing names for everyone and everything, calling me Joanie, Albert was Albie, Caroline was Caro, Stephanie was Stephie, and my daughter Pamela was Pammie. My favorite was when she would say, "Yes, indeedy!"

People who knew Grace before she became Princess of Monaco called her Gracie, but I always called her Grace, and my children called her "Aunt Grace." She did not mind being called by her first name and was not personally concerned with formality or protocol. After our "midnight snack," we found Caroline awake and listening to music at 3:30 a.m. I left them to talk and went to bed.

Monday, August 4, 1980

I went upstairs to breakfast at 10 o'clock to find Grace, Rainier, Albert and Caroline already at the table. We had bread, fruit, jam, honey and tea. Grace and Caroline went down to Monaco to pick up Caroline's things, as she had decided to leave her husband, Philippe Junot. Pam and I took photos and walked around the property. Then we went to the pool and enjoyed the breeze, the views of the mountains and the sea, and the tranquility.

At 1:30, a healthy, light lunch was served on the patio consisting of radishes, carrots, and new potatoes (all from their garden), with chopped steak, cheese, wine or beer, and fruit. Demitasse coffee was served on the lawn, as we stretched out on chaise lounges. Grace was knitting, Caroline was lying on the grass with her favorite dogs, Onyx and Tiffany, snuggling close to her, while Pam fell asleep next to Caroline. After the late night we had, Rainier also slept, and then went down to Monaco.

Sad and disheartened, Caroline talked seriously at length with her mother, as Grace was very concerned about her daughter's situation with Junot. The possibility of an annulment came up because the marriage had been rather brief. After quite some time, they were both worn out and went for a nap. I rested outdoors, enjoying the breeze, the sounds of the whispering poplar trees, and the contentment of having the privilege to be at Rocagel again. I was grateful to be there as a friend for Grace during such a challenging time.

Grace asked me to join her on the upper terrace for a chat while she did her needlepoint. She told me that she had tried to talk Caroline out of marrying Junot, but there was nothing she could say to dissuade a twenty-one-year-old girl who was so smitten and in love. When they married, he was a thirty-eight-year-old playboy bachelor, who perhaps was not too eager to change his ways. Caroline had been a devoted young bride who was now devastated and heartbroken, but she managed to be sweet and pleasant to us despite all of her pain and problems. (A few days later, Caroline issued an official statement announcing that her marriage with Philippe Junot was ending.)

Grace was busier than ever with all her duties, projects and charities. She loved going up to the ranch at Rocagel, where she could finally relax. She was juggling so many things at once, playing the role of wife, mother, and Princess. To the world, she made it look effortless, but she confided that she was quite exhausted.

Later that afternoon, Gant Gaither arrived; he was a talented Broadway producer and designer, who had been a long-time friend of Grace's (in 1957, he wrote the biography, *Princess of Monaco: The Story of Grace Kelly*). He and my daughter, Pam, were both celebrating their August 1 birthdays. He was given the airy guestroom next to ours, and he chatted brightly as he unpacked, while Grace and I listened, sipping tea on the lower patio outside his room.

That evening, we were going to a concert in Monte Carlo. I dressed in a black silk multi-colored dress with shawl, and Pam wore a white cotton dress and shawl. Pam was very concerned that she might fall asleep during the classical concert, but Grace told her not to worry about being embarrassed, because Uncle Rainier nodded off all the time! Before we left, we went to the upstairs terrace for a light dinner of fried squash flowers (a Mediterranean delicacy), cheese, a pear tart, and champagne.

Grace stayed behind at Rocagel to comfort Caroline, who was pale and upset by her pending divorce. Grace's chauffeur, Paul, drove Gant, Pam and me to the new Princess Grace Theatre, under the Loews Hotel. Gant praised Grace's good judgment and great common sense. Although we were disappointed that she and Caroline could not be with us, we were happy that she was able to give her daughter much needed support and advice at such a difficult time.

Prince Rainier joined us at 9 o'clock and showed us around the concert hall with evident pride regarding the design and acoustics of the building. That evening, world-renowned opera singer, Montserrat Caballé performed with the Monte-Carlo Philharmonic Orchestra. She was utterly fantastic, and the audience went wild, giving her a standing ovation. She sang six arias and an encore from *Madame Butterfly* – one of the most exciting moments of a lifetime!

I was seated to the right of Prince Rainier in the Prince's Box with Grace's Lady-in-Waiting, along with Gant and Pamela. At intermission, we were served champagne, smoked salmon, dainty sandwiches, physalis (a sugar-coated, small, yellow Mediterranean fruit) and petit fours in the private reception room behind the Prince's Box.

The Prince drove us back up to Rocagel at 11:30 in his Ford Ghia, expertly navigating the treacherous hairpin curves. He was gracious and charming all evening. Pam was very touched when we arrived and the Prince presented her with a package that he took out of the car. He had made a special trip to Monaco to pick up four tee shirts, as a gift for her birthday: "Monte Carlo Beach," "Grand Prix de Monaco," "Jubilee of Prince Rainier III," and "I Lost My Shirt in Monte Carlo." Pam was overjoyed. We still have them as souvenirs of a most memorable occasion.

Grace and Caroline had already retired to bed, so we said goodbye to the Prince and gave him a small Chinese lion curio. He responded, "Are you leaving so soon?" We packed until 1:30 a.m., and I used Rocagel stationery to write what would turn out to be my last letter to my mother before she died:

> *"ROCAGEL"*
> *August 4, 1980*

Dearest Mum,

Just a short note from Grace and Rainier's summer retreat perched in the hills overlooking Monaco, to let you know that we are having a fantastically good time.

We are being warmly treated as part of the family and are included in all activities including soirées at the Hôtel de Paris and a concert by Montserrat Caballé in Monte Carlo.

> *Much love, Joan and Pam*

Tuesday, August 5, 1980

We slept well, and went to breakfast at 8 o'clock with Grace and Caroline. We chatted leisurely and then Grace took our photo with Caroline before we tearfully said goodbye. As we walked to the car, we noticed a special arrangement of water and food for the dogs along the driveway; Caroline laughingly said, "That's a doggie drive-in!"

We were invited to come again and stay longer! It had been a delightful visit, with memories that we would treasure forever. The chauffeur, Paul, drove us to the airport in Grace's monogrammed Rover, complete with telephone (a rarity in those days!). This was the car that Grace herself drove down the same dangerous road on that fateful day just two years later. Upon our return to Canada, we were greeted by a sweet note from Grace: "…it was such fun having you with us & I so loved seeing Pam - She is lovely."

When my mother passed away that autumn, Grace wrote a loving and compassionate letter: "I was so sorry to hear of your mother's death and send my heartfelt sympathy - It must be terribly difficult for you, and the emptiness quite devastating - How wonderful for her that she had you near with the children these past years - that must have given her tremendous pleasure and joy - and a lovely consolation for you and Pammie…"

Rainier had written profound and poignant words when he experienced the loss of his own mother, Princess Charlotte, back in 1977: "I am indeed so sorry to have been so silent in writing to you, to thank you very much for your kind message of sympathy on the cruel occasion of my mother's death. But I have been trying to find time and tranquility to write to you, and up to now, found neither. These sad times leave one with a feeling of emptiness, where memories flock back mixed with regrets. Though one expects death, one never admits it, and it is hard to realize how completely definite it is!"

After my mother's passing, I also lost my father a short while later. I felt truly alone in this world, as I was an only child, and my friendship with Grace became even more like a cherished sisterhood. In June of 1981, I went to New York to meet her. She invited me to have cocktails in their suite at the Regency Hotel. We had white wine and caviar, with Albert serving the drinks and passing the hors d'oeuvres! He was very dear, especially for one who has been surrounded by servants his whole life.

On the night of June 4, we went to the Broadhurst Theater on Broadway to see Ian McKellen and Tim Curry in "Amadeus," the story of Wolfgang Amadeus Mozart. We arrived in a chauffeured limousine, to find reporters and photographers everywhere. Grace, Rainier and Albert were swarmed, and Prince Rainier finally had to push some of them out of the way in order for us to get into the theater. Nevertheless, Rainier was in great form that night, very pleasant and complimentary, and in remarkably good humor.

The play was absolutely fantastic, and the acting was powerful and unforgettable. We all thoroughly enjoyed it and went backstage to congratulate Ian McKellen, having champagne with him in his dressing room. He was on his way to receive an award that night, and would win the Tony Award for Best Actor in a Play a few days later. Upon leaving the theater, we again had to fight our way through the mob of reporters and photographers to get to our limousine. We drove to a nightclub in the West 50s, where we let Albert off to enjoy the rest of the evening.

Grace, Rainier and I went on to the 21 Club for dinner. Nobody knew they were coming, so the frenzy at the door was something to behold, and I think some people were actually asked to move. Strangely enough, we ended up at a table right by the kitchen. Rainier gallantly refused to let us ladies sit next to the swinging kitchen door, even though it practically hit him on the elbow every time it opened! Grace directed me to sit between the two of them, which was surprising because Rainier was always careful where he sat, in case someone took a photograph of him next to another woman, so they could crop Grace out of the photo and make false headlines in a tabloid.

Rainier and Grace celebrated their twenty-fifth wedding anniversary that year, and she told me, "I think we both deserve a medal for making it this far." A long-term marriage can be difficult enough for most people, but when your marriage and family are constantly in the media, with the whole world watching and gossiping about everything you do, it is even more challenging.

We had a wonderful time chatting for hours over drinks and dinner. It was a delightful and relaxed evening. Afterwards, I proceeded to get a taxi, but Grace and Rainier insisted on dropping me off where I was staying at 89th and First Avenue, which was out of the way from their hotel at 61st and Park. I was really touched that they cared so much about me, and treated me like family.

The next time I would see them, it would be on the trip of a lifetime. But tragically, for Grace, it would be her last...

August 1965, Grace in front of Rocagel

Hat's off to baby Stephanie!
Grace and Stephanie at Rocagel with Bahamian straw hat I sent her, August 1965

Prince Rainier visiting us in
Freeport, Bahamas for the
christening of Pamela-Grace
October 1967

Princess Stephanie with Princess
Grace, meeting her goddaughter
Pamela-Grace for the first time
June 1968

Greg, Stephanie, Grace holding her goddaughter Pamela-Grace, and Charles
at our New York apartment, June 1968

Grace visiting us at our home in New York, April 1973
with Greg, Eric and Pam (wearing a dress that Grace gave her)
3-year-old Eric was mesmerized and could not take his eyes off her!

Grace looking great at 40!
At Palace pool, June 1969

June, 1969 – Martin, Greg, Charles and Rainier
in the Palace pool that Rainier designed – large enough to accommodate a rowboat!

Grace and Martin by the Palace pool

Martin, David Niven, Grace, and Hjordis Niven in the Palace gardens

Charles with Albert in Monaco, 1974

Charles with Stephanie and Albert at St. Jean Cap Ferrat 1974

Pam's first visit to the Palace of
Monaco, in the *Galerie des Glaces*
(Hall of Mirrors) April 1974

Pam was awestruck by this extraordinary portrait of Princess Grace,
done in black pegs on a white background in the new wing of their private apartments,
with Grace's ever-present needlepoint on the sofa

Albert, Grace, Joan, Greg, and Charles
The last Christmas at our New York City townhouse, 1977

Princess Caroline's wedding to Philippe Junot, luncheon outside the Palace
June 29, 1978

Pam with Prince Albert at Rocagel, August 1980

Princess Caroline and Pam sitting on the grass at Rocagel, August 1980

Princess Grace and Pam by the pool house at Rocagel
Celebrating Pam's thirteenth birthday with her godmother

Pam, Princess Caroline and Joan with Caroline's guard dog in front of Rocagel
Photo taken by Princess Grace

❋

MY BOOK OF FLOWERS

❋

*To Pamela –
with love from
her god-mother –
Grace*

Christmas, 1980

PART FOUR:

THE LAST DAYS

In 1981, Grace wrote that she would be taking a seventeen-day cruise to the Arctic the following summer with Rainier and the children, sailing to Norway, Lapland, and Iceland. She sent me the brochure for the cruise and asked if I wanted to join them. I was very touched by the invitation, and of course, I said yes! I booked my trip immediately, as I was always eager to see Grace, and was grateful to spend this precious time with her.

I was to embark on Paquet Lines' ship *MERMOZ* from August 2-19, 1982, with Grace (age 52), Rainier (59), Caroline (25) and Albert (24). I had been looking forward to the cruise for months, knowing that it was going to be the memorable journey of a lifetime. It took me weeks to decide what to pack for this fantastic voyage, and, as usual, I brought along a travel diary:

Friday, July 30, 1982 – London, England

After planning and looking forward to this day, it has finally arrived! As the result of a great deal of preparation, I have two huge suitcases, one carry-on, and camera equipment – far too much! I left Canada and landed at Gatwick Airport in the South of England. The train trip to Victoria Station in London was uneventful, but on arriving with my two large suitcases loaded with clothes for a dressy cruise, I found pandemonium. There were no luggage carts available, and the one porter was being fought over by worn-out passengers eager to get home or to their hotels. It was hot and humid, with muddy water covering the platform of the station, which was under extensive construction. (Why is there always construction going on during peak tourist season?!) After helping several other travelers, the porter at last became available, and I managed to attract his attention and brave the madding crowd.

In front of the station, a seemingly unending line of people stood grumbling because of a shortage of taxis. The queue stretched around the corner and the wait felt eternal. As we shuffled along in line, I heard the people in front of me talking about the impending ferry and rail strike. They said that the ferry workers were due to strike in two days. That would mean I might not be able to get to France to board the ship in Calais! I quietly panicked. What to do? En route to my hotel at Sumner Place, my mind was whirring.

As soon as I got to the hotel, I immediately looked in the telephone guide to call Sealink, the company that operates the ferry between England and France. I had forgotten that the British telephone system was so much different than ours in North America. Was that a busy signal or a ringing tone? It was hard to tell, but I hung on to see if eventually it would be answered… Finally! I was told that indeed, the ferry workers were about to go on strike, so I cut short my visit to London, got on the last ferry before the strike, and booked the last room at a hotel in Calais. Luck was shining!

Sunday, August 1st, 1982 – Calais, France

The passage through the English Channel was typically beset with fog, so the ferry arrived quite late. And upon my arrival at the ferry terminal in Calais, my luggage was nowhere to be found! I was horrified, thinking to myself, "What will I do on the ship for three weeks with no clothing?" I had heard terrible travel stories of missing luggage; fortunately, I came prepared, just in case… In my carry-on bag I managed to fit three pairs of shoes, a long black dress, several stoles in silk, a bathing suit and robe, a nightgown, two blouses, a sweater jacket, a silk dress, a sports dress, lingerie, stockings, a blue wool coat, two light sweaters, silk scarves, cosmetics, cameras and film – plus the wool outfit I was wearing! Yes, I suppose I could have managed for three weeks, but it would have been a bit monotonous, especially on such an exceptional cruise, which would be quite dressy most of the time.

I looked everywhere in the terminal for my luggage and encountered the usual, *"Ah, Madame, c'est ici quelque part. Ne vous inquiétez pas!"* (Don't worry, Madam, it is here somewhere!) It was always the same story – four different Frenchmen, including the man in charge, told me: *"Patientez-vous, Madame, ils vont venir."* (Be patient, Madam, they will arrive.) They did *not* arrive! Had they put my bags on the train by mistake? Suddenly, I heard the whistle blowing – the train was leaving! I was panicking again. *"Allez à la consigne, Madame, peut-être sont-ils là-bas?"* (Go to the baggage checkroom, Madam, maybe they are there?) I rushed over and was told, no, they were not there... *"Attendez, les voilà!"* (Wait, there they are!) There were my bags, in a remote area where no one would ever have looked for them. What a relief!

I then had to get a taxi and was told, *"Il faut téléphoner."* (You must telephone for one.) I asked the man at the baggage checkroom if he could give me change for 50 francs, the equivalent of ten dollars. *"Non, allez au bar."* (No, go to the bar.) Luckily the barman was pleasant and gave me fifty centimes in exchange for some English coins. Then to the phone. I had such a feeling of frustration and helplessness, even though I spoke the language. "Keep your spirits up, Joan," I told myself. I dialed a taxi – wrong number! Finally, I got through and ordered the taxi to come to the *Gare Maritime*.

I looked all around, but again there were no porters. How was I going to get my luggage (with no wheels) to the front of the station? A cart, yes, I saw one across the tracks. I managed to get the cart and with difficulty put the two bags on it; still there were no porters, and no help was offered. I got to the front just as the taxi arrived... It seemed I was getting back into harmony.

The driver took me to the *Hôtel du Sauvage* and waited while I ran in to make sure they had held the room despite the ferry's delay from fog. I was in luck! I paid the taxi driver 22 francs, and he left my luggage on the sidewalk. A charming young lady from behind the desk went for a porter – again, NO PORTER! She and I struggled to carry the bags, until a friend of hers walked in and kindly carried my suitcases up to the room. I was very grateful, as there was no elevator.

My room was spacious and pleasant with striped and flowered wallpaper, a large armoire, a desk and chair, and a double bed with two huge pillows and a bolster. It had been a long trip, and I was hot and weary. I thought I would run cold water on my wrists and face in the bathroom. But where was the light switch? After looking and groping for five minutes, there it was – a minuscule switch, where else but below the sink! A handy place, and so easy to find!!

Monday, August 2nd, 1982 – Boarding the MERMOZ in Calais, France

I feel safe here in France; it is almost like coming home. I went out to pick up some things before boarding the ship, and the shopkeeper said that I resembled Princess Grace! I thanked her for the compliment. At lunch I sat next to two people from Monaco who were taking the cruise. They had known my husband, Martin, through business and thought I was related to Grace. I was feeling close to her already!

As I walked along the quay, which was slightly foggy, I could see the *MERMOZ* in the distance. While waiting for my embarkation time, I visited the Cathedral, which was still under repair from the bombing in World War II (after almost 40 years!). Then I went to a museum and was admiring sculptures by Rodin, when suddenly I heard *"On ferme."* (We're closing.) I looked at my watch, and it seemed early to me, so I asked why they were closing so soon. They told me that it was their proper closing time and then said, "Oh, Madame, there is a one-hour time difference between here and London." No one had told me; I could have missed the cruise! I dashed back to the hotel, grabbed my luggage and rushed to the ship.

I had requested a single outside cabin, and when I arrived on board, I was surprised to find that my stateroom was very close to Rainier and Grace's suite. I wrote a note to Grace telling her that I had arrived, and gave it to the steward who had shown me to my cabin. He insisted that I deliver the note personally right away. I was reticent and said that I should telephone her after the note was delivered, but he was adamant that I come with him. The steward knocked on the door, which was two doors away from my cabin. There was an empty Mark Cross suitcase in the hallway marked "Princess Grace of Monaco."

Grace opened the door and flung her arms around me, saying, "I was just going to phone you!" I entered their sitting room, and Grace said, "Look Rainier, talk about telepathy, here is Joan." Rainier kissed me on both cheeks and quipped, "Hello, Telepathy! You know my father's brother's son, Prince Louis de Polignac." I greeted Prince Louis, whom I had known from Monaco.

Their suite consisted of a sitting room and a bedroom with a large double bed. Grace took me into the bedroom, and we sat on the bed and talked for a long while. Grace mentioned that she had attended her annual Red Cross Gala the night before. She told me that, at her suggestion, André Levasseur had transformed Monaco's Summer Sporting Club into a replica of Grauman's Chinese Theatre in Hollywood, complete with the famous handprints and footprints of the stars. This was a perfect backdrop for Joel Grey, who provided the entertainment that evening (and who will always be remembered for his Oscar-winning role in *Cabaret*). Grace described his performance as a triumph, and said that the guests – including herself and the elegant Catherine Deneuve – were enthusiastically throwing flowers on stage.

Grace and Rainier had retired in the wee hours of the morning, only to arise again early to catch the train to Calais. They had already been on the ship for quite a while, so Grace had time to unpack. She remarked to me that she had not intended to wear her large, emerald-cut diamond ring on the cruise, but at the gala she had enjoyed the champagne and found that her fingers were slightly swollen in the morning, so she could not remove it! Grace never liked to wear much jewelry, and had a habit of leaving it lying around, much to her husband's dismay. Her trusting nature is such that I saw her just casually hand a jewel case full of valuables to a ship's steward whom she did not know.

It was very hot, and I was wearing a wool suit, having come from England. It was getting hotter and hotter, as Grace was telling me that she hoped she had done the right thing by allowing Stephanie not to come on the cruise. After a lot of soul-searching, she had decided to let Stephanie go to Barbados with her boyfriend, Paul Belmondo, and his parents (his father was the famous French actor, Jean-Paul Belmondo). Grace was a very caring and conscientious mother, and at seventeen, Stephanie really wanted to be independent. We chatted at length about raising children nowadays, and how they grow up before they can emotionally handle life.

With Stephanie verging on adulthood, Grace's job as a parent was nearing completion. She had been slowly changing from putting everyone else first, which is the usual lot for a wife and mother. Now that her children were grown, she could finally begin to take care of her own needs, ever mindful of her role as Princess of Monaco. She still had difficulty in saying no to certain requests, which sometimes taxed her energies to the limit.

Grace decided that the family should take the cruise, even if Stephanie did not join them, as she felt that they all needed a rest after so many duties, responsibilities and functions. She had been particularly concerned about Rainier's health, which she has constantly worried about ever since I've known her. Grace has a motherly attitude toward everyone and wishes that she could make everything all right in the world. She has invariably felt that she could do more, putting needless pressure on herself.

Suddenly, Grace said, "We are invited to cocktails with the Captain, and you must join us as you are sitting at our table." Grace was wearing an olive-colored cotton dress with a jacket. I had on my flat walking shoes and a wool Nina Ricci suit-dress, and did not have time to change. We went into the hallway and greeted Prince Albert, who was handsome in a blue suit, tie and blue striped shirt, and Princess Caroline, who looked striking in silk pants, a sleeveless silk blouse in bronze, and a colorful scarf.

We all went to Captain Guillou's quarters, where we had champagne, caviar, smoked salmon, and pâté de foie gras canapés. We watched the preparations for the ship to set sail, and the loading of vegetables and other food in massive quantities. It was fascinating. Crowds had gathered on the quayside, and, as we walked along the deck, the Prince and Princess went to the railing and waved to them. The people clapped and cheered, as Rainier and Grace were so warm and delightful.

Still without changing clothes, we went to dinner in the elegant Grill Room. There were just eight of us at our table, which was by a large window. I felt like part of the family, and I was thrilled and grateful to be included. I was seated close to Grace, between Rainier and Monsieur Biancheri, the Prince's Chief of Staff. Our table also included Albert and Caroline, Prince Louis, and Bettina Gray, who had been one of Grace's bridesmaids.

The Prince began joking with me right away, as we all chatted amicably in French and English. Caroline was her usual intelligent, witty, charming self, and she seemed very relaxed. Dinner began with a fantastic smoked Norwegian salmon and a superb Château Margaux wine, followed by filet mignon topped with foie gras, served with carrots and potatoes. We then had salad, more wine, and cheese.

In order to watch the ship set out to sea at 10:30 p.m., we rushed out on deck without having dessert. Everybody was in a party mood, as we had been served much wine and champagne at dinner. Albert had ordered dessert before we decided to leave, and our waiter somehow managed to deliver it to him on deck among the crowd of passengers. Albert stood quietly eating his cake, then looked at me and said, "Would you like some?" He very sweetly fed me a bite with his own fork. He put his arm around me, and I told him how dear he has been to me, and how I treasure fond memories of him and my boys together at the Palace of Monaco. He said that although he has friends who now live in the Ruscino, he still fondly remembers it as "The Dales' Building," where he used to come regularly to play with Charles and Greg since the age of two.

We found Grace and Rainier and walked to the bow of the ship, where we watched the tugboat inch the ocean liner out of the harbor. Grace was so excited; she had not been on an ocean voyage since July 1967, when the family went to Canada for Expo.

It was a lovely warm night with calm seas. Grace and I walked down one deck to watch the pilot nimbly leap off the ship onto the pilot boat. Then we all walked astern to have coffee outdoors, while everyone gawked at us. When we went to our respective cabins, Grace was so enthusiastic and eager, like a little girl. I said goodnight and Grace asked, "Will you be out on deck for exercises tomorrow at 8 o'clock?" I said, "Yes, I'll see you then."

My cabin was extremely small but adequate enough, as I would not spend very much time there – perhaps five hours a night – due to our rather encompassing schedule of activities. As I began to unpack, I noticed a complimentary bottle of Roederer Cristal 1976 champagne on ice... It is wonderful! I am merrily enjoying it, celebrating the journey ahead, as I write today's accounts in my diary at 2 a.m. I must write every day, or I shall forget these happenings on this fantastic cruise.

I am so fortunate to be here and feel that it is somehow ordained, though I do not know why yet. Perhaps I am here as a sounding board. Grace apologized for deluging me with her problems, but she was troubled. Little did she know how practiced I have been at listening to people's problems.

Tuesday, August 3, 1982 – At Sea

I woke up exhausted and still jet-lagged. I slept so well that I almost missed the 8 o'clock gathering; when I arrived on deck, everyone was already assembled. Grace brought along her aerobics audiotape, and there was an area where we could do our exercises without people watching. If they really wanted to, they could have, but people left the family alone for the most part. This was a public cruise, so it was announced to all those on board that the family was on a private vacation. Everyone was asked to please be considerate, and they truly have been.

After breakfast, I went to a lecture with Grace and Rainier, Albert, Caroline, Bettina Gray, Prince Louis, and Monsieur Biancheri in the Grand Salon, given by Professor Rey, an expert on Arctic exploration and the environment. He is President of *Le Comité Arctique International* (the International Committee on the Arctic), which is headquartered in Monaco under the honorary Presidency of Prince Rainier III. The Committee's focus is on the harmonious development of the Arctic region, while ensuring the preservation of its natural beauty and resources.

The subject of Professor Rey's talk was oil in the Northern Seas. He was a most knowledgeable and thorough speaker. He spoke for over an hour about oil rigs, pipelines, life on oil platforms, and the fantastic costs involved in the oil extraction process. He told us that economies have changed in various countries from fishing to oil production; however, oil extraction in the region would run out after thirty years. During the course of the lecture, he paid homage to Prince Rainier, and to his great-grandfather, Albert I, who had sailed north along the route we were taking at the turn of the last century. Unfortunately, Rainier falls asleep easily, and it was a bit disconcerting during the lecture (with all eyes on him).

At 12:30 p.m., I went to the upper deck, which was awash in a slight swell. It was enough to make one queasy if one looked out over the water long enough. Albert acted as though he were seasick and made everyone laugh, but some began to feel it!

It was a lovely sunny day, and after a buffet lunch on deck, Grace left to rest, Albert went to sunbathe, Caroline read, and Rainier slept. Prince Louis and I stopped by the post office for postcards, but it was closed, so we parted. I returned to my cabin and fell asleep deeply for two hours, overcome by jet lag.

Later, as I staggered out of my quarters, I bumped into Prince Louis, who had very kindly bought me some postcards. He said I needed a walk to "clear the cobwebs," so we went to the bow for fresh, pure air and talked at length about yoga, spirituality, life, and harmony. He was soon to retire from the *Société des Bains de Mer* in Monaco, but was still a part-owner of Lanvin Perfumes and had just sold his ownership in Pommery Champagne. He explained how difficult it was to keep up the château of his ancestors in this era, but he felt it was his duty. It kept him poor, he said; he would have been content with a small apartment. He is a very special and unique man.

At 6:30 p.m., I got dressed for the gala dinner. I wore a black Halston off-the-shoulder gown with a pearl pin. Grace was wearing a red chiffon long-sleeved gown with a full skirt, and her 10-carat emerald-cut diamond ring. Caroline had on a short navy chiffon cocktail dress with a soft petalled hem, in which she looked slim, chic and beautiful, as always. I complimented her on it, and she modestly said it was an "old dress."

There was a slight mix-up that evening. We were about to have a "Mermoz" cocktail in the Grill when the Captain hailed Prince Rainier and Prince Albert. Apparently, the Captain, the crew, and all five hundred and fifty guests had been waiting for us in the Grand Salon. The family was mortified that they had kept everyone waiting and wished that the Captain had told them that they were "expected" to make an appearance for this cocktail hour. I'm sure that all the guests were naturally eager to get a glimpse of the Princely Family.

After dinner, we went down to the cinema at the bottom of the ship, where the award-winning film *Diva* was playing, which Caroline recommended that we see. Despite the fact that the movie was in French, his native language, Prince Louis turned to me as we were watching and said, *"Je n'y comprends rien!"* (I don't understand a thing!) I agreed with him completely. Grace was aghast at the senseless killing and destruction throughout the movie, which was relatively tame in comparison to many other films. The cinematography was genius, but what message?

We had a long discussion about violence and the decline of the motion picture industry, a subject that Grace was very passionate about. She was concerned that the industry was degenerating by selling sex and violence as entertainment, to the detriment of society. We had a spirited conversation over a nightcap, and then retired at 1 a.m. I wrote postcards to family and friends, and then wrote in my diary until 3:30 in the morning.

Wednesday, August 4th, 1982 – Bergen, Norway

I called Grace to ask if she wanted to bring her tape to do aerobics on deck. "Yes!" she said, "In ten minutes," so off we went. Grace wore a Paquet Cruise Lines warm-up suit that Prince Rainier had bought for her in the gift shop. We went up to the top deck, which was enclosed on all sides but open on top. We did our exercises for half an hour in relative privacy; people looked but did not intrude, and no one took any photos! That was thoughtful. Grace and I were exhausted. She returned to her cabin, and I stayed on deck to enjoy a glorious day of warm sunshine on the Norwegian Coast.

It had not been so warm in Bergen since 1936! Our visit must have been foreseen, as it was usually cool and rainy in this area. In fact, we were told that the cruise before ours was beset with fog and never once saw blue skies. What a shame that would be on a journey to the "Land of the Midnight Sun." As Grace said, we were having "Princess Grace Weather," because the sun always shines for her wherever she goes.

Rainier, Louis, and I walked to the bow of the ship in the warm sunlight. Albert and Caroline joined us, and we took photos. The scenery through the fjord was extraordinary, with small isolated houses dotting the landscape, each with its own boathouse. It was a very long fjord, which was much more barren and eroded than I had expected. After lunch, we went out on deck to watch our arrival in Bergen. The princes were dressed in blazers and ties for an official visit to the mayor.

Grace, Caroline, Bettina, Monsieur Biancheri and I went on a minibus tour of Bergen with a charming Norwegian-French guide, who imparted a wealth of information. Grace was wearing a ruffled blouse with a pink suede skirt and a turban. Swarms of photographers followed us everywhere, and the long line of cars trailing behind us was incredible. The reporters were quite polite and, fortunately, not too pushy. We went into a department store that was supposed to close at 4 p.m. but stayed open for the Princess. To exit the store, we were led to a side door in order to avoid the photographers, but there they were! A quick leap into the bus, and we were off to the Hanseatic House Museum.

Rainier, Albert and Louis joined us to do some shopping in the city of Bergen after their visit to the mayor. Rainier wanted to go into a jewelry store, where he bought a ring in a Scandinavian motif for Grace. He loved to buy things for her and was one of the few men I knew who actually enjoyed shopping. The family, followed by hordes of photographers, went back across the street to the department store that had been kept open after hours, emerging thirty minutes later with many more packages in hand. Bergen did great business that day!

After a short drive in the minibus, we got out and walked through a tranquil beech tree grove. We arrived at an extraordinary wooden church, which had an extremely high roof that looked like an inverted Viking ship from underneath. Outside the church was a small opening where lepers used to receive the sacrament. A large crude stone cross stood on a mound. Photographers were everywhere, but thankfully not inside the church. We were then driven down a peaceful road to the summerhouse of Edvard Grieg, the famous nineteenth-century composer. Grace was enchanted by Grieg's music. She asked me to take a photo of an interesting lace curtain with a single red rose in a vase on the windowsill.

We returned to the ship at 7:30 and changed for dinner. Grace wore a blue tunic with black pants, and a huge Scorpio pendant with rubies and diamonds. Grace, Caroline, Bettina and I met at the Prince's table in the Grand Salon for martini cocktails and then went upstairs to the outdoor Grill Restaurant, where everyone joined us for dinner. I then went to the *Caverne* disco with Albert, Caroline and Prince Louis. Albert ordered special cocktails for us, and we danced until 1 a.m.

Thursday, August 5, 1982 – Geirangerfjord

I awoke at 6 o'clock and looked out at the calm seas as we entered the fjords – what a thrill. It was sunny and gorgeous, with the sun creeping over the mountains, as we passed a lighthouse and isolated houses amid green patches of land. I quickly dressed in my Paquet Lines warm-up suit and went on deck. The snow-capped mountains dropped sharply into the sea. This was the first time in years that the mountaintops could be seen without mist. It was gorgeously warm and breathtakingly spectacular – it defies description!

At 8 o'clock, I went to the outdoor gym, where I was joined by Grace, Rainier, Louis, and Bettina. We did exercises to Grace's aerobics tape – even Louis valiantly continued to the end.

I changed and had a light breakfast in my cabin, then went up on deck to take photos of the fjords opening before us, with craggy mountains on all sides. We entered Geirangerfjord, which is 15 kilometers long, with waterfalls coming down the mountains. It was somewhat reminiscent of the River Li in China. The sea was an amazing emerald green. Caroline was sitting in the sun at the bow, listening to her Walkman. She was very sweet, as I took a close-up photograph of her.

We had lunch on the upper deck near the pool. Rainier teased me about my decision to go on the bus ride up the mountain to 1,500 meters of elevation. He said I would have ear trouble, and asked if I had brought perfume to ward off the odor of people getting sick. I did not change my mind, although I wavered! Grace decided not to come, fearing motion sickness. Rainier wanted to avoid photographers, as did Caroline. Instead, they went for a swim and a walk, while Albert was the "red herring" for the reporters. I cannot imagine what their life must be like, being hounded by paparazzi wherever they go, even on a family vacation. I was getting just a small taste of what they must deal with on a daily basis. All eyes were always on them, and they really had no privacy. The paparazzi had grown more and more intrusive and relentless over the years. It ruled the family's life in many ways, and all but ruined it at certain times.

At 2:30, we took our warm clothing and went down two decks, where we boarded the launch to see Geirangerfjord. We were four: Albert, Louis, Monsieur Biancheri and me. The same photographers had somehow followed us from Bergen! I wondered how they had gotten to this area, as access seemed to be nearly impossible except by boat.

Once ashore, we entered a large, modern air-conditioned bus; Albert sat next to me and was very kind. He is always so dear and thoughtful. We stopped several times to photograph the *MERMOZ* in the fjord below, then the press caught up to us and recognized me on the road. I was beginning to feel like a celebrity myself. They found Albert and said they would leave if he would accord them an interview with photos. He said he would do so at the top of the mountain, as he did not want to make everyone on the bus wait. We drove up, and up, and up, to a lake with a glacier and a chalet restaurant. We continued driving endlessly up to 1,500 meters on a tortuous dirt road that had no guardrails! The bus just barely cleared the turns, but thanks to our excellent driver, we made it, albeit with white knuckles!

The view was spectacular down to the fjord far below, where our ship was just a speck in the distance. True to his word, Albert gave the interview and posed for photographers in his pleasant and competent manner. I took photos of him and Louis at the "top of the world." It looked like a desolate moonscape with mica-like rocks dragged by glaciers. Monsieur Biancheri found one solitary flower and some lichen for Grace – a touching thought, for her pressed flower collection, and as a souvenir of this cruise. Albert was leaping from rock to rock and taking pictures.

As much as I would have liked to have taken photographs of the beautiful scenery out the bus window, I asked Albert to sit in the window seat for the drive back down the frightening road. It was hair-raising, and I was glad Grace did not come, as she would have been fearful and worried about Albert's safety. Rainier had been wise to discourage her from coming. We stopped at the chalet restaurant on the way down for snacks and postcards.

Back at the ship, everyone met for cocktails. Grace wore tight ankle-length black pants, black high-heeled shoes, and a pale green Thai silk top with a mandarin collar and tiny jeweled buttons. Around her neck, she had a long crystal, gold, and diamond necklace. Caroline looked lovely in a royal blue silk pantsuit with a gold belt.

We had dinner at the Prince's table, where I was once again seated next to Rainier. We talked about Monaco's progress, the new Beach Plaza, nature, and the wonderful energy that trees impart. I told Rainier that I wished for harmony in life, and he responded, "How do you find it?" I said, "By standing aside from myself, not taking myself too seriously, and getting in tune with the infinite universal energy."

The men from our group then headed off to see the movie *Quest for Fire*, while the ladies opted for talent night in the Salon. It was such fun. We laughed and enjoyed watching the ship's guests being made up, with men dancing *Swan Lake* or the tango. It was delightful and relaxing. Grace said that Rainier had become more of a homebody lately and they did not go out as much anymore, so this cruise was a real treat for her. She and Caroline were very friendly and accessible to everyone; however, many people were too timid to approach them.

Afterward, we met the Prince and company in the hallway. Their description of the movie was priceless: "language primitive ape – ugh, ugh, ugh!" Prince Louis, with his thick French accent, said in English, "All they did in the film was 'fawk!'" I said, "Pardon?" He said, "Yes, that is what I said!" This was not his usual language, as he is such a gentleman, so it was very funny. We all went out on deck to enjoy the lovely fjords by moonlight, and then it was time to retire.

Friday, August 6, 1982 – Molde, Norway

On deck at 8 o'clock – the scenery around Molde is exceptional, with eighty-two mountain peaks and numerous small islands dotting the horizon. The Gulf Stream warms these waters, so all manner of flowers grow profusely.

At 8:10, Prince Louis arrived, then Grace and Rainier, so we began our exercises. Caroline arrived looking very tired. She said she had nightmares, because Albert had mistakenly unlocked her door and turned on her light in the middle of the night. The poor girl is constantly hounded by people and photographers who will not allow her any privacy, which can be unnerving after a while.

We were alone on deck and did our exercises rather strenuously, until we saw someone with binoculars and a long-distance camera in the hotel facing us. When Rainier noticed the man, he got his exercise by making angry gestures with his hands and arms, then stormed off. He gets so upset, but I do not blame him.

Grace, Caroline, Louis and I went to the dining room for breakfast, and then we all changed for our tour of Molde. Grace wore a black suede jacket, beige ruffled blouse, black linen pants, black espadrilles, and a smart beige Stetson hat. She looked great.

We went down the gangplank to the minibus. There were not too many people as we disembarked, but suddenly a crowd appeared out of nowhere. They surrounded our minibus and took photos of Caroline and Grace through the bus window. They were polite and waved, and Grace waved back.

Molde, "The Town of Roses," was a sweet town with a bronze statue of a young girl holding a basket of roses. The Town Hall had twenty thousand roses on the roof! We were shown the new church, which needed to be rebuilt after the Germans had blown up all of Molde during World War II. We drove past lovely houses, each boasting beautiful gardens resplendent with all kinds of flowers. We went on a long drive through soft alpine scenery dotted with streams, ferns and wildflowers. We were taken up to the top of a hill to see magnificent views of the town, our ship below, the surrounding islands, and the astounding mountains in the distance. It was spectacular!

We then went to a museum that featured groups of houses replicating Norwegian wooden homes from various regions. Some of the houses had turf growing on the roof, and an opening in the roof over the hearth to allow smoke to escape from cooking with pots suspended over a wood fire. There were benches all around the main room for sleeping and sitting around the fire. It would have been rather dark, but cozy. There were children doing a charming dance, dressed in black, white and red native costumes. Albert took a photo of a small boy sitting on a stump, which looked like a scene from a Hans Christian Andersen fairy tale.

Throughout the sightseeing tour, our bus was followed by a motorcade of *politi* (Norwegian police) and paparazzi – ten cars in all! In town, we bought a newspaper with photographs of their royal visit on the front cover. Photographers and reporters were everywhere, so the family agreed to pose nicely for photos but were still not left alone. We walked back to the ship, and the reporters continued to follow us. Finally, Rainier got upset and said to them, "We kept our bargain by posing for photographs, now you keep yours and let us enjoy our vacation!"

Anger seemed to be the only way to deal with the paparazzi. Grace usually kept her cool, but could not help getting angry eventually at being constantly stalked by them. She always tried to shelter her children from the ever-persistent media, but felt that she had sadly failed to protect their privacy over the years from the throngs of photographers who relentlessly pursued the family wherever they went. This was particularly true for beautiful Caroline. It was one thing for Grace, who chose to be an actress and a celebrity, but the children had no choice, as they were simply born in the spotlight. Prince Rainier, Albert, Caroline and Stephanie were all quite shy, and would probably not have chosen a life in the public eye, but it was their destiny.

The reporters were often ruthless and intrusive, but the adoring public was usually very kind, respectful, and excited to catch a glimpse of them. Back at the ship, a huge crowd had gathered, lining the approach to the gangway. The crowd cheered and clapped, as they saw the family arrive. I was walking with Albert, when a teenage girl gave roses to Caroline, who smiled and waved.

We had lunch on the top deck of the ship, admiring the gorgeous scenery, with clouds beginning to form as mist around the mountains. We were all relaxing in the sun on the ship's deck after lunch, when a fellow passenger approached Grace to show her the watercolor sketches that she had been doing throughout the trip. The woman was thrilled when Grace remarked how good they were.

That afternoon, I went with Grace, Rainier, Albert and Caroline to hear Professor Rey give a lecture on the Arctic. It was interesting, but quite long; we were all so tired and were nodding off, hoping no one would notice. Afterward, we all played bingo – Grace was two numbers away from winning $100, and she was so excited!

I rushed back to my stateroom to change for the Gala of the Ritz. I rested for ten minutes, and then quickly put on a long Chinese cheongsam dress, with a brown silk Chinese coat. Everyone loved it. Grace had on a green and mauve silk taffeta dress with a lovely Ungaro multi-colored scarf in the same tones. Caroline was wearing a smashing red, green and black taffeta dress with large sleeves, and a full mid-length skirt with a red waistband. Albert looked very handsome in black tie, with a lovely black velvet double-breasted vest.

It was clouding over and too cold to have cocktails on deck, so we went to the Prince's table and had a drink before dinner. I sat next to Grace, with Prince Louis opposite us. He told me that he was seventy-three years old. I was amazed; he looked and acted more like he was closer to Rainier's age of fifty-nine. He certainly is game, loves life, and does not want to miss anything. He said that although he had a girlfriend twenty years younger than him, he did not want to marry again, because he was too set in his ways.

We attended a special gala dinner, which was prepared by Chef Guy Legay, the Chef from the magnificent Ritz Hotel in Paris. We were served fresh foie gras, lobster, shrimp, salad, truffles, medallions of lamb, artichoke hearts, warm goat cheese, all accompanied by fine wines and Taittinger champagne. We were all very happy by the time we went down to the Main Salon to listen to a wonderful singer while we talked and had drinks until midnight.

Saturday, August 7, 1982 – At Sea

I woke up with a jolt at 8 o'clock and rushed to the gym at 8:10. I was the last one there! Grace, Rainier, Bettina, Louis and I went through our routine to the tape, but it was harder to do this morning.

Afterward, we all went down to the dining room for breakfast. A man from Paris sat down at our table, without noticing who was there. As soon as he realized it was the Princely Family of Monaco, he quickly got up to leave, but Grace asked him to stay, in her usual warm and welcoming manner. She has always loved to meet and talk to people; however, her position often makes her seem unapproachable, as most people gaze at her from afar without daring to speak with her as a person.

Over lunch, Grace asked me about the many rings I was wearing, and where I had gotten them. She relaxed on deck by working on her latest needlepoint project. Prince Rainier was teasing me about writing in my diary; he said it must be uninteresting, as I had fallen asleep. He then apologized for the remark, and I retorted, "Don't worry, you will never read it!" He said with a tone of gentle respect, "You know, Joan, you are the only woman who has ever dared to talk back to me." (Grace did stand up for important decisions that she valued as being morally right, but otherwise, the Prince's words were law.)

In the afternoon, we all went to see *The Third Man*, an excellent black and white movie, which I had not seen for a long time. Albert was thrilled and said he had not enjoyed a film so much in years.

After the movie, Grace and I went down to the dining room to have some tea. She talked me into sharing an almond pastry. Naughty! Caroline and Bettina joined us, and Grace told us about the "Night of 100 Stars." She had been at Radio City Music Hall with all of the major Hollywood stars to celebrate the centennial of the Actors Fund of America, and she enjoyed it immensely. She saw many old friends, including Gregory Peck, James Stewart, and Elizabeth Taylor, and rekindled feelings of camaraderie with those in the performing arts whom she loved and admired. Orson Welles apparently complained throughout the event. Grace said that when she saw him at the airport afterwards, he did not recognize her!

Sunday, August 8, 1982 – Hammerfest, Norway

There were no aerobics this morning. Instead, I went to Mass at 9:30 with Grace, Rainier, Albert, Caroline and Louis in the Grand Salon. At 11:00, we went into Hammerfest, the northernmost city in the world, where there is no daylight for four months of the year. There was only one group of TV reporters there waiting for us. At first I thought they were Laplanders, but they turned out to be Japanese! They were discreet, but they did follow us, especially Caroline, who was nice and answered their questions. I stopped in a shop to buy some postcards and then rushed to catch up with Grace and Rainier. All I had to do was follow the crowd! I found them at an outdoor market.

When we arrived in Hammerfest, the family decided to go fishing. Grace could not be on a small boat because she got seasick, so she and I opted for a walk up in the mountains after having lunch aboard ship. Grace and I enjoyed spending the day alone together. We chatted with the Captain, who was fascinating as he recounted his travels. He said, "The sea shows one humility," because one must always be aware of all the potential dangers.

Grace and I had lunch tête-à-tête at our large table. It was delightful. We were naughty and had two heavy dishes: *brandade de morue* (mashed cod and potatoes) and *cassoulet* (beans, meat and sausage). These dishes were not usually served for lunch, and especially not together. Grace and I both loved food, so we chose to indulge ourselves, but we agreed not to tell anybody what we had eaten because we still had to meet everybody for dinner. Somehow the Prince found out, and he joked with me later, saying, "As soon as the cat is away, the mice will play."

Over lunch, Grace and I talked about marriage and children, about friendship and kindness. I had been raised on the Golden Rule, "Do unto others as you would have them do unto you." I told Grace that my mother had told me, "One of the worst things one can be to someone is unkind." Grace became deeply immersed in thought at these words, and later she brought up the topic with our group, saying, "Unkindness is one of the great evils in our world," whereupon quite a lively conversation ensued. This obviously was a very important subject for Grace, who valued kindness, but she also knew that some people often did not realize that their words or actions could be hurtful. She felt it probably resulted from the way they were brought up, or from how they viewed themselves.

Grace is a great role model for me, because she invariably seems so serene. She has always embodied her title, Her Serene Highness, perfectly, even under difficult circumstances. As we sat talking over a cup of tea, I asked her if she ever felt anxious and out of balance within herself. She laughed her tinkling laugh and replied, "Oh, yes, often, but I try not to let it show." I think that reining in her feelings has taken its toll on her health. But she has always soldiered on, keeping much locked up inside herself.

After lunch, Grace and I headed into town, accompanied by our ship's steward Remy, and the Second Officer. We went shopping, and Grace lent me Norwegian money to buy a Lapland doll, some cards, and two pewter cups. I repaid her right away in francs. We then hiked up the mountainside on a steep, tortuous path, lined with wild flowers and wooden snow-break fences. We picked flowers for Grace to press for her dried flower arrangements. It was so peaceful there, with a stunning view of the quaint town of Hammerfest and the vast sea in the distance. Grace said, "We rarely have a photograph of the two of us taken together, Joan. Remy, would you take one, please?" We sat on a convenient bench and he took our picture.

(Grace passed by as I was writing this the next day in the Grand Salon. She asked if I were writing about "last night!" I shall get to that!)

We returned to the ship and watched the fishing boat with Rainier, Albert and Caroline pull alongside. They had caught twenty-three cod. Caroline came running up to her mother and said, "Guess what? There was a very nice sailor on the boat who asked me my name. When I said 'Caroline,' he said, 'Oh, what a pretty name.' He didn't know who I was!" She was so happy. She said, "I have found a friend." She ran to the top deck and waved down to her fishing friends. It was beautiful to see her sparkle, as the young man looked up at her like an adoring puppy.

It made Caroline's day to think she was just a normal girl to this boy. The whole family really would have preferred to be anonymous. Most people do not realize that privacy and anonymity are luxuries that we take for granted, but these are two privileges that royalty rarely get to enjoy. It is not always an easy situation. Caroline is so camera shy that even when friends take photos, she seems to wince. No wonder, as people are always poking their cameras in her face!

Later on, I played bingo with three cards given to me by Prince Louis. We nearly won! Grace did not come to dinner as she had throat and gland problems. She had some fresh cod sent to her cabin and slept, while the rest of us enjoyed the fish that the Prince had caught. After dinner, I went to the *Caverne* with Rainier, Louis, Albert, Caroline, and Monsieur Biancheri. On the way down to the disco, I congratulated the man who had won $120 at bingo, and he said, "I shall buy you all a drink," and promptly sat down with us. Rainier was stunned but enjoyed talking to this man, who reminded us of the gregarious French actor, Jean Gabin. They teased me after he left, saying that it was "all my fault," and spoke nicely of him as "my friend" for days.

I danced with Albie and Louis, and then I boldly asked Rainier to dance with me. He never dances unless he must, as he is somewhat uncomfortable in public. He agreed and really danced beautifully, seeming to enjoy it. I apologized later for daring to ask, but upon leaving, he thanked me profusely. Caroline was amazed that I had actually gotten him onto the dance floor. After Rainier and Caroline left, I danced with Louis, and we both left at 2:30 a.m. to retire to our respective cabins. Albert was still going strong!

Monday, August 9, 1982 - At Sea

No aerobics again this morning, so I slept in. At noon, the Captain gave a talk in English showing charts of Spitsbergen. At 12:30, we all met outside on the aft deck for drinks. It was lovely, sunny and cool. Louis did not appear until the afternoon, so I was teased about what may have happened after we left the disco together "last night." It was, of course, innocent.

There was to be a Ball that evening, complete with old-fashioned dance cards, where several different dances are listed, such as the tango, the waltz, the samba, etc. There is a line next to each one, where one writes the name of one's prospective partner for that dance. Before the Ball, the ladies approach the gentlemen to decide which dance they wish to dance together and then write down each gentleman's name. The dances are listed in order, and when the music starts, the partners seek each other out on the dance floor. Grace started off our dance cards for the evening with a bang by asking the Captain for a dance. When I approached the Captain, he chose to do the tango with me, which prompted Grace to say, "I'm going to keep my eye on you. I'm jealous!" She was joking, of course, but every woman on board the ship had fallen for the Captain! He was very charming. On my card, Albert chose the bolero, and Louis, the Charleston.

After lunch, Grace, Louis and I played a game. Then we went to hear Professor Rey's lecture on Prince Albert I of Monaco (1848-1922). Our cruise was commemorating the route that Albert I had taken on four successive scientific voyages, to explore and chart the seas and shores of the Arctic region from 1898-1907. He had made some of his journeys aboard his yacht, the "Princess Alice II," named after his wife, Alice Heine (1858-1925), an American heiress born in New Orleans, Louisiana. Grace was not the first Princess of Monaco who was American!

Albert I, known as the "Prince of the Seas," was a famous oceanographer in the Nineteenth Century, one of the early pioneers in the field. Until his accession to the throne in 1889, Albert I had devoted himself entirely to scientific research, and his discoveries in the fields of oceanography and paleontology earned him worldwide recognition and membership in the British Academy of Science. In 1910, he founded the world-renowned Oceanographic Museum of Monaco, which included an aquarium, a museum with all of the specimens he had collected on over twenty expeditions, and a library, housed in a palatial building perched on the rocks overlooking the Mediterranean Sea.

Albert I was also deeply committed to bettering the future of mankind. On February 25, 1903, he founded the International Institute of Peace, whose mandate was "studying the means of resolving disagreements between nations by arbitration, propagating attachment to methods of harmonious agreement and removing hatred from the hearts of people." This was a precursor to the League of Nations and the United Nations.

Princess Grace had previously spoken about the Institute of Peace, and how Albert I had done everything in his power to try to stop the onset of World War I. He could foresee that Europe was on the brink of war, and he invited the nations to Monaco for several meetings in order to resolve their differences in a peaceful manner. He knew Kaiser Wilhelm II of Germany quite well, as they used to go yachting together, so Albert I appealed to the Kaiser to maintain peace, but the Germans were already armed and prepared for war, so it was too late.

I have always believed that Grace was also a tremendous force for peace in the world, with her deeply caring nature and her serene manner. She can speak to anyone about anything, and people really listen to her wise and compassionate counsel. She has certainly championed so many causes dear to her heart and has made the world a better place in her own quiet way.

After the lecture, Grace and I had thirty minutes to quickly dress for cocktails with the Captain. She is a master of quick change after her modeling and acting careers, which has helped her a great deal in Monaco, when she has to change up to five times in one day to suit a variety of events. Grace looked elegant in a red chiffon gown, with her hair done softly. Caroline looked lovely as always in a short strapless white lace dress with white stockings. I wore a black and gold dress, with a green and red silk shawl that my son, Charles, had given me.

We had Krug champagne and caviar in the Captain's quarters. The Captain had to remain mostly on the bridge because we had encountered unexpected ice floes, and had to sail further south in order to avoid them. These "islands" of floating ice were thirty miles wide and quite impressive. As I looked out, I could see seals, walruses, and small penguins.

After having dinner, we all went to the Ball. It was great fun and very animated, as ladies hunted for their partners. I danced the last dance, the samba, with Rainier, then stayed with him for the conga line, and he really enjoyed the evening. Caroline said that my dancing with him at the disco last night had broken the ice, which made me happy. It can't be easy for the Prince to have people looking at him all the time.

It was still light out at 2 a.m.! I went out on deck to watch the calm seas and the midnight sun before going to bed.

Tuesday, August 10, 1982 – Spitsbergen, Norway

At 6 a.m., I went out on deck to see the extraordinary views of the island of Spitsbergen. There were very sharp mountains (in fact, "spitz" means sharp, and "berg" means mountain) with glaciers going into the sea. The blue-green water was calm like a lake, and the sun – forever sun! The cliffs were covered with green lichen. This area had once been tropical with ferns and lush foliage, as attested to by fossils found in coal deposits. A few hundred Norwegians and a couple thousand Russians inhabited the island. It was used for coal mining, in horizontal mines where one had to crouch or kneel to mine the coal. What a job in such an isolated place!

Up in the Captain's bridge, Grace, Rainier and I were given a demonstration of fjord navigation. These were dangerous passages, but the Captain was very efficient and careful. It was a joy to watch him. There were thousands of birds, including terns and small penguins nesting in rows on the cliffs, creating a cacophonous noise! The views were gorgeous, as blue-green ice chunks floated by. It was breathtaking. Albie arrived wearing a fur hat, and Caroline came later in "revolutionary" khaki. We told her all she needed was a gun!

I had breakfast with Grace and Caroline in the dining room. Rainier, Albert and Louis joined us for tea later, then Albert and Rainier went off in a helicopter with Professor Rey in search of the fjords that their illustrious ancestor had explored. I asked Grace what they were going to do flying over this deserted island all day. She replied, "Listen to Professor Rey!" We burst into laughter at the thought, because his lectures tended to be a little verbose.

Grace went for a nap, as this would be a long day, with the sun in the sky from 6 a.m. to 4:30 a.m. I wrote postcards and mailed them from Spitsbergen, where, in olden days, the islanders put the mail by a cairn and waited for passing ships to pick it up! I then went up to the deck in time to join Grace, Caroline, Bettina and Louis for tea in the Grand Salon. We all played a game of "Name the song from a movie," which was fun.

We were supposed to sail up to see the floating ice pack, but the warm weather was melting all the ice in the area. The ice pack was now too far north, so we had to turn back. We were disappointed, but we had seen part of it already the day before.

I met Grace and Bettina for a drink in the Grand Salon. At 8:15, we went ahead and had dinner without Rainier and Albert, who had not yet returned from their helicopter ride! It was still broad daylight at 10 p.m., and from the ship's deck, the *Baie de la Madeleine* looked extraordinary, with its glaciers and floating blue-green ice. When Rainier and Albert's helicopter finally arrived, they had to wait on shore until the crew built a boarding ramp using the ship's lifeboats and gangways! It was quite a job. Albert and Rainier had dinner on board ship with the Governor of Spitsbergen while Grace, Caroline, Bettina, Monsieur Biancheri and I took the launch to the rocky shore.

Grace had on a mink-lined raincoat. (This was the first coat that she had bought with her money from acting, and she was still wearing it thirty years later!) All of us were wearing warm clothes, although it was surprisingly not cold out, despite all the ice around us. It was an "out of this world" landscape of sand, rocks, lichen, and calm water. I took photos of Grace and Caroline sitting on the only log on the beach. We picked up rocks and enjoyed the spectacular glacier, then returned to the ship at midnight.

We met up with Rainier and Louis in the dining room and had pizza, red wine, and excellent apple pie. Caroline said it was the best she had ever had, "*et je m'y connais en tartes aux pommes!*" (And I know apple pies!) Rainier retired to bed, while the rest of us, including Albert, went to the upper deck. It was unbelievable to see the moon and the midnight sun in the sky together. Grace sent for brandy, while we enjoyed the astounding beauty.

At 3 a.m., we set sail again in full daylight. The "girls" – Grace, Caroline, Bettina and I – laughed and giggled in the hallways, while imagining what the other passengers were saying to each other about the photos that were displayed of our activities. When Grace saw a picture taken by the ship's photographer of herself and the Prince dancing, she remarked to me, "I am so glad Rainier's jacket camouflages my tummy in that photo. Joanie, we must continue with our morning exercises. There are good photos of you, though, Joan. You will be happy with them." I went to bed at 4 o'clock in the morning, with Grace's lilting words ringing in my mind: "Divine day. Goodnight, dear."

Wednesday, August 11, 1982 – At Sea

I went up to the Grill at noon, wearing blue slacks and the blue angora sweater that Grace had given me twenty years ago. Grace was surprised to see it, but delighted that I preserved things as well as she did. She and Bettina were out on deck wrapped in blankets. We all had the drink of the day, the "Troika"; Rainier said of these daily specials, "They all taste the same and have a cherry in them!"

Grace was not feeling too well, and Rainier was also ill with a fever, but he came to lunch and had some soup and gnocchi. Albert and Caroline joined us late. Caroline complimented me, saying how well I spoke French. I was flattered, as she does not give kudos easily! I always spoke in English with Grace, and she only spoke in English with her family, unless there were French-speaking people around. Rainier spoke English fluently, with a slight British accent, as he had been schooled in Great Britain. When my husband, Martin, worked for him, Rainier usually wrote to him in English. However, he would ask Martin to write any important information in French, as Rainier said that he did not want to "miss anything in the translation," so his mind obviously thought in French. In fact, in many of his letters, he often reverted to French sayings, then back to English in the same sentence. Caroline and Albert both spoke several languages fluently with impeccable accents.

I chatted with a nice midwife, who told me how much the family and I were admired, as we were modest, not arrogant people. She thought I was Grace's sister (again!). Many people came up to me throughout the cruise, saying, "You must be Grace's sister," and when I replied that I was not, they were quite surprised. The depth of our friendship truly feels like we are sisters.

At 5:15 p.m., I called Grace to ask her to join me for bingo, but she had a headache from the medicine she was taking for her throat and swollen glands. This was the night of the Costume Ball, but, unfortunately, Rainier had a fever, so he stayed in bed. It was such a shame, because he was going to come in a clown costume and do his own clown makeup. He loved clowns and the circus; every year in Monaco they had a circus festival, which he founded and always attended. The Prince even used to do paintings of clowns. We missed his clown that evening, and his warmth and humor.

Our group came to the *Bal Costumé* as pirates, with Louis as our mascot. At dinner, Louis was wearing white pants and a black shirt with a white cravat and looked very dashing. Afterward, Grace disguised Louis as a Norwegian troll, doing his makeup for him and dressing him in a costume that she made herself, with a paper skirt and a red wool wig. Grace dressed in black slacks, a white shirt, and a red sash. She artfully painted a scar on her own face and blackened out some of Albert's teeth, giving him a menacing look. I wore a bandana, a pirate hat, and an eye patch.

We had great fun acting out our impromptu pirate scene, holding up knives and swords, snarling and growling. The passengers were delighted that we all participated with such enthusiasm and vigor. Our fellow cruise-goers had expected the "royals" to be spectators only, but they got a real treat! (A group photo of all of us as pirates was published in several magazines, of course with me listed as "unidentified woman.") We danced and had a great time drinking champagne. Later, I went to the disco and danced with Albie and Caroline until 4 a.m. I was seemingly inexhaustible, fueled by joy… and bubbly!

Thursday, August 12, 1982 – At Sea – Spitsbergen to Iceland
I joined Grace, Rainier and Louis in the Salon to hear the news and events of the day. The Captain told us that the floating ice pack in the Straits of Denmark was creating a narrow, dangerous passage where the ice was closing in, so we would have to take another route to Iceland, which would take six to eight hours longer, with the ship going at full speed.

In the afternoon, I went to bingo with Grace and Bettina, then to a lecture on the Vikings, given by Professor Rey, with Louis and Albert. I changed into evening attire in twenty minutes to attend a piano concert of Chopin and Manuel de Falla. Unfortunately, Rainier was ill again and did not join us.

Grace and I spoke of how we had to steal time here and there to chat over a cup of tea or a cocktail, between our busy round of shipboard activities: exercising, attending lectures, going ashore, movies, cabaret performances, dancing, etc. As Grace put it laughingly, "We are having a difficult time just getting from one meal to another!" In fact, we had all gained a little around the waist with the delectable food of this superb French cruise line.

We went to dinner, which was again prepared by the excellent guest chef, Guy Legay, from the Ritz in Paris. We were served cold vichyssoise soup, filet mignon with truffles, sautéed mushrooms, stuffed potatoes, green salad, assorted cheeses, a basket of fruit, and a chocolate mousse with raspberries. After dinner, we heard an excellent poet and singer in the Salon. Then Grace, Albert, Caroline, Bettina and I danced in the disco until 3:30 a.m.

Friday, August 13, 1982 – At Sea

I went up to the Salon for a "mime" game and then listened to the news. Later, Professor Rey gave a talk on Greenland, describing it as being two thousand kilometers long and covered with ice that is several kilometers thick. He told us that the glaciers move one hundred meters per day, and that icebergs are filled with air bubbles, which create a sound that can be heard and located by sonar.

I had the "Rêve d'Amour" cocktail of the day with Grace, Rainier and Louis. The sea was rough enough to knock Louis over, even though he was seated! And it was not because of the drink du jour! That afternoon, I went to Professor Rey's lecture on Iceland and saw Grace there; she was wearing a lovely wine-colored pantsuit. It seems the Vikings named the islands of Iceland and Greenland in order to deceive potential invaders: Iceland is actually lush, green and beautiful in some areas, while Greenland is virtually covered in ice!

We had cocktails before dinner in the Stern Room of the ship to celebrate Bettina's birthday. Rainier was feeling well again, so he joined us and livened up the evening with his good mood. We were served an Indonesian dinner, as most of the waiters and cabin boys are from that area. (They sign up for sixteen months and work 365 days a year, with a few hours off here and there.) The ship is very well run and efficient, everything is perfect, and the table service is excellent. After dinner, we went out on deck, where the seas were calm, and the volcano of Iceland was visible.

Later, we enjoyed *Journey to the Center of the Earth*, based on a Jules Verne story, starring James Mason. I sat next to Rainier, who got very involved in the story. He left after the movie, while the rest of us went up to the Grill for a drink. We danced, and anybody was invited to sing onstage. Caroline did not want to sing, so we talked about opera instead. Captain Guillou sang beautifully, with a rich voice that sounded almost professional. The Captain announced while he was singing, "Don't worry, the ship is in good hands – the priest and the cook are on the bridge!"

We turned our watches back one hour as we crossed into a different time zone. Louis, Caroline, the Captain and I went to the *Caverne* disco where we danced and talked until 3:00. Caroline told me that I would die dancing!

Saturday, August 14, 1982 – Reykjavik, Iceland

I met Rainier, Louis, and the Captain for a talk by Professor Rey, during which we drank Singapore Slings. I watched the ship dock as we arrived at Reykjavik at 4 p.m., several hours late, because of our detour to avoid the ice pack. We were supposed to go to the airport to fly over Greenland, but there was no longer time for that as Grace and Rainier were expected to attend a formal dinner, given by the female President of Iceland.

Instead of our aerial tour, a chauffeur was waiting at the dock to take us sightseeing by car. The press was everywhere, but they were more respectful than in some other places. Everyone in Iceland was polite and well educated, even the taxi drivers. They all spoke many languages. We strolled through quaint shops, where I bought Icelandic wool hats, sweaters, and a sheepskin rug.

We went back to the ship, and everyone got ready for the formal dinner ashore. Grace looked lovely in a long white gown with a white mink jacket. Bettina and I were the only ones left at the Prince's table for dinner. I was tired, so I went to bed relatively early at midnight.

Sunday, August 15, 1982 – Iceland

The Consul General of Iceland for Monaco came to pick up our group for a tour in a minivan. He brought his wife, who looked very chic in leather jodhpurs, high boots, a tweed jacket, and tweed hat. We had a police escort, along with five cars of reporters, and a mysterious white van following us.

Our caravan visited a replica of a Viking settlement, with sod-covered roofs and interiors of wood that were like wooden igloos. We drove across the country on unpaved roads, past lava fields and sweeping vistas of barren and grassy land with the sea beyond. It was an unreal countryside, almost lunar in feeling. We saw sheep, cows and ponies (Iceland is famous for them), along with moss, and lichen, which they use for throat medicine. We stopped at a stream, where

Rainier tried his hand at fly fishing for salmon, while Grace, Caroline and I walked through wild willows and hot springs, which are used to heat houses.

The group had a rest stop at a rustic inn and then proceeded to a wild and rocky area, where Iceland held its first parliament. The wind was so strong that it almost knocked us off our feet. We stood for over half an hour in the cold, blustery wind listening to the history of the first parliamentary meeting, but I never managed to understand why this significant event would have taken place in such a barren and forbidding location.

We drove out over stark land that was gray-black with lava outcroppings. It felt eerie and desolate. Here, of all places, where it was so windy and without any trees, we stopped. Suddenly, the mystery of the white van that followed us was revealed: out came a tent, tables, chairs, place mats, crockery, silverware, red napkins, and an incredible assortment of food! We were served drinks on a silver tray as I watched silver wine coolers on pedestals being unloaded for the French white wine. It was incomprehensible to be experiencing such splendor in this harsh place, which was nothing but lava rock and wind!

The elaborate spread of food was amazing. There was herring and potatoes mashed together and served in an iron fish mold, whole smoked salmon, Scandinavian gravlax, smoked salmon marinated in dill, red and black Icelandic caviar, whole poached salmon with sauce, shrimp in aspic, potato salad, trout salad, fruit and cream salad, Icelandic cheeses and bread. All of this was accompanied by a drink called "Black Death," an aquavit with cumin flavoring, which we needed in order to get warm!

Then came the Icelandic delicacy, buried shark's fin, which was passed with great reverence in a tightly closed jar. Albert was the only one who had the courage to try it. When he opened the bottle, a terrible odor of rotting fish escaped and permeated the entire tent. I was sitting across from Albert, and I thought I would pass out from the stench.

Albert gamely proceeded to take a piece of the fin and put it in his mouth, quickly sealing the jar again. I saw him chewing it, and chewing it, and chewing it. It appeared to have the texture of rubber. Finally, unable to swallow it, Albert very subtly removed the piece from his mouth and dropped it on the dirt floor behind him. He was being very careful not to offend the hosts, although they had warned us that this delicacy was an acquired taste! Suddenly, Grace whispered to him, "Albie, you have got to get rid of that thing, the smell is making me ill." So Albie quietly picked up the offending fin and deposited it outside the tent.

Life for a royal family is first and foremost about duty and dedication – going to parties, charitable events and official functions night after night after night; even functions such as this smorgasbord while they are on holiday. They must meet and make conversation with hundreds upon hundreds of people, many of whom are dignitaries who speak foreign languages, with foreign customs and barely pronounceable names. It is interesting and exciting at times, but it can become exhausting eating luncheons and dinners whether one is hungry or not, being offered "delicacies" that can have unusual tastes, but one cannot insult the host by refusing. Prince Albert once said to me, "So many of my friends envy my position, but they wouldn't if they could spend one day with me."

We were served coffee in ceramic cups made out of lava, and then we all went outside the tent. Suddenly, a lone pony just happened to wander our way in this deserted landscape. I wondered if the pony's visit had been carefully orchestrated like everything else? I couldn't help thinking to myself that perhaps this is why the Consul General's wife was inexplicably wearing jodhpurs.

Our minibus continued across barren land to a huge waterfall and then on to the geysers for which Iceland is renowned. There was an enormous geyser that erupted every few minutes and then fell back into the ground in clouds of steam. We made a much-needed rest stop, as there had been no facilities (and no trees!) throughout the entire day.

We returned to the ship at 6:30 p.m. and boarded a small plane for an aerial tour of Greenland. The plane had engine trouble, so we flew quite low over ice packs, fjords, and mountains, before returning to the ship. The scenery was spectacular, but a little too close for comfort! It was a very harrowing and rather frightening experience, to say the least. Grace went to bed without dinner, and I was not feeling too well myself.

The ship set sail from Iceland, anticipating rough seas ahead with force eight winds. I went with Rainier, Albert, Caroline, Bettina, Louis and Monsieur Biancheri to see the staff of the ship perform *Man From La Mancha*. I had a Fernet-Menthe digestif, which Rainier recommended for my upset stomach, then went to bed at 11:30, exhausted.

Monday, August 16, 1982 – At Sea

At 10 o'clock in the morning, Grace tapped on my door to go do exercises. I had a sore throat and could not go. The sickness of the *MERMOZ* strikes again! I made reservations for the bus to Paris and got the last available seat. Grace said that I should go with them on the train instead.

In the afternoon, Grace joined me in the Salon, while I had the cocktail of the day, "Yellow Bird." She was abiding by her yearly tradition of abstaining from alcohol for six weeks from August 15 to September 30, which took willpower when everyone else was enjoying wine, champagne, and cocktails. Bettina, Grace, and I sat in the sun with blankets, admiring the calm, rolling seas and the gorgeous clouds. Rainier was enjoying talking to Professor Rey and Captain Guillou; he was more at ease in male company.

We went to the Captain's quarters for champagne and caviar, then on to dinner at the Captain's table, where we had more caviar with vodka. Grace looked stunning in a black pantsuit with a ruffled chiffon neck. Caroline wore black, green, and red taffeta. I wore a pink cheongsam dress, with a burgundy, ultra-suede, long coat-vest designed by Vera Maxwell. The menu consisted of scallops in a golden Neptune sauce, seafood flan, roast beef with artichoke hearts, salads, cheeses, ice cream with meringue, and fruit, all accompanied by Mouton Cadet 1979 and champagne. After dinner, I joined Grace, Rainier, and the group for dancing at the Grill until two o'clock in the morning.

Tuesday, August 17, 1982 – At Sea

After five hours of sleep, I heard Grace knocking on my door at 8 a.m. to do exercises with her tape. We were the only ones who showed up, and it was delightful. Our little fitness group swelled and waned according to the activities of the previous night, until finally only she and I were left. I took a photo of Grace climbing on a ladder marked "Do Not Glimb Up" – the spelling error made us both giggle, as Grace mischievously said that she was not "glimbing."

We then went to the dining room for breakfast, where we talked in depth. I have felt a real closeness with Grace on this trip, as if we are a happy family. We have been enjoying chatting about everything under the sun in the friendly manner born of long acquaintance. Grace and I have a true friendship that has grown as the years have passed. It is the kind of friendship that often needs no words. We are so similar in many respects that understanding seems to happen effortlessly.

People at the top are never sure whom to trust, and unfortunately, they are often betrayed. It is easy to forget that those in exalted positions – sometimes not by their own choosing – are real people with needs, wants, and feelings, just like everyone else.

Although she and the Prince have a good marriage, it is difficult for them to find quiet time together, due to their hectic schedules. As partners, they complement each other in every way, even to their respective fair and dark looks. Where one leaves off, the other fills in, without effort or words necessary, whether in their roles and duties or in their personal lives.

Being in the public eye also presents its own set of stresses, tensions, and difficulties. Sometimes, as with any couple, they have a tug-of-war, but they quickly go on to the resolution of the problem. Rainier, being European, has the final say in the family, but he listens to her wise words before making a decision. Grace has often said that couples married for many years deserve an award. She and Rainier have had their problems just like everyone else, but Grace turned to me, and, looking directly into my eyes, she said, "You know, Joan, I know that Rainier loves me." She said it so sweetly that it brought tears to my eyes.

We went up to the Lido Deck for a celebration of Indonesian Independence Day. All the waiters and the cabin boys lined up wearing red and white, the colors of their flag (also the colors of Monaco). It was very ceremonial. I was standing with Grace, Rainier, and Louis. Albert arrived late and was very upset that no one had told him about the occasion. He is always very conscientious and really was quite annoyed at himself.

Afterward, we all played bingo. It was the last game of the cruise, but no one from our group won. I had lunch with Grace outside on the deck, but it was cold, and I was beginning to feel it in my chest, so I decided to take it easy for the rest of the day. We went to Professor Rey's last lecture, on the future of the Arctic, in light of issues like Russian missiles and oil drilling.

We had dinner at Grace and Rainier's table with the Captain and three officers. Then we went to the Salon for an evening of Jacques Brel songs. Everyone else continued on to the Indonesian evening, while I had a Fernet Branca to help my chest and went to bed. The cruise was almost over, and I did not want to miss a moment of it, but I was sadly not feeling well.

Wednesday, August 18, 1982 – At Sea

The hot water bottle that Grace lent me really helped my chest, so I slept quite well. I packed, hoping that everything would fit in my luggage (including the heavy sweaters and sheepskin rug that I had bought!). I went up to the Grill for lunch and met Grace. She asked me how I was feeling as we sat down at the table, waiting for everyone else to arrive.

I went to the movie studio for a poetry and mime show by the staff, with exceptional presentations by Caroline and Albert. Caroline has a beautiful voice and spoke her three poems with feeling. Albert mimed playing a marionette marvelously, his eyes were huge and his movements were controlled – it was a very poignant and polished performance. Everyone was astounded that they would join in. Grace and Rainier were so proud. They had not seen their children on stage since they were little. It was very touching.

In the evening, we went to the Captain's cocktail party. I wore a long black dress with a Chinese stole. Grace was in a three-quarter length, "Joan Crawford" style black crepe dress with a Galanos silk stole in many colors. We were the last ones to arrive at the cocktail party, and we sat down at our usual booth in the center of the room. The Captain gave an eloquent speech to say "au revoir" with humor, pathos and humility.

We went to our table at the Grill for our farewell dinner, where Professor Rey and his elegant wife joined us. The menu consisted of foie gras in golden aspic, lobster, grilled scallops flaming in Armagnac, confit of duck with Parisian potatoes, green salad, cheeses, and ice cream flambé with aquavit and fruit. For dessert, there was an amazing igloo made of ice cream, complete with marzipan seals, polar bears, penguins and Eskimos in a kayak.

Afterward, we went down to the Salon to see an excellent magician. Caroline had been grinning all day, saying that she had a big surprise for us. She excused herself from the table, and we certainly were surprised to see her appear onstage. The magician put Caroline in an upright box and passed rods through it, and then he pushed out the middle section. Everyone gasped, especially Grace. Caroline was great! She later told us that even though she was slim, she had to slip her entire body into an impossibly small space, but it was fun and exciting. She is always enthusiastic and game to try anything, which is a refreshing attitude and approach to life. It was wonderful that Albert and Caroline joined in activities like other people. They made five hundred fans!

I talked Grace into going to the *Caverne* disco to enjoy our last night together. Rainier retired to their cabin, so she and I trekked down and were almost alone. We chatted for a while, until Louis arrived, followed by the Captain's aide, then Albie and Caroline. We had a wonderful time dancing disco and samba. Grace and I left everyone there at 2 a.m. and returned to our cabins, giggling like schoolgirls!

Thursday, August 19, 1982 – Calais to Paris

At 10 a.m., I watched the tugboats pulling us into the dock at Calais. I finished packing, but nothing seemed to fit as well as when I came! I said goodbye to people on board the ship; some mistook me for Grace, but I said nothing to disappoint them. I felt flattered. Several passengers had purchased pictures of the family that had been taken by the ship's photographers and asked me if I would have her autograph them, which they were most grateful for. Grace gave me a lovely signed stamp folder with commemorative Prince Albert I stamps. It was dear of her.

It was sunny and beautiful on the Lido deck for our last lunch together. All of the officers were present, as was the Captain, who was now joined by his wife. Rainier remarked that he had never seen so many women with sad faces. Grace replied that all of the women on the ship had fallen for the Captain, and were jealous to see his wife.

We said goodbyes all around to the officers and crew and were ready to disembark. Cars and the press were waiting at the bottom of the gangway. Photographers especially wanted photos of Caroline, who was wearing a pink linen pantsuit with a beige embroidered blouse. Grace looked chic in an olive-colored suit and a beige hat. Rainier was dashing as always in a suit and tie, and Albie and Louis were in sports coats with ties.

I rode in a car with Professor Rey and his wife to the train station in Calais. All of our baggage was brought into the first class car; between the eight of us, we had thirty-five pieces of luggage – plus hand carry-ons! This included Grace's four paper parcels and a plastic shopping bag. Rainier always teased her about looking like a bag lady, when she could afford to carry the finest luggage.

On our three-hour train ride to Paris, Caroline, Grace and Rainier sat opposite Albert and me. Albert had been up dancing until 4:30 and then had to pack, so he took a nap. He was concerned that his long legs might bother me, as he is over six feet tall. He is a dear and thoughtful young man.

Albert is most kind and attentive, affectionate and courteous. I felt at peace with his gentle but strong personality, and captivated by his depth of perception and his devotion to duty. On board ship, he threw himself into all the activities with enthusiasm, including performing for the other passengers. He was always one of the last to leave the discotheque at night. He enjoyed dancing, even with his mother and myself, thus flattering our older egos with attention from one so young and handsome.

I have heard it said that Albert is "too nice," but I know that, although this trait is the basis for his winsome character, when necessary he can be firm and unerring in his decisions. Albert knows who he is inwardly as a person, as well as being well aware of his role and position in this life, a duty and responsibility that he takes very seriously. He is quietly empowered from within, like his mother. He will be a great Prince for the Monégasques.

Grace and Caroline read during the train ride to Paris, while Rainier also slept. Louis lost his voice, another victim of the "*MERMOZ Maladie*" and late nights. We were all coughing. I took some photos of the lovely scenery from the train and then slept a little, but the car was very hot. Grace and I stood on the back platform of the train to get some air at Amiens.

We arrived in Paris ahead of schedule. Photographers on the train insisted on taking photos, especially of Caroline. Grace said, "What good are these photos, as we are hot and tired?" The reporters then went onto the platform and waited for us to come off the train, photographing Grace with her shopping bags. Louis was adorable, but he looked so ill with his laryngitis, and I hoped he would take good care of himself. He was so conscious of his age and wanted to push to show he was still young. (And he certainly was in spirit.)

There were only two porters at the *Gare du Nord* to handle our mountain of luggage. Prince Rainier surveyed his one suitcase and carry-on bag, into which he had packed everything necessary to look impeccably dressed throughout the cruise (including formal clothes and a thick parka!), plus numerous gifts for his secretaries and others. He obviously was a master at packing. He noticed Louis's five matching suitcases, each one on wheels, with straps cleverly attaching them together, and could not help but tease his cousin about his "luggage train." Louis was always elegantly dressed and very dapper. It is said that the Duke and Duchess of Windsor traveled with sixty pieces of luggage or more, so five pieces did not seem to be too outlandish for a prince! They loaded everything into a minibus for the family. The Monaco diplomatic representative offered to drive me to the *Hôtel St. James & Albany*, on the Rue de Rivoli facing the Louvre and the Tuileries Gardens.

Grace and I hugged each other. She said, "We were so happy to have you on this cruise with us, Joanie. Please give hugs to the boys and Pammie. Our next cruise will be to Alaska, and you must join us. Then we will come and visit you in Victoria." She got on the minibus with the rest of her family to catch the train that would bring her back to Rocagel. I got into the official Monégasque diplomatic car, and, as we drove off in our separate directions, I waved goodbye to my dear friend, Grace... for the last time.

Photo taken by Grace
on the cruise ship *MERMOZ*
Joan writing her diary!

Grace on deck with her latest needlepoint project, August 1982

Prince Albert above Geirangerfjord, Norway, with *MERMOZ* below in the distance

Grace with tiny icebergs in broad daylight at midnight!
Spitsbergen, Norway, August 1982

Grace, Prince Louis and Joan on deck for exercise in matching warm-up suits

"Do Not Glimb Up!" Grace couldn't resist 'g'limbing!

Grace and Joan dressed as pirates
for the ship's costume party, where
the whole Grimaldi family
got into the act as pirates

Prince Rainier clowning around in a
broom closet near his stateroom

The family on deck on the last day of the cruise (L to R):
Prince Louis, Joan, Princess Caroline, Princess Grace, Prince Rainier, Bettina Gray

Grace and Joan in Hammerfest, Norway – last photo taken of the two of them together

To Joan -
in souvenir of our
wonderful trip.
Love - Grace -
1982

Princess Grace's last gift: a set of stamps commemorating Prince Albert I of Monaco
inscribed, "To Joan - In souvenir of our wonderful trip – Love – Grace –" 1982

Joan and Grace on deck of the *MERMOZ* – Grace doing needlepoint
Photo sent posthumously by Grace's Lady-in-Waiting
in an envelope marked "Joan Photos" in Grace's handwriting 1982

Grace and Rainier enjoying their last vacation together in Bergen, Norway
with a woman dressed in traditional Norwegian costume

Photo sent to me by mistake from the
photo lab, instead of the photo
of Grace and Rainier above
A stone cross... just a few days before
her tragic accident

Pamela-Grace, Prince Albert and Joan in New York City, 1987

Joan with Prince Albert
at Charles's wedding
in Aspen, Colorado 1997

EPILOGUE:

THE DAYS AFTER

When I returned home to Canada after our wonderful Arctic cruise, I ordered duplicates of some of my photographs to send to Grace. Instead of printing the picture of Grace and Rainier posing with a lady in Norwegian costume in Bergen, the photo lab "mistakenly" printed the one next to it – a photograph of a stone cross! Grace died tragically a few days later, after her horrendous car accident on the treacherous road that we had driven together so many times.

Grace Kelly, wife of Prince Rainier III, died on September 14, 1982. The whole world grieved, as 100 million people watched her funeral on television. I could not bear to go – I wanted to always remember my dear friend as the vivacious, beautiful woman that I had spent seventeen wonderful days with just the month before. My heart was broken, and my spirit was crushed, as were those of her bereaved family. I don't think any of us ever recovered from her loss – Prince Rainier certainly never did. There was no doubting the love he had for Grace, seeing him devastated, torn apart by grief. Even people who never knew her felt the pain and emptiness of a great light that had been extinguished from our world. We never really know what we have until it is no longer there, but Grace's enduring legacy will forever live within people's hearts, because she made such a lasting impression.

My only solace was in knowing that Grace and her family had a truly special time together on their last vacation, filled with so much love, joy, and laughter. She had enjoyed the cruise immensely and was like a sparkling young girl in her enthusiasm. I was so profoundly grateful to have shared that time with her and with the family. I could never have imagined that would be the last time I would see her.

Losing Grace was one of the greatest losses of my life. The pain has been deep, and only my memories and photographs fill the void. Shortly after her death, Grace's Lady-in-Waiting sent me an envelope that was marked in the top right corner "Joan Photos" in Grace's distinct, bold handwriting, with her "Double G" insignia on the back. Inside, there were two photos from our cruise: one of Prince Louis with a fish in Norway, and one of Grace and me sitting informally on the deck of the *MERMOZ*. She was a dear and thoughtful soul, who lives on in my heart…

In our serious, modern world, Grace was a beacon that could draw people into her warmth and light-heartedness. Her laugh was melodious, endearing, and reassuring. Her voice was lilting and soothing. She enveloped you in her cloak of safety. Grace's childlike innocence and joy in everything drew everyone into her little bit of heaven.

Part of her irresistibility was something many people could not recognize in her, and that was her love and enjoyment of everything. Grace loved to have fun and was not jaded by her surroundings. She loved people; she remembered everyone's name, and was always interested in what anyone had to say. She loved little things, like flowers, nature, needlepoint, and a treasured collection of Royal Danish porcelain sea children. For a woman who could have champagne, caviar, and foie gras – she also took great delight in peanut butter sandwiches. She preferred simplicity to glamour, did not put on much makeup or jewelry, loved to be casual in espadrilles, and often wore a scarf on her head. She personified understated elegance, and loved beauty in all its forms.

In the years since her passing, there have been countless tributes to the beauty that was Grace, and many memorials made in her honor. The Franklin Mint produced a line of jewelry inspired by Princess Grace, recognizing her as a rare gem: "*There will never be another woman quite like her. Her Serene Highness, Princess Grace of Monaco. A woman who attained the glamour and attention of celebrity, yet chose to live her life with quiet dignity. A woman whose breathtaking physical beauty was surpassed only by the beauty of her loving spirit.*"

Grace left a legacy of loving kindness. She made you feel welcome and drawn into whatever was happening in her world. Her light of love still shines for all who knew her and even for those who did not. Her name was aptly chosen, for she embodied all the graces. In fact, it would be difficult to find fault in her character. I am sure there must have been some, but my own personal knowledge of her over the years did not reveal any flaws, except perhaps that she worried too much about other people's well-being, sometimes to her own detriment.

Princess Grace gave her last interview with Pierre Salinger for ABC's *20/20* on June 22, 1982, less than three months before her death. Salinger: "I know it is much too early in your life to ask you this question, but at some point, someone is going to ask it to you... How are you going to want to be remembered?" Grace: "I would like to be remembered as trying to do my job well, being understanding and kind." Salinger: "Are there any things about your career that you would like to have remembered? They will be remembered anyway..." Grace: "Well, I don't know... I don't feel as though I achieved enough in my career to stand out more than many other people. I was very lucky in my career, and I loved it, but I don't think I was accomplished enough as an actor to be remembered for that particularly. No, I'd like to be remembered as a decent human being and a caring one." She certainly was all of that, and so much more.

Would Grace have believed that she would become a legend? I don't think so – she never wanted to be put on a pedestal and was always very humble. I feel that she was somewhat mystified by her appeal to so many. Her rise to fame as a movie star was meteoric in such a few short years, but it was her fairy-tale marriage to a charming and handsome prince that catapulted her into a realm known by few in our world. The fact that she was stunningly beautiful, approachable, and compassionate endeared her further.

Grace could have just lain back and enjoyed being a princess, letting others serve her and fawn all over her. She could have led a frivolous and superficial existence, but she chose to use her position as an opportunity to be of service, to help others, and to champion worthy causes. Grace worked tirelessly night and day; she was busier than anyone I ever knew and was always taking on more and more projects and responsibilities. She sacrificed precious time with her family and children to do what she felt might make the world a better place, in whatever way she could.

Grace often said, "One person touches many lives," which indeed she did – the ripples that Grace left in her wake touched more people than she could ever have imagined, even to this day. When a person is famous, their fame precedes them and outlives them – Grace always tried to live up to other people's expectations of her. She was a true role model of graciousness, despite those who would seek to somehow tarnish her loving image.

The only time I ever heard Grace complain was about the "paparazzi" – not the legitimate reporters, but the growing epidemic of stalkers hiding behind cameras and the "freedom of the press," who would literally jump out from behind bushes and descend like locusts wherever they went. They became a parasitic cancer in her life, and in the lives of her children, robbing them of privacy, and sometimes of dignity. She often felt like prey being hunted for sport. Grace was always willing to give interviews or pose for photographs, but she became so hurt when the tabloid press would intentionally print malicious lies about her and those she loved in order to sell papers. Grace could never understand why anyone would choose to be unkind to another human being, particularly one they did not know.

Grace always tried to protect her children, but she could never have imagined how much worse it would get after her passing, especially for young Stephanie, who not only endured the trauma of the car accident that killed her mother, but then ended up being repeatedly questioned about it by some in the press. Knowing Grace, I could never believe that she would have broken the law to let her underage daughter drive; in fact, there were witnesses, including a *gendarme* (policeman), who saw Grace driving behind the wheel of her 10-year-old Rover.

On our cruise the month before the accident, Grace had been showing signs of tremendous stress and strain from all of her duties and responsibilities, and from the pressures that this world placed on her. I believe this led her to have a stroke that ultimately claimed her life. Seventeen-year-old Stephanie lost her beloved mother on that terrible day, but rather than having support and compassion from the world, she was horribly and unjustly victimized. Stephanie was not only emotionally scarred forever from that unimaginable tragedy that she narrowly escaped from, but also from the abuse of the heartless press that has followed her ever since. The family has endured more than their fair share of pain and heartbreak.

Above all else, Grace was a loving mother, who cherished her family as the most important thing in this world. She tried everything in her power to give them as "normal" an upbringing as possible under the circumstances, but she knew that the life they were born to meant that everything they did would be scrutinized. She told her children: "You will make your mistakes, but try not to make too much of a mess of it. You will have to learn your own lessons and live your own life."

Grace left many great legacies, and her three beautiful children – beautiful physically and spiritually – are perhaps greatest among them. They are each kind, caring, and compassionate, carrying on Grace's work, as well as projects that are near and dear to their own hearts, to make this world a better place. They all continue to be dedicated to duty and service to mankind, as well as to the planet, while they keep alive the legacy of love that Grace represented. She would be more than proud and happy to see her family's loving determination to make a difference in this ailing world. They each do so much good work that often goes unseen. They are real human beings, simply normal people with beautiful hearts and souls like their mother, who have great joys and sorrows in life, just like everybody else.

Whenever I have visited Monaco, the family has always been very kind to me, going out of their way to welcome me. I have watched them over the years, gamely carrying on, despite their deep, deep grief. Each has emerged stronger and capable of withstanding life's many challenges in positions of leadership. The light that Grace shone so brightly now seems to light their path. When I look at them, I see her smile shining in their eyes, and I know that she is with them, guiding them in her loving way.

Grace and Rainier were married for twenty-six years (half her life!), and when I returned to the Palace to visit Rainier, memories of her were still present everywhere, and nothing had been moved. The regal early portrait of Grace was still hanging, the bronze bust of her was still in the living room of their private apartment, and her Oscar was there, too. Grace will always live on in the hearts of all who knew and loved her, for she touched everyone deeply, whether one knew her for a moment or a lifetime.

Princess Grace's presence remains throughout Monaco, with buildings and streets named after her. When I walk along the streets, I have so many happy memories of "the good old days," as Rainier called them. All that is missing is Grace herself... That warm and welcoming energy that she exuded, her sparkling yet serene radiance, and her unforgettable, playful laugh are no longer present, and I feel lonely. Monaco is the jewel of the Mediterranean, a clean, chic, elegant enclave, shining in the radiant sunlight. I see it thus, too, but inside, I feel an emptiness and a longing for the way things used to be.

My dear Grace, how deeply I miss you! I am a far richer and deeper person for having known you, and I am grateful for the everlasting gifts of your being, which live with me in memory. You were always there for everyone else – a pillar of inner strength, a shoulder to cry on, a fountain of wisdom.

Each time I return to Monaco, I visit your tomb at the Cathedral. There are fresh flowers in vases, in bunches, and sometimes a single flower is placed with gentle care on top of the stone set in the floor, marked "Gratia Patricia." I sit in the main part of the Cathedral, where I had so often sat on joyous occasions and I return to the memories of you and the times we shared. Tears fall quietly, as I realize that deep within me there is a part of you, Grace, that will always remain

– the sister I never had, the loyal friend, the wise counselor. Our bond is deep, and I feel your presence.

I think of your memorial card, which said you that would like to be remembered as "a kind and caring person who made a difference in the world." You certainly were that, and much, much more. You were a woman of devotion, of loyalty, of duty and service, dedicated to peace and values. Your greatest gift, as your deeply mourning husband said, was your "legacy of love." And that, sweet Grace, few have achieved.

As I leave the Cathedral, I quietly whisper, "Goodbye, my dear friend. I shall love you always..."

RR

Oct 2nd [1982]

Dear Joan –

Thank you so much for your lovely letter. And thank you also for sharing so much our great grief and sorrow.

These were horrible days that will remain as a nightmare forever. It was all so sudden! Why? And yet Grace was such a beautiful person and such a wonderful human being, full of love and kindness, that maybe she was not really made for this world of violence and misery. And so God took her in his Kingdom. We have lost so much with Grace's departure from this world, the void left is terrible. Yet her presence is everywhere, where we look, what we touch, what we talk about.

The children are wonderful and such comfort, we are very closely united in our sorrow and the wonderful memory of our darling Grace.

Grace was very fond of you, and I know she was happy that you shared our holiday cruise this summer.

Please share with your children all our grateful thoughts in these times of pain.

With affection

Rainier

ABOUT THIS BOOK

Co-Author's Note by Grace Dale

Some years before my mother, Joan Dale, passed away, I was helping her to sort through various boxes of memorabilia. As we came across programs from elegant galas in Monte Carlo and menus from luncheons and dinners at the Palace, she recounted stories from her past, especially from the years that she had lived in Monaco. I had heard some of these stories before, and many of them corresponded with photos of Princess Grace and her family that were interspersed among the framed photographs around my mother's home and throughout our family photo albums. However, I was hearing many of these extraordinary accounts for the first time and was amazed to discover what my mother's remarkable life had been like.

My mother was a wonderful storyteller who had a great memory for details. There were so many amazing anecdotes that I asked her if we could record them to preserve these memories for my brothers, and for future generations of our family. Although my older brothers had lived in Monaco and had been the first playmates of Princess Caroline and Prince Albert, they had been very young and perhaps were not aware at the time of how extraordinary their life was, having birthday parties and watching first-run movies at the Palace, being privately tutored with the young Prince and Princess, swimming in the Palace pool, playing and riding ponies at their private ranch of Rocagel, etc.

As my mother and I continued to sort through boxes, we came across hundreds of letters that she had written to her parents, recounting the events of the day as they were taking place. These letters served to refresh her memories, and triggered more fascinating stories. It was interesting to read my mother's letters written from the point of view of a naïve newlywed embarking on adventures in Europe as the wife of a young Consul in the U.S. Diplomatic Service, followed by letters written from Monaco describing their glittering life there. She wrote to her parents regularly, as most people did in those days. She was an only child who was very close to her mother, openly sharing everything that was happening in her life, so these letters also provided a diary of her lifelong friendship with Princess Grace. (Of course, these letters have been excerpted to include only what is relevant to this book.)

Over the years, Princess Grace had written over a hundred warm notes and chatty letters to Joan, sharing her thoughts and details of her family life and her endless duties as Princess of Monaco. These were almost always handwritten in her unique writing style, often on her monogrammed stationery. She also wrote postcards from her many travels around the world. She never forgot our birthdays, and always sent me gifts with loving notes to her goddaughter.

Prince Rainier also wrote about one hundred letters to my parents, mostly to my father until my parents divorced, then he carried on writing to my mother, especially after Princess Grace's tragic death. Even after my father, Martin, left his service as Privy Counselor and Economic Advisor, the Prince often wrote to him asking for his advice and counsel, repeatedly saying that my father was one of the only people he could trust.

The crown came with very heavy burdens for Prince Rainier, which he shared candidly with my father. His letters were full of deep philosophy, wistful regrets, endless frustrations and concerns, tremendous humor, and pride for his children. Many people think that royals can do whatever they want, but his letters often expressed that he was not a free man but was bound by duties and responsibilities, and committed to a small nation of people who depended on him. He devoted his life to protecting their rights and welfare to the best of his ability, and securing the future of his country.

In Prince Rainier's last letter to my mother shortly before he died, he sent a beautiful photograph of her and Princess Grace dressed in gorgeous gowns for a gala, with a note saying, "Dear Joan, going through old memories and pictures of those 'Good old days.' I think this shot would amuse you. Affectionately, Rainier."

Princess Grace visited us many times in our various homes in New York City, and we were invited to the Palace and to stay as guests at their private mountain retreat, Rocagel. However, most people did not know about my mother's connection to Princess Grace, and even fewer knew that I was her goddaughter. (I have always kept this very private, and have hardly ever told anyone.)

Until I read the letters that my mother had written to her parents, I did not fully know the extent of how close Grace and Joan were before I was born. I was amazed that my mother was at the Palace several times a week, that they watched movies together, did ballet, played golf together and even went bowling! I knew that they raised their eldest children together, but until I saw the home movies, I did not realize that my family went on month-long vacations with Princess Grace's family.

What has now become a book began from my desire to know more about my mother and my godmother. Aunt Grace died when I was fifteen years old, and I felt a profound sense of loss and a deep void in the world. It happened during my first week at boarding school at Philips Exeter Academy, and I was overwhelmed with grief, as I loved her dearly. I was named Pamela Grace in her honor, and although all the letters in this book refer to me as Pam, I have preferred to be called Grace for over twenty years. I was blessed to have spent time with Aunt Grace on many occasions, including celebrating my thirteenth birthday as her guest at Rocagel, two years before her untimely death. She was very loving and affectionate with me, and I was always excited to see her.

Princess Grace was an exceptional human being, and the experience of her love and light left an indelible impression on one's heart and soul. The only person I've ever encountered whose energy is similar to hers is His Holiness, the Fourteenth Dalai Lama. I have had the good fortune to meet His Holiness and be in his presence several times, and they both exude warmth, welcoming, generosity, kindness, love, wisdom, compassion and humor. Perhaps these qualities are the hallmarks of true greatness.

Some people may think that Princess Grace was "too good to be true," and some have dug deep in muddy waters in order to sling dirt on her memory. I may have been quite young when I knew her, but I have always been very good at sensing the true essence of people, and hers was as exquisite as they come. Princess Grace had a brilliant aura that shone so brightly, it could light up a movie screen and come right through the television, which is why her light has continued to shine in the world for decades.

The energy around Princess Grace was warm and cool at the same time, calm like a placid lake and soothing like a gentle breeze. She spoke gently in her slow and thoughtful manner, with a voice that was almost hypnotic (her voice was so unique that one can easily still recognize it as hers to this day). She giggled and laughed often; when she laughed, she was even more radiant and enchanting. The only time that she was not smiling was when she was concerned about someone else's well-being, or when she was speaking about any form of injustice in the world.

Prince Albert shares many of his mother's best traits and qualities. I did not spend much time with Princess Caroline, other than at Rocagel the week before she announced her divorce from Philippe Junot; she was very sweet and kind to me at that time, despite her terrible sadness and heartbreak. When my mother passed away suddenly, Princess Caroline wrote me the most touching note that I read over and over again to get me through my endless grief. I only spent time with Princess Stephanie when I was a small child, but I had the pleasure of visiting with Prince Albert on several occasions. He was at Rocagel when I was there, and he came to our home in New York with his mother a few times. He also came to Charles's wedding in Aspen (and Charles attended his wedding to Princess Charlene in Monaco in 2011).

Prince Albert is known to be warm, charming, friendly and open, like his mother. He has her smile, and her fair complexion. Prince Albert is very sincere and committed to bettering this world. He has a quiet strength, and a passion for causes dear to his heart, like sports, the environment, the oceans and humanitarian efforts. He is extremely intrepid, enjoying skydiving, participating twice in the Paris-Dakar Rally, and being a five-time Olympian in the dangerous four-man bobsleigh (although Prince Rainier wrote to my mother: "I wish he had gone for Ping-Pong!"). He has a willingness to try new things, and he will step up to do what other people won't.

Of course, His Serene Highness Prince Albert has now taken over the roles and responsibilities of his father as Sovereign Prince of Monaco, and he has also taken on many of his mother's causes. He is a different type of Prince than his father was; he has a more diplomatic quality, wanting to keep and maintain peace wherever possible. Like Prince Rainier, he is a forward thinker, and a Prince for the Twenty-First Century. Prince Albert is a voice for reason and peace in the world, especially as Monaco is a member of the United Nations. He is the best combination of both of his parents: he has his mother's kindness, caring and compassion, with his father's visionary thinking, courage and sense of adventure.

My mother, Joan, started writing this memoir while Prince Rainier was still alive and ruling Monaco. Over the years, every time she got upset at the nonsense and lies printed about Princess Grace and her family, she would pick up her pen to write the truth – ultimately leaving copious pages. When Prince Rainier died in April of 2005, my mother felt that it was the end of an era... and for her, it was the end of the world as she knew it. My mother died unexpectedly of a brain hemorrhage a few months later (which is what ultimately had caused Princess Grace's death as well). Grace had been the glue that held everyone together, and although they all drifted apart somewhat because of time and distance, my mother had been treated as part of the family, and indeed, loved them as such.

This book was created as a result of sharing many wonderful days with my mother, who was sharing her memories of many wonderful days spent with Grace. Her Serene Highness was the perfect title for her, for she was the very embodiment of Grace and Serenity. As an Oscar-winning actress, she has become an enduring icon of style and beauty, and her Hollywood legend has long outlived her; but there were many more dimensions to her, and it is my hope that this book gives insight into the multi-faceted woman beyond Grace Kelly.

This memoir was originally intended for my nieces and nephews, so they could know who their grandmother was, because they were born very late in my mother's life, and she was well aware that they were too young to really know or remember her. In honor of my mother and my godmother, I feel called to share these loving memories of two lovely women who led extraordinary lives in an extraordinary place at an extraordinary time.

Portrait of Joan Dale in Monaco
by Alejo Vidal-Quadras 1964
www.alejovidalquadras.com

Additional Information at:
www.PrincessGrace*of*Monaco.com

CPSIA information can be obtained at www.ICGtesting.com
Printed in the USA
LVOW11*2256030815

448669LV00015B/371/P